To our dear friends
Dennis & JoAnn Lundeen
May you always continue to be a blessing
in God's Kingdom and may he
Sing over you with joy!
    With love,
        Jack & Carol

Imagine your
"Goofy" friend can
pay something un goofy"
    —Love,
        Gloria, "Goofy" friend.

# Tough Questions- Christians' Answers

*AuthorHouse™*
*1663 Liberty Drive, Suite 200*
*Bloomington, IN 47403*
*www.authorhouse.com*
*Phone: 1-800-839-8640*

*First published by AuthorHouse 8/22/2008*

*ISBN: 978-1-4343-8855-1 (sc)*

*Library of Congress Control Number: 2008906282*

*Printed in the United States of America*
*Bloomington, Indiana*

*This book is printed on acid-free paper.*

# Credits

1. The cover page picture is a photograph of a crown of thorns in St. Andrew's United Methodist Church in Syracuse, Indiana. The photograph was taken by Carolyn Clark. Cover design by Jack Clark.
2. Thanks to the St. Andrew's United Methodist Thrift Shop of Syracuse, Indiana. They sponsored the publishing costs of this book to promote the spreading of Jesus Christ's good news.
3. Scripture references indicated in footnotes are as follows:
   A. JBP = J. B. Phillips translation. *The New Testament in Modern English for Schools.* J. B. Phillips, © J. B. Phillips, 1969, 1960, printed in Great Briton by Cox and Wyman, Ltd, Reading for the publishers Geoffrey Bles, Ltd, 52 Doughty Street, London, WCI and distributed by William Collins Sons & Co. Ltd 144 Cathedral Street, Glasgow, C4.
   B. KJV = King James Version
   C. NAS = the *New American Standard Bible,* Copyright © 1960, 1962, 1963, 1968, 1971, 1972, 1973, 1975, 1977, 1995 by the Lockman Foundation. www.Lockman.org
   D. NCV = *The Inspirational Study Bible*, Max Lucado General Editor, © 1995, Word Publishing, all rights reserved, *The Holy Bible, New Century Version*, Scriptures quoted from the *Holy Bible, New Century Version,* © 1987, 1988, 1991 by Word Publishing, Dallas, Texas 75234. Used by permission.
   E. NEB = New English Bible
   F. NIV = New International Version. Scripture taken from the HOLY BIBLE, NEW INTERNATIONAL VERSION®. Copyright © 1973, 1978. 1984 by International Bible Society. Used by permission of Zondervan. All rights reserved.
   G. NLT = *Holy Bible, New Living Translation*, Copyright © 1996. Used by permission of Tyndale House Publishers, Inc., Wheaton, Illinois 60189. All rights reserved.
   H. RSV = The Holy Bible Revised Standard Version, Published by the World Publishing Company, © Copyright 1962 by the World Publishing Company
   I. TM = *The Message,* Eugene H. Peterson, © 2002. Scripture taken from *THE MESSAGE, copyright* © 1993, 1994, 1995, 1996, 2000, 2002. Used with permission of NavPres Publishing Group.
   J. TNIV = Today's New International Version[TM] TNIV®. Scripture taken from the Holy Bible, Today's New International Version[TM] TNIV® Copyright © 2001, 2005 by International Bible Society ®. All rights reserved. Used by permission of Zondervan.

# Dedicated to

**Jesus Christ,** the author and perfecter of our faith[1]

## All the people who authored and translated the Bible –
Those who experienced God in their lives and shared the experiences with us, and those who made the scriptures available for all of us, often at great personal cost.

## Those who have passed the faith to us and sustained our faith –
Our spiritual mothers and fathers in the faith.

## Those who will pass the faith to others –
Those who are continuing to make disciples and keep the faith growing.

---

# *We claim for Jesus Christ the following:*

*Our lives, His gift to us, and our gift to Him*

*Our homes, our families, and our friends*

*Our congregations*

*Our towns, cities, states, nation and the world*

*We proclaim they are all His and ask only that we be used to further His Kingdom*

---

[1] Hebrews 12:2 (TNIV)

## Contributing Authors

Betty Berger
David Berger
Arlene Berkey
Josephine Butler
Betty J. Byers
Becky Campbell
James Chupp
Bruce Clark
Carolyn Clark
Jack Clark
Robert Craig
Dean Culbertson
Sherry Doherty
Mark Eastway
Gloria Frew

Matthew Gunter
Judy Hardy
Donald Impey
June Laudeman
Gary Lewis
John Munson
Michael Neff
Gary Phillips
David Schramm
Joyce Schramm
George Shaffer
Larry Sheets
Harlan Steffen
Cathy Ann Turner
Jonathan Ummel

## Group study contributors

The Fairplain Presbyterian Adult Church School Class of Benton Harbor, Michigan

One of the small group fellowships at St. Andrew's United Methodist Church, Syracuse, Indiana

# Table of Contents

**(Table of Contents Continued next page)**

**(Table of Contents Continued next page)**

**(Table of Contents Continued next page)**

---

[2] John 14:12-13 (NIV)
[3] Matthew 10:38, & 16:24, Mark 8:34, & Luke 9:23 (NIV)
[4] Mark 11:24 (NIV)

**(Table of Contents Continued next page)**

# Introduction

The world asks tough questions of Christians. Sometimes it's because the questioner wants to know, and sometimes the questions are scornful. Some answers can help the questioner be more open to the Holy Spirit and help establish a relationship with God. We ask tough questions of ourselves, and the answers can help us grow in our faith.

One hundred-thirty-six deeply committed Christian Brothers and Sisters were contacted and asked to consider helping to write this book. Twenty-nine Christians of seventeen denominational backgrounds and an agnostic are contributing authors. All but one of the contributing authors live in or have lived in northern Indiana. Those Christians who contributed were asked to consider the Apostle Peter's urging: "Always be prepared to give an answer to everyone who asks you to give the reason for the hope that you have."[5] In addition to the individuals, two groups have helped evaluate using the material for devotions.

Contributing authors include nine clergy and twenty-one lay people. Three of the laypersons are wives or widows of pastors. Eighteen contributors have been teachers (grade school, middle school, high school, special education, Bible and Sunday school classes, college, technical college, university, and adult education). There is one certified lay speaker, two certified Christian counselors, two people who have worked with large publishing houses, a former journalist, three who have been lay delegates to their church's annual conferences, two who have been congregational lay leaders, and one who was a district lay leader in their denomination. One has been a leader of Emmaus Walks and another has been a participant. One has been a presenter at Marriage Encounters and six others have participated in these events. Two presently have their own businesses doing home maintenance including considerable carpentry work perhaps giving them a professional as well as a spiritual affinity with their Savoir. Our views are our own; we do not presume to speak for our denominations in any official capacity.

Contributors could pose tough questions and if they felt called, to answer the tough questions. Each person asked could contribute as many or as few questions or answers as they wished.

Some who were asked had too many obligations to respond. Some did not feel qualified. Some saw the questions as a challenge to accepting their relationship to God by faith. Some felt they should be spending their energies elsewhere. Some weren't interested in the project.

For those of us who accepted the challenge of responding to the questions, the responses were the result of our faith, much study, contemplation, and inspiration by the Holy Spirit and others who have played a role in our faith. It was in the hope that the Holy Spirit will use this work to stimulate thought and a deeper faith in others and ourselves that we have written this book.

Each contributor worked independently of the others with the exception of two obvious questions. Some of the answers can be rather involved. One very special answer succinctly summarizes it all with one word. There was no attempt to form a consensus of understanding. You will likely find areas where you do not agree with us. This is not surprising. After all Saint Paul observed that now we know only in part the full picture of God's perfection. It was surprising that there weren't more differences among the contributing authors. Where we did have understandings that were different they were accepted in the spirit of John Wesley who is quoted as saying, "If your heart is as my heart, give me your hand." Those who were able to make a contribution to the book have a short biography at the end of the book to acquaint you with them.

All proceeds from sales of this book above production costs will be given to mission projects.

Jack Clark, contributing author and coordinator

---

[5] First Peter 3:15 (NIV)

## Suggestions for using this book in small group or personal devotions

This book certainly may be read without using it as a basis for devotions or a basis for a small group study. The Fairplain Presbyterian Adult Church School Class in Benton Harbor, Michigan played an early role in the development of the material. They found that the material does lend itself to personal devotions or group study, and the following suggestions have been reviewed with Rev. Dr. John Munson, their pastor, and are offered if it is wished to be used in such a way. After the completion of the book, one of the small group ministry fellowships at St. Andrew's United Methodist Church, Syracuse, Indiana also reviewed material and study methods confirming that it was adapted to this use. Below are suggestions about this type use.

1. Start by reviewing the table of contents to pick a question or challenge that is especially interesting. Do this on your own for an individual project or with the total group if a small-group study is chosen. Try to have a group small enough that there will be time for all members to participate. Being a Christian demands active participation. No one should be on the sidelines. If this is to be a group study, choose how many weeks you will be meeting and pick one less total subjects than the number of weeks. (For a twelve week study pick eleven challenges.)

2. Choose one of the questions/challenges in the table of contents of the book, read it aloud to the group (or to yourself if using the material for personal devotions) with the associated comments (if any). Take a short time to consider what your response might be if you were presented with this question/challenge. Share your own thoughts with others if in a group setting.

3. At a later time (perhaps the next day), review your thoughts. Read the comments by the author or authors in the book. This would be between sharing times in group settings.

4. Think about the authors' comments. Where do they make sense? Where do they seem out of line with your understanding? If your understandings differ, is it possible to see enough common ground to respect each other's understandings as brothers and sisters in Christ? If the study is in a group, share your thoughts at the next gathering. End this session by repeating steps 2 and 3 to consider the next question or challenge.

# Is there a God?  How can we be sure?

When we're challenged by an atheist who says, "There is no God!  Religion is a narcotic of the masses designed to stupefy them,"[6] or an agnostic who says, "How can you be sure there is a God?" How can we answer?  How can we be sure of God's nature?

*(An answer by Jack Clark)*

I can only answer for myself that my being sure of God's existence boils down to three things: I see evidence that God exists everywhere I look – in the things He has created. Creation testifies that there is a creator.  I see the evidence of His ongoing concern for His creation, and through His personal interest in me by His Holy Spirit, I conclude that He believes in me!

Theology in the minds of some is the study <u>about</u> God.  It would seem more accurate to say that theology is the study <u>of</u> God.   To share in an observation of Frederica Mathewes-Green, a theologian is often thought of as one who has acquired intellectual understanding of religious theory.  Probably a better understanding would be "a theologian is one who has approached union with God and been flooded with light.  A theologian is not one who grasps the truth but who has been grasped by the truth and has been transformed."[7]  This process of being grasped, held, and transformed by the truth of God plays a large role in my belief.

How can I prove God exists?  Some proofs are by convention.  We prove that the sun comes up in the east by the convention that east is where we see the sun rise.  This was the understanding of mankind for thousands of years until it became obvious that the sun doesn't rise at all – the earth rotates and gives the impression that the sun rises.  From the perspective of the earth, the sun is the immovable center of our solar system.  (The sun would rise over many, many years if observed in its rotation from near the black hole at the center of our galaxy because our galaxy does rotate around its center.)  Another long-held convention was that the earth is flat.  Very few believe this today, so long-held convention cannot be looked on as proving anything.  No skeptic about God's existence or

---

[6] This was the sentiment of the early leaders of the Communist Party in the Soviet Revolution to justify their suppression of religion and dedicate the efforts of the people and the economic assets of the Russian Orthodox Church to the advancement of the state.

[7] *At the Corner of East and Now,* Frederica Mathewes-Green, p. 153, copyright © 1999, Published by Jeremy P. Tarcher/Putnam, 375 Hudson Street, New York, NY 10014. (This book is about understanding Eastern Orthodox faith.)

nature would be convinced on the basis of long-held beliefs. They are certainly not the proof he seeks.

I would suggest that the thought occurs to me: "How can I be sure of anything at all?" How can I be sure my wife, Carol, loves me? In answering this seemingly easier question, I might answer, "I'm sure that Carol loves me because she tells me so." On reflection I have to confess that this isn't much of a proof, because as much as I enjoy hearing it, I have to recognize that people say these same words to each other when they don't really mean it or even when they're telling an outright lie. So I might qualify my answer – "I'm sure Carol loves me because she tells me so, and I'm persuaded that when Carol tells me something that it's the truth." A scoffer could well come back with, "Do you think there was never a person who was told by someone that he or she was loved and was convinced that it was the truth only to find out it was a lie?" I would have to confirm that this too has happened not once, but multiple times to other people I have known. As much a treasure as these words of Carol's are to me, I must recognize they don't prove her love.

Ultimately I am forced to the admission that I cannot prove Carol's love as one would prove a mathematical problem. I have to accept that she loves me because I have experienced the effects of that love. I have been buoyed by her love when I have been tired beyond going on or defeated by overwhelming problems. I have been forgiven by her love when I have been less than loving or considerate to her. I have shared her love as we have worked together to meet problems or to build our dreams, or to share each other's pains. I have experienced my love for her growing as I revel in her successes and as she supports me in my efforts and failures and as she helps me to grow and become a better person than I have been in the past.

The same type of process is involved in my coming to the realization that the Bible verse my Grandmother taught me a long time ago is true: "God is love."[8] God gives me the same transforming proofs of His love – the experienced effects, the support when I don't know where to turn, the forgiveness, the chance to share my hurts and dreams and God's sharing His dreams and disappointments with me spiritually, and the

---

[8] I John 4:8 (KJV)

encouragement He has given me to grow. I have chosen to return God's love to the best of my ability and in the expectation that He will help me to become more like Him.

If a friend had not told me about Carol many years ago, I would have never responded by calling her to ask for that first date. If I had not responded to her suggestion that I call her back, we would have never had the second date. If this had not occurred (in spite of a gap of time resulting from my being ill after – not because of – the first date) we would never have held hands. If that had not happened we would have never shared the first of many delightful kisses. If there had been no first kiss, there would have never been the conviction that Carol was the right woman with whom to share my life. If this had not happened, I would not have proposed to her, she would not have accepted, and we would have never been married. The growth of relationship with God follows parallel paths of development that result in commitment and life-changing events in the person who accepts God's love.

We often start by hearing about God. It's sort of like hearing about someone that you've never met – just a name – perhaps like the name Carolyn Shaffer was to me at one point. In itself, the name has very little meaning. But as others tell us more about the person the name represents, it comes to mean more. Perhaps there's enough interest that we make an effort to learn more, and the name becomes more than words. The name becomes a person. As things progress as they did in Carol's and my relationship, there might come a time when we meet the person and find them to be ever so much more interesting than the things we've read and heard. This same process often happens with God. With God there will come a time when He offers to be our friend. There comes a time when He says in effect, with a few changes and a different focus you could really have a better life. Then as friends do, you share adventures and activities together. One day God says, "How about letting me do the leading?" Because you've learned to trust and love Him and learned to admire His ways, you're pleased to say, "Yes." It's surprising where He'll take you. Sometimes it's even scary. But it's always an exciting experience; it's something new all the time. As with a lot of adventures, you learn to pack light and leave the excess baggage. God is always doing a new thing, and with him in the driver's seat, you'll not have need for a lot of "things."

The Bible records the experience of many people becoming aware of God and God's nature and God's fully reliable love, yet only one individual at a time can become convinced of God's existence and nature. I can only pass on my experience – not to be grafted onto another person but as an account of what God has shown me and as what I am convinced He will show to others if given a chance.

Scriptures have several things to say about a person who ignores God or denies His existence. "The heavens are telling the glory of God, and the firmament proclaims his handiwork."[9] "In his pride, the wicked does not seek him; in all his thoughts there is no room for God."[10] "The fool says in his heart, 'There is no God.'"[11]

God's nature – His essential qualities actually involve a great many attributes. He is holy – perfect, separate yet approachable, above all things. He creates – in the beginning he created the universe by His word – His thought – His energy (I think these mean the same thing where God is concerned). Not only did he create things then, He continues to create now: "Jesus said to them, 'My Father is always at his work to this very day, and I, too, am working.'"[12] Not only does he create, he re-creates. Some of the physical universe seems to have cycled through the "big bang," the formation of the galaxies and stars, the explosions of super novae, and using the material to form new stars. In addition to this re-creation of the material universe, God re-creates sinners – fallen human kind – into born again beings by the action of His son's redemption. Another characteristic of God's nature is that He reveals Himself; another is that He offers Himself and walks with us through life's experiences in a very personal manner. He does the revealing and offering through the inspiration of the prophets who were led to understand Him and write their understanding into the scriptures. He does it through the revealing of His nature through the life and teaching of Jesus, God's Messiah, and He does it by awareness given to people by the Holy Spirit as He meets us in the chaos that living in the world involves and through being with us and sharing in our pain and sufferings. Another characteristic of His nature is that He seals the offers He makes with covenants that can never be broken and with his everlasting love. Probably the greatest and certainly the most referred to aspects of His character are covered by the Hebrew words *sedeq* and *hesed*. *Sedeq* is God's righteousness, and *hesed* is His steadfast love.

---

[9] Psalm 19:1 (RSV)
[10] Psalm 10:4 (NIV)
[11] Psalm 14:1 (RSV)
[12] John 5:17 (NIV)

How can I prove these are characteristics of God's nature?  Only by experiencing them myself or by accepting the experience of those I trust.  After all I cannot prove on my own most of the facts I accept.  Most of the facts about any subject are passed on to us from others.

It seems obvious that God has created us for fellowship with Him.  "God created man in his own image.  In the image of God he created him; male and female he created them."[13] God could certainly have created human-kind so that we <u>had</u> to love Him, so that we <u>had</u> to obey His laws, so that there was no choice.  Superficially this may sound appealing – it certainly would exclude evil and sin from our lives.  But the consequence would be that we would be puppets or automatons – robots with no free will.  What kind of a relationship would that be?  What kind of a relationship would it be if Carol had no choice but to be my wife and no choice but to obey my every whim?  The relationship would go from freely accepted and mutually desirable to that of slave and master.  How could I ever be assured it was a relationship of her choice and because she chose it and that she desires and cherishes it?  How could I ever be convinced that it was not just forced on her?  God seeks to have a deeply intimate relationship with mankind – a relationship more deeply intimate than the best imaginable marriage but without the physical aspect.  The only way this can happen is that it must be by mutual choice.  This isn't to say that the depth of the relationship won't grow with shared experiences.  Certainly Carol and my relationship grows deeper with each year of our marriage, and our relationship with God grows deeper with time.

The Bible says: "Seek the Lord."[14]  "See and taste!"[15]  These are not suggestions. They are imperative sentences that demand response.  Seek indicates that the person who wants to know God must make an effort.  "The man who approaches God must have faith in two things, first that God exists and secondly that it is worth a man's while to try to find God."[16]  The person who seeks Him has a promise: "Those who look to him are radiant."[17]  Carol and I have had several people ask us, "What's different about the two of you?  You always seem so happy and seem to enjoy each other and what you're doing so

---

[13] Genesis 1:27 (NIV)
[14] Psalm 34:4-5 (NIV)
[15] Psalm 34:8 (NIV)
[16] Romans 11:6 (JBP)
[17] Psalm 34:5 (NIV)

much." God does make a difference in our lives, and what a great chance it is to share the source of our joy and to share that it's available to anyone who asks for it.

See and taste indicate that the seeker must experience God. It's a sensual experience to come to know God, just as it is a sensual experience to come to know the love of another person. Intellect can be involved in either relationship, but a successful relationship has to involve more than intellect or creeds or ritual or disciplines. All of these may play a successful role in the knowing of God or a human lover, but in themselves they are no substitute for the depth of understanding and commitment that comes from experiencing another's love – whether that other be your human lover or God, the lover of your soul. Just as a person in love with another person has his thoughts and dreams filled with the one he loves, we come to experience the same type of longing for God as the psalmist did: "As a deer pants for streams of water, so my soul pants for you, O God. My soul thirsts for God, for the living God!"[18] This was written by a person who lived in a desert country where a dry waterhole could send the deer on an intense search for that which was crucial to sustain life. The reason for this is that God has built into us this same intense need for seeking Him that He built into the thirsty deer to know what it needed to preserve its life.

When we give ourselves and our love to God, He responds by heaping blessings on us. This is an important characteristic of God's nature. I don't know the mechanism of God giving me blessings any more than I understand the blessings given by my wife in response to my loving her, but they are certainly there.

There are a lot of less involved things that we accept based on the observation that it's just how things work. When I was in medical school, we didn't know how aspirin worked. We knew that it relieved pain, inflammation, and fever, and could cause stomach irritation; however, at that time we didn't know of the existence of prostaglandins and their effects or that their production was decreased by aspirin. We could observe and use the effects of this powerful drug without understanding exactly how it worked. These uses and side effects were understood on an empirical basis. Likewise God's actions in nature and in our lives can be observed. When we give our lives to God, we can see the effect in the

---

[18] Psalm 42:1-2 (NIV)

changes in what is important in our lives, the change in our esteem of others and ourselves, and the change in our actions. Our lives become full, rich, and complete. If we have committed ourselves to God and stray from him, as all of us have done at times, we can see the effect, we can feel the effect, and others can detect the resulting shallowness and lack of completeness. Christians have noted the effect of God on our lives to be so great that, over the years, we have described it as being born again.[19] How more graphically could the effect of something be noted and this giving characteristic of God be revealed?

It is a characteristic of this great God, this creator of the universe and everything in it, including you and including me that He requires that we relate to Him. The sad consequence of not doing so, involves the loss of all He has hoped to give us. If I choose to reject God's love and gifts and the relationship He has devised for me, I can lose these things. He will urge me to accept them. He will go to great lengths to let me know the benefits of accepting them and the consequences of not. He will devise means for me to be made worthy to accept them even when I could never be worthy on my own, but ultimately He will not force you or me into the acceptance. In the words of the scripture, "Choose for yourselves this day who you will serve... But as for me and my household, we will serve the Lord."[20]

It is in the nature of God to supply our needs, to guide us, to watch over us, and to urge us to achieve the most we can in this life. This aspect of His nature is reflected in the following: "'I know the plans I have for you,' declares the Lord, 'plans to prosper you and not to harm you, plans to give you hope and a future.'"[21] This paternal attitude led Jesus to suggest we think of God as Abba. We in the English-speaking Christian church are used to having this translated Father as in "'Abba, Father,' he said, 'everything is possible for you. Take this cup from me. Yet not what I will, but what you will.'"[22] This is the term Jesus used for God when he taught the disciples how to pray, "Our Father which art in heaven..."[23] Actually the true sense of the translation seemingly should have conveyed a

---

[19] John 3:3 (NIV)
[20] Joshua 24:15 (NIV)
[21] Jeremiah 29:11 (NIV)
[22] Mark 14:36 (NIV)
[23] Matthew 6:9-13 (KJV)

less formal, tenderer, closer, more dependent relationship. It would seem that probably a better rendition of the word Abba would be Daddy.

A friend of our grandson Jonathan told us about some of her experiences in Israel. She explained that Abba is still the word used for Daddy. One day, she watched a toddler eagerly dash with up-stretched arms toward his father, repeatedly expressing his delight with cries of Abba! Abba! Abba! As he rushed to meet him, his daddy smiled widely, bent down and scooped the child up into his arms. The daddy pitched him up into the air and caught him. Both laughed with irrepressible joy, and in that instant she was given a new appreciation of the delight we should feel about Abba, our Father God, and the joy He feels about us.

Another aspect of the nature of God is that He is the one who spoke and everything was created. This is the God who is Holy—sacred, venerated, revered, separate, set apart, unapproachable based on our efforts, perfect, so perfect that He cannot stand imperfection, awesome, high, not fully understandable. This is the God who, although holy, at the same time made himself approachable totally through his son, Jesus Christ. This Holy God though high and perfect, loves each of us so much that He would literally give up anything to convert our imperfections into perfection through Christ in order to bring us to Him. This is the God who sent His angel to Hagar, an abused Egyptian slave girl in Abram's camp. She was pregnant at her mistress Sarai's bidding to produce a surrogate child for Sarai by Abram. In Hagar's misery and rejection, God took mercy on her and comforted her, naming her son Ishmael (God hears). In her response she gave God one of the most telling names attributed to Him in the Bible: "She gave this name to the Lord who spoke to her: 'You are the God who sees me.'"[24] I can picture Hagar huddled in the corner of the tent, abused, impregnated but not loved, an object to be used to satisfy the longing of her mistress, but unnoticed as an individual—not even seen by anyone but God Himself. Many, many Bible accounts tell us this is just the kind of person God does see; God does give His compassion, and God does reach out in love to help. Later when Hagar and Ishmael were thrown out of the camp to die in the wilderness, this same God heard the dying boy's crying and his broken hearted mother's sobs because she couldn't bear to watch her son die of thirst. He gave them water; He gave them life,

---

[24] Genesis 16:13-14 (NIV)

and He gave them the promise that they too would have a great nation spring from them. This God who is both holy and separate demonstrated his total involvement in Hagar's life in this brief vivid depiction. By extension, this God "who sees me" demonstrates His total involvement in my life and in your life and the life of every other person He has created.

I usually think of Abba as the creator. This certainly is true, but in some way it is obvious that the son also was involved in the process of creation. "In the beginning was the Word, and the Word was with God, and the Word was God. He was with God in the beginning. Through him all things were made; without him nothing was made that has been made."[25] Paul spoke about the nature of God when he was introducing Him to the Greeks who had been worshipping a pantheon of gods including an "unknown god." Paul identified this unknown god as Yahweh, the true God, and indicated that he was there more to expand their knowledge and get rid of some mistaken understandings than to destroy their beliefs. "Now what you worship as something unknown, I am going to proclaim to you. The God who made the world and everything in it is the Lord of heaven and earth and does not live in temples built by hands. And He is not served by human hands, as if He needed anything, because He himself gives all men life and breath and everything else. From one man He made every nation of men that they should inhabit the whole earth; and He determined the times set for them and the exact places where they should live. God did this so that men would seek him and perhaps reach out for him and find him, though He is not far from each of us. 'For in him we live and move and have our being.'"[26]

Part of being Holy is to be completely without sin. Sin is totally repugnant to God; He abhors sin.[27] This is why God, by His very nature, cannot tolerate sin. This is why mankind, who cannot avoid sin, cannot be acceptable to God without the plan He and His son devised to remove all our sins from us. To allow us to be acceptable in God's presence, Jesus Christ volunteered to take all the sins of the world onto himself. "The wages of sin is death, but the gift of God is eternal life in Christ Jesus our Lord."[28] It was to establish the fact that he indeed had taken our sins on himself that Christ did die on the cross. We could not have comprehended the grace without it. My sins require me to be

---

[25] John 1:1-3 (NIV)
[26] Acts 17:23-28 (NIV)
[27] Psalm 26:5 (NIV)
[28] Romans 6:23 (NIV)

separated from God, and this is death. Only through Christ making himself a substitute for me could this fate be avoided. Even then, I must accept the gift; God and Christ will not force it on me.

My perspective is constrained by finite measurements of time and space analogous to a photograph that can record only a two dimensional view of what is seen. God, on the other hand, has no such constraints. His existence is from everlasting to everlasting. He is the beginning and the end. He is in a state of everlasting present, so right now He is at the beginning of our time, at the end of our time and at all points in between. This concept is probably more difficult for most of us than it is for physicists who view space-time as the fourth dimension of the known universe (the other three being up-down, forward-backward, and right-left). God views everything that happened at the beginning, in between and at the end all at once. This is why He knows what will happen; He sees it as happening now. This is why his edicts, such as the defeat of Satan outlined in Revelation, are accomplished facts even though in human history they will occur sometime in our future. He knows where we have been, where we are now, and where we are going, because all these aspects of our existence are in the present tense to God. There is no past to God. There is no future in God's perspective. The finite future from our perspective, in which we hope, with God and His Christ and His Holy Spirit is accomplished now in God's perspective. With God, there is only an everlasting present that encompasses our concept of the past, present and future.

Christ says, "I am the Alpha and Omega,[29] the beginning and the end."[30] He didn't say I was the Alpha and will be the Omega. The verb is present tense. God, in speaking to Moses, referred to Himself as "I AM."[31] Spiritually God and Christ are now at the beginning, at the end and at all places in between. This is why David could write, "A thousand years in your sight are like a day that has just gone by, or like a watch in the night."[32] Likewise Peter wrote, "With the Lord a day is like a thousand years, and a thousand years are like a day."[33] This perspective allows God to know everything; we call this omniscience. An interesting aspect of this is that God even knows what I will pray for

---

[29] Revelation 1:8 (NIV)
[30] Revelation 21:6 (NIV)
[31] Exodus 3:14 (NIV)
[32] Psalms 90:4 (NIV)
[33] Second Peter 3:8 (NIV)

in the future. A result of this could be that a friend in another town may go to surgery without my knowing about it. If I get a call after the surgery is over, God can respond to my request that the result of the biopsy turns out all right. In my past limited understanding, I would have reasoned that the result was already determined even before the offending tissue was noted and long before the biopsy was done. But because God exists and knows everything in the present tense, He knew of my prayer before the involved tissue had become a tumor and before the tumor was discovered, and before the surgery was completed, and so well before the pathologist determined the nature of the tumor. Now this aspect of God's nature is certainly a blessing!

God is a spirit. He cannot be tied to a physical existence.[34] He is in everything He has created, but He is not bound by the material nature of His creations. As a spirit, one of His qualities is that He can be found everywhere. He is to be found in the depths of the earth, in the most distant solar system, beside a quiet brook, or in a roaring factory. More important than the places God can be found are the spiritual conditions in which one may find Him. These range from the darkest hell of despair of the person who has removed himself from God's love to the quiet joy of the person who is doing God's work. We can find Him wherever we are and in any spiritual condition. He is omnipresent, present everywhere.

He is also characterized as omnipotent, all-powerful. Not only did He create everything, He can change what has been created, He can perform miracles, He has vanquished death and defeated Satan. This latter event is in our future but has been decreed by God, and, so even though it is in our future, the action is completed. He can protect us from anything, or if He chooses will go with us through anything if it can be for our betterment or the advancement of the kingdom. He can open our eyes and understanding through all these events for our spiritual growth and for His glory. As the Bible says, "If God is for us, who can be against us?"[35]

To me, one of the most telling scriptural references to God as all knowing, all powerful, and all present is written by David: "O Lord, you have searched me and you know me. You know when I sit and when I rise. You perceive my thoughts from afar. You discern

_____

[34] John 4:24 (NIV)
[35] Romans 8:31 (NIV)

my going out and my lying down; you are familiar with all my ways. Before a word is on my tongue you know it completely, O Lord. You hem me in–behind and before; you have laid your hand upon me. Such knowledge is too wonderful for me, too lofty for me to attain. Where can I go from your Spirit? Where can I flee from your presence? If I go up to the heavens, you are there; if I make my bed in the depths, you are there. If I rise on the wings of the dawn, if I settle on the far side of the sea, even there your hand will guide me; your right hand will hold me fast. If I say, 'Surely the darkness will hide me and the light become night around me,' even the darkness will not be dark to you; the night will shine like the day, for darkness is as light to you. For you created my inmost being; you knit me together in my mother's womb. I praise you because I am fearfully and wonderfully made; your works are wonderful, I know that full well."[36]

The Jewish people speak of the *Shekinah* (the Presence of God), a visible sign of God's being in a location, or, as they also referred to it, the Glory of the Lord. They were especially aware of the His Presence as related to the Ark of the Testimony, and the Holy of Holies.[37] Of course, God's Presence was also especially evident in the cloud that led Israel by day and the pillar of light that led them by night while they were in the wilderness[38] and in the cloud that covered the tent of the meeting as Moses would go in to commune with God.[39] With a small amount of insight, I maintain God's Presence, His *Shekinah,* may be witnessed in the glories of His creation and in the joy of fellowship with Him.

Although it is true that our Holy God can never be fully known, He gives thrilling partial understandings of his nature. In the words of Paul, "Now we see but a poor reflection as in a mirror; then we shall see face to face. Now I know in part; then I shall know fully, even as I am fully known."[40] One day while driving to Goshen Hospital to see patients, I turned west on US 33 near Benton, Indiana. It was early in the day, and a lovely orange sun shown directly behind me. As I changed the setting of my rear view mirror to decrease the intensity of the beautiful reflection to a level I could tolerate, it occurred to me that this was exactly what Paul was talking about. God's full majesty is not

---

[36] Psalms 139:1-14 (NIV)
[37] Exodus 25:22, Leviticus 16:2, Second Samuel 6:2, Second Kings 19:14-15, Psalm 80:1, Isaiah 37:16, Ezekiel 9:3, and Hebrews 9:5 (NIV)
[38] Exodus 13:21-22 (NIV)
[39] Exodus 33:9 (NIV)
[40] First Corinthians 13:12 (NIV)

withheld from me now because of God's selfishness or because of His not wanting me to know, but because my senses cannot encompass Him in His full greatness. Instead of overwhelming my senses and my understanding He gives me what I am able to grasp and increases my understanding as I become capable. In-so-far as we can comprehend, He reveals Himself to us through our study of the scripture, through understanding gained and shared by other brothers and sisters in Christ, and through interaction with His Holy Spirit. As God unfolds His nature to us, we can come to appreciate His plan for His creation, and come to develop insight into where we fit in that plan. Theologians, in trying to understand God, speak of the Mind of God, the Heart of God, and the Will of God. They also speak of three aspects of the will of God: His intentional will, His situational will, and His ultimate will.

To understand the Mind of God means to comprehend His thoughts. Of course no one but Jesus Christ has fully understood the thoughts of the Father; however, it is possible to develop a great deal of insight about His thoughts from study of the Bible. Several places the scriptures confirm we cannot ever fully know God's mind. "God's voice thunders in marvelous ways; He does great things beyond our understanding."[41] "'My thoughts are not your thoughts, neither are your ways my ways,' declares the Lord."[42] On the other hand, the Bible also indicates that God will reveal much of His intentions and thoughts if we seek to know Him. "If you call out for insight and cry aloud for understanding, and if you look for it as for silver and search for it as for hidden treasure, then you will understand the fear of the Lord and find the knowledge of God."[43] Of course to know God is a deeper relationship than to know about God. It seems to me that we can determine that it was in the mind of God to make mankind in His image to foster a relationship with the beings He made. It seems that He intentionally gave us a free will knowing that we would abuse the privilege (since He knows everything). The reason He gave this free will becomes obvious as we read of His relationship to the people in the testaments. He didn't give it so He could catch us in mistakes and punish us as some seem to suggest. He didn't give us free will so that we would fail. The reason He gave us the free will was so that we could voluntarily come into a deep, loving, intimate relationship with Him not by coercion but by our own choice.

---

[41] Job 37:5 (NIV)
[42] Isaiah 55:8 (NIV)
[43] Proverbs 2:3-5 (NIV)

Rev. George Lohman related a story from the Civil War that, from a human standpoint, illustrates the action of a righteous father and so illustrates in parable the heart of God. A young Quaker boy was determined to join the Union Army. Because of their religious beliefs in pacifism his family strongly opposed this action. Not to be deterred, the boy joined anyway. Almost two years went by without any word. One day the family received word there had been a great battle nearby and it was thought their son was a causality. Without hesitation, the father set out for the battlefield. He located the Union commander and sought word about his son. All the commander could tell him was there had indeed been a terrible battle with many causalities and many of the dead and wounded were still in the trenches. The father went to the front, picking his way through the mangled, bleeding men, some of whom were crying, some moaning, and some eternally silent. As he walked through the night, he would call out, "Jonathan Smythe, thy father seeketh thee." Repeatedly he called, "Jonathan Smythe, thy father seeketh thee." Many men would respond, "I wish you were my father." On and on the search went. Finally there was a weak response, "Father, father." The father and wounded son were reunited. The son declared, "I knew you would come." So it is with our Father in heaven. Even when we reject His advice and leave him, He stands ready for our return, and if trouble ensnares us, He stands ready, to search us out and rescue us. Abba God is a lover of our souls; He is not willing that one of us should be lost. He seeks for us, and He and all the angels in heaven rejoice when one of us is found and returned to the family of God. "Blessed is the man who trusts in the Lord, whose trust is the Lord. He is like a tree planted by water."[44]

To further understand the heart of God, we need to try to see others as He sees them. This was illustrated in our family when Carol took our granddaughter, Katie, who was twelve at the time, to visit my mother in the nursing home. Katie was expressing how nice it was to see "Mammaw." Mother responded, "Why would anyone want to see a dried up old prune like me?" Katie, without a moment's hesitation, responded, "Oh, Mammaw, in God's eyes you're a fresh plum." Great grandmother looked to Carol with, "Is she a minister?" Of course Katie had been brought up in the tradition that all believers are

---

[44] Jeremiah 17:7-8 (RSV)

ministers, so the answer would be yes. And it would seem that she is a pretty good one too.

In helping to understand God's aspirations and plans for us, C. S. Lewis suggests that God will, in the long run, be satisfied with nothing less than absolute perfection that will only be achieved when we are in heaven. But he also suggests that God will be delighted with the first feeble, stumbling effort we make. He noted that George MacDonald, another Christian writer, points out that every father is pleased with a baby's first attempt to walk, but that no father would be satisfied with anything less than a firm, free, manly walk in a grown-up son. He quotes MacDonald: "God is easy to please, but hard to satisfy."[45]

The will of God is understood as occurring on several levels. The intentional will of God is that every person would live in a deep relationship with Him, a relationship in which our perfection would be the same as His, a relationship with no separation from Him or from others. Because of our imperfections, this can't occur. God's situational will comes into play when our rebellion, our foul-ups and our self will, our sin separate us from Him or when circumstances or the sins of others would ruin our relationships or the quality of life for us. God can take these disasters of life and turn them into something positive that can be a blessing for us, a blessing to others, further the kingdom, or bring us closer to Him. This situational will is what the author of Romans had in mind when he wrote, "We know that in all things God works for the good of those who love Him, who have been called according to His purpose."[46] His ultimate will is that each individual will have the opportunity to overcome the destruction that would result because of our imperfection and be redeemed, washed clean in the blood of Christ, and be brought into relationship with God. What a plan! What excitement in being able to recognize even a fragment of God's mind, His heart, and His will! How exciting to realize that God had planned all this with the son even before the world was formed![47]

God himself gave an indication of His nature to Moses. "He passed in front of Moses, proclaiming, 'The Lord, the Lord, the compassionate and gracious God, slow to anger, abounding in love and faithfulness, maintaining love to thousands, and forgiving

[45] *Mere Christianity*, C. S. Lewis, © 1980 by Arthur Owen Barfield, Touchstone Books, Touchstone Rockefeller Center, 1230 Avenue of the Americas, New York, NY 10020, p. 174.
[46] Romans 8:28 (NIV)
[47] First Corinthians 2:6-16 (NIV)

wickedness, rebellion and sin. Yet He does not leave the guilty unpunished; He punishes the children and their children for the sin of the fathers to the third and fourth generation.'"[48] On the surface of things, this pronouncement might suggest God has a compassionate and an unfair side to His nature. Where is the justice let alone the compassion to be found in punishing children for the sins of their fathers? On reflection it seems to me that what God is saying is that sin by its very nature inherently has a pernicious aspect that harms and affects all that come into contact with it. My sin distorts the lives of myself and all those around me, and it does indeed affect my children and even their children. This observation recognizes the nature of sin rather than indicating a perverse side to God's nature.

As I think back over the answer to the nature of God, I return again and again to the great advice my Grandmother Prow gave me when I was a child: "Jack always remember that God is love." That seems to summarize it all.

*Another answer by Jim Chupp*

The debate between atheists and Christians is merely a question of what is real and what is unreal. The atheist says God is not real. I would say the atheist is not real. If you place the Christian in a place of torture to cause him to denounce his faith in God, you will find someone willing to die with his faith in God intact. Put an atheist in the same torturous condition in order to move him to denounce his faith in himself and he will most likely cry out to God. Religion may indeed be the "opiate of the masses", but religion is not Almighty God. It is not the real power of God being lived out in an individual's life that drives the atheist into intellectual assault on faith. It is the religion of God with all its distortion, corruption, and deception that fuels the atheists' resolve. When anyone, whether atheist or agnostic, crosses paths with Almighty God there is an awakening. Just ask the son of Madeline Marie O'Hare.[49]

*(Another view by Dean Culbertson)*

To answer an agnostic, I would ask, "How can you not be sure?" Honestly, I'm concerned for agnostics. If I were not a believer, I could only be an atheist. This doubt doesn't work for me.

---

[48] Exodus 34:6-7 (NIV)
[49] Madeline Marie O'Hare was a dedicated, aggressively atheistic person who fought against religious beliefs in many court battles. Her son became a dedicated Christian.

36

Regarding the atheist, I would acknowledge his or her freedom not to believe. I would also point out that disbelief is a choice. Atheists demand proof that there is a God. God demands faith. The fact of the matter is I don't have to "shoot down" atheism. I would tell an atheist that even drug and alcohol programs refer to a "higher power." I know people who have quit drugs, stopped drinking, and had changed hearts. The atheist simply can't produce that – nor can he or she explain the changes. It does truly take faith to be an atheist.

*(Betty Byers' thoughts)*

I have felt His presence in my life. He is alive! The Bible says it, and I believe it because I have experienced it.

*(Arlene Berkey's thoughts as presented to a spiritual growth event in her congregation in October 2007)*

Concerning God . . .

I think one of the interesting things about Bible study is that it seems the more I study, the less I know. It's much like the moral person who accepted Christ – he thought he was a pretty good fellow until he found out what the standard actually is!

Looking at God is much the same. The more I learn, the bigger I realize He is, and, to a certain extent, the less I can truly grasp Him. But I think it's important that I continue to try. A. W. Tozer said, "What comes into our minds when we think about God is the most important thing about us." [The Knowledge of the Holy]

So what do I know about God? Can I understand Him? What comes into *my* mind when I think about God?

God is all those things we've studied – omnipotent, loving, gracious, merciful, faithful, good, wise, holy . . . and much, much more. I'm glad I'm not responsible on my own to turn myself into His likeness. It will never happen! And I'm glad I don't have to fully understand how all those attributes work together – that won't happen either, because my finite brain can't comprehend the infinite God.

But one thing I know, and one of the things I love best about God is this: In spite of the vast difference between Him and me, God wants me to know Him! And He's made Himself *knowable* by giving us the Bible. The Bible is one long love letter from God to me, telling me who He is, what He's like, what He's done. He reveals Himself in the Bible so we can know about Him, but more importantly, so we can know how deeply He longs for a relationship with us, and how He's made that relationship possible.

Creation convinces me that God exists, but the Bible teaches me what He's like. I can learn a lot about God by reading and studying the Bible . . . but just in case I couldn't understand it all . . . God came to earth Himself in a special way to show me exactly what He's like. Jesus told Philip, "He who has seen me has seen the Father." [John 14:9] Jesus is the express image of God the Father. I can gain more understanding of God by learning about Jesus, and how He lived His life on earth. He said to Thomas, "No one comes to the Father except through me. If you really knew me, you would know my Father as well. From now on, you do know him and have seen him." [John 14:6-7] Of course, He came to save us, but He also came to reveal His Father.

Another thing I love about God is that He's *approachable!* I think of the High Priest of the Old Testament, who had a rope tied about him when he entered the Holy of Holies . . . so others could pull his body out just in case he hadn't done everything right and didn't survive the encounter! How grateful I am that I don't need such a rope! No, because of Jesus, no matter how much I mess up, no matter how far I fall short of His standard, no matter when or how I call on Him, He's delighted to respond to me. I don't have to be cleaned up first or go through elaborate rituals – He's always there when I come to Him.

It's astonishing that the God who spoke the universe into existence would condescend to listen to me – and not only that, be delighted to do so.

Zephaniah 3:17 always amazes me: "The LORD your God is with you, he is mighty to save. He will take great delight in you, he will quiet you with his love, *he will rejoice over you with singing.*"

So as I continue to learn more about God, I fully expect to be more amazed, more confused, more awe-struck, more humbled, and more grateful that this incomprehensible yet knowable God . . .

"Who lit the sun and fixed it in the sky,

Who flung the stars to the most far corner of the night?

Who rounded the earth in the middle of his hand; this great God . . ." [50]

. . . This Great God knows me and loves me and wants me to know Him and love Him back. And maybe – just maybe – that's the thing that's hardest of all to understand about God!

---

*(A presentation by Gloria Frew at a spiritual growth event for her congregation in October 2007)*

## OMNIPOTENCE

God grant that I speak suitably. May my words be in your hands to your glory and honor. Amen.

The word omnipotence does not appear in scripture as far as I have researched with the help of friends.

As I began to consider this presentation, I wondered about my personal definition of omnipotence and came up with the following: Wider than the widest, taller than the tallest, deeper than the deepest, smaller than the smallest, the Alpha and Omega – beginning and end, infinity and beyond, and all points in between. In Revelation 1:8 we find: "I am the Alpha and the Omega says the Lord God, who is, and who was, and who is to come, the Almighty."

Webster says, omni "all" and potent – "able" having unlimited power or authority – all powerful – the omnipotent God. The boundlessness of God, for anything we say is limited and in a sense wrong because there is no way it can go far enough. The overlap of each of the characteristics of God is ever present for each of the attributes are rays of light coming from the same source. To quote a seminary professor of my husband Phil's, "It would be easier for a dog to understand algebra than for humans to comprehend God." I promise to keep my barking to a minimum.

---

[50] From *The Creation* by James Weldon Johnson

We use words to explain God's omnipotence and we run into problems, particularly as language changes and meanings of words change. Take the word, "awesome" for example. Phil bought his new truck and he was really pleased – drove it home and three teenaged boys came up and said, "Man Rev. Awesome Truck!" I about came through the windshield with several thoughts which I kept to myself. The main one being, God is awesome, Trucks are not!!! It makes me sad, and I miss that word being associated with God only.

One has to give the devil his due though. If words which we have reserved to describe God in his majesty change to include the stuff of this world, we have to look and carefully consider how we describe God, and then remember that Revelation 21:5 states: "He who sat upon the throne said, 'Behold, I make all things new.'"

In many ways He is the unnamable by us, for the names we apply to him are as limited as we are. Giving his name to Moses the Almighty said I AM WHO I AM which is really an incomplete action. We want to name Him, for as we name another we come to believe we know them, at least in part.

The one area in which I could not find direct information was in the connection of omnipotence with God's humbleness. For me this is one of the great mysteries, an omnipotent God, who when he sent the Messiah, his son, to earth sent him as an infant, to a young virgin girl to be born in a stable with animals in a place called Bethlehem. At the time, not many got it, so to speak. The shepherds did with some help from a great light and an angel who appeared with the words, "Fear not for behold...." How I love that phrase. It is one of my touchstones which in my darkest times I turn to never knowing what will follow the "behold," but always reminded that God knows. And then there was the angel choir, which no doubt helped the shepherds, and they went to Bethlehem.

Mary and Joseph got it. They knew it was the Messiah. Elizabeth, John the Baptist's Mother got it; the Wise Men got it and brought gifts. Herod got it as evidenced by his slaughter of the innocents, the infants. Somehow I think even the animals got it: an omnipotent God sending his son into the humblest of circumstances.

In Jesus' ministry, his disciples were not the great learned men of the day, but humble, some disliked by society, and the folks he spent time with besides the disciples were the sinners. Those he raised from the dead as far as we know were not well known, but common people.

His death on a cross, like our Electric Chair of today, was used for the worst of criminals. His burial place was a borrowed tomb.

And then something happened. Women (note the lesser members of society) were the first to be at the empty tomb, and God's omnipotence was revealed, in the Risen Lord, His son. Not all "got that"" either for here again, the all powerful mighty God gave all free will, allowing choice to follow Him and accept Him or not.

Through the ages there have been many attempts to express God's omnipotence in architecture for example, the great cathedrals of the world that were commissioned by kings, and in spite of that a glimpse of God's glory is seen, so much so that we feel like a cinder on the sidewalk of life – so tiny and small when we enter them. For example, when I visited the Cathedral of St. John the Divine in New York City, where it is said that a baseball cannot be thrown from the floor and hit the ceiling (why would one do that?). I realized that I am grateful to the designers of that cathedral for it is a reminder of how small and insignificant I am particularly in relation to the Mighty God, and I need that reminder.

God's omnipotence is expressed in the great art of the world. I had the opportunity to go to the New York Metropolitan Museum of Art. It was memorable in many ways, but the one which hit me the most was a painting that I encountered. It was huge. As I recall, it had giant hands at the top, one of which held strings with people dangling from them over what appeared to be a pit of hot coals. In the other hand was a pair of scissors. The title of the painting was "Sinners in the hands of an Angry God." (There is a sermon by Jonathan Edwards from July 1741 by the same title that is 3,751 words and would be fourteen pages printed out.) As I stood there speechless, briefly, I did say, "Oh my, I'll be so good!" and promptly walked away. It was the first time in my life that I encountered the omnipotent God's wrath and what it really means. Of course it is tempered by His son, who died for us sinners in the hands of an angry God.

It takes little searching in scripture to find references to the mighty God, powerful God, the Almighty.

In music we have many reminders of omnipotence, Handel's Messiah, Vivaldi's Gloria (I must admit I do like the title). In the Praise songs: "The Majesty and Glory of Your Name," "How Majestic Is Your Name in All the Earth," "Great and Mighty is the Lord," "Our God is an Awesome God."

In the hymns, "A Mighty Fortress is our God,"

> "Immortal, invisible God only wise,"
> "I sing the almighty power of God who makes the Mountains rise."

And of course those of you who know me know that I rarely miss an opportunity to mention my favorite hymn specifically (the 3$^{rd}$ verse. "Dear Lord and Father of Mankind :")

> O Sabbath rest by Galilee,
> O calm of hills above
> Where Jesus knelt to share with thee
> The silence of eternity interpreted by love.

A silence of eternity, impossible to comprehend and it is interpreted by an omnipotent love; and it reaches deep within me.

This almighty God was not in the Wind, Earthquake or Fire, but in the still small voice. This has always surprised me for it is always in the silence that my deepest experiences with God have been found. Amazing that this loud mouth old sinner, the mighty God chooses to meet in the deepest silence, for he is everywhere.

I recall a 5 year old cousin, who with his father was showing his little friend the church and answering his questions about God. His friend asked, "Where is God?" Greg answered, "He's everywhere, behind the altar, in the balcony, outside, right next to you; but don't lean on Him because you'll fall down." Greg had not matured enough to understand the meaning of the everlasting arms.

An omnipotent God who cares for the fall of the sparrow. I remember asking the question, "Who is the sparrow?" And I have discovered that we don't get to pick and choose. We simply must care.

I think one of the better quotes about God's omnipotence comes from Martin Buber; it's a term that I have never had the opportunity to use until now. He says, "God is the Mysterium Tremendum that appears and overthrows, but he is also the mystery of the self – evident, nearer to me than I am to myself."

Closer to me than I can be to myself, He reaches down into a part of me that I am unable to reach on my own. This all-powerful God who is always so near to each one of us. That is one of the great mysteries for me of Omnipotence,

---

*(An answer by Gary Phillips)*

Philippians 3:7-9a "But whatever was to my profit I now consider loss for the sake of Christ. What is more, I consider everything a loss compared to the surpassing greatness of knowing Christ Jesus my lord, for whose sake I have lost all things. I consider them rubbish that I may gain Christ and be found in him."

2 Timothy 1:12b "I know whom I have believed."

As we come out of the Spiritual Dark Ages known as the Age of Enlightenment or Age of Reason the question of "Is there a God?" becomes important to society. There are many who claim the question is irrelevant and/or superstitious for Modern Man. Much of the reasoning of the age of Enlightenment/Reason begins with the assumption there is no God or if there is a God he is impotent and cannot interact with the physical world. This has been described as beginning with the assumption there is no God and arguing in a circular manner to the point where you claim we have proven there is no God and to believe in a God is to be ignorant or superstitious. People holding this position will discount any statement to the contrary. It is said, "I will not believe anything that cannot be proven scientifically or mathematically." This has become the standard by which all things are measured.

To this we need to ask a simple question. Can this statement itself be proven true by scientific or mathematic methods? I don't think so. What does this mean? The standard by which all things are measured fails to pass its own standard. What is it then? It is an unproven and at this time, a statement of belief that cannot be proven, i.e. a matter of faith.

What can our response to the question, "Is there a God?" be? I think there are two ways to respond. First is to attempt to use logic and reason to prove there is a God. Some can do this very well and I salute them.

There is a second way to respond. This is simply to proclaim "I know Him." To our ears which have been steeped in modernity, this is a statement which will cause many to question our sanity. Yet it has been proclaimed by many Christians through the millenniums of Christianity.

This is what Paul was saying to the church at Philippi and to Timothy. "I know him whom I have believed and this knowing is more important to me than anything else in the world."

The sensation I had when I read <u>The Confessions of St. Augustine</u> was that I was reading the personal love letters of someone to the desire of his love.

Brother Lawrence in <u>Practicing the Presence of God</u> teaches us not only to know God intimately but how to live in God's presence constantly. He knew Him whom he believed.

The British preacher W.E. Sangster published a compilation of his sermons in 1960. He chose the sermons based on the written responses to his sermons over his career as a preacher. His first sermon and the title of the book was <u>Can I Know God</u>. Hear what he says on page 16;

> "Put into precise terms, the experience which is claimed is one of immediate acquaintance. It is not "knowledge about" as I might have about, say, Bouvet Island in the South Atlantic (where I have never been and am never likely to go) but immediate acquaintance such as I had for years with my father, at whose side I grew up, on whose strength I relied, and to whom I could turn for help every day.

44

The heart of religion is not an opinion about God, but a personal relationship with him."

Is there a God? How can we be sure?  To these questions I answer, "Yes there is a God!  Because I know him!"  I have read of his love for me in the Bible.  He has shown his love for me by the ways he has helped and strengthened me in times of trial.  I have been bathed in his loving presence.  He has told me Person to person that He loved me!  I know Him, and He is worth knowing!

# Is the God of the Old Testament the God of the New Testament?

How can you say the God of the Old Testament is the God of the New Testament?  How does killing whole groups of people in ethnic cleansing match up with the affirmation that "God is love?"

*(An answer by Jack Clark)*

One of the things that I have become increasingly aware of in my relationship with God and in my study of the scriptures is that God has a plan.  It's increasingly obvious that the plan is that as many humans as possible will choose to be in relationship with Him and choose to let Christ's saving power allow us to be a part of His Kingdom.  This was His plan before creation.  This was His plan from the very beginning of mankind's awareness of the possibility of such a relationship.  It was His plan when he led Abram to leave his ancestral home and start the wanderings that would lead to a newness of relationship that later lovers of God would call being born again.  The recognition of that new relationship involved the changing his name to Abraham.  This was God's plan throughout the events recorded in the Old Testament.  It was His plan in the life events and teachings of Jesus, God's Messiah, and it is God's plan in the history and events of the church and in the lives of the saints (followers of God) since that time.

God offered Abram a special relationship for him and his descendants.  The relationship is called a covenant.  Seemingly Abram accepted this covenant with enthusiasm, but I know from personal experience, that when God makes an offer and the recipient of the offer is less than willing to accept it, that God tends to exert more and more pressure to get His way.  He doesn't make the offer compulsory or give threats to get His way, but His will becomes increasingly irresistible.  Scriptural references to such offers include God's offering to send Moses to free Israel from Egypt.  Moses was certainly less than willing to accept the assignment, and he certainly had numerous reasons why he thought it was a bad idea, but God got His way.[51]  Certainly Jonah wasn't interested in God's assignment to go to Nineveh, the capital of Assyria, and lead them to repentance.  As an Israelite, Jonah had every reason to want nothing to do with Assyria.  Rarely has there been a nation crueler to another nation than Assyria had been to Israel.  Jonah resisted to the point that he had to be chewed up and spit out (whether figuratively or literally) to get him to agree to the offer.[52]  Hopefully God will not need to do this with

---

[51] Exodus 3-4
[52] Book of Jonah

any of us when He has an assignment, but He does have methods to get His way when we have accepted Him as ruler of our lives.

When God offered Abram the special covenant relationship for himself and his descendants forever that made them God's Chosen People, He made clear what that plan was: "I will surely bless you and make your descendants as numerous as the stars in the sky and as the sand on the seashore.  Your descendants will take possession of the cities of their enemies, and through your offspring all nations on earth will be blessed, because you have obeyed me."[53]  The blessing was not just to benefit Israel; it was to benefit all people.

Not every person in Israel was a pillar of faith or a pillar of strength that could resist temptations.  When it came time to have a homeland for God's chosen people, there weren't great expanses of empty uninhabited spaces available for free homesteading.

God recognized that Israel with all its short-comings was the most capable of all people to eventually get to the point that His son could make his entrance into the world among these people.  It would take centuries, false starts, good kings and bad kings, wandering away from their faith, wars, deportations, and ignored prophets to prepare this people to reach the point where a few would understand and accept the message that Jesus would bring.

It was also essential in God's plan that the location of the Chosen People would be at the crossroads of the civilized world, so that the message could spread throughout the nations.  Such a location was in the Fertile Crescent.  This was already occupied by many small city states whose citizens worshiped idols, fertility cults that employed temple prostitutes as part of their worship experience, and even Molech, a god to which the inhabitants made a fiery sacrifice of their first-born children.  You wouldn't have to be an all-knowing God to understand that to put your Chosen People into such a situation would have spelled disaster for the plan.

If there was any doubt about Israel's difficulty in handling enticements, it was certainly

---

[53] Genesis 22:17-18 (NIV)

confirmed when Moses went up on Mount Sinai to receive the Ten Commandments. When Moses came down with God's Laws, the people had melted their gold and made a golden calf to worship! If ever there was a group of people for whom it was imperative that they not be led into temptation but delivered from evil, it was God's Chosen People. To have put them into daily contact with the people who occupied the land when they came from Egypt would to have been to doom the plan God had voiced to Abram to total failure. They could not have become the nation into which God's son could have come and where a group of followers would be attracted to him. This group of followers would become those who would ultimately fan out from the Fertile Crescent to bring Christ's good news to the rest of the world.

Did God hate the Canaanites, the Hittites, the Amorites the Hivites, the Perizzites, the Girgashites, and the Jebusites who lived in the land that God gave to Israel? I don't think so. The book of Hebrews in the New Testament makes the statement that God "wants all men to be saved and come to a knowledge of the truth. For there is one God and one mediator between God and men, the man Christ Jesus, who gave himself as a ransom for all men–the testimony given in its proper time."[54] This last phrase indicates to me that Christ gave himself spiritually for our redemption long before that gift was manifest on the cross at Calvary. The letter to the Hebrews makes the claim, "Jesus Christ is always the same, yesterday, today, and forever."[55] And Jesus said, "anyone who has seen me has seen the Father."[56] From these statements taken together, I take it to indicate that God's will is that all humankind would be saved. I also take it that this was God's will at the time the people were displaced from the Promised Land to make way for the Hebrews. So it logically follows that God loved the people who were displaced and would have chosen that they would have chosen to be a part of His Kingdom and have been saved.

I get a deep sense of Christ's (and by inference God's) feelings toward those who reject the offer of relationship from an account of one of Christ's statements: "O Jerusalem, Jerusalem, you who kill the prophets and stone those sent to you, how often I have longed to gather your children together, as a hen gathers her chicks under her wings, but you were not willing. Look your house is left to you desolate."[57]

---

[54] I Timothy 2:5:6 (NIV)
[55] Hebrews 13:7 (JBP)
[56] John 14:9 (NIV)
[57] Matthew 23:37-38 (NIV)

It would certainly seem that God mourned over the people who had to be removed to allow Israel to develop into what God had planned for them, but it certainly wasn't because these depraved people were without any knowledge about God. In the New Testament it is reported what God feels in respect to those who have chosen never to become a part of His plan. While the situation refers to events at this later time, it is obvious that it applies to all times by indicating the same things have been the situation from the creation of the world. "The wrath of God is being revealed from heaven against all the godlessness and wickedness of men who suppress the truth by their wickedness, since what may be known about God is plain to them, because God made it plain to them. For since the creation of the world God's invisible qualities – his eternal power and divine nature – have been clearly seen, being understood from what has been made, so that men are without excuse. For although they knew God, they neither glorified him as God nor gave thanks to him, but their thinking became futile and their foolish hearts were darkened. Although they claimed to be wise, they became fools and exchanged the glory of the immortal God for images made to look like mortal man and birds and animals and reptiles. Therefore God gave them over in the sinful desires of their hearts to sexual impurity for the degrading of their bodies with one another. They exchanged the truth of God for a lie, and worshiped and served created things rather than the Creator – who is forever praised. Amen. Because of this, God gave them over to shameful lusts. Even their women exchanged natural relations for unnatural ones. In the same way the men also abandoned natural relations with women and were inflamed with lust for one another. Men committed indecent acts with other men, and received in themselves due penalty for their perversion. Furthermore, since they did not think it worthwhile to retain the knowledge of God, he gave them over to a depraved mind, to do what ought not to be done. They became filled with every kind of wickedness, evil, greed, and depravity. They are full of envy, murder, strife, deceit, and malice. They are gossips, slanderers, God-haters, insolent, arrogant, and boastful; they invent ways of doing evil; they disobey their parents; they are senseless, faithless, heartless, ruthless. Although they know God's righteous decree that those who do such things deserve death, they not only continue to do these very things but also approve of those who practice them."[58]

Those whose lives are lived in a moral cesspool will show its effect, and those who

---

[58] Romans 1:18-32 (NIV)

constantly associate with them are likely to absorb the odor. In fact the history of Israel records such consequences repeatedly. I can often best understand God by thinking of Him as Christ asked us to do – as our Father. What would a Father do if he was faced with a situation where he had two sons - one that was evidently totally depraved and without hope of redemption and one who had such great potential that he could benefit people throughout the world for all time and bring them fabulous blessings? Additionally suppose the Father, who loves both sons, knows that the evil son has the wish and the ability to destroy the other son's potential. I think the Father would, with great sadness, do exactly what God saw had to be done. The evil son would have to be deposed and displaced to protect the son with the potential.

I get a sense of God's feelings from the book of Joshua when Israel was just starting to take the Promised Land. "When Joshua was near Jericho, he looked up and saw a man standing in front of him with a drawn sword in his hand. Joshua went up to him and asked, 'Are you for us or for our enemies?' 'Neither' he replied, 'but as commander of the army of the Lord I have now come.' Then Joshua fell facedown to the ground in reverence, and asked him, 'What message does my Lord have for his servant?' The commander of the Lord's army replied, 'Take off your sandals, for the place where you are standing is holy.' And Joshua did so."[59] When the commander advised he was neither on the side of Jericho or Israel, it indicates to me that he was totally there to do God's work in order to further God's plan. It shows that he, and by inference God, felt no personal difference toward the two peoples. Since we know that God stated, "When Israel was a child, I loved him,"[60] it would seem that God also loved the people who had to be removed from the country to let the plan proceed.

Later on, many of God's Chosen People would be influenced by the very people from whom God tried to protect them. "Therefore the Lord's anger burned against this land, so that he brought on it all the curses written in this book. In furious anger and in great wrath the Lord uprooted them from their land and thrust them into another land."[61] Israel had to go through the awful purification of deportation to get back on course to be working toward the completion of God's plan. My earthly father and many other earthly fathers have told

---

[59] Joshua 5:13-15 (NIV)
[60] Hosea 11:1
[61] Deuteronomy 29:27-28

us when administering punishment, "This is going to hurt me more than it hurts you." The clearing of the land of those who would destroy the plan was painful to God. The sending of Israel into bondage to get them back into the plan hurt God, and when I have to be corrected to get me back into sync with God's plan, it certainly hurts me, but I am absolutely sure that it hurts my heavenly Father even more.

It's the plan! God has worked, is working, and will work to include as many humans as possible in His fellowship and His Kingdom. God wants as many as possible to be a part of that plan. If we choose to be a part of the plan and respond like our savior, "Thy will be done," God will be pleased to use us. If we persistently choose not to be a part of the plan, God will sadly respond that we can have things our way if we demand it and will move us aside, so that the plan can proceed.

*(From Betty Byers)*

The Old Testament predicts a Person (Christ), and the New Testament presents Christ. The Old Testament is explained in the New Testament.

*(Mark Eastway's answer)*

The Old and New Testaments are a two parts of a single book: the Bible. The Bible describes a unified plan of salvation, as revealed through the promises made and fulfilled by God. Similarly, the attributes of God in both Testaments are the same.

In Genesis, after the fall of humankind into sin, God revealed, in part, His plan of salvation. We read in Genesis 3:15 *And I will put enmity between you and the woman, and between your offspring and hers; he will crush your head, and you will strike his heel.* Satan would one day strike the heel of Eve's offspring, causing Him harm, but He would, in turn, crush Satan. Later, in Genesis, God promised to Abraham (Genesis 12:3), *I will bless those who bless you, and whoever curses you I will curse; and all peoples on earth will be blessed through you.* Somehow, through Abraham, all people on earth would be blessed. Many years later God said to King David (Psalm 89:4), *I will establish your line forever and make your throne firm through all generations.* God promised that a descendant of David would rule on his throne, whose kingdom would never end. Other details about the coming King include: He will be born of a virgin (Isaiah 7:14), a Savior to the Gentiles (Isaiah 49:6), and will come from the town of Bethlehem (Micah 5:2). Many other prophecies were made and fulfilled regarding the details of Jesus' ministry. Although written by many authors over a long period of time, the Bible describes a single plan of how, after humankind fell into sin, God would and did raise up a Savior.

Regarding the attributes of God, in both the Old and New Testaments, they are the same. For example, God is faithful: Moses writes in Deut. 4:31 *For the Lord your God is a merciful God;* **he will not** *abandon or destroy you or* **forget the covenant** *with your forefathers, which he confirmed to them by oath.* Paul writes concerning the faithfulness of God in Romans 15:8, *For I tell you that Christ has become a servant of the Jews on behalf of God's truth,* **to confirm the promises made** *to the patriarchs.* God of both Testaments has not and will not forget the covenants or promises He has made.

On the other side of the spectrum, God is just: Moses wrote in Deut. 32:4, *He is the Rock, his works are perfect, and all his ways are just. A faithful God who does no wrong, upright and* **just** *is he.* Likewise, the Apostle John states in Rev. 15:3, *Great and marvelous are your deeds, Lord God Almighty.* **Just** *and true are your ways, King of the ages.* In addition to many of the other attributes of God, such as loving, good and merciful; He is also just, jealous and wrathful.

Many people read about a God of the Old Testament who commanded His people to kill others. They contrast this with Jesus, who taught us to be merciful, peacemakers and meek. However, such a perspective requires both a selective and allegorical reading of the New Testament. We should not overlook the fact that Jesus introduced and developed the concept of hell, a fate far worse than physical death. Likewise, the God of the New Testament will judge us and determine our eternal destiny (Revelation 20:11-15).

Jesus, Himself, made it clear that He fully supported the Old Testament. He states in Matthew 5:17-18,

> *Do not think that I have come to abolish the Law or the Prophets; I have not come to abolish them but to fulfill them. I tell you the truth, until heaven and earth disappear, not the smallest letter, not the least stroke of a pen will by any means disappear from the Law until everything is accomplished.*

In conclusion, the two Testaments portray a God with a single plan of salvation, revealed progressively through the Bible. He is a God whose attributes remain unchanged through both Testaments. And the One through whom the promise of salvation was fulfilled, Jesus, Himself, confirms the writings of the Old Testament, down to the smallest stroke of a pen. So the answer is, "yes," the God of the Old Testament is the God of the New Testament.

Challenge 3

# Maybe there was a creator, but after the universe was formed, it seems to be left on its own.

There are people who concede that it's possible that a "Supreme Intelligence" designed and created the universe, but then left it on its own. Even if there is a God, what makes you think he's interested in you?

*(Some observations by Jack Clark)*

When I was fifteen years old I very much wanted a Mossberg 22 rifle and a 12-gage Stevens double barreled shot gun. My Dad enjoyed hunting, and I was eager to share time and experiences with him. I got a job working as an assistant to an older teen in our community helping with construction work. One of my jobs was to dig dry wells – hot, dirty and tiring work, but I earned enough over the summer to buy the guns I wanted. Dad, the older boy, his father and I went pheasant hunting in South Dakota that fall. I was pleased with my gun and really upset when I accidentally hit it against the ground breaking off the stock. A local welder was able to make repairs, but I was especially careful with my gun after that. It seems those things for which we've planned and worked are more important than the things that come easy.

Well, as I understand it God planned and worked to create mankind. Following that effort, a lot more work went into revealing himself and planning for our development to the point that we would be able to fellowship with Him. I don't think that God would be likely to work so hard to create something that He desired and then just cut loose of us and the rest of His creation. I think that God would cherish what he created like I had cherished what I'd worked hard to earn. I think that if something went wrong with what He created, He would be at least as concerned as I was when I broke my gun, and I think he would make every effort to make right our brokenness and be very pleased when things are made right again – just as I was.

The thing that makes me most sure of God's continued interest in His creation is that I've been persuaded of his interest in me. I am convinced that He loves me. I am convinced that he pursued me – sometimes relentlessly – to save me from the separation from Him I one time had allowed to occur and from the spiritual death that results from such separation. I've felt Him helping me to grow in my understanding and cheering me on as I strain toward the goal of becoming more like Him.

From a less personal standpoint I see the continuing evolution of what he has created. If I had created something as vast, complex, and personally pleasing as what God has created, I would have a continued interest in it. On a much smaller scale, I am interested in the garden Carol and I have made in our front yard. I help her weed it. I cultivate it. I prune the bushes, and keep it watered. I delight in the result. I think God delights even more in His creation. I think He's concerned with His creation and that He takes an active part in its ongoing development. It seems that God thinks of Himself as our Father (probably better translated Daddy) according to our Christian understanding. I certainly wasn't nearly the Daddy to my children as I believe God is to us, but I can remember my delight in their achievements. I can remember some disappointments when they fouled up. I can remember being eager to help them straighten out a few messes. As the co-creator of my children, I can't conceive my not being interested in doing these things. Likewise I can't conceive of God having gone to the trouble to create in the first place not being interested in or taking part in the continued process of creation that goes on – physically, mentally and spiritually. I feel certain that God loves us and is much more interested in our development than I have capacity to be even with my children.

These folks that suggest there had to be a creator but that perhaps creation has been on its own since then have a great deal of insight compared to those who don't believe that God exists at all. They recognize that the universe, life itself, the kitten playing at their feet, and the flowers bursting into bloom in a spring woods are too complex and too fabulous to have been an accidental occurrence. They recognize that all these and thousands of other things sing out and shout in joy: "I exist. My existence proves I have a creator. Listen to me, and I will identify my creator and urge you join with us in our hymn of unending praise and glory."

These people are like the citizens of Athens who Paul addressed. He noted that they were very religious because he had seen an alter to an unknown God in their city.[62] Of course, Paul went ahead to proclaim the God who he had come to know through God's own son.

---

[62] Acts 17:23

These people, like the Athenians, recognize that God has to exist. They simply haven't seen the evidence that he continues to be active in the universe, and especially they haven't seen the evidence that He is concerned with what He has created. They need to feel God's presence in their own lives. Having already been convinced that God exists, now all they need is the realization that it is worth their trouble to try to find Him and know Him.

Perhaps their problem is that we haven't shared our experiences. Perhaps their problem is that they have been so discouraged with disappointing things in their lives that they haven't been able to see God working for good in everything – even converting life's tragic events into something positive in association with those who love Him. Maybe they have never come in contact with someone who has experienced the presence of the living God in their lives and shared the experience with them. Maybe the one who tried to share their experience did a lousy job and turned the person off. I understand Gandhi was warmly attracted to Jesus' beatitudes, but was turned off by the imperial attitude of some of the people who professed to be Christians but didn't love their neighbor let alone their enemies and didn't care for the fatherless and the widows.

Jesus gave us quite a responsibility when he told us to spread the good news of his redemption and salvation. We need to ask for the guidance and wisdom of the Holy Spirit as we take on the privilege of doing so. Our sharing must include not only that God is alive and active in the world and in our lives, but it must include the realization that He wants to be an active part of everyone's life. We need to get across that we have been brought to our relationship because God is a great and good God – NOT because we are anything special or because of our goodness. We need to pray for the action of the Holy Spirit in the lives of others. Those in this group of people who recognize God exists are very near to gaining a much lovelier and complete understanding of His nature that only the Holy Spirit can give to each individual. We have been given the job of being tools for the Holy Spirit's efforts. What a gift!

---

*(Betty Byers' understanding)*

God is still in the Heavens and is in control. God is interested in me and loves me. I can pray to Him, and He answers my prayers.

---

# How can anyone believe in miracles?

How can you believe in miracles?  Since God made the rules of the universe, why would He break them by performing miracles?

(Jack Clark's answer)

A miracle shows God's presence in the world—usually in an intense, unexpected way. Miracles have a purpose.  Any miracle should bring glory to God as well as often meeting a human need.  A miracle may be defined as an event that cannot be explained by known laws of nature.  (Although Saint Augustine observed that miracles are not contrary to nature, but only contrary to what we know about nature.  When he made this observation certainly such things as the transmission of voice and even pictures over the air waves to be picked up by devices in individual homes would have been thought to be entirely beyond any realm of possibility.)

A second definition is that a miracle is a marvel.  Probably more Christians would think of the first definition, but to me using the second one helps me appreciate a wider scope of God's activities and doesn't leave out any event that would qualify as one of the first type of occurrences.

There was a time when I was spiritually dead.  My first marriage was a failed one.  I was existing (as opposed to living) in a morass of depression, self-pity, and lack of any personal objectives in life.  I literally felt myself to be in a hell of my own making.  The Holy Spirit convicted me of my sins.   Jesus Christ defines divorce except for unfaithfulness as being the same as adultery.  The marvelous miracle that the Holy Spirit worked in my life was to literally drive me (I didn't have the energy to do it on my own) to read and read and re-read the Bible until one day while reading First Corinthians Chapter 13, I realized that this was how God feels about me and any other sinner who will turn to Him.  Of course I knew that Paul had originally written it to tell Christians how to deal with each other, but I was fully convinced that it also applies to our relationship with God.

I had the joy of being reborn in Christ before meeting and marrying Carolyn Shaffer with whom I am privileged to share in our faith walk with the Lord.  We have made our marriage a triangle with Christ as the head, and do our best to keep the other person before ourselves in importance.  God has answered my prayer that I grow to love Carol more each day, and we have been privileged to raise my four children in our home. Through Carol's love and their acceptance and love, they have become _our_ four children. We are blessed with thirteen grandchildren and seven great grandchildren. We look on each one of them as a special gift from God.

Some might say this wasn't a miracle. No law of physics or other law of nature was set aside to accomplish the results. I can only respond that from my perspective going from spiritual death to spiritual life was as miraculous as going from physical death to physical life would be. God can and did even use my sins to result in a good outcome.

In the same process, the gaining insight about God and His ways that has been an ongoing result of these events has been another miracle to me. I'm reminded of the account of the man who had been blind from birth and had his sight restored. The disciples understood such problems resulted either from the person's sins or the parents' sins. Jesus answered, "Neither this man nor his parents sinned…, but this happened so that the work of God might be displayed in his life."[63] Later the Pharisees examined the young man accusing him of fakery and of being born in sin. They also claimed that Christ was a sinner, as he had healed the man on the Sabbath. Such a confrontation would be terrifying, knowing the power of the Pharisees, but the man had the courage to respond, "Whether he is a sinner or not, I don't know. One thing I do know. I was blind, but now I see!"[64] In my own personal miracle, the understanding even in part of the mind of God lets me also affirm, "One thing I too know. I was blind and now I see," even if my blindness was spiritual and my seeing fits in with the Apostle Paul's observation: "Now we see but a poor reflection as in a mirror; then we shall see face to face. Now I know in part; then I shall know fully, even as I am fully known."[65]

I know of a young man whose family had been wrecked by the effects of his father's alcoholism. The father had lost multiple jobs. The family suffered humiliation and privation because of the father's problem. The mother had barely been able to hold the family together. The father eventually was able to overcome his affliction and attributed his ability to do so to his faith in Jesus Christ. On an occasion when a scoffer raised

---

[63] John 9:2-3 (NIV)
[64] John 9:25 (NIV)
[65] I Corinthians 13:12 (NIV)

doubts about Jesus' miracles, the son responded, "I don't know about turning water into wine, but I know of a time when Jesus Christ turned wine into groceries and furniture for our family."  The renewal of wrecked lives, the rebirth of those who were spiritually dead are truly miracles as great as can be cited anywhere.

To me every recovery from an illness represents a miracle built in by God in our immune and cellular regenerating systems.  Ambrose Paré was a French military surgeon who devised using ligatures rather than boiling oil to stop the bleeding after military amputations.  He observed, "God heals.  I only change the bandages."

Going on to what is reported in the scriptures – those events that most people would think of when they ask this question.  There are miracles of nature, miracles of healing, miracles of conception, miracles of protection and conquest of enemies within and enemies without, miracles of restoration to life, and miracles of forgiveness.

Some miracles require faith and desire of the recipient such as the healing of the thirty-five year invalid at the pool of Bethesda where the blind and the lame, the disabled, and the paralyzed would lie hoping to be healed.[66]

Some miracles require no faith on the recipient's part.  For example the casting out of demons from the man who lived among the tombs.[67]

Some miracles were to meet a desperate need such as God parting the sea to save Israel from the Egyptians.[68]  Some seem to involve filling a rather minor need such as the feeding of the five thousand.[69]  This involved a lot of people who certainly were hungry, but they could have returned to their homes and met the need themselves.

Some miracles produce a grateful response such as the man blind from birth and the demon possessed man.  Some are a disappointment such as occurred after the healing of the ten lepers with only one returning to give thanks.[70]

---

[66] John 5:2-14 (NIV)
[67] Matthew 8:28-32 (NIV)
[68] Exodus 14:1-31 (NIV)
[69] Matthew 14:13-21 (NIV)
[70] Luke 17:11-19 (NIV)

Some people try to explain the miracles as natural events. They are convinced God never works outside the natural laws, and some want to detract from the truthfulness of the Bible. I have heard it argued that perhaps in the time of Abraham and Sarah that time was counted differently and they were not really as old as is recorded when they had their child. Perhaps the miracles of Moses done to impress Pharaoh were nothing more than copies of the tricks of the court magicians Moses had seen when he was a child. Perhaps when the sea was parted, it was the result of a seiche, a strong wind that can blow enough to pile up water against a lee shore and in some cases uncover a shallow area. Perhaps the drying up of the Jordan River that allowed Israel to cross over on dry ground was due to a landslide upriver that cut off the flow. Perhaps the star the wise men followed was due to a conjugation where several stars are aligned and are additive in their brightness. Perhaps Mary was not truly a virgin, but only a young girl caught in a desperate circumstance. Perhaps the miracle of feeding the five thousand resulted from the fact that the assembled people had plenty to eat and were just moved to share it when they saw the generosity of the boy with the fish and loaves and the attitude of Christ and the Disciples. Perhaps Christ's death was feigned.

To those of us convinced of the miracles, it would seem that some of the above explanations could be correct. God's use of a seiche to part the sea or a landslide to stop the flow of the Jordan certainly could have been a possible mechanism for these miracles, but one would have to admit that the timing was pretty good and the natural occurrence pretty unusual; therefore, I would still maintain that they would fall into the classification of miracles. Those who would detract from Moses' miracles would be hard-pressed to explain the death of all the first born of Egypt as a trick. If the feeding of the five thousand did take place as proposed, it would still be a miracle of change in persons to get that level of sharing to occur, and changing people is one of the greatest miracles of all. Some of the other proposals are not possible to refute except to say that they were predicted in Old Testament prophecy, an argument that would not convince the scoffers.

Certainly the disciples were convinced Christ calmed the storm; again this could have been happenstance, but it is difficult to explain Christ's walking on the water as any natural phenomenon. The healing of the lepers and the giving of sight to the man blind from birth cannot be explained by any such occurrence. Certainly the Pharisees tried to discredit the latter event, and certainly the man who had been blind was convinced enough to withstand the terrible pressure applied and even to accept being cast out of the temple, an awful thing for a Jew. In the case of Christ's resurrection, the disciples were changed from a cowering group of people fearing for their lives and avoiding the authorities to a thoroughly convinced group of men ready to testify to their faith and ready to defy the direct edict of the same authorities they had so feared before. Certainly their changed response is testimony to me that they believed in Christ's resurrection and that it was not a made-up affair.

Do I believe that God can change the rules and cause miracles of this second type? Yes! This doesn't seem to happen often and not nearly as frequently as we might wish. I believe that God created the universe and everything in it. As such I believe that He created the rules that govern nature. Just as the rules governing basketball are set by the National Basketball Association that can change the rules governing its play, I believe that God who made the laws of nature can change those laws. Even scientific discoveries point to the possibility of such unexplained changes in natural laws. One example would be that there is irrefutable evidence in the alignment of magnetic particles in rocks that there have been many times over millions of years when there has been a switching of the earth's magnetic poles. This results in the north magnetic pole ending up near the geographic South Pole and the south magnetic pole near the geographic North Pole.[71] This would not be related to any known miracle, but certainly would involve a sudden and marked change in the natural laws of the universe. There are water striders, North American insects, and Central American lizards about ten inches long that I have seen walk on water using the surface tension of water to support their weight. If God can change the magnetic polarity of the earth, it certainly doesn't seem such a stretch of the imagination to think that He could temporarily increase the surface tension of the Sea of Galilee to allow Jesus to walk on it as a possible mechanism to explain Jesus' walking on the water. I have no insight that this is what was involved; it is suggested only as a possibility.

There are certainly instances recorded in the scripture where even believers doubted that God could perform miracles. Sarai laughed in disbelief when she eavesdropped and heard that God planned for her to have a baby at her advanced age. When she realized

---

[71] *National Geographic Traveler* magazine, April 2007, Vol. XXIV, Number 3, p. 112

she had been found out, she even lied about it. The Lord responded to her disbelief with, "Is anything too hard for the Lord?"[72] As hard as it was for her to believe, Isaac's birth must have clinched it for her. I am especially drawn to God's response to doubters of his ability to perform miracles on two other occasions. The first occurred when Moses doubted that God could furnish meat for 600,000 men and their families who he had led out of Egypt into the Sinai desert. They were at the point of rebellion – not because they were hungry (they had already been given the manna), but because they wanted meat. God, in His anger, said he would give them so much meat over a month's time that they would become sick of it, it would come out of their nostrils and they would loathe it. Moses responded that whole flocks and herds of animals or all the fish in the sea wouldn't be enough to do the job. The second episode involves Israel's disbelief that even God could save them from their disastrous situation. In both cases God responded to those who believed that He didn't have the ability to supply the miracle with the words: "Is my arm too short?"[73]

I've seen several other things in my own life and in my medical practice that seem to be miracles. When I was nine years old in 1942, I developed appendicitis. My appendectomy was followed by multiple complications: pneumonia, a kidney infection, and a post-operative wound infection that drained for weeks. Sulfa was very new and was used. Antibiotics weren't available yet. When I was the most ill there were two successive days when the hospital records show I had a fever of 107. It would be rare to live through such an illness and even rarer not to have permanent brain damage from the high fever.

When I was in my middle teen years, early one spring, my younger brother and I took the family rowboat out on the lake. All we had was a hand-cranked trolling motor. Foolishly we didn't also take oars along. A strong wind came up and blew us away from our home. We ended up in a swamp on the other side of the lake. Swamps have soft spots, into which one could sink. The weather was quite cold, but I waded to shore without mishap. I'd told Jerry to wait in the boat, but on our return the boat was empty. Fortunately he also got to shore safely. I think this was another miracle.

---

[72] Genesis 18:1-15 (NIV)
[73] Numbers 11:4-33 and Isaiah 50:1-11

In adult life, my wife Carol and I had been sailing for a week on the gorgeous North Channel of Lake Huron in our 24-foot sloop. Strong winds made 12 to 15 foot waves coming from the direction we had to go. The waves were cresting and foam was blowing off the top of the waves. The ship would make a steep climb to the top of a wave and literally fall into the trough. The boat would shudder for several seconds with each impact. This happened over and over. Because we couldn't make headway sailing, I decided to use our boat's 9.5 horsepower outboard. Unfortunately, the waves were so steep that on three occasions the motor was snuffed out. In order to keep headway and avoid the rocks, the jib (foresail) had to be raised until the motor would dry out and could be restarted. I suggested to Carol that she steer and I would go forward to raise the jib. She responded, "If this is going to capsize, it's not going to be my fault. You steer, and I'll put up the jib." Three times she had to fasten her lifeline, go forward to raise the jib with the waves breaking over her head and almost pulling off her deck shoes. She allowed that the metal railing at the bow of the ship was aptly named the pulpit, because she did a lot of praying up there on that day. The bilge of the ship had taken in a lot of water when we finally reached port. I feel that it was truly a miracle that we made it through this event.

Back when chemotherapy for cancer was fairly new and there were no nearby oncologists to which referrals could be made, and there were limited therapeutic drugs available, I had two patients with extensive colon cancer that had spread to their livers and lungs. One was a retired pastor, and one a church member who was inactive because he had been discouraged by some arguments in the church. Although the typical time of response to the only available agent at the time (5-fluorouracil) that I gave them intravenously at weekly intervals is a matter of a few months at best, both lived over five years. The areas of spread in both in their livers came to the point they couldn't be seen on the scans, and the base-ball size area of spread in one of the patients' lungs became no longer visible on x-ray. Both eventually died of the problem, but both contributed joy to their families, their churches and their doctor in the five years given them that I interpreted as a miracle. The man who had withdrawn from active participation in church became active again, enjoying Bible study and being one of the most cheerful Christian witnesses I've ever known. The minister was a blessing to everyone he met, helping others with serious health problems and encouraging people wherever he went.

My brother-in-law had a critical heart problem. He was born with a heart murmur. One day he collapsed at work. He was found to have a dissecting aneurysm of the arch of the aorta. In this condition the layers of the main artery leading from the heart split apart from each other. This caused multiple tiny clots to shower into the brain resulting in multiple strokes. The valve leading from the heart to the aorta was destroyed. At surgery, the valve was replaced as well as repairing an opening between the right and left chambers of the heart and repairing some of the vessels that emptied into the wrong chamber. My sister asked for prayers from family and our church. He was in a coma several weeks. He had fluid drained from around the heart and from the chest several times. We had fears that if he lived trough the event, the strokes would produce severe damage. He eventually made a good physical and mental recovery and was able to return to work. After he was well, he told us that during the event he could see as a spectator the people working on him, and at one point was told that he had died. His response was, "I can't die. I've got to go back to help my wife with the kids." To me this qualifies as a miracle.

The most recent miracle I've seen involves our youngest son, Bruce, who has written an article for this book about how he felt about a sin of omission. Bruce has had long-term diabetes. He has been critically ill with heart and kidney failure. He became so swollen that he couldn't get up or sit on his own. He was ready to be put on dialysis to help the swelling. A considerable increase in his medication was able to reduce the swelling (he lost thirty pounds of fluid in about two weeks). That was unexpected and a blessing, but could have been attributed to the change in medicine. What was so startling and couldn't be attributed to this was that he had been using over 150 units insulin daily in four to six injections to control his diabetes. Over a four week period the need for insulin steadily decreased and finally stopped with his blood sugars remaining in normal to very slightly elevated range. I had asked the Holy Spirit to pray for Bruce, because I didn't know for what I should pray. Logically it seemed that he was at the point where he could not get better. I even suggested that if he couldn't be better that I would be at peace for the Holy Spirit to pray that Bruce go on to his next life. I would probably have been skeptical enough, that I would have attributed the congestive heart failure improvement to the medication change, but the diabetes improvement couldn't be attributed to that. I claim this is a miracle. Along with the other miracles, I can only say to God be the glory!

I've prayed for many other friends and patients without the result I would have chosen, so I'm certainly not a faith healer, but sometimes things do happen that seem to be outside the realm of what we could expect.

I believe that God's arm is never too short to reach us wherever we are and in whatever condition we find ourselves. After all, He reached me in my self-made hell. When he does reach us He can choose to change the situation or to change us. Often when we ask for something that would constitute a miracle God grants something else. For example I think of when the Apostle Paul asked three times for relief of the "thorn in his flesh." God's response was, "My grace is sufficient for you, for my power is made perfect in weakness."[74]

The direct and indirect testimony of the writers of the Bible is helpful in getting me to believe in miracles. Perhaps the most telling conviction comes from having been changed myself, but if we look around us there are miracles to be seen everywhere – the unfolding of a new leaf and flowers in the spring, each and every conception and new birth, changes in people brought about by the Holy Spirit, the joy and fulfillment found in the gift of shared love, and the occasional healing or long-term remission of a condition that medical science cannot explain.

If we are to recognize God's miracles we have to be open to perceiving them. In the words of Elizabeth Browning:

> "Earth's crammed with heaven
> And every common bush afire with God
> But only he who sees takes off his shoes.
> The rest sit round it and pluck blackberries."

*(Another answer by Jim Chupp)*

"Because He can," may be the simplest explanation for the issue of miracles. However, the problem of miracles is in the mind of natural man. Miracles just don't fit our limited grasp of natural law and order. When it comes to rules that govern the Universe, it is the natural mind that must put logical order and law over everything. It gives us a greater sense of security and

---

[74] Second Corinthians 12:9 (NIV)

intellectual dominance to know that what we can scientifically know about death, blindness, disease, and physical science as a whole, is neatly packaged and conceivable. God is in the business of doing inconceivable things outside of our neat intellectual packaging in order to reveal Himself to a blind humanity. Therefore, it may require supernatural work in a natural world, if for no other reason than to draw people to God.

*(Another understanding by Betty Berger)*

Paul says, "Even as my preaching has been accompanied with the power of signs and wonders, (and all of it by the power of the Holy Spirit)."[75]

All through the New Testament, signs and wonders followed the preaching of the Word. It's the witness to unbelievers. Plus we have experienced several miracles in our family. "Jesus Christ is the same yesterday and today and forever!"[76]

*(Betty Byers' understanding)*

I have seen miracles. I know people who have been cured of cancer. I have seen people delivered from alcohol and drug addiction. Birth is a miracle.

*(Sherry Doherty's answer)*

I can believe in miracles because of what I see both in my personal and professional life as a nurse. I feel that God's rules are black and white, so when He chooses to override those rules, it is because He sees the need to do so. In doing this, He demonstrates to me that He is the ultimate love, the ultimate giver.

*Some observations by Becky Campbell about the importance of miracles)*

## Considering the 1st recorded miracle of Jesus - John 2:1-11

There is some thought among theologians that recognizes the "firsts" of God, when He says or does something new, as especially important. As we look at the first miracle of Jesus, there is much more God is teaching us than simply turning water into wine. In this

---

[75] Romans 15:19 (A B)
[76] Hebrews 13:8 (NIV)

account we recognize three very important things. First, this was the beginning of signs Jesus did in Cana of Galilee. Secondly, it was a manifestation of His glory, and finally because of this miracle, His disciples believed in Him.

The only gospel that records this first important miracle is John, the one who is known as the disciple that Jesus loved. We know Jesus and His disciples had been invited to a wedding, along with His mother Mary. He saw fit to attend this social gathering celebrating love and marriage which speaks to the importance of the marriage covenant, an institution established by God. Also significant is that this, the first of His recorded miracles involved sharing food and wine with His disciples. Later we learn that His last gathering with His disciples before His death, a Passover meal, also was a moment of sharing bread and wine with them. Passover was also time of gathering and social celebration for the Jews, as well as a Holy Day commanded by God.

Perhaps attending this wedding was the Lord's way of saying to his disciples, "One day I will be your bridegroom and you will be my bride." In Matthew 25:1-13 Jesus tells the parable of the wise and foolish virgins, going to meet the bridegroom. Later in Revelation 19:7-9 John records the marriage supper of the Lamb (Jesus) and His wife (believers).

It's evident that a need arose, because Mary said to her son Jesus, "They have no more wine." Mary had for these many years, pondered the greatness and the upcoming ministry of her son in her heart. Now He is 30 years old, and she is asking, Son will you fulfill this need?" Even though Jesus seems to say, not yet mother, she said to the servants, "Whatever He says to you, do it." Jesus, the one who can fulfill every human need, and is moved by human need, now steps into action.

As we get to verse 6, John records that six stone water pots used for purification of the Jews, and usually containing twenty or thirty gallons apiece were sitting nearby. They apparently were empty, because Jesus commanded the servants to fill them to the brim with water. His next command was simply, "Draw some out now, and take it to the master of the feast." "And they took it." Later, when the master of the feast had tasted the water that was made wine, he commented that it was good wine.

There is great significance in these verses that surely speaks about the condition of humans after sin entered the world. Because of sin we are like those stone jars, cold, hard, and empty.

At the moment we come to understand that we are sinners in need of a Savior, and cry out to Jesus asking Him to come into our lives, our Redeemer comes. He begins a work that births a change in the hard, cold, emptiness of these earthen vessels. He moves to fulfill His promise from Ezekiel 36:26 that states, "I will give you a new heart and put a new spirit within you; I will take the heart of stone out of your flesh and give you a heart of flesh." Jesus begins to speak to the substance of who we were created to be, sons and daughters of the Most High God. He turns what is plain and tasteless in us into fine wine. The Song of Solomon 1:2 states, "for your love is better than wine." With great tenderness and love, He begins to write His commandments on our hearts, similarly to how He wrote with His finger on stone tablets and gave them to Moses. We become new wine in new wineskins, a new creation.

Interestingly, it was not until the jars were dipped into, or poured out so to speak, that the change from water to wine was known. As Christians, we need to realize that as we give of ourselves and make the love of Christ known, even as weak, poor, and cracked earthen vessels, we are being used by God in this broken world, changing water into fine wine. Praise God that we have such a high and pleasurable calling!

---

# Since God knew people would sin and created us anyhow, how can He blame us for sinning?

If God knows everything in advance of it happening, He must have known people would sin before He made them. Since He knew they would sin, and He created them anyway, why did He blame them?

*(Jack Clark's perspective)*

As they used to say in logic class in college – the premise is right, it's just the conclusion that's wrong. God does know everything in advance. God certainly knew the people would sin before He made us. God does hold us responsible for our actions, but He doesn't blame us. God's not into the blame game. I think the best understanding of God was given when his son asked us to think of God as our Father and related the parable of the prodigal son (also known as the parable of the lost son in more recent Bible translations).[77]

I don't remember specifically thinking such thoughts before any of my children were born, but looking back, I must have known that they would not be born mature, perfect individuals. I must have known that I could impart some of the things I knew to them, but they wouldn't absorb it all. I must have known that I would set down some rules and make many suggestions in the hope that it would help them to mature, fulfill their potential, and avoid some of the mistakes and circumstances that could lead to physical, emotional or spiritual problems for them. If I had thought through the reasons for these guidelines, they would have involved the love of and hopes for these precious gifts – my children.

Understanding God as our Father, it seems to me that He has the same hopes and aspirations for us that I have and had for my children. It also seems that He had the same purposes in setting guidelines. I knew that my children wouldn't avoid running into the street just because I said so. I knew that having had pets to love, they might not understand the inadvisability of presuming every dog in the world wanted their affection and attention. I knew that at times when I wanted to guide them, they would respond, as every child I have ever known: "I do it myself." God certainly knew these things before he created us. God certainly knew that we would need to be reminded again and again. He knew that sometimes even though He had thoroughly instructed us we would forget. He knew that flashy things might draw our attention away from what we should have known

---

[77] Luke 15:11-31

and end up with us being in a real mess. He knew that sometimes we too would be rebellious, stomp our foot and defiantly shout, "I do it myself."

Well my Mom and Dad didn't give up on me; I didn't give up on my children, and God didn't give up on any of us. He doesn't see us only as we are. He sees all our potential. He sees all that we can become, and He works with us to reach the goals we choose and the aspirations He has for us. Our purpose in setting boundaries and rules wasn't to catch or punish our children, and our heavenly Father's purpose in establishing boundaries and rules for us was to help us choose on our own to see that His way is best, and to want it for ourselves.

No, God isn't in the blame game; He's in the love game, the redemption game, the encouragement game, and the game that lets us choose to be on his team because we want to – not because we're forced to. He's in the game of life. He's going to win the game, and He invites each and every one of us to be on His winning team! Sometimes He reminds us of the rules of the game. Sometimes there are penalties (consequences) for not following the rules – designed to make the game fair for all the players including us. Blame doesn't enter into the equation, and the only reason anyone is ever thrown out of the game is because they absolutely refuse to be a part of it.

---

*Another answer by Jim Chupp*

Coming from a position of a finite and severely limited part of creation I don't think I would have bothered creating humanity at all. But that is the point isn't it? God, as limitless and omnipotent creator, sets mankind in the middle of an amazing creation. I think we make the mistake of thinking that creation itself is somehow the ultimate achievement. Some may consider it the "crown jewel" of His magnificent creative power. It's not whether humanity was a rebellious, bull-headed, obstinate collection of fools, but rather it is what John saw in his vision recorded in the book of Revelation that is the sole objective of God's creative effort in mankind. The redemptive revelation of Himself through Christ is what fulfills all of God's intention in the universe. Rebellious though we are, it is the worth and work of God through Jesus Christ that illustrates the reason and purpose of humanity: the establishment of a union between created man and the creator Himself. It is this single end that makes all of human history meaningful and hopeful.

---

72

I feel that sin is simply stated a mistake. We as people are not perfect, so we make mistakes or sin. I also feel that God truly blames us for not learning from our previous sin – for it is from making a mistake that many times we learn our deepest lessons in life.

# How can there be only one God when Christians say the Father, Son, and Holy Spirit are all God?

How can you claim there is one God and still say that the Father, the Son, and the Holy Spirit are all God?

*(An answer from Jack Clark)*

The term trinity doesn't appear in the Bible. It is a concept that Christians use to identify different aspects of one God.

In Genesis God is speaking and says let <u>us</u> make man in <u>our</u> own image. These plural pronouns aren't clearly preceded by a noun to let us know to what the pronouns refer. Is it God speaking to heavenly beings such as angels? Is it God speaking to other gods? Or is it God speaking to the aspects of himself that we call the trinity?

In fact the Scriptures speak of other gods. Even the Ten Commandments direct that we shall have no other gods before God. But as we study the Scriptures, it seems clear that the other gods aren't truly gods in the sense that God is God. They aren't the source of all creation. They have no power. Far from being our creator, they are the creation of humans. They usurp the place of the true God. They may be made of wood or stone or metal, or they may be such non-physical things as power, money, or fame. They may be even things that don't have a physical existence such as devotion to country or even family. Anything devised by mankind or imagined by mankind or given devotion by mankind to excess to the point that it becomes first in importance in our lives is a god.

As we understand the Trinity this God is the source of all creation – not the idea of created beings. The concept of a triune God seems to be a recognition of various aspects of God. Perhaps the concept can be helped by recognizing that every person is known differently to various people. So I am known to Carol as a husband. I am known to my four children as a father. I am known to my patients as their physician. To my friends I am known as their friend.

In general the Abba or Father aspect of God is thought of as the creative aspect – not only of the physical universe but also of the moral laws and physical laws under which we function. The Son aspect of God or the Messiah or Christ (meaning God with us) aspect is the recognition of the saving and redeeming aspect of God – that aspect in which God most fully reveals Himself to humans.  The Holy Spirit aspect of God is generally thought of as that aspect that continues to relate to people and guide us in various ways.

And yet, there is overlap in the function of the persons of the Trinity.  John affirms that nothing was created without the action of the son.[78]  Genesis proclaims that in the process of creation that the Holy Spirit was hovering or brooding over the face of the waters,[79] and the Holy Spirit interacted with God's people throughout the Old Testament.  Jesus told his disciples that after he left them to return to the Father that, in response to Jesus' prayers, the Father would send them another comforter – the Holy Spirit.  Although this Holy Spirit would be available to guide us, rebuke us, remind us, and to even pray for us, Jesus said that whenever two or three are gathered together in his name, that he would personally be there.[80]  This overlapping of function should not be surprising.  On a personal note, overlapping of function occurs in our lives also.  While I am attending to my patient's needs, I am often aware of and concerned with being a good husband, so I try to let Carol know if I expect to be home late for dinner.

Even though there is overlapping of the various aspects of God's functions, there are also hints of some areas in which they are not identical.  When the disciples questioned Jesus about the time of his return, he responded that only the Father knows the time.[81]  At times it helps my understanding of the trinity to compare them to individuals who combine to function as one.  Examples would include the very best imaginable marriage characterized as the two becoming one flesh.[82]  They might even be compared to a flock of birds that are so attuned to each other that they act as one unit rather than individuals – each immediately responding to the rest of the flock in a change of flight.  Or they might be compared to a great athletic team who so know and understand each other that they function as a unit rather than individually.

It's helpful to see what the Scriptures have to say on the subject.  They proclaim there is one God: "Hear, O Israel: The Lord our God is one.  Love the Lord your God with all

---

[78] John 1:1
[79] Genesis 1:2
[80] Matthew 18:20
[81] Matthew 24:36
[82] Matthew 19:5 and Mark 10:8

your heart and with all your soul and with all your strength."[83]   Jesus taught us to pray to the Father: "Our Father who art in heaven."[84]   Jesus said, "Anyone who has seen me has seen the Father." [85]   A voice from the heavens heard at the time of Jesus' baptism declared, "This is my son whom I love.   Listen to him."[86]   When the disciples were unhappily facing the prospect of not being with Jesus, he offered the following: "I will pray the Father and He shall give you another comforter that He may abide with you forever.[87]

Well there are a lot more verses that suggest some aspect of the nature of the Father or of the Son or of the Holy Spirit, but it seems that these verses give a pretty good understanding of how God is at the same time three distinct parts, yet combined to make the whole.

*(Betty Byers' thought)*

I believe in the trinity or Triune God.  The Bible supports this belief.  All aspects of God are important and have different duties.

*(David Schramm's thoughts)*[88]

A study of the Hebrew version of Genesis chapter one gives intriguing indications of support for the concept of the trinity.  To understand this, one must understand that in the Hebrew language the verb and the noun in a sentence may be singular or plural, and in the usual sentence structure a singular verb would go with a singular noun, or a plural verb would go with a plural noun.

Now let's consider the very first sentence of Genesis: This is usually translated, "In the beginning God created the heavens and the earth."[89]  In this sentence there are several interesting things to note in the Hebrew version.  First of all, the first word "the" is not present in the Hebrew, but the other words rendered as "the" in the sentence are present.  This suggests something unusual.  It suggests that the action was not confined in time.  The second interesting thing is the word used for God is the generic term for God, Elohim.

---

[83] Deuteronomy 6:4-5 (NIV)
[84] Mark 14:36 (KJV)
[85] John 14:9 (NIV)
[86] Mark 9:7 (NIV)
[87] John 14:16 (KJV)
[88] This insight was shared in January 2008 with a Hebrew class being taught by Rev. Schramm to a class at St. Andrew's United Methodist Church in Syracuse, Indiana.  He has also taught this class in multiple other settings in the past.
[89] Genesis 1:1 (TNIV)

God does not reveal His personal name, YHWH (I Am) until later in Genesis. It is used for example when He is speaking to Moses at the burning bush. The next interesting thing is that the verb and the noun do not agree. The noun "God" is plural; but the verb "created" is singular. This would indicate that a plural God (not plural gods) had done a singular act. If gods were plural the verb should have been the plural form also.

This now leaves the sentence, "In beginning Elohim (plural) created (singular referring back to the subject noun) the heavens and the earth." This suggests that there are multiple aspects to this one God, and certainly would be very compatible with the concept of one God who at the same time has multiple natures – the Father, the Son, and the Holy Spirit.

---

Challenge 7

# What supports Jesus' claim to be one with God?

Even if there is a God, why would you think Jesus is a part of God?

*(Jack Clark's view)*

By far the best answer to this question came from Jesus himself as a suggestion to those who were skeptical but open to possibly believing in him: "If I am not doing the works of my Father, then do not believe me, but if I do them, even though you do not believe me, believe in the works, that you may know and understand that the Father is in me and I am in the Father."[90]  In other words, he was suggesting that they let his actions prove who he was.  Similarly he still asks us to let his actions continue to prove to us who he is.  Ultimately, when we have had the opportunity to know him through what he does in our lives and what he has done in others lives, he will ask us for a decision and a commitment.

Some people have suggested that Jesus was a man of God, a great teacher, a good guide for moral principals, or a great philosopher, but not the son of God.  Moslems accept him in their holy book, the Koran, as a prophet of God, but not the great prophet who, in their understanding, was Mohammad.

If we consider what Jesus had to say about himself, it is obvious that he claimed to be the son of God.  This was what so infuriated the Jewish authorities that they determined to kill him.  One of the most significant references Christ makes about himself occurs as he and the Pharisees are talking about his place in the nation Israel.  The Pharisees, true to form, try to trap him and indicate that he cannot hold a superior place or superior knowledge to Abraham.  "'I tell you the truth' Jesus answered, 'before Abraham was born, I am.'"[91]  This is such a profound statement that it almost startles me even after I have read it many times.  Jesus was using the name of the Holy God, the name by which God identified himself to Moses at the burning bush: "God said to Moses, 'I AM WHO I AM. This is what you are to say to the Israelites: "I AM has sent me to you.""[92]  Jesus in his statement to the Pharisees was fully identifying himself with God.  He was affirming that not only is he God's son[93] (son of the Most High[94]), but he is God himself.  This is the

---

[90] John 10:37-38  (RSV)
[91] John 8:58 (NIV)
[92] Exodus 3:13-14 (NIV)
[93] Matthew 26:63-64 (NIV)

basis for the formulation of the Christian concept of the trinity. Either his statement is true, or he is the world's most mild-mannered paranoid schizophrenic, or this is a lie of historic proportions confirming the Pharisees' allegation of blasphemy. There can be no middle ground. Based on this statement alone, no one can offer the compromise that some would like to propose of accepting Jesus as a good person or example but not a part of God or anything other than the possibilities given: what he claimed to be, or a liar and blasphemer, or a psychotic. The Pharisees fully understood the import of this statement and their response was furious anger and denouncement.

This understanding of Christ as being one with the Father must be tempered by his assertion that, "My Father is greater than I,"[95] and when the disciples were asking him about his return, he responded that no one knew except the Father–not even the son.[96] It would seem that they are truly one but that they have some areas of separate and distinct existence.

Another time when Jesus spoke of his oneness with the Father was in the account John gives of Jesus' prayer time just before he was arrested. Of additional significance to us as his followers he also prays, "I pray also for those who will believe in me through their (the disciples') message, that all of them may be one, Father, just as you are in me and I am in you. May they also be in us so that the world may believe that you have sent me."[97] This would seem that Christ is praying for a four-part unity between the Father, himself, the Holy Ghost and his followers. What a great blessing! What a mind expanding thought! What an honor! What a responsibility!

In studying the oldest Greek texts of the New Testament the same thought is clear in other areas of the scripture. Where verses are translated "believe in Jesus," the more literal translation would be "believe into Jesus" suggesting a transformation of the believer into an oneness with Christ.[98]

There can be no uncertainty about Jesus' words recorded at the time of his trial by the

---

[94] Luke 1:32 (NIV)
[95] John 14:29 (NIV)
[96] Matthew 24:36 (NIV)
[97] John 17:20-21 (NIV)
[98] Rev. David Schramm's lecture on Hebrew given on Feb. 25, 2008 to a class at St. Andrew's United Methodist Church, Syracuse, Indiana

Sanhedrin: Caiaphas, the high priest, was frustrated because he couldn't get believable testimony from his witnesses. Failing in these attempts, "the high priest said to Jesus, 'I charge you under oath by the living God: Tell us if you are the Christ, the Son of God.' 'Yes, it is as you say,' Jesus replied. 'But I say to all of you: In the future you will see the Son of Man sitting at the right hand of the Mighty One and coming on the clouds of heaven.'" Well, there certainly could be no doubt about what was claimed here. For whatever reason, Jesus certainly supported the claim, and because of his testimony, the Sanhedrin considered that he deserved to die.[99]

The Moslems side step this claim by saying it was falsified by the Apostles and those who wrote the books of the New Testament. This is certainly an interesting claim, as Jesus lived and was crucified long before Mohammad lived. It was, of course, Mohammad who established the Moslem faith and wrote the Koran. Mohammed lived from A.D 570 to 632, so the only basis for conferring the status of prophet on Jesus that Mohammad would have had at the time he lived would have been the New Testament – the exact same source that the Moslems claim was falsified by Christ's followers.

So, according to scripture, Jesus certainly claimed that he was the son of God and a part of God. Such a claim can only be accepted as true, a lie, or the ravings of a lunatic. The rest of his calm and compassionate life focused on serving others is not compatible with what any psychotic I have dealt with in my medical practice would have done. His works reported in the Bible and in the lives of many people including my life certainly support his claim that he and God were a part of each other. I think that if you will observe his works and allow him to play a role in your life that you too will be convinced that he is indeed one with God.

---

*A viewpoint from Dean Culbertson*

Jesus didn't just speak of being one with the Father. He <u>proved</u> it by being raised from the dead. He promised the Holy Spirit would come. He stated He and the Father are one, and later passages linked the Spirit to Jesus and to the Father. The Trinity is <u>not</u> a man-made idea. It came from God!

---

[99] Matthew 26:57-67 (NIV). Also reported in Luke 22:66-71

I believe Jesus is one with the Father because I believe in the Trinity-God the Father, Son, and Holy Spirit.

# Why didn't the Messiah come to earth as a conqueror?

When the Messiah came to earth, why was it as a "suffering servant" instead of the conquering person that so many of the Jews expected?

*(An answer by Jack Clark)*

It's certainly true that most of the nation of Israel was expecting a conquering Messiah who would restore the glory of the time when Kings David and Solomon ruled. They had relished their designation by God as being His chosen people, and after years of defeats, subjugation, humiliation, and then being second class citizens in the Roman Empire they were eagerly anticipating having the days of glory restored. There was one flaw in their expectations. They remembered that they were (and are) indeed God's chosen people, but they sometimes forgot that the reason they were chosen was for another purpose than just receiving God's blessings for their own people. God had made it clear to Abram at the very beginning of His covenant relationship with Israel: "I will make you into a great nation, and I will bless you. I will make your name great, and you will be a blessing. I will bless those who bless you, and whoever curses you I will curse, and all peoples on earth will be blessed through you."[100] Later in the Bible we read, "I will give you as a light to the nations, that my salvation may reach to the end of the earth."[101] I'm sure that you notice that a very important part of giving of God's blessing was that Abram's descendants were to be a blessing to all people throughout the earth.

To understand Jesus' manner of operating when he came to earth, we need to try to understand his objective. In his own words, "I came that they may have life, and have it abundantly."[102] The apostle John said, "The reason the Son of God appeared was to destroy the devil's work."[103] The work of the devil is to seduce mankind away from their love of and acceptance of God; it was this with which Jesus came to do battle. It is indeed rare that a military conqueror wins the hearts and allegiance of those he conquers, but this is exactly what Jesus Christ' intentions were. He came to let people know just how much he and the Father love us and to let us know the extent to which they are prepared to go to convince us of that love. God had and has a plan. That plan is to reach every person possible, convince them of His love, His redemption and acceptance, and salvation and

---

[100] Genesis 12:2-3 (TNIV)
[101] Isaiah 49:6 (RSV)
[102] John 10:10 (RSV)
[103] I John 3:8 (NIV)

persuade every person possible to want to accept the relationship offered and made plain through the life of His son.  Jesus did not come to destroy us or even to destroy sin (the destruction of sin will come with the second coming); he came to win us by the greatest love the world has ever known.  That's been God's plan all along.  It was even His plan when Israel itself had turned away: "The Lord appeared to us in the past, saying: 'I have loved you with an everlasting love; I have drawn you with loving kindness.'"[104]  It was to draw us; it was to offer redemption and salvation that Jesus, God's Christ, came to earth, and he came to conquer us by love and persuasion rather than force and military might.

*(Betty Byers' thought)*

It was not in the plan of God to have Jesus come as a conqueror.  He came as a humble servant.

(Sherry Doherty thoughts)

Maybe in Biblical times the message of a conqueror would have made a larger impact.  I truly don't know about that.  But God in His infinite wisdom realized that the world was still young, and by sending the Messiah as a "suffering servant" would teach His ultimate love of His people.  Personally, by leading me with love, Christ has enriched my soul, for in this way I have found that serving is a better role model than taking over.

---

[104] Jeremiah 31:3 (NIV)

# Since Jesus had no sins why was he baptized?
Why was Jesus Christ baptized?  (Submitted by Josephine Butler)

*(Jack Clark's answer)*

John the Baptist said that he was baptizing with water for repentance.[105]  He also indicated that he was only preparing the way for God's Messiah (which means God with us in Aramaic just as Christos means in Greek or Christ in English).  He indicated that the Messiah would baptize with the Holy Spirit.  Jesus said we need to be baptized by water, fire and the Holy Spirit.

Of course we Christians understand Christ to be perfect and therefore to have no need for repentance, so it would seem he didn't need the baptism of water.  The baptism by fire is understood to result from trials in life and to result in purification by removal of the impurities in our life.  Jesus Christ is understood as having no need for purification and no impurities; however, he certainly underwent trials in his life.

Baptism by the Holy Spirit is understood to be the receiving of power from the Holy Spirit such as the disciples received after Christ's resurrection, and the forty days he spent with them before his ascension.[106]  We understand the Father (creator), Jesus, and the Holy Spirit to be three distinct parts making up the one indivisible God, so it wouldn't seem that he needed the baptism of the Holy Spirit, but despite this the Holy Spirit was reported to have descended on Jesus after his baptism with water accompanied by the words from the Father, "You are my Son, whom I love; with you I am well pleased."[107]  From these records, it would seem that Jesus, God's Messiah, had all three baptisms even though he needed none.

John the Baptist is reported to have told Christ that he had no business baptizing him – that it was John who Christ should have baptized.  Jesus answered, "Let it be so now; it is proper for us to do this to fulfill all righteousness."[108]

Righteousness can be defined as being made right with God.  Jesus certainly didn't

---

[105] Matthew 3:11 (NIV)
[106] Acts 2:1-40
[107] Mark 1:11 (NIV)
[108] Matthew 3: 14-15

need this, as he is one with God.  Righteousness many also be defined as acting or being in accordance with what is just or moral, or the state of being morally excellent.

It would seem that the underlying reason for Jesus to be baptized was in order that people who would believe in him would be able to accept him as both fully God and fully man.  He seems to have been demonstrating his oneness with us through the act of baptism, and to be demonstrating the value of baptism in our lives if we identify with him.  As we Christians understand baptism, it is an outward sign of an inward spiritual condition.  Some are convinced that it is an absolute requirement for salvation, but it would seem to others of us that if the person has accepted Christ as his savoir but not had the opportunity to be baptized that God would have provided for their salvation.  Certainly the thief on the cross next to Jesus didn't have an opportunity for baptism with water, but Jesus assured him, "today you will be with me in Paradise."[109]  Likewise for the person who had never had an opportunity to know and accept Christ as their savior, it seems possible that Jesus likely will make provision for them to be saved through his efforts.

So it would seem that Jesus was baptized in order that we may recognize that he was one with us as well as one with the Father and to recognize the importance of the inward state righteousness in our lives that baptism represents.  Having recognized the importance of these things and with Christ as our example, he intended that we would seek baptism – even more importantly, he intended we should seek the inward state of righteousness that he offers us through his redemption and salvation.

_(Another answer by Betty Berger)_

Matthew 3:13-17 explains why.  Jesus said it was to fulfill what was right.  He didn't minister until after He was baptized.  Then He went about preaching, teaching, and healing.  Baptism is an outward witness.  He was and is our example.

_(The answer of Betty Byers)_

Jesus was baptized at the beginning of his ministry to "fulfill all righteousness."[110]  It is reported that God was well pleased.

---

[109] Luke 23:43 (NIV)

[110] Matthew 3:15 (KJV)

# Some of the roles of Jesus seem to be in conflict.
The Bible describes Jesus as our redeemer (the person who pays our bail), our advocate (our lawyer), and our judge.  Isn't this a conflict of interest?

*(Jack Clark's thoughts)*

This seems like a fun question to consider.  In your imagination, can't you just visualize Satan hopping up and down ready to prosecute his claim that any one of us is a sinner and totally deserving of condemnation and worthy to be turned over to him for eternal punishment?  In this situation I'm sure that he could very well raise this objection.

I can also imagine the Son of God calmly responding, "That's all true.  They are sinners.  They do deserve to burn in hell.  It is a conflict of interest for me to serve in all these capacities based on worldly standards and certainly on your standards, Satan.  But I have another plan, another solution to my friends' problems, and I'm the one who makes the rules.  Objection overruled!"

*(Betty Byers' understanding)*

These three roles aren't a conflict of interest, because we need all three to have eternal life.

# Challenge 11
# Why does sin kill?  How does sin kill?

*(An answer by Jack Clark)*

Bill Cosby has a monologue comedy routine where he portrays a lady (I think it was Geraldine) who was tempted beyond resistance by a beautiful red dress she saw in a shop window.  She tried to resist, but was drawn – compelled – to go into the store and simply try it on.  Then she was tempted even more, responding with, "Get behind me, Satan!"  The clinching line in her downfall was Satan's remark, "It looks pretty good from back here too."  There is a lovely song about sin.  It starts, "I was sinking deep in sin, far from the distant shore..."  There is a parody of the song that goes: "I was sinking deep in sin.  Wheee!"  Satan is truly the great liar and the great deceiver.  He not only leads us ever so gradually astray, he makes it oh so easy and inviting.

First it's important to understand what sin is.  On the surface, this may sound silly, but a good many people believe that this only means not obeying one of the Ten Commandments.  While this is sin, it certainly doesn't fully define sin.  It's important to realize that the commandments aren't arbitrary or capricious rules set down by a god who wants to see us fail.  They are God's letting us know how He has morally devised the universe and how, the closer we can come to following the commandments, the richer our lives and the lives of everyone around us will be.  Another major purpose of the Commandments is to eventually let us find out that we cannot earn our salvation.  If we are to receive salvation, it must be accepted as a gift from God through Jesus Christ.  People who have never heard of the Ten Commandments sin.  There was sin before Moses was given the Ten Commandments.  Anyone from the very first person onward who disobeyed God or who acted in a way to not respect God or another of God's creations was guilty of a sin.  Jesus even pointed out that evil thoughts can be sins as well as our actions.[111]

Someone is sure to ask, "How could a person be guilty of sin if they didn't know God's laws?"  Paul answers this: "When the gentiles, who have no knowledge of the Law, act in accordance with it by the light of nature, they show that they have a law in themselves, for they demonstrate the effect of a law operating in their own hearts.  Their own consciences

---

[111] Matthew 5:21-32

endorse the existence of such a law, for there is something which condemns or excuses their actions. We may be sure that all this will be taken into account in the day of true judgment."[112]

Some people break down not following God's plan and rules into sin, transgression, and iniquities. Sin refers to things we fall into by accident - not by our design. Transgression refers to those willful, thought out things we do even though we realize ahead of time that this isn't what God wants for us. Iniquities refer to those things we do and then, in rebellion, respond to God with: "You don't have any business telling me how to run my life!" While the transgressions and iniquities might seem to be bigger problems than sin, I cannot find much in the Bible that indicates that God views them differently. Perhaps one indication in this area would be: "He (God's redeemer) was pierced for our transgressions; he was crushed for our iniquities. The punishment that brought us peace was upon him, and by his wounds we are healed."[113] This might be taken to indicate that iniquities require a greater saving redemption than transgressions.

The next thing is to understand what is meant by death and what is meant by life. Again a lot of people might chuckle at such an obvious question, but close study of scripture seems to indicate to me that life is being with God and death is being apart from God. Take it from one who has experienced being so separated from God that I characterized the experience as being in Hell, that a person may breathe and have a heart beat and consciousness but still not feel or be alive. I would characterize the situation in which I found myself as existing, but not even close to living.

So how does sin kill? It kills by separating us from God, the very source of life!

Why does sin kill? Some people visualize a wrathful God looking down on us watching for us to slip up and ready to stamp out our lives with a gleeful, "Aha! Gotcha!" When I read the account of the prodigal son in Luke,[114] this certainly isn't how the father (who I understand to represent God in the account) reacts to the errant son. The Father is concerned. The Father is eagerly hoping that the son will come to his senses and return

---

[112] Romans 2:14-16 (JBP)
[113] Isaiah 53:5 (NIV)
[114] Luke 15:11-31

90

home – of his own choice – not because he was forced to by the Father or the servants. The Father is looking eagerly for the son to return home. The Father is delighted when his son returns home. And the Father and the household celebrate when the son returns home. Jesus confirmed that our Father God feels the same: "I tell you that in the same way there will be more rejoicing in heaven over one sinner who repents than over ninety-nine righteous persons who do not need to repent."[115]

Many times Jesus tells us to consider how we react to our own children, as imperfect as we are, when we are trying to understand how God reacts to us. I certainly know that I have broken my earthly parents' rules and greatly disappointed them and not honored them at times. They let me know of their disappointment. They would punish me in various ways, but eventually, when their wrath subsided, I wasn't expelled from the family. I have found God has dealt with me in the same way.

The Bible indicates that God is ready and willing to forgive any sin except one – blasphemy against the Holy Spirit. This used to concern me more than a little. I knew I had a lot of sins to be forgiven, and I didn't want to be guilty of one that was impossible to forgive. I asked Phil Frew who was my pastor at the time exactly what this is. I remember his response: "Don't worry about it, Jack. If you're concerned, you haven't committed it." The dictionary describes blasphemy as irreverence toward God or anything sacred. It was Jesus who said that blasphemy against him could be forgiven, but not blasphemy against the Holy Sprit.[116] As I now understand blasphemy against the Holy Spirit, it can involve a life-long, never-renounced denial of the Holy Spirit's existence. It can also involve willfully attributing actions or attributes of the Holy Spirit to Satan or attributing actions or attributes of Satan to the Holy Spirit.

Sin separates us from God. Eventually sin can separate us from God to a degree that we cannot return to Him. This isn't God's choice. This isn't God's wish, but sin can become so chronic that we can't bring ourselves to go back to God. God will pursue us – he has even been called the hound of heaven. God will work to try to get us to return, but he won't force us to return to him against our will. Some have felt the weight of their sin so greatly that they come to the mistaken conclusion that their sins can't be washed away.

---

[115] Luke 15:7 (NIV)
[116] Matthew 12:31-32

Jesus spent a lot of time with fishermen. He even invited that we followers could become fishers of men. Perhaps those who don't see any chance of being relieved of their sins should remember that we don't have to be already clean to come to Christ. Like any good fisherman, he cleans the fish <u>after</u> he catches it. It's been said that many are called but few are chosen, but the truth of the matter is the only ones not chosen will be those who refuse to be. Eventually the situation comes down to each individual looking to God and responding like our Christ did when he said, "Your will be done."[117] In other words, you're in charge because I choose to have it that way; I want it to be that way; I literally thirst and hunger to have it that way. If an individual never comes to the place where they will choose this option, the only other alternative left to our God who gave us the free will to choose to be a part of His Kingdom or to refuse to be a part, is for God to look at the individual with great sadness and respond to the lost person, "<u>Your</u> will be done!"

So often when we sin we react like Cain did after he killed his brother, Able – we deny it, or we try to hide from God. What a childish thing to try to hide from God who is everywhere (omnipresent), or to try to lie to God about it when He knows everything (omniscient). When we sin we shouldn't run away from God. We should run to him, because that's where the forgiveness is!

The Bible indicates God's reaction when we come to Him and seek His forgiveness and to be made new by his love: "I, even I, am he who blots out your transgressions, for my own sake, and remembers your sins no more."[118] "As high as the heavens are above the earth, so great is his love for those who fear him; as far as the east is from the west, so far has he removed our transgressions from us."[119]

Moses made the following observation: "This day I call heaven and earth as witnesses against you that I have set before you life and death, blessings and curses. Now choose life, so that you and your children may live and that you may love the Lord your God, listen to his voice, and hold fast to him. For the Lord is your life."[120]

Sin doesn't have to kill us. God doesn't want sin to kill us. God has gone to every

---

[117] Luke 22:42
[118] Isaiah 43:25 (NIV)
[119] Psalm 103:12 (NIV)
[120] Deuteronomy 30:19-20 (NIV)

possible effort to be sure that sin will not kill those of us who don't choose that result. "The wages of sin is death, but the gift of God is eternal life in Christ Jesus our Lord."[121] God sent his very own son to tell us of his plan for salvation and to convince us that he had the ability and the right to offer us salvation and redemption. Jesus said, "I came that they may have life, and have it abundantly."[122] He also said, "I am the way, the truth and the life."[123] He has provided the way; he has shown us the way; he has told us the truth. He has offered us life!

---

[121] Romans 6:23 (NIV)
[122] John 10:10 (NIV)
[123] John 14:6 (NIV)

# The Bible says that Jesus paid for our souls' ransom. To whom was the ransom paid?

*(Jack Clark' thoughts)*

We know that one of the reasons for the cross was to draw mankind to Jesus Christ. We also understand that the main reason for the cross was to pay for our sins. By offering himself as a sacrifice to pay for our sins, Jesus, God's Messiah, redeemed us just as one might have redeemed a pawned treasure from a pawnshop.

Did you ever stop to think about to whom it was necessary to pay the ransom? Christ says about himself, "The Son of Man did not come to be served, but to serve and to give his life as a ransom for many." It doesn't take a great deal of insight to understand for whom the ransom was paid. It was paid for me; it was paid for you; it was paid for everyone. Anyone who will accept the fact that the ransom has been paid can receive the free gift, the mercy, of salvation.

The Bible commentator William Barclay points out that for many years men have asked the question, "To whom was the ransom paid?" He pointed out that if the ransom was paid to God who required a blood sacrifice and death to atone for our sins that this hardly fits with the characterization of "God is love."[124] It would seem that Christ didn't die in order to make God love us or accept us;[125] He already loved us with an everlasting love,[126] and He and His Son had already planned before the beginning of time how they would provide for making us acceptable in the Kingdom.[127] Barclay also pointed out that Origen had no doubt that the ransom was paid to the Devil who would not release us from his grasp until he received the payment. Gregory of Nyssa saw the fault with this conclusion, because it means that Satan could dictate terms to God. Barclay concludes that there is no answer as to whom the ransom was paid – only that it was paid.

I'm reminded of an event that happened a few years ago in the United States. A revolutionary group, the Symbionese Liberation Army, kidnapped Patty Hearst in February 1974. Patty was the granddaughter and heir of publishing giant William Randolph Hearst. It was initially expected that the group would demand a huge ransom or kill the young lady to make their revolutionary statement against her family. Instead months drug by without the intensive manhunt being able

---

[124] First John 4:8 (NIV)
[125] *The Attributes of God,* Arthur W. Pink, p.103, © 1975 by Baker Books
[126] Jeremiah 31:3
[127] Titus 1:2

to bring about her release. During this time the gang was brain washing her and sexually abusing her. Later in 1974 the group committed a bank robbery. Patty was recorded as having taken part. It seemed that there would have been an opportunity for her to break for freedom during this event, but she didn't. Was she too scared? Had they effectively turned her into one of them during these months? Did she choose to identify with them? Were there other reasons that kept her from bolting for freedom?

The gang was finally apprehended in 1975. Patty was tried and convicted of bank robbery and sentenced to seven years in prison. She served twenty-two months at which time President Jimmy Carter commuted her sentence. Seemingly something held Patty Hearst in the clutches of her evil captors even when she might have escaped on her own. The efforts of those who wished to free her were directed as much against her will as against those who had kidnapped her. The letter of the law convicted and condemned her. The compassion of President Carter could look beyond the facts of the case and her participation in the event of the robbery that seemingly involved some willingness on her part. He could even understand how the things to which she had been subjected could have led to her having aligned herself with her captors and helped to result in resistance to her deliverance.

In the Old Testament, Gomer had become enslaved to her masters. She had initially been lured to them by the false love of lust. She had initially left Hosea and gone to them by choice. Under God's direction, Hosea determined to buy her back, and determined to re-win her love and faithfulness even though there was no evidence that she desired this at the time he paid the ransom.[128] The fifteen shekels of silver and homer and lethek of barley Hosea paid ended up in the pocket of her owner, but they were also the first installment paid to her in the process of regaining her love. God in the context of dealing with unfaithful Israel did the same thing. "I led them with cords of human kindness... How can I give you up?"[129] He also states, "I desire mercy, not sacrifice, and acknowledgment of God rather than burnt offerings."

It would seem to me in both the cases of Patty Hearst and Gomer that the effort spent or the ransom paid was as much to win the enslaved prisoners' acceptance as to defeat those who enslaved them. So it would seem that the ransom Jesus Christ paid for my salvation and for your salvation is paid to those of us who were held in bondage. It was necessary as the first step in drawing each of us back into relationship with God with cords of human love so that we would

---

[128] Book of Hosea
[129] Hosea 11:4, 8 (TNIV)

participate in our escape by accepting it.

I note that when God speaks of drawing Israel back into relationship in Hosea, He speaks of using cords of human love. When a ship at sea has lost power and is in danger of being washed onto the rocks, lines are passed from a rescuing tug to the disabled ship. An important factor in this rescue at sea is the fact that those on the foundering ship have to accept the lines thrown from the tug. They have to be convinced that there is hope for the rescue being offered or they won't make the effort to attach the lines. The cords of God's love for mankind were always there; the connection had to be reestablished from man to God, and we couldn't do it on our own. Jesus had to become man to re-establish the life-saving connection. I would agree that the ransom paid by Christ was not paid to a vengeful, bloodthirsty God, because this is not His character; He still desires mercy, not sacrifice;[130] He is love. I would agree that the ransom was not paid to Satan, as Satan could not have held onto any sinner that God chose to wrest from his grasp. The ransom was paid not only for us. It was paid to us! May your heart be filled with the understanding of God's and Christ's boundless love!

---

[130] Hosea 6:6

# Was it really necessary for Jesus to be crucified?
What is it that the crucifixion accomplished?

*(An answer by Jack Clark)*

In a word, yes. It was necessary that Jesus be crucified.

Jesus himself gave the reason: "I, when I am lifted up from the earth, will draw all men to myself."[131] This was absolutely necessary to show us a glimpse of his unfathomable love that prompted him to forgive our sins. His resurrection was also absolutely necessary to show us that he had the power to forgive our sins and offer us everlasting life.

A very parallel event is recorded in the Bible. You will recall that a paralyzed man was brought to Jesus. Jesus said," Your sins are forgiven." I doubt this is what the crippled man had in mind when he asked his friends to take him to Christ. I doubt that it's what the friends had in mind when they brought him there. Of course some of the teachers of the law responded with the assessment that Jesus was blaspheming. Jesus knew their thoughts, and asked, "Why do you entertain evil thoughts in your hearts? Which is easier to say, 'Your sins are forgiven,' or to say 'Get up, and walk'? But so that you may know that the Son of Man has authority on earth to forgive sins…" At this point, Christ said to the paralyzed man, "Get up. Take your mat and go home."[132]

Anyone could have <u>said</u> to the paralyzed man, "Your sins are forgiven." I could <u>say</u> that; you could <u>say</u> that; actually doing it is something else entirely. The teachers and everyone else there knew that only God actually had the power to forgive sins. Only through the act of curing the man's physical problem, could Christ show that he had the ability to forgive the man's sins. Only through the demonstration of his unsurpassed love for us in accepting his suffering on the cross and in his power to defeat death, could we be convinced that he has the power to forgive our sins and offer us eternal life.

God and His son knew of peoples' sins even before any of our race was created. They devised and completed the solution – love and forgiveness – before the beginning of

---

[131] John 12:32 (NIV)
[132] Matthew 9:2-7 (NIV)

time.[133]  But it was beyond mankind's ability to comprehend this free gift until Jesus made it so totally obvious that there was no way it could have been mistaken.

This timetable of events will no doubt be a surprise to some.  I'll point out where scripture confirms this.  "(God) has rescued us from all that is really evil and called us to a life of holiness-not because of any of our achievements but for his own purpose.  Before time began, he planned to give us in Christ Jesus the grace to achieve this purpose, but it is only since our savior, Christ Jesus, has been revealed that the method has become apparent.  For Christ has completely abolished death, and has now, through the gospel, opened to us men the shining possibilities of the life that is eternal."[134]  Paul also wrote, "He (Jesus) chose us in him before the creation of the world to be holy and blameless in his sight."[135]

Jesus' role in our being made right with the Father is to be a substitute for the punishment that you and I should have received.  Matthew and Mark record that he gave his life as ransom for many.[136]  The Apostle John noted that, "He takes away the sins of the world."[137]  Conventional Christian understanding usually thinks of our redemption as having taken place on the cross, but in the book of Isaiah written about 760 years before the birth of Christ, the author uses the past tense in recording what Christ had already done: "He took up our infirmities and carried our sorrows...  He was pierced for our transgressions; he was crushed for our iniquities; the punishment that brought us peace was upon him, and by his wounds we are healed.  We all, like sheep, have gone astray; each of us has turned to his own way, and the Lord has laid on him the iniquity of us all."[138]  Isaiah can only be speaking of what had already taken place in the mind of God before Christ's coming to earth.  It would seem that Christ's time on earth and the events that occurred then were so that we could understand, believe, and accept what had already been done.

Put yourself in God's place for a little while.  Jesus has said that we should think of God as Abba.  In our scripture Abba is translated Father.  It should have been probably

---

[133] Second Timothy 1:8-10
[134] Second Timothy 1:9-11 also see Titus 1:2-3 (JBP)
[135] Ephesians 1:4 (TNIV)
[136] Matthew 20:28 and Mark 10:45
[137] First John 2:2 (NIV)
[138] Isaiah 53:4-6 (NIV)

more accurately translated Daddy. Just as we earthly parents know that when we have children they will do things that are destructive and mean and need to be corrected and even punished, God knew before He created any of us the things we would do. Our natural parents may have said to us, or as we may have said to our children when punishment was needed: "This is going to hurt me more than it will hurt you." God certainly loves even more than a human parent, and just as a human parent, He is interested in the restoration of relationships. Read the story of the prodigal son[139] to understand how much God longs for our return and how much He celebrates when it happens. Have you ever known someone who had a wayward child? Some of us have been wayward children and have been welcomed back with open arms. God loves us. God loves you. God loves me. He will go to any length to salvage our broken ties!

The love of Jesus showed in coming to earth where he knew he would be reviled, abused, and crucified is almost beyond my comprehension. As I think about this, some perspective occurs when I realize that on any day I would give my life if there were no other way to save the life of a family member. Most days I can conceive of giving my life to save the threatened life of a good friend. On a very good day, I can envision possibly giving my life to save that of a stranger. I can ruefully say that I doubt that I would ever give my life to save that of an avowed enemy. Before accepting our gift of salvation we have been described as enemies of the cross of Christ.[140] It was in this state of enmity that Jesus made his sacrifice to save us. It is after we accept the salvation that he calls us friend.[141] Jesus indicates that after we have become part of the Kingdom of God, that God is our Father. If God is our Father, then Jesus must be our brother. It is obvious that after we accept our salvation that we are family and friends, but it is equally obvious that Christ paid the ransom for us while we were still enemies.

Looking at the role of God the Father in the great drama of our salvation and restitution into relationship, He did something I could never do. While I can conceive of giving up my own life to save at least some other people, I could never bring myself to be part of a plan that would sacrifice the life of one of my children to save anyone's life. This points out one of the many significant differences between God and me! "God so loved the world that He

---

[139] Luke 15:11-31
[140] Philippians 3:18
[141] John 15:15

101

gave His one and only son that whoever believes in him shall not perish but have eternal life."[142]

I have suggested that redemption was devised by God and by Jesus before the beginning of time and have quoted Bible verses to support this view. Otherwise Abraham, Moses, and the many others indicated as being saved by their faith could not have been saved before Christ's crucifixion. Having been a determined course of action by God, it was a completed event only waiting on its manifestation in the life, death, and resurrection of Christ.

Well, if salvation was a completed event, was the cross necessary? It seems that the spiritual sacrifice was made before the beginning of time and long before the crucifixion. Jesus knew this, of course. I would suggest this may be why he prayed in the Garden of Gethsemane, "My Father if it is possible, may this cup be taken from me. Yet not as I will, but as you will."[143] I don't think Jesus would have prayed this if the spiritual requirements for our salvation had not already been met. That is not to say that salvation without the cross such as Abraham and Moses received would have been cheap grace. As painful, degrading, and awful as the physical act of crucifixion on the cross was, I would suggest that the spiritual act of redemption was even more degrading, painful, and awful to our Holy God and His Holy son. The physical act of the crucifixion still was essential.

When mankind realized that God had expectations and rules to follow but broke those rules, God devised the sacrificial system to restore humans' relationship with Him. Since breaking God's rules resulted in spiritual death, the sacrifice involved a substitute death of an animal that was important to the sinner. That is the sinner had to give up a life that was important to him as a substitute for his own life. To eliminate the necessity of repeated sacrifices and make one final sacrifice that was so great that people could understand its significance as eliminating any need for future sacrifice, God and his son himself devised the son's crucifixion as the ultimate sacrifice that would wash away the sins for all time of those who would accept it.

Probably most Christians think of Jesus' death on the cross as being the act of

---

[142] John 3:16 (NIV)
[143] Matthew 26:39 (NIV)

redemption. I have suggested that as difficult as that was for the Son and the Father, that the act of redemption occurred much earlier on a spiritual level and that as terrible as the crucifixion was that the spiritual event was even more terrible and costly to God. Many of us lustily sing of being washed in the blood, or the cleansing power of the blood. In no way do I want to minimize the physical sacrifice that God and Jesus made to redeem my soul and the souls of all believers. The physical act of the crucifixion was essential to prove to people who would never have been convinced of the gift of redemption through the love of God without such proof. The crucifixion was the proof of the love. The resurrection was the proof of Jesus' power to have the right to forgive our sins; these events drew mankind to Jesus because of the demonstration of both his love and his power. I think of a person imprisoned in a dungeon separated form God by sin. If the person was forgiven and during the night while the prisoner was asleep and the prison doors were unlocked without the prisoner's knowledge, they wouldn't know of their release. Jesus came to convince us of our release. Otherwise we would never have been convinced that the debt had been paid by him as our substitute. In truth we were and are washed in the blood of Jesus, the lamb; not because of his, or the Father's requirement or Satan's demand, but because we could not have believed it without the astounding evidence. Even when we were convinced of his love and his intention, we would have been skeptical of his right to pardon our sentence without his demonstration of the power to take up his life again.

Christ's crucifixion was not necessary to appease a blood thirsty God – that's not His nature. It wasn't necessary to grab us out of the clutches of Satan – Satan could never resist an all powerful (omnipotent) God. It was necessary to convince <u>us</u> of God's and Jesus' love and what he and the Father had already done and to convince us that we have a chance to escape the snare, the death trap, of sin in which we were entangled!

---

*(Betty Byers' answer)*

Yes, it was really necessary for Christ to be crucified. His blood had to be shed, so we could get eternal life.

---

## Challenge 14
# How could Jesus be dead three days and possibly live again?

We know that somewhere between three to five minutes with no heart beat results in irreversible brain death. How can it logically be claimed that Jesus died on Friday and took up his life again on Sunday?

*(Jack Clark's answer)*

Well the fact is that it can't be logically claimed from a human perspective. It can only be claimed as a God event. Other God events can't be understood logically from our perspective. How could it logically be claimed that the complete universe was at one time a tiny dot of substance that had formed and before that had been only the energy of God's thoughts and desires? And yet science confirms back to the tiny dot that burst forth to make the universe, and certainly science has no explanation of what went before that event. This leaves us with the God-centered explanation. How can it logically be conceived that God is aware of and concerned with everything going on in every person's life and everything going on down to the atomic and subatomic level of existence in every individual speck of dust throughout this universe, and yet that's exactly what we have the temerity to claim about God. Many of us are certainly convinced of this level of involvement of God in our lives by the events we've experienced.

Paul in First Corinthians gives one of the best explanations of how existence after death occurs in discussing what our resurrected bodies will be like. He points out that when we plant a seed it is different when it sprouts and matures. He suggests there are heavenly bodies and earthly bodies each with their own splendor. He goes on to say, "So it will be with the resurrection of the dead. The body that is sown is perishable; it is raised imperishable... It is sown in weakness, it is raised in power. It is sown a natural body; it is raised a spiritual body... I declare to you, brothers and sisters, that flesh and blood cannot inherit the kingdom of God, nor does the perishable inherit the imperishable... We will be changed. For the perishable must clothe itself with the imperishable and the mortal with immortality."[144]

Certainly it's no stretch for those who believe that Jesus existed as a part of God before anything was created to realize that as a spiritual being with a spiritual body he became an earthly individual with an earthly body. We believe his purpose in this

---

[144] First Corinthians 15:35-54 (TNIV)

transformation was to relate to humans and tell us fully of God's love and plan of salvation. At the time of his resurrection it seems that he was transformed back to his spiritual body's state of existence. Certainly a savior who could enter a room through barred doors but who could offer to let Thomas put his finger in the nail holes of his hands and into the spear wound of his side had to have a physical body that was somehow different than it had been. He was not only a spirit without a physical body, but he surely had different physical properties than he had before. In a God-determined event, Jesus had gone from a spiritual existence and a spiritual body to an earthly body and back to an imperishable spiritual body. With each transformation the essence of his being was transfigured into the changed existence along with the total essence of his personality, his memory, his power, his emotions, his love, his ability to perceive, and his reasoning and intellectual abilities. He still knew his friends. He still loved his friends. He deeply understood and restored the brokenness of his friends. He could prepare a picnic lunch for his friends along the seashore. He could walk with his friends along the road to Emmaus. He could share additional knowledge with his friends. He could give his friends courage. In short, although he was physically changed, he remained very much the same. The wonder is that, through what he is, he made it clear that he offers the same possibility to each of us, if we will accept the free gift.

---

*(Thoughts of Matthew Gunter)*

Jesus was dead. There is no doubt whatever about that. As Dickens writes of Jacob Marley's death, this must be distinctly understood, or nothing wonderful can come of the story. Thomas knew he was dead, and a large chunk of Thomas had died with him. Jesus had inspired Thomas. Jesus had set Thomas's heart on fire. But now that fire had been extinguished on the cross, and Thomas is left with cold ashes in his heart. Jesus is dead. No wonder he was reluctant to believe the others. Wouldn't you be? No wonder he wanted to see for himself. Not just see, but feel. "I want to poke my finger in the holes in his hands before I'll believe." He had hoped so much, and that hope had died. It was not going to be resurrected by hearsay.

Then it happened. Jesus appeared to Thomas and offered to let him feel the wounds. It doesn't say whether he actually did, but it doesn't matter. He was changed forever. "My Lord and God!" Thomas and the others had sensed and believed that Jesus was special before. But you get the feeling in the Resurrection stories that they were encountering something new; something so awesome they could barely speak of it. In some versions, they don't. This was more than some kind of story you might read in Ripley's Believe It Or Not. It was more than a case of someone's heart stopping for a few minutes on the operating table. The Mystery of life and death, the Mystery at the heart of the universe, had broken through and declared itself. It had acted decisively in history on behalf of humanity. Now that Mystery had a face, the face of Jesus Christ. So Thomas, almost as a reflex, says, "My Lord and my God."

But the others got to see it for themselves. What about us? We don't get the proof that Thomas was granted. We have the records of the appearances in the Bible, exciting and confused, as you'd expect under the circumstances. We are grateful for them. We can read them and allow the Holy Spirit to nourish our spirits through them. We can study them and try to figure out if it happened this way or that. But sometimes it feels like a long time ago and far away.

Yet Jesus says, "Blessed are those who have not seen and yet have come to believe." Why? Because, the Resurrection is not, primarily, about something that happened 2,000 years and half a world away. It is about the presence of the Risen One in our lives here and now. It is about the promise of resurrection in our lives here and now. It is about the promise of that final Resurrection of which Easter is but the foretaste. We do not see him like Thomas did. But the Resurrection isn't just something that happened in Palestine some 19 ½ centuries ago. Christ has become present to us in a new way through the Holy Spirit, and we can know that presence.

The French poet Paul Caudel wrote, "Christ did not come to the world to end suffering; he did not even come to explain it. He came to fill suffering with his presence." In his death and Resurrection, Christ dealt the forces of death and suffering a mortal blow and became present to us in our suffering. It is significant that, after the Resurrection, he still bears the wounds of crucifixion.

God is not out there somewhere, while we struggle with our lives and the death and suffering that are a part of them. He is present in the rubble in Oklahoma City. He is present in the refugee camps of Rwanda. He is present wherever there is suffering, both great and small.  He has entered in, taken on the wounds of suffering and death, and transformed them into life.  He has filled them with his presence.  The power of his presence is available to those who believe and open themselves to it.  It is the power of self-giving love and renewal of life.  "Blessed are those who have not seen yet have come to believe."

It is the promise of resurrection in our lives here and now.  To believe in resurrection is to believe no situation is hopeless, no relationship is beyond redemption, no just cause is ultimately lost.  It is to believe that our lost hopes and dreams are not really lost.  Because they are now filled with the presence of the Risen Christ, every disappointment, every discouragement, every loss can become a reminder of the promise of resurrection by which we can start again.  Each is a sort of death from which we can rise to new life through Christ.  And the ashes in our hearts become fire again.

Christ's Resurrection is the promise and foretaste of the final Resurrection in which the victory begun during Holy Week will be completed.

I remember sometimes at family gatherings after things had settled down but people were not ready to leave, we would watch television.  As I recall, we usually watched Lassie.  I have an uncle, Lavon, who liked to tease us.  He would wait until the part in the story where it seemed Lassie had gotten into a hopeless situation.  Then he would say with all seriousness, "It doesn't look like she's going to get out of this one.  I think Lassie is done for this time."  There would then be a station break during which we would all worry about Lassie's future.  As we got older, we began to catch on; no matter how bad things looked or how dire my uncle's predictions, we knew that Lassie would make it in the end, and all would be well.

Part of Easter is the promise that in the end all will be well.  The story is not over yet.  We each have our own part in it.  And certainly each of our stories will take many turns, and involve some close calls, some too close.

But because we believe God raised Jesus from the dead, we hope for the consummation of that work in the final Resurrection of all creation.  We are not told how he's going to do it.  But somehow, on the cross Christ absorbed all the sin, and suffering and sorrow everywhere and always.

Christ's Resurrection was the foreshadowing of the promise of the day when it will be all transformed into joy.  And as Julian of Norwich wrote, "... all will be well, and all will be well, and every kind of thing will be well."  On that day we will stand before the Risen Christ and be able to join Thomas without any doubt in saying, "My Lord and my God."

# How do we know the resurrection wasn't a fake?
What supports the resurrection of Christ, and refutes the assertion of the authorities that Christ had not actually died at the time of his crucifixion, or that his disciples stole his body and made up a great lie that he rose from the dead?

*(Jack Clark's answer)*

First I'll address the suggestion that Jesus had not actually died. The Roman soldiers were well-trained. They knew how to crucify a person. They were no friends of Jesus. They were the ones who beat him and mocked him and spit on him and crammed the awful crown of thorns down on his head. They wouldn't have risked their necks to not do their jobs. Sure, they were surprised that he died so soon and that they didn't have to finish him off by eventually breaking his legs like they usually did. But he had been through grueling beatings that would have made him more quickly go into shock and die from the added pain and the inability to get a good breath without having to heave himself upward by pulling against his pierced hands while on the cross. And then there was the spear wound to the side. It wasn't just a surface wound, or the body fluids wouldn't have gushed out. The soldiers were experienced. If they said you were dead, then you were really dead!

Then there were the times of appearances after his resurrection. We're told that somehow his body was different – transfigured. He could appear in a locked room. He was reported to have taken a long walk with some followers (not a part of the eleven, as they later reported to them) along the road to Emmaus.[145] Have you ever stepped on a nail and removed it and then in a few days tried to walk? I have. Believe me, it hurts. And the nail I stepped on was a relatively small shingle nail. It wasn't a spike that had gone completely through both feet. For sure if I had been crucified but not killed and transfigured, I would have never been able to make that hike along the road to Emmaus.

It seems to me that the most telling evidence is not the direct testimony of the believers; although, this is certainly important. To me the most telling proof comes from the indirect testimony of their actions. I've mentally tried to put myself in their place. Perhaps if you do the same thing it will be significant to you too. Imagine yourself one of the remaining eleven disciples who were left after Jesus' crucifixion and Judas' suicide.

---

[145] Luke 24:13-35

You had all pledged to follow Jesus wherever it led. Thomas had said let's go with him to Jerusalem even if it means our death. Peter had pledged that he would never deny Christ and had been willing to do battle with the group (including soldiers) who came to arrest Jesus – he even cut off the ear of the servant of the high priest. Then every one had run away just as Jesus had predicted. Peter had denied he knew Jesus the three times even throwing in a curse for good measure. Every disciple was terrified for his own life. They were behind locked doors. If we were part of the eleven we would have done the same thing. We both know that we would. John alone stood at the foot of the cross at the crucifixion and was given the care of Jesus' mother Mary. It most surely was love rather than bravery that brought John there, because he too was later found quaking behind the locked door trying to avoid the authorities. All of a sudden the picture changed. The disciples were out in the street proclaiming a risen Lord. They weren't trembling any more. They weren't hiding any more. They were out where the Romans and the Sanhedrin, and the Sadducees, and the Pharisees could hear them. Then they were brought before them and threatened and whipped (and this wasn't a few whacks on the legs with a switch – it was a cruel beating designed to really get a person's attention), but they didn't shut up or fade away. What would have led you or me if we had been part of that group of disciples to have changed like that? What would have sent us into the streets in defiance of all that power? If we were a part of the group who would be known as the Apostles, what would have eventually led ten of our group of eleven to accept martyrdom when all we would have to do would be go back to our fishing or our tax collecting or other employment and avoid all that? (Judas had committed suicide, and of the remaining Apostles only John died a natural death.) I am persuaded that each disciple was totally convinced that Jesus, God's Christ, was actually raised from the dead. Nothing else would have convinced them or us to have taken this course of action. No conspiracy or lie could have held up without having been exposed by one of us.

An awful lot of people were reported to have seen Jesus after the resurrection to assign the reports to mass hysteria. "He appeared to Peter, and then the twelve." (Judas had been replaced.) "After that, he appeared to more than five hundred of the brothers at the same time, most of whom are still living, though some have fallen asleep. Then he appeared to James, then to all the apostles, and last of all he appeared to me" (Paul) "also, as to one abnormally born." [146]

Could the grief of the disciples have led to a mass psychological breakdown that resulted in a few having a delusion that Jesus was risen and the rest of us being convinced? When my brother died climbing Mount McKinley in Alaska, I didn't have any hallucinations or delusions that he was still alive, but I did have some very realistic dreams of him being found alive. When I would wake, I would realize what the dream was and cry again. Do you think a few of the stronger ones could have convinced the rest based on their wishful thinking or their dream, or their delusion, or their hallucination? It certainly doesn't sound like Thomas believed it without irrefutable direct proof which he was given. "Unless I see the nail marks in his hands and put my finger where the nails were, and put my hand into his side, I will not believe it." A week later Thomas had his chance. Jesus said, "Stop doubting and believe." Thomas responded, "My Lord and my God!" Then Jesus told him, "Because you have seen me, you have believed; blessed are those who have not seen me and yet have believed."[147]

Well I say again that to me the most telling testimony is the change in the lives of the disciples. I'm one of those who were not there to see Christ in person, but I have experienced him in my life, and I do believe. Do you?

---

*Dean Culbertson's answer*

First, the resurrection is clearly discussed in the Scriptures. The fact of the matter is Jesus endured a horrible beating. He was flogged. Then they put a robe on Him and mocked Him. The blood would have stuck to His robe. Then they ripped the robe from Him. He bled again. A crown of thorns pierced his scalp. This caused more bleeding. Finally, they nailed his hands to a cross and left Him to die. The law required that prisoners had to die before the Sabbath. At some point, a Roman guard put a spear in His side. Not just blood came out. Water did too. I think this suggests some type of heart failure. Anyway, they came by later to break His legs if necessary... the fact is, He had already died.

---

[146] I Corinthians 15:7-8 (NIV)
[147] John 20:25-29 (NIV)

Of course, His resurrection was indeed a miracle. Yet several dead people were resurrected upon the death of Jesus. Further, Golgotha was a huge hill. As Jesus died, it went pitch black in the middle of the day. And yes, the earth shook. God gives us this kind of miracle to show Himself to us. (By the way, I would <u>not</u> want to have been mocking Jesus on that hill!)

They feared hoaxes, so when He was entombed in a burial site given by Joseph of Arimathea, they sealed the door to the cave with a large rock. The rock was put there to keep "visitors" out. The Bible records that the stone was rolled away and that Jesus indeed appeared to Mary, Peter, and later to the rest. Honestly, this is just too much to fake.

*(Betty Byers' answer)*

We know the resurrection wasn't a fake based on the Bible accounts. There were those who witnessed the crucifixion, the empty tomb, the eyewitnesses who saw and visited with him, and the preaching of the Apostles.[148] Jesus showed Thomas his hands and feet.[149]

*(Matt Gunter's thoughts)*

## Risen To Interfere and Transform

Scriptures: Jeremiah 17:5-10; Psalm 1; 1 Corinthians 15:12-20; Luke 6:17-26

"If Christ has not been raised, then our proclamation has been in vain and your faith has been in vain."

Occasionally you'll come across an author, perhaps a preacher or a theologian, even a biblical scholar, who will say that if by some chance an archeologist stumbled upon the tomb of Jesus and found in there the bones of Jesus, their faith would not be particularly affected. That begs the question what exactly their faith is based upon in the first place. Then you will find others who will say, "The Bible says it. I believe it. That settles it." These will write books seeking to prove beyond any reasonable doubt that all sensible people must agree that Jesus rose from the dead.

---

[148] Mark 16:14, Luke 24:31, Acts 4:2 and 17:18 and 24:15, and 26:8, and Romans 6:5 (KJV)
[149] John 20:27 (KJV)

The problem with those kinds of books is that it is hard to imagine what criteria one would use to prove or disprove something like the resurrection. Either the resurrection is the most fundamental fact by which all else is measured or there is something else more fundamental on which we base our examination of the resurrection. Sooner or later we must declare ourselves and declare what we believe is most basic.

That's not just true of resurrection, though. On many things it is difficult to figure out what criteria we use to demonstrate for sure what we believe. Is peace really better than war? Many cultures in history have not believed so. The way of the warrior has been valued in many cultures, in many places, and many times, and the way of peace has been seen as the way of weakness. Is forgiveness really better than revenge? Again, that has not been obvious to all people, in all places, in all times. In fact, in many cultures revenge is an obligation and a duty. Or, more basic and more puzzling perhaps is the old philosophical and theological question: Is what we experience as reality really real, or is it all an illusion? By what criteria do we measure and evaluate such questions? By what criteria do we measure and evaluate resurrection?

We are left with the choice to either bet our lives on the resurrection of Christ as the fundamental fact – the fundamental criterion by which we measure everything else – or we decide there are other more solid facts and criteria by which we measure things and measure the resurrection. Those criteria will inevitably be based on some philosophical or theological commitments other than the resurrection.

At least some scholars are honest about those commitments. One in particular is Marcus Borg, a New Testament scholar who has made a fair bit of money writing books about Jesus. Writing about the resurrection in *The Meaning of Jesus*, one of his books about Jesus, Borg admits that when it gets right down to it his problem with the resurrection is not primarily about historical or scientific evidence. He's honest enough to admit that it's almost impossible to prove or disprove something that happened two thousand years ago. But Borg is prejudiced against the resurrection from the beginning. He writes (in a footnote, but it is nonetheless clear) that he is inclined to reject the resurrection as traditionally understood because of his theological presuppositions about how God has to be.

First of all, Marcus Borg believes that God does not interfere in the world. And what is the resurrection of Jesus Christ except the most basic interference of God in the world? It is interfering with the usual course of things. People die, and people stay dead. If Jesus didn't stay dead, then God really interfered in our history, in our world, in our reality.

Marcus Borg also says he has a problem with resurrection because if Jesus rose from the dead then one might conclude that Jesus is superior to all the other religious and spiritual and political and philosophical leaders in world history. If Jesus did not stay dead that gives him place preeminence; and for Marcus Borg, all religions, all faiths, all philosophies must start out on an equal footing.

Marcus Borg and those like him sound sophisticated. They will tell you what intelligent people can and cannot believe today. But the conclusions of their scholarship are shaped by their intellectual prejudices. In that, they are really no different – no more honest, no more sophisticated, no more objective – than a fundamentalist whose intellectual commitment to inerrancy dictates that he find "evidence" of Noah's flood. There are many careful, thoughtful scholars who reject both the simplicities of naïve literalism of the fundamentalist and the pseudo-sophistication of the likes of Borg.

But Christians believe in the resurrection. We bet our lives on the historical, physical reality of the resurrection of Jesus Christ. We believe God did interfere with history – and with all reality – in the resurrection. Because Jesus Christ is risen and lives, he is present in our present. His presence interferes with our presence. Just as he interfered with Peter, James and John at their nets on the Sea of Galilee, just as he interfered with Zacchaeus and his money changing, just as he interfered with the woman caught in adultery and with the Pharisees who were about to stone her, just as he interfered with the Samaritan woman. He interferes with our world and he interferes with our lives if we allow him. Not only interfering, but transforming, as he transformed Peter, James and John, Zacchaeus and others. Jesus Christ, alive and present, interferes to transform our lives – to transform our lives, to redeem our lives, to change our lives, to bring healing, wholeness, forgiveness and life. Christ is risen and alive and he interferes. And once we believe that, he interferes with the way we see the world.

And, Marcus Borg is right. If Jesus is risen, if Jesus alone did not stay dead but rose again and is seated at the right hand of God – which means sharing the power at the heart of the universe – then he is unique and incomparable. Mohammed, wise and insightful as he was, died and stayed dead. Gotama Buddha, wise and influential as he was, died and stayed dead. Plato, Socrates, Aristotle, and Confucius – each died and stayed dead. George Washington and Abraham Lincoln, who we celebrate, died and stayed dead. If Jesus rose from the dead and left an empty tomb behind, he cannot be ignored or accommodated to other ways of understanding reality. All other understanding must be accommodated to that basic reality. However offensive to Borg and many others, that is what it means to say Jesus is Lord.

If Jesus died and stayed just as dead as all the others, then who is Lord? Part of the appeal of making sure that Jesus stays just as dead as everyone else is this: You know who is Lord if Jesus is dead – you are. I am. If Jesus is as dead as everyone else, then we can look at Jesus and Mohammed and Confucius and Buddha and Abraham Lincoln and John Locke and anyone else you want to include and we get to measure and evaluate what they said and did as it fits into our scheme. If I don't want God to interfere, then I can just make sure that those who say that God doesn't really interfere are the ones I listen to. I can pick and choose based on my own prejudices, or the prejudices of my culture, who it is that fits the way I see things. I get to be Lord. If Jesus Christ is risen; *he* is Lord. And he will interfere with the way I see the world. He will come to me, challenging me to allow him, through his Spirit, to transform me.

Paul wrote to the Corinthians telling them that if Christ is not raised, then everything that he told them was nonsense. The Corinthians, or at least some of them, wanted to be Lord. They wanted to be more spiritual than God. They wanted to be wise. They wanted to escape. They had a bias against the material world. They had a bias against bodily existence. What they most wanted was to escape.

There are only a handful of ways of seeing our situation. One is to simply say that what is is, and there is nothing more. There is no escape from the reality around us so you might as well make the most of it. Eat, drink and be merry because tomorrow you die. Or, you can say there is an escape. We have immortal souls trapped in this earthly, bodily, existence with all the historical misfortunes and vicissitudes and what we need to look for is escape. It might be that death is our escape. By and by we will die and then all the suffering will be over. If that's the case, the best thing to do is try to manage with whatever suffering you can't avoid and try to avoid as much suffering as you can until you get to die and be put out of your misery. Of course, some ways of seeing reality – ways like Hinduism and Buddhism – suggest that death is no escape. Then the challenge is to figure out how to escape the cycle of birth, death and rebirth.

But resurrection is not about escape. Resurrection is about transformation. If God interfered in our history, in our reality, then transformation has broken in on us. Transformation has come and our reality, our history, our world and our lives are redeemable and can be transformed. It is not just escape that we are promised; we are promised the transformation of all of our lives, all of our reality, all of our bodily existence with all of the hurts that we have experienced and all of the hurts that we have inflicted. All of creation transformed by God in Christ; that is the promise of resurrection.

If all that we are about is escaping – shuffling off the mortal coil – then all the suffering and death in the world have the final word. If Christ is not raised, everything that we do here is empty. If the tomb is not empty, our faith and our hope are empty. If Christ is not raised, we can look back on all that he said and all that he did as being perhaps interesting but, in the end, sort of quaint and sentimental. If Christ is not raised, who in their right mind would say that it is blessed to be poor, to be hungry, to weep? If Christ is not raised, who would seriously believe that to be wealthy and well-fed and happy are dangerous? But Christ *is* risen and those words are as true for us as they were for those to whom he spoke them two thousand years ago. Christ is raised. Christ is alive. Christ is present in our midst by his Spirit to interfere with the way we see the world, to interfere with the usual way of things, but also to bring transformation, healing and redemption. And this is not simply a matter of our individual selves. All creation and all human structures are destined for the resurrection transformation begun with Jesus. And we are called to live into that now.

When we are baptized we are made a participating part of Christ's death and resurrection. If Christ is not raised, then that too is meaningless and has no more ultimate significance then being initiated into the Lion's Club or learning the handshake of a secret society. If Christ is raised, we who are baptized are incorporated into his living presence

118

right at that time. If Christ is raised, all of us are subject to his interference and his transformation. Christ is raised. God, through Christ, interferes in our world. God, through Christ, brings transformation.

It makes a fundamental difference in how we see the world if we believe God is about resurrection and transforming our reality rather than just providing some way for us to escape the suffering of this world. Several years ago I went to the Holocaust Museum in Washington, D.C. Perhaps some of you have been there. It is three stories of pictures and descriptions and artifacts from one of the most horrific periods in history, a testament of human evil and human suffering. One part in particular that is very poignant is a glassed in room that is full of nothing but shoes, shoes that were taken off of the people who were led into the concentration camps. Many of the shoes are shoes of children. Children, women, men, herded into concentration camps, often herded into gas chambers and killed. I guess if all we're about is trying to escape the suffering of the world, we can say that at least they were put out of their misery. But there can be no real justice for them. And there can be no ultimate forgiveness for those who participate in such evil. If, however, what we are about is resurrection and transformation, then their suffering is not meaningless or lost. It will be caught up in God's resurrection reality, caught up in Christ who entered in to the suffering of the world on the cross and raised it up in transforming, redeeming power. No suffering is ever lost. No evil is ever forgotten. Both are caught up in Christ for judgment and transformation where there is forgiveness, justice, and healing.

Whether or not finding the bones of Jesus somewhere outside Jerusalem would affect our faith depends completely on what it is – or who it is – we have faith in. Whether or not it would affect our hope depends entirely on what it is we are hoping for. Let us live in the hope of Christ's interfering and transforming presence in our midst. And, let us bear that presence, through his Spirit, in the world around us.

## Challenge 16
# What if Jesus' burial site has been found?

In 2007 a "bombshell" claim was made in the TV documentary "The Lost Tomb of Christ" that Jesus' casket (ossuary) had been found in a Jerusalem suburb along with ossuaries of Mary, Joseph, Mary Magdalene and "Judah son of Jesus." If true this challenges the basis of Christian belief.

*(Thoughts of Jack Clark)*

Many people who would be detractors of the Christian faith have challenged the basic beliefs from the very first. In the early church history, some said Christ was only a spirit. The Sanhedrin claimed that the disciples had stolen Christ's body and that there was no resurrection. This is another such effort to diminish Christ. It would make no difference in my personal faith if Christ had married and had a child or children, but I'm convinced that if he had the Bible would have reported this. It certainly would be difficult to work into faith the finding of Jesus Christ's casket containing "decomposed human residue." Certainly this is impossible to prove one way or the other. Those who want to detract from Christ will see it as proof that we Christians are a deluded bunch. Those of us who are convinced that Christ is the son of God will see it as an attempt to gain fame and make money through controversy.

There are several observations that can be made. First, these were very common names in that time. It is certainly possible that the caskets of this family shared the same names as our savior's family and friends. We should recall that the man who was released by Pilate on the insistence of the yelling mob was also named Jesus – Jesus Barabbas (meaning Jesus son of the father). Second, Stephen Pfann, a Biblical scholar at the University of the Holy Land in Jerusalem, is not convinced that the name on the ossuary is even Jesus. He suggested the name is actually Hanun.[150] A third factor to consider is that Amos Kloner, the first archaeologist to examine the site when it was uncovered in 1980, told the Associated Press after the release of the film that the filmmakers' assertions are false.[151] The third observation I would make about the subject is the indirect testimony of the early disciples (followers) of Jesus Christ. After Christ's crucifixion they were huddled together behind barred doors in fear for their lives. I find it impossible to believe that Peter and the others, if they knew of Jesus' burial site in an ossuary where his body decomposed instead of being resurrected, would have become

---

[150] Netscape March 4, 2007.
[151] *Ibid*

121

the revolutionaries that would turn the Jewish nation and the Roman Empire upside down. They wouldn't have risked their lives for a lie. Ten of them wouldn't have accepted martyrdom as the price of being apostles (those who attempt to convert others).

*(Betty Byers' comment)*

Someone is always coming up with ideas that make people doubt the Bible. If you doubt one area, it's easy to doubt many areas.

Challenge 17
# Why are there so many names for God?
Does it really matter what we call our heavenly Father?  Which name should be used at what time?
(Submitted by Fairplain Presbyterian Adult Church School class in Benton Harbor, Michigan)

*(Jack Clark's thoughts)*

For those of us who are the male parent of children – does it matter what they call us? I expect that most of us are delighted any time they speak to us in love or respect.  Dad, Daddy, Father, Pop – anything will do.  We delight in our relationship.  Only if they are disrespectful are we hurt or angry – the name used disrespectfully may even be the same as the one used in love at other times.  God seems to feel the same way.  That seems to be why one of the Ten Commandments is not to take the Lord's name in vain.

In his Pulitzer Prize winning book, *God a Biography,* Jack Miles suggests that the various names encountered in the Bible represent changes in the nature of God during the period of Israel's development.[152]  To those of us who understand that God never changes,[153] this doesn't seem to cover the reasons for various names.

One of the most important names for God is the name by which He identified Himself: YHWH.  The Hebrew language did not use vowels in its written form, and devout Jews avoid saying this personal ritual name of God out of respect and a concern that they might accidentally use it in an irreverent manner.  Most commonly when modern writers insert vowels, the name is written YAHWEH.  When translated to English it has become Jehovah.  Most commonly this ritual name for God is felt to mean I Am or He Causes to Be.  YHWH is the name by which God identified Himself to Moses at the burning bush when He said "I am who I am" that has also been translated I cause to be what comes into existence."[154]  The name YHWH especially refers to the creative power of God.  It's interesting to note that the word hallelujah comes from combining the Hebrew words hallel (praise) and YHWH (God).

Because of the Israelites' not permitting themselves to say the name of YHWH to avoid possibly debasing it, they usually referred to God as ADONAI meaning The LORD.  They would also refer to Him as HA-SHEM meaning The Name.

---

[152] *God a Biography,* Jack Miles, © 1995 by Jack Miles, First Vintage Books Edition, April, 1996
[153] See Hebrews 1:10-12
[154] *Abingdon Bible Handbook*, p. 425, Edward P. Blair, Abingdon Press, Nashville & New York.

EL and ELOHIM (meaning Almighty) were also used especially in the Northern Kingdom of Israel in reference to God, but could also be used as a generic term to include other gods besides YHWH.

EL ELYON means God Most High or the Most High God.

EL ELOHEY YISRAEL means The Mighty God of Israel and was a title given at a consecrated place by Jacob.

EL SHADDAI is usually translated Almighty and literally means The Mountain One. It has also been translated The All-Sufficient One, Omnipresent God, and God Almighty.

YHWH (Jehovah)-JIREH indicates that God Will Provide.

YHWH (Jehovah)-RAPHA means The Lord Who Heals.

YHWH (Jehovah)-NISSI indicated The Lord is My Banner.

YHWH (Jehovah)-MEKODDISHKIM means The Lord Sanctifies You (makes you Holy).

YHWH (Jehovah)-SHALOM means The Lord Is Peace.

YHWH (Jehovah)-RAAH translates The Lord Is My Shepherd.

YHWH (Jehovah)-SABAOTH refers to the aspect of God that declares Him to be The Lord of Hosts.

YHWH (Jehovah)-SHAMMAH means The Lord Is There.

YHWH (Jehovah)-TSIDKENU translates to The Lord Our Righteousness.

Jesus when asked how we should pray suggested we address God as Abba. In English this is usually translated Father, but many believe it was a much less formal and more intimate word and could perhaps be better thought of as Daddy.

One of my favorite names for God was given by the slave girl Hagar. She called him EL ROI, The God Who Sees, because she perceived His caring for her and His concern for her. Interestingly God also instructed Hagar to name her son Ishmael. Again the –el part of the name refers to God and the total name means "The God who hears." These names indicate the involvement of God in the lives of those who everyone else discounts as being of no importance.

Other names in the Scriptures tell something of God's concern, function, or some special quality attached to God. These include Fountain of Life,[155] Comforter,[156] Rest and Victory,[157] God Forever and Ever,[158] Portion Forever,[159] Judge, Lawgiver and Life,[160] King,[161] Rock and Redeemer,[162] True God,[163] God of gods and Lord of Lords,[164] and Joy and Delight.[165]

In addition there are Scriptural references referring to various qualities, characteristics, and attributes of God. These include: our Confidence, Hope, Defender, Inheritance, Warrior, and the Shade at my Right Hand. They also include creator, maker, provider, healer, refuge and savior, protector, shelter, leader, stronghold in times of trouble, fortress and deliverer, and teacher. He is also called shepherd, strength and song, helper, light and salvation, shield, and power.

Why are there so many names for God? Because our heart, our mind, nor our language can encompass the magnificence nor the Grace nor the power of our deity. They are attempts to describe some aspect of His being even though we cannot choose any one term that can totally describe Him.

Perhaps we shouldn't be too surprised. After all, many different names can be used to identify any one of us. While most people would know me as Jack Clark there are those who might refer to me as Fred and Alice Clark's son, or son, or Dad, or Dr. Clark, or Dr. Jack, or in the case of my wife as Honey or Sweetheart. I think you get the idea.

It seems that any of the names of God may be properly used in various situations. I think that God is ready, willing, waiting, and eager to hear from us at any time, and is delighted to be talked to or talked about to others by any of the names that fit the situation.

---

[155] Proverbs 14:27
[156] Psalm 23:4,
[157] Proverbs 21:31
[158] Psalm 48:14
[159] Psalm 73:26
[160] Deuteronomy 30:20
[161] Isaiah 33:22
[162] Psalm 19:14
[163] Jeremiah 10:10
[164] Deuteronomy 10:17
[165] Psalm 43:4

People walking with God in faith in the time of the Old Testament were always learning new names for God because they were constantly learning something new about God, coming closer to Him, and expressing the new-found understanding.[166]

---

[166] Rev. Schramm shared this understanding in a Hebrew class he taught at St. Andrew's United Methodist Church in Syracuse, Indiana on Feb. 25, 2008

# What should we really understand it to mean that "God is love?"
(Submitted by Fairplain Presbyterian Adult Church School class in Benton Harbor, Michigan)

*(An answer by Jack Clark)*

God loves you! I know it's so, because the Bible tells me, and I know it's so because I have experienced the wonder of that love in my own life and in the lives of others!

I like comics. Most of them simply give a little amusement or a chuckle, but once in awhile one has a really profound message. I recall a week-end issue of the comic strip *B. C.* It was near the time of Resurrection Sunday (most people call this Easter). One of the characters is shown in a situation where he does something less than what he should have done. The result is indicated by dirt on his clothing. Rubbing the dirt only spreads it. He goes to a river and tries to wash it out on his own with no success. He wades in deeper; still no cleansing, but a rivulet of red starts flowing toward the river from a cross on a hill behind the person. When the red reaches the river, it spreads and soon the total river is red and the garment itself is covered in red. As the bewildered comic strip character steps ashore, the garment becomes a gleaming white. It is only as you and I are washed in the blood of our savior, Jesus Christ, that we can be cleansed from our sins! There could be no greater love than this!

"Your name is more delightful than wine." "Your name is like perfume poured out." "We rejoice and delight in you." "We will praise your love." These are some of the first lines from the Song of Songs, otherwise known as the Song of Solomon. It's at the same time a sensual song of love between a man and a woman, and an allegorical song of the love of God for His people and our love of God.

Love means many things to many people. You can love chocolate. You can love your dog or your cat. You can love your husband or your wife or your children. You can love other family members. You can love God. You can love your neighbor. The physical act of sexual relations can be termed making love – that can actually involve love or simply be an act of lust.

Is it any wonder people become confused when the word love is mentioned? The word love when applied to a garment or an item of food or a movie or a piece of music isn't what is referred to when we talk about God's love. This actually refers to liking something, and although God likes us much of the time, His feelings are a lot stronger than this. And His love is still there when He doesn't like us at all.

The Greeks had at least three words for what is referred to in the scriptures as love. First there was the love of a person for another close person. This is the love for our family members or even our neighbor. This is the love that wishes good for the other person and sometimes may go to a great deal of effort to help them and be sure good happens for them. This is brotherly love known by the Greeks as *philos*. From this word we derive Philadelphia, the city of brotherly love.

Then there is the Greek word for the love between a woman and a man. This word is *eros*. While this relationship usually implies a physical sexual relationship, illness or disability does not cancel out erotic love in a good marriage. Although many scriptural references refer to a marriage relationship between God and Israel or between Christ and the church, erotic love is not what it's talking about. God's love certainly includes the tenderness, compassion, mutual respect, and regard that go with a great marriage – but not the physical or erotic love that is a part of human erotic love relationships.

Then there is the third Greek word for love: *agape*. This is a love that gives without regard for return to the giver. This is the love that holds the recipient's interests always higher than the giver's interests. This is the love that delights in the growth and achievements of the beloved without any tinge of jealousy. This is the love that will even sacrifice one's own interests for the other party. This is the love that would even give up its own life for the other if necessary. While this *agape* love can be added to brotherly or erotic love in the best of human relationships, and while this is the type of love Christ asks us to show to others, it is best expressed in the love of our God, our Christ, and the Holy Spirit for each of us and for all of their creation.

Hosea is one of the most deeply moving books of the Bible. The Song of Solomon tells us of God's delight in his love of His beautiful bride who returns His love with passion, grace, and exquisite pleasure. I can understand this kind of love, because, in a somewhat more sedate manner, it is the same feeling I share with my own beloved wife Carol when she tells me how precious I am to her and that she loves me. I can relate to this love through my frequent prayer that I be allowed to grow in my love of Carol every day. I can be the lover and the beloved on a human level in the Song of Solomon, and so can catch something of the love of God for his people and for each of us individually.

Hosea shows a different kind of love, a level I can only begin to understand in its infinitely greater beauty. I rarely have the ability to show the grace Hosea and God show in this book. I can only identify with Gomer and be the recipient of this love. Only rarely can I emulate it to a slight degree.

God asked Hosea to live a parable. Parables in the spoken form are one of the most effective forms of teaching. A parable lived is certainly the most powerful form of teaching. Hosea, son of Beeri, who lived in the Northern Kingdom of Israel, was asked to show us the very heart of God through his interaction with his unfaithful wife Gomer.

It is obvious that Hosea loves Gomer. It is equally obvious that Gomer is a tramp. Gomer repays Hosea's love and tenderness with total disregard and unfaithfulness. In her own words, "I will go after my lovers who give me my food and my water, my wool and my linen, my oil and my drink."[167] This is erotic love run amuck. This is love degenerated into lust and self love.

Hosea, in his role of husband while living this parable, is hurt beyond understanding and enduring. In his anger, he punishes Gomer. He also anguishes over his lost love. His suffering can be shared from his own words: "She decked herself with rings and jewelry, and went after her lovers, but me she forgot."[168] He actually divorces her but then determines to win her back–not through force but by alluring her. "I will lead her into the desert and speak tenderly to her. There I will give her back her vineyards, and will make the Valley of Achor (trouble) a door of hope. There she will sing as in the days of her youth."[169]

It's interesting to note that it was against Jewish law to remarry a person after divorcing

---

[167] Hosea 2:5 (NIV)
[168] Hosea 2:13 (NIV)
[169] Hosea 2:15 (NIV)

them. Hosea's plan is not to destroy his unfaithful wife or to degrade her, or even to never have anything to do with her again. His plan is <u>not</u> to bring her back into a relationship with him where he will constantly punish her for her misdeeds or throw them up to her when there are difficult moments. His plan is to win her love, to save her from the tragic results of her unfaithfulness and the evil that her thoughtlessness, will, and misdirected sensuality have caused. God instructs Hosea, "Go show your love to your wife again, though she is loved by another and is an adulteress. Love her as the Lord loves the Israelites, though they turn to other gods and love the sacred raisin cakes." Hosea responds, "So I bought her for fifteen shekels of silver and about a homer and lethek of barley. Then I told her, 'You are to live with me many days; you must not be a prostitute or be intimate with any man and I will live with you.'"[170]

Since Gomer must be purchased, it is obvious the kind of love which was involved in her illicit relationship. It was a love of bondage, a love that brought about slavery to her sin and slavery to the one who now owned her, a love that thought so shallowly of her value that her owner was willing to sell her and be done with her for a price. How pitifully and disgustingly low Gomer had sunk.

In this lived parable, it becomes obvious how pitifully and disgustingly low Israel and each of us have sunk! This is not only the story of Hosea's personal relationship with Gomer. It is not only the story of God's relationship with the nation Israel. It is the story of God's relationship with each one of us who have rejected at some time the love of God for the enslavement by other lovers who think no more of us than Gomer's lover did. I stand in awe of Gomer's and my shared depravity. I stand in awe, with tears in my eyes contemplating the unfathomable love of God which would redeem me from the stupidity I have demonstrated in the horrible life choices I have made at times.

The observation is made, "They sow the wind and reap the whirlwind,"[171] and "Their sins engulf them; they are always before me."[172] This is totally tempered with Hosea's and God's free gift of unmerited redemption—their indescribable grace. "I desire mercy, not sacrifice, and acknowledgment of God rather than burnt offerings."[173] God's great

---

[170] Hosea 3:1-3 (NIV)
[171] Hosea 8:7 (NIV)
[172] Hosea 7:2 (NIV)
[173] Hosea 6:6 (NIV)

tenderness and mercy toward Israel and all other sinners is so beautifully expressed throughout the eleventh chapter, and is summarized: "I led them with cords of human kindness... How can I give you up?"[174] It's revealed that God, through the covenant terms, was legally bound to give up His relationship with Israel. It is revealed that although God judges in righteousness, He still loves. It's revealed that God feels an unimaginably deep pain at our rejection, and that He suffers for His love and redeems the ones He loves even though we are not worthy of that love. "I will ransom them from the power of the grave; I will redeem them from death. I will heal their waywardness and love them freely, for my anger has turned away from them."[175] Only in the life and redeeming death of Jesus Christ is the depth of God's love shown more clearly than it is shown in the lived out parable of Hosea's life and grace. To know Hosea is to understand God's unconditional agape love.

One of the most outstanding examples of agape love that I have ever seen in humans involved a brother and sister in my medical practice. The sister, who was about ten years old, had acute leukemia. Back when I started practice, this diagnosis carried a 100% fatality outlook, but by the time of this event, there was a fair chance for a cure. The youngster had been cared for by cancer doctors at Indiana University School of Medicine's Riley Hospital. She had undergone months of chemotherapy with all its unpleasant side-effects – hair falling out, bruising from low platelet counts, weakness, tiredness, infections from impaired immunity and low white blood cell counts. When she would come to the office, she would always greet me with a smile – occasionally enthusiastic – more commonly a wan smile of resignation but friendship. It eventually became obvious that she was not going to have the hoped-for response. Her only hope for recovery would be to find a suitable donor of bone marrow and give the patient a marrow transplant after giving a super dose of radiation and chemotherapy to totally destroy her diseased cells. Months went by trying to find a compatible donor. Finally they determined that her brother was the best match. The parents explained the problem to the brother who was only a little older than his sister, and he agreed to undergo the procedure.

In all their concern about the daughter's condition and chances, it wasn't made clear to her brother what the consequences of the bone marrow donation would be to him. After

---

[174] Hosea 11:1-11 (NIV)
[175] Hosea 14:4 (NIV)

the procedure, their mother was talking with him relating how his sister was doing and commending him for his willingness to undergo the pain of the transplant to help his sister. He very calmly looked into his mother's eyes asking, "How soon will I die?" In his mind, his giving the possibly life-saving donation to his sister meant that he would no longer have any bone marrow. Having heard the discussions, he knew that bone marrow was essential for life, so he logically concluded that he would die. His only question was how soon. Of course, his misconception was corrected, but this in no way diminished the magnitude of his gift. The graft was not successful. The patient died. She was very brave. I was not. I wept for her bravery, for the joy of her life lost to those who loved her, for the potential of all she would have been, and for her brother's disappointment, because despite his willingness to sacrifice everything in trying to save his sister, he could not accomplish it. He is a true hero. "Greater love has no one than this that he lay down his life for his friends."[176]

How much does God, the son and the Holy Spirit love us? A story that illustrates the point suggests that someone comes to Jesus and asks, "How much do you love me?" Jesus in the story stretches his arms full length and responds, "This much." Then his hands are nailed to the cross. The Bible also records how much Jesus says he loves us: "My command is this: Love each other as I have loved you. Greater love has no one than this, that he lay down his life for his friends. You are my friends if you do what I command."[177] How much does the Father love us? "I have loved you with an everlasting love."[178] "No eye has seen, no ear has heard, no mind has conceived what God has prepared for those who love him."[179] "God so loved the world that He gave his only begotten son that whosoever believeth in him should not perish but have everlasting life."[180] God has sent the Holy Spirit in response to Jesus' prayer. He has many functions, but one of the dearest and most loving is that He will pray for us when we don't know what to pray.[181] What a comfort this is when I'm at the end of my ability to even know for what I should ask.

This love of God asks each of us for a response. About two thousand years ago Paul

---

[176] John 15:13 (NIV)
[177] John 15:12-14 (NIV)
[178] Jeremiah 31:3 (NIV)
[179] I Corinthians 2:9 (NIV)
[180] John 3:16 (KJV)
[181] Romans 8:26

realized this when he wrote: "As God's chosen people, holy and dearly loved, clothe yourselves with compassion, kindness, humility, gentleness and patience. Bear with each other, and forgive one another if any of you has a grievance against someone. Forgive as the Lord forgave you. And over all these virtues put on love, which binds them all together in perfect unity."[182] Three hundred years ago Isaac Watts wrote the hymn *When I Survey the Wondrous Cross.* It ends with the words, "love so amazing, so divine, demands my soul, my life, my all.

So, now back to the question. When we say, "I love you," are we sharing God with another person? The only answer I can give is: "Maybe." When that sharing is the agape love such as we've seen in God's love of us, then most certainly it is sharing God with the recipient. Someone has suggested that we are the only Christ some people will ever see. When we're sharing brotherly love and seeking what is the best for our brother or sister, then yes we're sharing God with the other person. If we're speaking of erotic love that also involves the brotherly love or the agape love, then yes we are sharing God with the other person. If we're speaking of liking, or desiring or lusting, then it isn't a sharing of God.

One thing is for certain, God does love you, and when He tells you so, He most positively is sharing himself.

---

*(Thoughts of Gary Lewis)*

Love in Action is the Only Kind of Love that Matters

In the movie, *A Walk to Remember,* Jamie Sullivan agrees to help Landon Carter overcome some obstacles in his life. Landon, a typical popular high school bad boy is having difficulty in classes and trouble staying out of trouble. Jamie places one condition on her help. Landon cannot fall in love with her.

Thinking this is easy since she is a school geek, he agrees to the condition. As you suspect this is the one condition he cannot meet. He does fall in love with her and as his life changes so does his focus, from himself to her. In doing so he helps her develop a list of things in her life that she desires to accomplish. The twist comes when she finally

---

[182] Colossians 3:12-14 (TNIV)

reveals to him that she is dying of leukemia. He decides the priority in his life should be to help her accomplish her list for life. His love takes over as he continues to live for her. Because of his love for her, when she dies he continues living as she has taught him.

We also have someone who loves us to this extent. He is committed to doing everything to benefit and bless us. However, instead of living our life for us after we die, He gave his life away on a cruel cross so that we may have life. We can have a real life in the present and in eternity.

He loved us before we knew Him and before we were created. Even before we could love He loved us. His love has always gone before us, inviting us to experience a deep kind of love that is out of this world. Our entire existence comes from Him choosing to love us.

"I chose you before I formed you in the womb; I set you apart before you were born. I appointed you a prophet to the nations."[183]

"For I know the plans I have for you" – this is the Lord's declaration – "plans for your welfare, not for disaster, to give you a future and a hope."[184]

Our church recently completed a spiritual growth emphasis that involved reading devotions dealing with various "one another" passages in the Bible. The idea was to find ways to show love in practical ways to the community – both the community of faith within our church walls and the community outside our church walls.

I learned a valuable lesson about how small actions can make a big difference in developing faith. I was initially opposed to the suggestion of going out and removing debris from abandoned properties. I felt we were making the Gospel message cheap by picking up downed limbs and mowing the grass "in Jesus' Name." *Is this what Jesus' death on the cross and His coming to life means to us? We get to clean-up some abandoned properties?"*

---

[183] Jeremiah 1:5
[184] Jeremiah 29:11

I guess I wanted to feed 5,000 needy people at a free meal, or build 54 Habitat houses, or …. some grand gesture that would be more fitting to the name of Christ in our community. Yet, when I saw about 60 church folks gather in the parking lot at church on that Saturday morning; when the weather cooperated fully and when I drove around afterward to view the cleaned-up properties, I realized those small actions really did make a difference. We made deposits of hope throughout the city.

It is so easy to allow our pre-conceived notions of what is right to cloud our definition of love. Love is the most overused word in our society. It is used and misused on a daily basis. We have a plethora of songs about love. All one has to do is shop at any bookstore and find an entire section of romance novels. There are how-to books about being loved, making love, how to love yourself and how to let others love you.

The Bible offers the best definition of love. Probably the most quoted portion of Scripture is First Corinthians 13 where the Apostle Paul describes love as an action. "Love is patient and kind. Love is not jealous, it does not brag, and it is not proud. Love is not rude, is not selfish, and does not get upset with others. Love does not count up wrongs that have been done. Love takes no pleasure in evil but rejoices over the truth. Love patiently accepts all things. It always trusts, always hopes, and always endures. Love never ends." (1 Corinthians 13:4-8)

In other words, people recognize God in our lives only when our actions do the talking. Our actions must speak louder than our words. Words are vital, words are important and our speech can reveal the intent of our hearts. But when it comes to love, true love, it is something different than just a feeling, emotion, desire, or thought. This love makes requirements of us.

Romans 12:9-14; 1 Corinthians 16:14; 2 Corinthians 8:24; Ephesians 5:2; 1 Timothy 1:5, 4:12, Colossians 3:14; 1 Thessalonians 4:9; 1 John 3:11; Hebrews 10:24, 13:1; 1 Peter 4:8. All of these passages require actions beyond thoughts or wishing.

In order to see that we have love we must get off our couches, leave the pews and go into a loveless world and love others. A nail will never penetrate wood unless we apply a hammer to the nail. Our love will never be felt unless our actions demonstrate it to others.

135

If we love someone then we want to know that person, to spend time with that person. That's what our time with God needs to be like. We want to spend time with God, enjoying what God enjoys and bask in God's love. When we love someone we are willing to pick up the trash, rake the leaves and pull out the poison ivy. When we love someone we will look at the list of things they want to do and accomplish and work at helping them accomplish their list. When we love someone we will be like Landon Carter from the movie *A Walk to Remember.* Our focus will change from us to them. Our lifestyle will change. What we think of as fun will include what they think is fun.

To what extent do you love God? Do you find out what is on God's list and work to help God accomplish this? Do you want to spend time doing what God enjoys doing? Do you find solace in doing menial tasks for God's glory? Do we love enough to lay aside our wants, our wishes, our loves and focus on the ultimate Lover's wants and wishes ... to give up the selfish love we have and love God's way?

---

## Challenge 19
# Is salvation possible for a non-Christian?

How do we answer a Jewish friend who claims salvation according to the covenant of God with Israel? (Submitted by Fairplain Presbyterian Adult Church School class in Benton Harbor, Michigan)

*(An answer by Jack Clark)*

I've given an answer that considers salvation for other than Christians in response to the question who is going to be in heaven? That covers in general any non-Christian, but to specifically answer this question about a Jewish person I'll expand on that discussion. Of course since the answer to this earlier question would suggest that being a part of the Kingdom of God is a possibility for a person who is outside the Christian faith, it would certainly include Jews, but it seems that the Jewish people would constitute an even more special case. My understanding of the nature of God is that He will never break a promise, and a covenant is a very special, sacred promise. So I would say that when God said that Israel was special to Him, he meant it, and he will never go back on His word.

When the author of the book of Hebrews in the New Testament speaks of a great cloud of witnesses that surrounds us and gives testimony to us, he specifically mentions and includes a great many people who have been saved by their faith. Those mentioned are all Israelites or early ancestors of the Israelites. Included by name are Able, Enoch, Noah, Abraham, Sarah, Isaac, Jacob, Joseph, Moses' parents, Moses, the Israelites who passed through the Red (Reed) Sea, those who brought about the fall of the walls of Jericho, Rahab, Gideon, Barak, Samson, Jephthah, David, Samuel, the prophets, and those who had suffered for their faith. The author of Hebrews states they are made perfect along with us through Jesus Christ.[185]

We all recognize that none of these Jewish saved had heard of Jesus by name or knew of his teachings after his incarnation, but the Apostle John affirms that Jesus, the Word of God, was present with God from the very beginning.[186] So then these witnesses who are perfected and therefore saved had faith in the Messiah as well as the Father even though they did not know Jesus by name.

Recall that Jesus said, "I am the way and the truth and the life. No one comes to the

---

[185] Hebrews 11:4-39
[186] John 1:1

Father except through me."[187]  To take the concepts together would seem to indicate that the Messiah (Jesus or Yeshua in the Hebrew) had to have been the way by which these witnesses achieved their salvation through their faith.  Jesus knows and perfects and saves these witnesses even though they only knew him through God's promises.

Now comes the harder part.  Remember that Jesus said, "Whoever acknowledges me before men, I will also acknowledge him before my Father in heaven.  But whoever disowns me before men, I will disown before my Father in Heaven."[188]  I would venture to say that a person (Jewish or otherwise) who still has never heard of Jesus can be saved through their faith in God that would include His Messiah.  I would venture that a person who may have heard of Jesus, but doesn't know enough about him to make an assessment that he is God's Christ could still be saved by their faith.  I suspect that it is likely that someone who has been presented a distorted or false understanding of Jesus through imperfect witness on the part of those of us who are supposed to spread the good news could still be saved by Jesus in accordance with their faith.  A significant thing Jesus said on this subject is, "I tell you every sin and blasphemy will be forgiven men, but the blasphemy against the Spirit will not be forgiven.  Anyone who speaks a word against the Son of Man will be forgiven, but anyone who speaks against the Holy Spirit will not be forgiven, either in this age or in the age to come."[189]

I would agree that a Jewish friend could still achieve salvation through the old covenant.  This, if based on their actions only, would require perfection, and Jesus has said only God is perfect, so achieving perfection would still require the intervention of the Messiah (which means God with us).  If the person in question had only a distorted view of Jesus, it still seems that Jesus in his great love might very well intervene for them and they could have salvation.  On the other hand I would really be concerned for a person who has an untarnished understanding of Christ and still denies him.  I would say that only Christ himself can and will judge this case.  Jesus said that he is our redeemer (the one who pays our bail), our advocate (lawyer), and judge.  I believe I will one day stand for judgment.  I believe that every person will do the same.  I know I need every bit of help available to qualify for a not-guilty verdict.  I also believe that having Jesus Christ give a

---

[187] John 14:6 (NIV)
[188] Matthew 10:32-33 and Luke 12:8-9
[189] Matthew 12:31-32, Mark 3:28-29, Luke 12:10 (NIV)

character witness testimony about me is the best defense that could be offered. I believe that there is the possibility of such a character witness for those who never knew (confessed as their savior) Jesus, but he's promised this to anyone who believes in him and confesses him.

If I were building a bridge I would want the best engineer available to plan and oversee the project. When I am being judged for eternity, I want Jesus testifying for me.

Back to the Jewish friend in the original question. I have had a couple Messianic Jews as friends. I greatly enjoy the magazine *Friends of Israel* written by Messianic Jews, so I know that it is possible to be a Jew, hold to their traditions and faith and to still believe in Jesus. I have also had another Jewish friend who was interested in my faith. We shared our faith in depth, and he ultimately responded that while he greatly respects my faith, he cannot leave his own traditions. Jesus said there is a danger if men "nullify the word of God by your tradition that you have handed down."[190] I can only hope that I have planted seeds that others will water and others will harvest for this Jewish friend of mine.

*(Betty Byers' answer)*

No! There is only one way to salvation, and that is believing on the Lord Jesus Christ and accepting him as your personal savior.[191]

---

[190] Mark 7:13
[191] Romans 6:23, John 1:12, and Revelation 3:20 (KJV)

## Challenge 20

# What? You want me to do something special, God? You're kidding. Right? I'm not even sure I qualify to be called a Christian.

Most people who give our lives to Christ at some point in our journey come to realize that God has some surprises for us. While God seems to have a sense of humor, it doesn't seem that kidding is part of the relationship. The second part of the challenge comes because we realize we're not good enough to measure up to the standards of God

*(An answer by Jack Clark)*

Sometimes it comes out of the blue – completely unexpected. Sometimes an awareness gradually overtakes a follower: here is something God wants done, and He wants me to be the one who does it! Often it's something that hadn't entered our minds before. Often it interrupts what we had in mind for that day or that segment of our life. It may be something that we're really not excited about at all.

Bill Cosby has a great comic routine about Noah. Noah is going about his business when a deep voice calls his name: "Noah. Noah." Cosby playing the part of Noah responds, "Who's that." "It's the Lord." (pause) "Sure it is. (pause) Who is it really?" Eventually the Lord convinces Noah of who it is and tells him to build an ark including that he's to make it out of gopher wood ("What's gopher wood?"), and make it a specified number of cubits ("What's a cubit?"). In the process the imaginary Noah has to deal with an unhappy neighbor who wants him to move the ark so it's not blocking the driveway. It's a fun routine, but it points out some of the very real problems that can show up when God "puts us on assignment."

There is no record of how Abram felt when God told his father Terah and him to gather up his family and flocks and leave Ur of the Chaldeans (in modern Iraq) for the Promised Land. I expect he had some misgivings. If he didn't I expect Sarai did. Can't you almost imagine her response? "You want me to do what? You want us to leave our home and most of our belongings not to mention our friends and our neighbors and hike to a new promised land?" It's almost certain that later when Abram was afraid that the local king might kill him because of Sarai's beauty and Abram told her to pretend she was his sister to save Abram's life that Sarai must have wondered about this God-directed venture. Still later when she was very old and had not been blessed with children, she was convinced that God had a sense of humor when the word came that she would be having a son. God changed their names at this point. Sarah laughed in the tent, but the Lord heard her and confronted her. Sarah lied about the laugh, but the child came on schedule. Abraham had laughed at the thought too. After all, it seemed impossible that he would have a son when he was 100 and Sarah was 90 years old. Even if you had longed for a son as a young woman, who would want a pregnancy, childbirth and the raising of a child to start at these ages?[192] I can almost guarantee they had some qualms about accepting the "blessing."

We certainly have recorded Moses' hesitancy to accept the honor and assignment of returning to Egypt for a face-off with pharaoh about letting the Hebrews go free. Moses had all kinds of arguments and excuses to try to wiggle out of the job. First he suggested, "Who am I that I should go to pharaoh and do this?" Then God promised he would be with him. Then Moses asks, "Who are you." God then tells Moses He is the God of their fathers and goes on to give his personal name: "I AM WHO I AM." Moses was less than convinced. He asks what if they don't believe me and God gives him a staff that converted into a snake and back into a staff. God showed him also how he could show a leprous hand and heal it and how he could convert water from the Nile into blood. Moses then comes up with a speech problem and God says He will be with him and send his brother Aaron to speak for him. I've wondered why God didn't suggest that for someone with a speech problem, Moses sure talked a lot. God had gotten pretty ticked off with Moses by this time, and Moses did what he was told.[193]

I recall when my brother Jerry, an agnostic, was getting ready to climb Mt. McKinley in Alaska also known as Denali, the highest mountain in North America, the Holy Spirit urged me through an inner awareness of increasing intensity to write Jerry about the reasons for my faith and the difference it had made in my life. I really didn't want to. Jerry was a fine, moral man despite his lack of faith in God, and he knew of my shortcomings. I didn't want it to appear that I thought I was better than he was. I resisted writing, but finally gave in much as Moses had done. I wasn't even sure Jerry got my long letter until I went to Oregon with our Mother to clean out his living quarters after receiving word of Jerry's death and the death of fellow climbers in a huge storm that buried them after reaching the summit. They are still there on Denali. Several weeks later while driving to the hospital to see patients, my depressed mood was interrupted with the sense that, "Jerry's better off than you are." Notice that the words in the awareness were you are – not I am. I was convinced that Jerry had received and read my letter and that at some point before his death, he had accepted Jesus Christ as his savior. I am convinced the Holy Spirit was

---

[192] A summary of Genesis 11:27-18:15
[193] A paraphrase of Exodus 3:1-4:17

142

aware of the upcoming danger for Jerry and directed events to lead him to accept Christ's salvation. Since then I have had a sense of awareness and urgency to share the good news of God's salvation with others. There comes a time when, if too many opportunities are missed, the time will run out.

The next such event in my life was when our daughter was a member of a religious group that did not believe in the use of medicines or doctors. After delivering seven children without any apparent complications, I was moved to write her and her husband about all the Biblical reasons they seemed wrong to me. I really didn't want to do it, because other families had alienated their loved ones by similar efforts. Again I resisted (slow learner). Again the Holy Spirit applied more and more pressure. Finally the situation came to the place where I had a very distinct awareness that a pertinent Bible verse applied: "Anyone who loves his father or mother more than me is not worthy of me; anyone who loves his son or daughter more than me is not worthy of me, and anyone who does not take his cross and follow me is not worthy of me."[194] I wrote the letter. It was well received and eventually helped change their thinking – I found out they had been thinking along many of the same lines themselves. It's good to realize at times like these that God doesn't leave us on our own; he's working at such times in multiple ways.

Well, it's almost certain that God is going to have some assignments for all His followers. Some may be dramatic, and some mundane, but they're all important.

Sometimes I wonder why God would choose me to be a part of His kingdom. After I convince myself, unlikely as it seems, that He did choose me, I could be very satisfied to simply sit by His feet and learn and bask in His glory. Jesus said, "You did not choose me, but I chose you and appointed you to go and bear fruit–fruit that will last"[195] When it came time for me to consider this, I realized I had enough shortcomings and foul-ups in my life that I didn't seem to be a likely choice. But wonder of wonders, God did choose me. Frankly if I had been on the selection committee, I doubt that I would have made the cut. Happily God has a different list of selection criteria. I'm honored, pleased and filled with gratitude at this unexpected turn of events. I'm also convinced that once elected God has plans for us. The plans don't seem to involve passive praise. God wants players in the game of life – not spectators.

---

[194] Matthew 1037-38 (NIV)
[195] John 15:15-16 (NIV)

Have you, like I have, ever wondered why in the world God would choose you? If you think it's strange that God has chosen you to be a part of his kingdom, think of some of the other strange choices He's made. Rahab was a foreign Jericho prostitute, and Ruth was a Moabite woman. The Moabites were despised by Israel with good reason. Who would have guessed God would have chosen these two women to become ancestors of King David and Jesus? Amos was a shepherd, a farmer. Who would have expected God to have chosen this man to be one of His prophets? Which one of us would have picked Zechariah and Elizabeth, barren and well beyond childbearing age to have a son, John, who would prepare the way of the Lord? For that matter who of us would have picked a young girl, Mary, and Joseph, to be the parents of Jesus? Jesus was the son of a young woman who hadn't even completed her wedding vows to a common carpenter–hardly a great beginning.

Why did God pick Israel to be His chosen people? Why did God choose the individuals He chose to carry out His plan? What was His purpose in choosing any of us? Why in the world would God choose you? God let it be known that He chose you because He found pleasure in you. "He will take great delight in you, he will quiet you with His love; He will rejoice over you with singing."[196] God also gave the reason for his choices to Abraham in Genesis, "I will bless you; I will make your name great, and you will be a blessing."[197]

This then is why God chose Israel. It is why God chose the patriarchs and the good kings, and the prophets, and Elizabeth and Zechariah, and Mary, and Joseph, and the disciples of Jesus, and each of us. In God's great wisdom, He could see beyond the shortcomings of each of us and see our potential to return His love, accept Him, and accept the blessing. In turn, he could see in each of us the potential not to hoard the blessing for ourselves but to pass it on to others in our community and in His church. Just as Abraham was chosen, we are chosen for blessings in order that we may bless others, and in order that the kingdom may grow!

Are there things that inhibit you in your responses to Christ's call in your life? Are there things that threaten to block your effectiveness?

---

[196] Zephaniah 3:17 (NIV)
[197] Genesis 12:2 (NIV)

Do you see yourself as too old?  Are you older than Abraham or Sarah or Noah or Elizabeth?

Do you see yourself as too young to be taken seriously by others?  Are you younger than David when he dealt with Goliath?  Are you younger than Mary when she became the mother of God's son?

Do you see yourself as too busy?  Are you busier than Levi who had a very important job as a tax collector or Simon and Andrew who were an essential part of their father's fishing business before they became Matthew, Peter and Andrew, disciples and then apostles of Jesus Christ?

Do you see yourself as too poor?  Are you poorer than Job after he had lost all his worldly possessions and sat on a trash heap still praising God or poorer than the beggar who was blind from birth.  He acknowledged Christ before the Sanhedrin–a really scary thing to do.

Do you think you don't know enough?  Jesus said we can pray for the gifts of the Holy Spirit, and two of these are knowledge and discernment.

Are you concerned that you can't speak well?  So was Moses, and God promised he would be with him when he spoke.  Jesus promised that the Holy Spirit will be with his followers when we speak.  What better speech coaches are there than these?

Does Satan give you doubts as to your abilities because you're a sinner?  So are all the rest of us, but Jesus says he has washed us white as snow.  Will you believe the great liar, Satan, or will you believe Christ?

Are you concerned that you don't want to make yourself out to be better than others are? Don't. Be open. Share your shortcomings.  Spreading the Gospel has been likened to one beggar telling another where he has found bread.

Are you concerned that you can't sing?  The song in you heart and the song the dove of the Holy Spirit sings through you are the important songs.

Are you concerned that you have no talent or that you can't teach or that you aren't trained? Paul said that the church is a body made of many parts and with many functions – all equally important. Besides he said we can pray for and develop our talents.

Are you concerned that you have too much family responsibility? Andrew, John, Peter, and James all had recorded pressing family obligations. I find that when I put Christ first in my life, my family is better off than when I put them first, and much, much better off than when I put myself first.

Does Satan put impediments in your way? Do you feel not appreciated? Are you physically or emotionally ill? Are you overburdened, tired, or struggling to make ends meet? Do you have family problems? Do you have an addiction to tobacco, alcohol or drugs or a bad past that people will remember? Every time you try to do something for God, does it seem to blow up in your face? If you plan to go to church do you have an argument with your spouse or your kids? Satan loves situations such as these to discourage us or sidetrack us, but Satan can be resisted through prayer, study, the power of the Holy Spirit, and with the help of Christian friends.

If you or I feel discouraged by the weaknesses that would inhibit us or the road blocks Satan throws in our way, we can take heart in realizing our brother Paul also had weaknesses and obstacles. He recounts them for us in the Bible.[198] He even referred to himself as not deserving to be called a disciple because he had persecuted the church of God before his conversion on the road to Damascus.[199] The implication is that if he can be a witness despite all these deficiencies and problems, so can I – so can you.

One of the people I contacted about contributing to this book decided not to contribute, but told me about a friend from high school days who in middle age thought she had been such a sinner that there was no way God could ever accept her. As a child she and her sister had been sexually molested by their father. As many such victims do, she felt that somehow this was her fault – her sin – not the father's. She was at the present time a professional woman who had been in a very unhappy marriage, had an affair with a married man, become pregnant in the affair, and had an abortion, and then divorced. One of her grown children was in prison, and she felt responsible for his failures. She still had a responsible job in her profession, but was filled with anger, loosing long-time friends,

---

[198] First Corinthians 4:12-15 and Second Corinthians 11:23-30 (NIV)
[199] Acts 22:6-11

and had turned to alcohol to try to avoid her feelings of guilt and rejection. She made the statement that she had broken every one of the Ten Commandments. She could see no hope of redemption for herself. She and everyone else who feels this way need to be gently confronted with some very special understandings from the Bible. God is love.[200] God loves us with an everlasting love.[201] Love covers a multitude of sins.[202] God has great plans for you.[203] All have sinned and fallen short of the glory of God.[204] There is no one who is righteous; our righteousness is like filthy rags.[205] And of greatest importance they need to put themselves in the place of the woman drug before Jesus to try to trap him into defying the Law of Moses. She had been caught in the very act of adultery. The law required that she be stoned to death. Jesus wrote something on the ground, and said, "Let him who is without sin cast the first stone." The accusers left one by one, and looking up Jesus asked the woman if no one condemned her. She responded, "No one, sir," and Jesus said, "Then neither do I condemn you. Go and sin no more."[206] The same love and the same salvation are available to any of us sinners who will accept it.

Why in the world would God choose Paul or David or Ruth or Abraham or Sarah or Moses or Rahab or Amos or Zechariah or Elizabeth or Jack Clark? Why in the world would He choose you? The answer isn't in the world. The answer is in the heart and mind and will of God.

God chose you because of His immeasurable love of you. He chose you because He longs for your love. He chose you because He sees in you the potential to further the kingdom. He chose you to bless you in order that you could be a blessing to others. He chose you that your joy might be complete and so that His joy might rest with you. He chose you to take great delight in you, to quiet you with His love, and to rejoice over you with singing.[207] He chose you because He sees in you the potential to follow His commands to love one another and to go and make disciples. He chose you that you might be the daughter or the son of the King. He chose you that the great plans He has for you might be fulfilled. He chose you to cherish you. He chose you to spend eternity living with Him, His son, His Holy spirit, and all the others who accept His salvation.

---

[200] First John 4:8
[201] Jeremiah 31:3
[202] First Peter 4:8
[203] Jeremiah 29:11
[204] Romans 3:23 (NIV)
[205] Isaiah 64:6 (NIV)
[206] John 8:3-11
[207] Zephaniah 3:17

# GOOD FRIDAY STORY

Thanksgiving, November 2007, 1 A.M. I was awakened from my sleep. I felt as if God was telling me that I needed to do something. I prayed and asked for guidance and wanted Him to know that I would do whatever it was. I wanted His will in my life. After praying and confessing my intentions, I was able to return to sleep.

The next couple days went by and I didn't mention my Thursday evening events to Barb, but felt whatever it was that He wanted me to do would be made aware to me. That Sunday, church started with a picture of a cross on the screen. This was very unusual because to my knowledge this hadn't been done before. Usually there were upcoming events on the screen. When I saw the cross, I felt a very special feeling inside. This wasn't uncommon since the first time I viewed the PASSION OF THE CHRIST movie and have become aware of the immense pain our Lord went through for us all on the cross. One of the pictures displayed many different crosses.

The same start to our worship happened the following Sunday. During the ride home I decided to tell Barb my story and see how she would take it. Barb was unsure how she felt about it and said she would pray for guidance. That night during my sleep I was awakened with the thought of the cross and suddenly thought about the two pieces of logs that had been lying in our loft for the past eleven years (it's a log home). I thought I would be able to make a cross from these and that I should carry it on GOOD FRIDAY to our church.

The next Sunday at church everything started the same way (about the cross). I felt a real peace about what I had decided to do. I looked at Barb and began to cry. She smiled and pointed at the cross on the screen. On the ride home that morning, we talked about this. She was very understanding and supportive and felt that I was making the right decision. She said God would help me complete the walk. We talked about my plans many times and wanted to make certain this was God's will. I decided to talk to our pastor, John Drexler. He said this was an awesome thing to do, and he asked how far I was going to carry the cross. When I told him seventeen miles from our home in Syracuse, he had a real frightened look on his face. He asked, "Are you sure you can go that far? Should you put wheels on it?" I felt very strong and confidant that I could do this with God's help. The most important thing about all of this was that it wasn't about me, but all about Him! Pastor said he would pray about this and see if he received any direction against this decision. Pastor John told me a concern he had would be for negative people or hecklers along my trip. I hadn't thought about that, so he prayed that His will be done and to give us a sign if I shouldn't carry the cross.

The following Sunday we met together again. Pastor John said he didn't have any strong feeling against my trip and asked what we were feeling by this time. Barb and I both felt confidant and had no reservations. I told Pastor I would be doing some walking trips to prepare for my journey.

That afternoon I walked around the lake 8.5 miles in two hours and twenty minutes. Therefore, I thought I could make my Good Friday journey in four to five hours to the Goshen First Brethren Church at Clinton and Second Streets. I had planned to do a practice walk to Goshen without the cross to prepare for Good Friday.

These were things God planned ahead of time to prepare me for the journey. On January 30, 2008, I was able to go on a mission trip to the Dominican Republic. While there, I participated in a very strenuous job of carrying eight inch concrete blocks (50 lbs. each) to the second floor of the Goshen House, carrying two at a time to keep the weight even. I was quickly surpassed by most everyone else carrying anywhere from four to eight blocks by very impressive young men. There was a time when I would take the challenge, but that was many years ago! Also, I had been doing a winter remodeling project on our house. Putting up Styrofoam and drywall on several walls to cover the dark knotty pine and to help control the draftiness. I also installed floor batting insulation between the floor joists in our very tight crawlspace. All of these projects prepared me for the task to carry the cross to Goshen.

Something that was very important to me was that I asked Pastor and Barb to keep this to ourselves, because I didn't want anyone to think this was about me. It was all about our Lord and Savior. I wanted no appreciation or accolades. The week of Good Friday: I had no reservation. I didn't feel that maybe I was wrong or misunderstood His direction. I had a real peace and even felt confidant I could do it with His help.

The evening before Good Friday: the only thought I had was His understanding my commitment. I decided to start my walk on County Road 500 North at the top of very steep Boliver Hill. This would reduce my journey by one mile. I told Barb, and she agreed that this made good sense. I asked her to drop me off with my cross at 8 A.M. to start my journey. I also asked her to stay home with her cell phone on and pray for me. I had asked Pastor John to pray for me throughout the trip. I thought I should be at the church between two and three P.M.

We (Jesus and I) arrived at 2:45 P.M. I say Jesus because there was no way I could have completed the six hour and forty-five minute trip without Him. The following is a list of people that stopped and encouraged me during the trip. Along with all these people, I also had many people honking their horns and doing thumbs up.....absolutely no negatives!

**1.** One mile into my journey a very excited man drove up to me and said he couldn't believe what he was seeing. He called his wife on his cell, and told her there was a man carrying a cross (in this day and age)! He didn't realize how encouraging it was for me to hear his comments! I shared my testimony with him, and he said, "God bless you."

**2.** Fifty more feet – a lady pulled up in her car and said how encouraged she was when she saw the cross. I shared my testimony and Matthew 16:24-25. "If anyone would come after me, he must deny himself and take up his cross and follow me." This sweet lady also energized me with her comments. She said she worked at Quaker Haven Camp, not far from my house. I thought, "Yes, I can do this," and began to sing and pray during my walk. After this encounter, I made my way to the Wawasee High School. I called Barb, and asked her to bring me better shoes and socks. I changed them at the school's tennis courts. Was the devil making my feet sore? A neat thing happened at the railroad crossing beside the school. There were two trains crossing (opposite directions) at the same time. Just as I got to the crossing, both trains separated and the way was clear for me to cross without even stopping. I felt I didn't want to stop for any reason, because maybe the devil would try to convince me I couldn't go any further.

150

**3.** Two miles more, and a car pulled up with two ladies, and just said, "Power to you, sir." I yelled, "Thank you," and they gave me thumbs up as they drove away.

**4.** One hundred more yards, and a van pulled up in front of me. (My whole trip I walked against traffic and had absolutely no problems!) A lady got out and walked up to me and said she was from a local paper and asked why I was doing this. I explained the verses and gave my testimony. She wanted to take my picture, and I asked her to take from the back and not print my name, because it was not about me but about our Savior.

**5.** I walked about another three fourths mile and came to US 6. As I was crossing the highway, there was a car pulling up beside me. It was a lady that had worked with Barb at the physician's office, Jana Wolf. I was happy to see a familiar face, and she said, "This is just too cool. What are you doing?" I said thanks and that it was all about my Savior and how He has meant so much to me especially for the last two years. Ever since I studied *The Purpose Driven Life*[208] book in small groups at our church, I've gotten real direction for my life and have felt a real purpose. She began to cry as she drove away, and I again was so encouraged with her stopping to talk! I had to call Barb and tell her all my stories. She was too excited and mentioned she had thought about asking me to make a small cross for her so we could have made the trip together. I was just overwhelmed by her comment. To think my lovely wife would do this with me! I praise God for her!

**6.** I went another half mile, and it began to blow and snow, so I just sang and prayed to God to help me make it. Another man pulled up beside me and asked, "Are you on a tour or something?" I kind of laughed and explained my testimony and asked him if he believed in God. He said yes, and as he left he said, "God bless you."

**7.** I went another half mile. I was now half way there. Eight miles to go. I went a little further on CR 29, and a gentleman in his van with his son in a child seat in the rear asked why I was doing this? I again was able to give my testimony, and he said many positive things. Our conversation was cut short because of traffic, and he had to move on.

**8.** Shortly after that I saw a young man on the other side of the road heading toward me. I was a little concerned because of what the Pastor said about negative people. We got closer. He came to my side and wanted to talk. To my surprise he asked if he could bear my burden. I was so surprised by his statement, I messed up and said, "Oh, I'm ok, but can we continue to walk and talk together for a while?" Of course he agreed (the awesome person that he was). He told me his name, and as we walked together, he

---

[208] *The Purpose Driven Life,* Rick Warren, © 2002 by Rick Warren, Zondervan Press

explained he saw me carrying the cross and felt the need to talk with me. He had just had a fight with his wife and was feeling pretty sad. We talked and shared as we walked to his car that he had parked a quarter mile ahead in the direction I was heading. TOO COOL! We had a great conversation, and I've tried with no avail to contact him. I've prayed that if the Lord wants us to meet again, we will. So until then I just pray for him. I went another quarter mile, and you guessed it. There was a real large mean dog coming toward me. He wouldn't leave me alone! He was almost run over by a car (no luck). He finally gave up. Even though I was on the down side of the trip, my shoulders were getting real sore. I just kept switching the cross from side to side, and it seemed to help. I went another half mile and decided I needed to take off my fleece sweatshirt and put it on my shoulders under my Carhart Jacket. (Sounds easy enough. NOT!) I still remember doing this, because I thought it would be a real struggle because of the bulkiness. Would you believe it went right on the first time? It was by the small things that I knew my Lord was with me!

9. By then I was at US 15. My son, Jered, called to see how it was going. I was real happy to hear from him. I had told him in advance of doing this trip with the cross. He couldn't understand why I felt the need to do something so drastic! I asked him to just try and understand me, pray for me, and support me. He said he could and for me to be careful. I know Jered understood because of the influence of his grandparents, Woody and Catherine Puckett. After Jered's call, I called Barb to say I would be at the church by 2 P.M. It was then 12:15 P.M. I also told her the stories of my stoppers-by, as I had many times, and she was in awe! As I was going north on SR 15 against traffic, the vehicle exhaust fumes were starting to make me sick. But with horns still honking and many thumbs up, I was able to keep going. After making the curve, I saw a car pull over and a man get out to talk with me. His name was Loren, and he wanted to know my story. It was a great conversation. He mentioned he doesn't attend any particular church but meets each week with others to praise God and learn more about Him.

10. As I continued past the Old Mill Inn, a car was backing out of their driveway. A woman was getting out of her car, and her son was in the back in a child's seat. She was explaining to him that she would be just a minute. She then came and asked my story. After giving my testimony and explaining why I was doing it, she asked if she could carry the cross for a while as Simon of Cyrene did for Jesus. I didn't mess up this time and say no. I was very pleased she asked, so she took it from me and carried it about seventy feet. She shared with me that she was the pastor of Waterford Mennonite Church. Tina was her name, and she would be sharing this story that night at their Good Friday Service.

She was quite overwhelmed with my love of Christ for this to happen. I was very blessed to be a part of this on such a great day!

**11.** As I left Tina, another van stopped beside me, and the driver asked my story and said she was so taken with the sight of the cross that she had to stop and talk with me. I was so blessed to have another Christian take the time and talk with me. It encouraged me again that I could do this! As I was crossing County Road 38 I was struggling to walk normally and getting real tired. When I passed Yoder-Culp Funeral Home, I decided to call Barb to tell her to come then, because I should be at the church in thirty minutes. As always in every conversation with her she was concerned about how I was doing, and I said I think I can make it but was pretty exhausted.

**12.** As I went past Goshen College, I thought it would be best to get off the highway and onto the sidewalk. I thought by then it was the last mile. (YEA) Going down the sidewalk was a little bumpy, and some branches were hitting the cross. I endured it, because I was almost there. Close to Southside Soda Shop, I saw a family by the sidewalk taking pictures of their eight kids. I wasn't sure what was going on but would soon find out. They had seen me coming and were waiting to ask what I was doing. I explained my reason, and he still was surprised that I would do this. They were from the Ukraine. His wife didn't say anything; she was busy taking pictures. The kids wanted to try and lift the cross, so they all lined up beside it with me while mom and dad were busy with the movie camera. After the fact I found out they were Jewish, and his name was Bejermine. TOO COOL! I was starting to get cold because of the time at the photo shoot. HA!

As I crossed SR 119, I was really having problems keeping my step, but I was almost there. Only one half mile to go! I was running a little late for my schedule, but oh well! As I came up Third Street and SR15, I saw someone taking my picture at the Chase Bank. I looked over, and it was Barb! She asked how I was, and I said I was pretty whipped, and she asked if she could carry the cross to the church parking lot. Then she would give it back to me to finish the last fifty feet. Remember, I learned after the first flub up. Of course you can if you want to! As Barb made her way down the sidewalk, she was really making good time. I was unable to keep up with her! We passed the jail, and turned toward the church parking lot. Barb gave the cross back to me to finish the last fifty feet. At the church and pretty exhausted, I laid the cross down, and Barb went to get a ladder, so we could stand the cross at the church entrance for Easter Sunday. It was 2:45 P.M. It had taken six and three quarter hours on that March 21, 2008 wintry day to make the very memorable, worthwhile, and unforgettable journey.

Many people have suggested that I write my story on paper, as I am now documenting this sometime later on April 21, 2008. This is now complete, but I still must emphasize that none of this was about me, but was all about MY LORD AND SAVIOR. He is the one deserving of everything. Without His help, I could not have completed the journey.

On the following Monday, I picked up the cross from the church and brought it home. I had asked Barb if I could erect it on our side yard. She graciously agreed. Since the trip, I've been able to reflect on many things. I'm reassured that this was an act of God for many reasons:

- The many previous scenes at church of the cross to help me realize His will in my life.
- The two pieces of logs in the loft for eleven years. Why hadn't we discarded them many times before, as they were in our way and not needed. The two pieces were exactly the length needed for the cross!
- The weather forecasted for Good Friday was five inches of snow. (There was none)
- The most important were the twelve people I talked with during the walk. I've felt that Jesus and the eleven disciples sent them to be an encouragement to me.
- Without His help and being by my side, I would not have felt so confident in the beginning. I was overwhelmed by the heaviness of the cross after taking it down at the church. HOW IN THE WORLD WAS I ABLE TO DO THIS? I think I completely understand now.

## Challenge 21
# What's the most important question to answer?
Of all the questions you've ever answered, which one do you think is the most important?

*(An answer by Jack Clark)*

At last, an easy question instead of a tough one. How vividly I remember the time in my spiritual journey when I was confronted by Jesus Christ for a commitment to him. Spiritually it was just like the exchange between Jesus and the Disciple Peter. I felt the same sense of a fixed gaze deep into my very being that I am sure Peter felt when Jesus looked into his soul and gently, but very firmly asked, "'What about you? Who do you say I am?'" Out of the same unshakable assuredness, I answered with the same response Peter and so many others have given: "You are the Christ, the Son of the living God." [209] That conviction, that response, that certainty has made all the difference in my life!

For me life's greatest adventure has been coming to realize that God knows me fully, and despite this that He loves me anyhow. The second greatest adventure is my coming to know God. Even if it's only in part, I can look forward to the time I am assured that I will know Him as He knows me.

Being sure of this lets me live life to the fullest. "This is the day which the Lord has made; we will rejoice and be glad in it."[210] The reason for this is shared with the author of the book of Romans: "I am convinced that neither death nor life, neither angels, nor demons, neither the present nor the future, nor any powers, neither height nor depth, nor anything else in all creation will be able to separate us from the love of God that is in Christ Jesus, our Lord."[211]

---

*(An answer by June C. Laudeman)*

It took me a long time to sort out my priorities. I wanted everything just so. Then one day my son said, "Mom, you never have time to do anything with us. Don't you love us?"

That really hit me. I reshuffled my priorities and decided that my husband and son

---

[209] Matthew 16:16 (NIV)
[210] Psalm 118:24 (NIV)
[211] Romans 8:38-39 (NIV)

were far more important than dusting and dishes and clubs and parties. Later when my son was grown I had time for these other activities, but then I wanted to be with them.

I have a close relationship with God and am still active in my church. I keep my faith uppermost in my heart. My husband and son were happier then and now as we enjoyed and enjoy activities together.

There is no greater joy here on earth than being loved in a loving family circle. The choice is always before us. We must decide on our priorities.

I pray: Loving Father, help us choose you today, for you are love. May our priorities include you and our family and friends, so that we may enrich their lives. Amen.

The choice is always before us – the way of Christ or the way of darkness.

*(Betty Byers' answer)*

The most important question I ever answered was to believe in the resurrection of Jesus Christ. Our salvation is based on it!

*(An answer by Matt Gunter)*

## Little Floaty Things That Say "No" (Answers to the Questions of Doubt)
### Scriptures: Acts 3:12a, 13-15, 17-26, Ps.118:19-24, 1 John 5:1-6, John 20:19-31

"Dad, do you ever have little floaty things in your head that say, 'No'?" My daughter, Becca, was in second grade when she asked me this question one night as I was putting her to bed. Taken a bit aback, I asked her what she meant. She elaborated, "Well, like when I say to myself there is a God and the floaty things say, 'No, there isn't.' Or I say God loves me and they say, 'No, he doesn't.'" It dawned on me that the "little floaty things that say, 'No'" was her second grade way of describing her early experiences with doubt. I assured her that I was also familiar with the little floaty things and had been since I was about her age.

This gospel referred to above is the famous episode in which Thomas earned the name "Doubting Thomas." There is more to Thomas than his doubts and this passage is

156

about more than doubt. But, it is clear the little floaty things were in Thomas' head and they were saying, "No". No to all that he had been living for the last three years. No to all that he had come to believe about Jesus. No to all his hopes. Following Jesus, Thomas had come to have great hopes about what God was doing in his world and his own life. He had seen those hopes nailed to a cross and buried in a tomb. The little floaty things in his head and heart shouted, "No!"

I suspect that most of us have had some experience with the little floaty things - with doubts. Most of us, at one time or another, have wondered about the existence of God or his goodness or his love for us personally. And doubt is not limited to the theoretical. On a more practical level, it includes questioning whether the way of life revealed in Jesus Christ is really the way to our fullest life and deepest joy. Whether they are theoretical or practical, and no matter what image we use to describe them, the questions are bound to arise at one time or another. What do we do with the little floaty things that say, "No"? Here are some suggestions:

1. Do not be ashamed, embarrassed, or afraid of your doubts. They come with the territory and actually act as a spur to spiritual growth. Buechner calls doubts, "The ants in the pants of faith."

2. On the other hand, beware the snare of pride. It is easy to become self-satisfied for being so clever and sophisticated as to see all the difficulties with faith for "thinking" people.

3. Talk to God about your doubts - even if it means starting your prayer with, "I'm not even sure I believe you are there . . ." God is not afraid of your doubts or offended by your questions. After all, Jesus invited Thomas to examine and touch his wounds. He has promised his love to you. No matter what. God would much rather have you spend time with him asking hard questions than have you not spend time with him at all. Taste and see that the Lord is good (Ps. 34:8). Spend time with God in prayer and worship. An intimate realization of God's presence and love puts to rest a lot of the questions. Such a realization does not usually happen without some discipline and time on our part. We need to be trained to pay attention spiritually. As with physical discipline, it usually takes time to see the effects.

4. Remember that you are part of a community of faith. You are not the first person to ask questions about faith. It is helpful to find out, through reading or conversation, how others have answered or learned to live with particular questions.

5. Be skeptical of your own skepticism. We live in a skeptical and cynical age. It is quite easy to be a complacent skeptic. But, the bases of many doubts are also subject to doubt. In the areas of science and history, for example, many are realizing that the methods used are not as objective or certain as was once claimed. They are themselves based on assumptions that cannot be proven and are shaped by the biases of the researcher. And they are unable to answer every question. Nothing that matters can be proven beyond a shadow of doubt. The truth can only be demonstrated by the living of it. This is no more or less the case with the truth of faith.

6. It can also be helpful to recognize that while faith has its difficulties, so do unbelief and apathy.

For example, the persistence of evil and suffering has been a perennial problem for those who believe in a loving God who desires our good. The problem is not solved, however, by removing God from the equation. The question is only changed to "If we are no more than the most recent byproduct of a cosmic accident, why do we care so much about the suffering of others?" Or, even more problematic, "Why *should* we care?" There are people starving and dying in Ethiopia. If there is no God and life is accidental anyway, why should I care?

7. Don't be surprised by doubt. It is part of the conversion process. The gospel is after all foolishness and a stumbling block. When the values and prejudices of the gospel conflict with the values and prejudices into which we have been acculturated, there will be tension. That is true whether the prejudices are intellectual, moral, or theological. That tension leads to doubt. It also leads to a choice. Whose prejudices am I going to live by?

8. Do not use doubt as an excuse not to follow Christ or respond to the Spirit's call. If I neglect to apply for a job because I doubt I will get it, I surely won't. I can remain unchallenged and comfortable right where I am. Anabaptist Hans Denk suggested this

basic axiom of the life the Spirit is, "You cannot truly know Christ without following him in life." Jesus calls us to follow just as he did the first disciples. We are left to choose whether we will or not. Thomas exemplifies this earlier in John's gospel (chapter 11) when Jesus heads back toward Jerusalem to raise Lazarus. The disciples counsel Jesus not to go because those who want to kill him are there. Jesus goes anyway. Thomas' response is, "Let us also go, that we may die with him." He had come to believe that following Jesus was the way to his deepest joy and was committed to follow him and share his fate. The knowing comes in the following.

9. Recognize that there is mystery at the heart of it all. As Christians, we believe that God has spoken and acted definitively through Jesus Christ and the Holy Spirit. But God has not seen fit to provide answers to our every question. And even the answers we've been given contain mystery. At some point, we can only rest with humility in the presence of the Mystery.

Following these suggestions will not silence all the little floaty things once and for all. They are natural companions of faith. But, these suggestions can lead to some answers. They can also take away some of the power of the floaty things. And even when our questions are unanswered, the struggle with them leads us deeper into the mystery of God where the "No" of the little floaty things is countered by God's resounding, "Yes!"

Challenge 22
# Why be a part of the Christian church?

So many people who say they are a follower of Christ fall short of what they should be. Why would anyone want membership in such a miserable group of failures?

*(Jack Clark's thoughts)*

Some people use this question to justify not being a Christian. It's true; all of us who follow Christ fail him. Isaiah recognized the problem: "All of us have become like one who is unclean, and all our righteous acts are like filthy rags; we all shrivel up like a leaf, and like the wind our sins sweep us away."[212] Every one of the Disciples failed Christ when he was arrested – it wasn't only Peter who denied him three times.[213] All the others who had pledged to follow him even to the death if necessary had fled in terror and gone into hiding.

It's true that some well-known TV evangelists and pastors have been swept away by scandal. It's equally true that I too have fallen short of God's plan for my life. Paul had the same problem: "My own behaviour baffles me. For I find myself not doing what I really want to do but doing what I really loathe… I often find that I have the will to do good but not the power. That is, I don't accomplish the good I set out to do, and the evil I don't really want to do I find I am always doing."[214]

To those who would be discouraged from being a Christian because of the failures of those of us who are Christians, I would observe that when a follower of God and Christ fails, nothing of God or Christ fails. To those of us who feel the weight of our failures, I find consolation in the Grace of God expressed in the Book of Romans: "There is now no condemnation for those who are in Christ Jesus."[215] I find a depth of understanding of what is important to those of us who are "Followers of the Way," as Christians were called in early times, in another observation of Paul: "I do not consider myself to have 'arrived,' spiritually, nor do I consider myself already perfect. But I keep going on, grasping ever more firmly that purpose for which Christ Jesus grasped me. My brothers, I do not consider myself to have fully grasped it even now. But I do concentrate on this: I leave the past behind, and with hands outstretched to whatever lies ahead I go straight for the goal

---

[212] Isaiah 64:6 (NIV)
[213] John 18:25 (NIV)
[214] Romans 7:15 & 18-20 (JBP)
[215] Romans 8:1 (NIV)

– my reward the honour of my high calling by God in Christ Jesus."[216]

Thinking of the church as the body of Christ can be both humbling because of the honor of being selected and aggravating when one sees how poorly the body performs at times. It's exasperating to look at myself and others, realizing that so many parts of this body are paralyzed or covered with warts and blemishes. On reflection, I've understood that this is another example of God's power being manifest in our weaknesses. God can take this imperfect body (the church – including me) and accomplish great things. Also I need to be a part of this body because there are those who are weak who can benefit from my strengths, and there are those who are strong who can strengthen me when I need help. Most congregations are poor organizations, but they are the places Christ has chosen in which He intends us to grow.

So to those who might hesitate to become a Christian because of my failures or the shortcomings of others, I would urge that they certainly do not follow me or my example. Follow the one true God and his Messiah. "Do not conform any longer to the pattern of this world, but be transformed by the renewing of your mind."[217] The result will be that we will "all reflect the Lord's glory, being transformed into his likeness with ever-increasing glory, which comes from the Lord."[218] Being made into the likeness of Christ is not a one step process. It's not a sprint. For most it's not even a long-distance run or a marathon. It's more like a struggle up a steep and shifting sand hill. With every step forward, there is a risk of sliding back several feet only to keep striving. Eventually, with God's help, we have been promised that we too will be perfected. Come on! Jesus can always use another person fishing for men.

---

*(Another answer – from Cathy Ann Turner)*

How is it possible that a Christian can do "bad things" or live an awful life and have those actions (sins) forgiven and go to Heaven, but someone who has lived a good life but is not religious can't expect to go to Heaven. In the words of our Faith, how can Salvation/the Blood of the Lamb wash a sinner clean?

---

[216] Philippians 3:12-14 (JBP)
[217] Romans 12:2 (NIV)
[218] 2 Corinthians 3:18

My short answer to that is: I don't know how! – I just believe it in Faith because Christ Jesus proclaimed it. When I decided to believe that Jesus was my PERSONAL Savior I had to buy the "whole package" – that doesn't mean that I don't question some things or that I find all of the answers but that I believe that whether or not I understand a thing to be so doesn't really matter – it still is so for God, for all of Christendom and for me too.

My Faith tells me that no actions I ever take or works I ever do can earn me Salvation – except the action of Proclaiming Jesus to be my Savior – because I can never make up for every wrong; simply because I can never declare or even know all that I do that drives a wedge between me and others or myself and God or others and God (such actions and thoughts are the definition of "sin"). That's the basis of the Christian Faith – the aspect that sets our Faith apart from all others – Scripture tells us that Salvation does not come by "works" but by Faith and that our Faith is to be in Christ Jesus. To my knowledge, all other religions are based on an angry God (rather than a loving one) and the works of a man himself in his own attempt to "earn" eternity, or in some cases the works and actions of other men on someone's behalf.

To my mind, far worse than relying on myself to get myself into heaven would be the need to rely on someone else to do the right thing in the right way at the right time. I understand that Mormons believe salvation comes from baptism and that you can be baptized multiple times to gain salvation for others and a "better room in the house" in the kingdom of heaven for yourself. First I don't believe that Baptism "wins" a person salvation but if it did, what if you forgot to get it done and thought "oh, well, so and so will do it for me" and that other person never got around to it either? Might be bad news!

_(Betty Byers' thoughts)_

The church is for sinners.    All who are saints are first of all sinners too.

# How does God feel about people?

*(Observations by Jack Clark)*

Almost everyone who has ever heard of Jesus Christ recalls that he told his disciples that we should think of God as our Abba, our Father or our Daddy. God had spoken to His people long before that through the prophets suggesting the same thing: "I myself said, 'How gladly would I treat you like my children and give you a pleasant land, the most beautiful inheritance of any nation.' I thought you would call me 'Father' and not turn away from following me."[219]

God reportedly spoke through his prophet Samuel to King David: "I will raise up your offspring to succeed you, who will come from your own body, and I will establish his kingdom... I will be his Father and he will be my son. When he does wrong, I will punish him with a rod wielded by human beings, with floggings inflicted by human hands. But my love will never be taken away from him."[220] Bible students point out that the promise extends not only to Solomon, King David's immediate successor, but to all David's descendants who would succeed him. This again speaks of God as Father, but also explains the reason for the punishment of God's people when necessary and how the punishment would take place.

I can tell you how God thinks about you, because I can tell you first hand how God thinks about me, and I know that He feels the same about every other person. He loves me! He loved me so much that when I had drifted away from Him in my earlier life and became more and more self-centered and really messed up my life that he let me suffer. As I understand it now, he handed me over to Satan in order that I could come to my senses and choose voluntarily to make the choices that would lead to my salvation. After I had suffered enough that I was thoroughly miserable and depressed, He sent his Holy Spirit to hunt me down and help me to realize that life could be better than that. I can really identify with the story of the Prodigal Son.[221] Unlike the prodigal son, I didn't have enough good sense on my own to repent and go to my Father and ask forgiveness. The

---

[219] Jeremiah 3:19 (TNIV)
[220] Second Samuel 7:12-15 (TNIV)
[221] Luke 15

Holy Spirit had to put some pressure on me and force me to turn to the Bible. I read and read and read. The process took literally months. Eventually while I was reading First Corinthians Chapter 13, the Spirit let me understand that this is how God feels about me. Oh, I know that Paul originally wrote this to tell Christians how to deal with each other, but there was equally meaning in there for God's offered relationship to me. It speaks of a love that is patient, and years before my Grandmother had taught me that God is love. It speaks of a love that isn't proud. It isn't too proud to love me when I haven't been at all lovely; it isn't so proud that although God is perfect that He can't accept my very marked imperfections and make up for them. God's love for me was anything but self-seeking. He didn't want to disgrace me or punish me, or even scold me; He wanted to hold my self-wounded soul tenderly in His arms and heal me. He didn't want to keep a record of my wrongs; He wanted to remove them as far as the "East is from the West."[222] He didn't delight in the evil I had done, but rejoiced in the truth that His son had already ransomed me from that spiritual death in which I had found myself and offered me a chance to be born again! Tears rolled down my cheeks, as I realized that this Holy God was eager to always trust me, always hope that I could do better, and would always persevere in his efforts to help me "strain toward the goal with outstretched arms."[223] The verses promised that love never fails. In spite of the fact that I can only see a poor reflection of what God's total aspirations are for me, the part I am able to understand is fabulous!

Paul made it plain that if God could love him and that if Jesus could redeem him and save him, that the offer was good for anyone. My experience lets me give the same assurance.

Some of the things God has revealed to those who wrote the scriptures that deal with this subject of how he is concerned with and feels about us are among the most beautiful things ever recorded:

"Before I formed you in the womb I knew you; before you were born I set you apart."[224] "You made my whole being; you formed me in my mother's body. I praise you because you made me in an amazing and wonderful way. What you have done is wonderful. I

---

[222] Psalm 103:12 (NIV)
[223] Philippians 3:12-14 (JBP)
[224] Jeremiah 1:5 (NIV)

know this very well. You saw my bones being formed as I took shape in my mother's body. When I was put together there, you saw my body as it was formed. All the days planned for me were written in your book before I was one day old."[225] "I am fearfully and wonderfully made."[226]

"I have loved you with an everlasting love; I have drawn you with loving kindness."[227] He offered that He would be our God and that we could be His people.[228] He wants us to be bound to him "by cords of human kindness, with ties of love."[229] "Mercy and truth are met together; righteousness and peace have kissed each other."[230]

To let us know of his plans for watching over us: "The Lord thy God in the midst of thee is mighty; He will save; He will rejoice over thee with joy; He will rest in His love; He will joy over thee with singing."[231]

To let us know that God is always there for us and that in a world with no more stability than quicksand that He's unshakable: "God is our refuge and strength, an ever present help in trouble. Therefore we will not fear, though the earth give way and the mountains fall into the heart of the sea, though its waters roar and foam and the mountains quake with their surging.[232]

To let us know that there is absolutely nothing that can ever come between Him and us with the exception of our own rejection: "I am convinced that neither death nor life, neither angels nor demons, neither the present nor the future, nor any powers, neither height nor depth, nor anything else in all creation will be able to separate us from the love of God that is in Christ Jesus our Lord."[233]

---

[225] Psalm 139:13 &16 (ISB)
[226] Psalm 139:14 (NIV)
[227] Jeremiah 31:3 (NIV)
[228] Exodus 6:7
[229] Hosea 11:4 (NIV)
[230] Psalm 85:10 (KJV)
[231] Zephaniah 3:17 (KJV)
[232] Psalm 46:1-3 (NIV)
[233] Romans 8:38-38 (NIV)

To let us know that whatever happens we will ultimately be on the winning team: "If God is for us, who can be against us?"[234]

To let us know that God will work in anything the world may dump on us: "We know that in all things God works for the good of those who love him, who have been called according to His purpose."[235]

To reassure us that despite anything we have been or done, that we really can be a part of God's Kingdom: "Therefore, there is now no condemnation for those who are in Christ Jesus."[236]

To remind us that God is at work. He has created; He is creating, and He will create. He is also re-creating that which He has already made. He is working with us to help us become the persons who He planned us to be. "He who began a good work in you will perfect it until the Day of Christ Jesus."[237]

To let us know just how much He treasures us: "We have become gifts to God that He delights in."[238]

"'I know the plans I have for you,' declares the Lord. 'Plans to prosper you and not to harm you, plans to give you hope and a future.'"[239] "No eye has seen, no ear has heard, no mind has conceived what God has prepared for those who love Him."[240]

---

(Another answer by Cathy Ann Turner)

When I was a child after my parents divorced, and while I was living with my Mother, I was hungry for church fellowship and would walk by myself to a Baptist church some distance from Mother's house. When I was in high school, I lived with my Dad and was active in MYF, Sunday school, church, and choir. In college I was sporadic in church

---

[234] Romans 8:31 (NIV)
[235] Romans 8:38-39 (NIV)
[236] Romans 8:1 (NIV)
[237] Philippians 1:6 (NAS)
[238] Ephesians 1:11 (TLB)
[239] Jeremiah 29:11 (NIV)
[240] First Corinthians 2:9 (NIV)

attendance – sometimes going to a Presbyterian church and sometimes to a Catholic church. After I married we moved often because of the demands of my husband's engineering job. Over the years I have attended or been a member of nine Christian denominations.

In spite of all these church experiences, I was forty years old before I had a personal understanding and relationship with Christ. That right there is a telling statement. To have been a part of church life all those years, to have "head knowledge" without "heart knowledge" is now absolutely amazing to me. There was a time – a day, an hour when suddenly I knew the amazing truth that Jesus went to the Cross for me – and in a profoundly Spiritual sense, he went for me alone. He went to the Cross 2000 years ago because He knew then that I would need Him to do that for me. He did it for all other believers too, but what an amazing thing to realize that He would have (if need be) done it just for me - therefore in that Spiritual sense, he did it just for me!

My spiritual growth after this time has led me to the understanding of God's plan. Getting to know the Holy Spirit was a tempestuous and challenging experience. My husband Tom and I were challenged to give control of our lives back to God, to learn to not only accept God's spiritual gifts, but to welcome them, to come to the place where I could say, "If you want me to have this gift, then I welcome it." (And more importantly, to mean it and to convince God that I meant it!) What a challenge that was, mostly due to past family experiences and the fears and anger that they engendered. God led us into the places I could grow because of His love and concern: adult Sunday school, small share groups, care ministries and small group ministries where not only did I grow, but found myself contributing to the growth of others. That tells a lot about how I have found God feeling about me and other people.

*(Betty Byers' idea)*

God loves everyone. He wants everyone to accept Christ, and He is interested in every area of our life.

# Free will versus predestination

We talk about God's plan and we talk about predestination. Where do these fit in with free will? How do we know what God's plan is for us? (Submitted by Carol Clark)

*(Jack Clark's answer)*

People have some differences in understanding the will of God. My wife Carol is convinced that it was God's specific intention that we meet in response to her prayer to find a Christian husband. She does feel it was our choice as to whether we should marry. While it is at the same time humbling and enthralling to consider that one could be the answer to a maiden's prayer, I suspect God may have created several other men who would have made an equally good husband for such a graceful, lovely, fun-filled, exciting woman as Carol. Susan, one of our daughters, expands on Carol's views and has spent considerable time in study, contemplation, and prayer to determine God's will for her life. Personally it seems good to me to seek God's will, because He is delighted to know that we want to do those things that please Him, and we will be blessed if we do. However, it would seem while God may occasionally have picked one specific path for a person to follow throughout their life and may often pick short-term projects for many of us, that in many instances He is equally happy when we make any one of several good choices.

Perhaps it's significant that Susan married a Presbyterian minister. Traditionally, the Presbyterian fellowship has believed in predestination. This doctrine holds that God has foreordained all things; especially that God has elected certain souls to eternal salvation. When I'm in a teasing mood, I may ask why, if someone holds to this view, they would bother to check traffic before pulling onto a busy highway. The status of the traffic would seem to make little difference if all things are predestined.

In respect to the view that some persons are predestined to salvation, all the efforts of God and Christ suggest that if such a thing does exist, it must apply to all persons, and that those who do not achieve this destiny of salvation do so because they have thwarted God's plan through their rejection. I am fully persuaded that God indeed has great plans for each of us. In fact the Bible even says so: "'I know the plans I have for you,' declares the Lord, 'plans to prosper you and not to harm you, plans to give you a hope and a future.'"[241] In the view of some, these plans are very specific with each detail decided. In others' understanding, these plans consist sometimes of very specific courses of actions, but often only of a sketchy outline that may allow much amplification and many personal choices by the individual. Regardless of their understanding of the course of each individual's life, both groups of believers would agree that God has other long-term plans that will come to fruition no matter what we or others do as individuals. His kingdom will come. Jesus Christ will return to rule over the nations. Satan and his cohorts will be thrown into the pit. There will be a new heaven and a new earth, and a New Jerusalem. We may choose to be a part of this, or we may choose to decline being a part of it. God has given us the choice (free will); although, it's evident that He yearns for each of us to voluntarily make the choice to be a part of this great plan. He has offered us the privilege of playing a role in this sweeping and exciting adventure. In doing so, we have the thrilling chance to imprint His kingdom with our efforts, to be co-creators with God of the nature of eternity in a small but significant way if we so choose. We cannot frustrate God's ultimate plans, but we can be a contributing part of them. "Many are the plans in a man's heart, but it is the Lord's purpose that prevails."[242]

The Bible does have several things to say about destiny and predestination. In Job it's noted that the destiny of those who forget God is to perish because they are like reeds without water and like those who lean on a spider's web clinging to what can't hold them. [243]

Perhaps one of the more difficult references is: "Those God foreknew he also predestined to be conformed to the likeness of his Son, that he might be the firstborn among many brothers. And those he predestined, he also called; those he called, he also justified; those he justified, he also glorified. What, then shall we say in response to this? If God is for us, who can be against us?"[244] Also, "In love he predestined us to be adopted sons through Jesus Christ, in accordance with his pleasure and will – to the praise of his glorious grace, which he has freely given us in the One he loves."[245] To some students of the scripture these verses signify that God has planned and directed and orchestrated

---

[241] Jeremiah 29:11 (NIV)
[242] Proverbs 19:21 (NIV)
[243] Job 8:12-16
[244] Romans 8:29-31 (NIV)
[245] Ephesians 1:14-16 (NIV)

who will be a part of those saved and those who will accept salvation. To others of us it indicates that because God is all-knowing, and exists in an eternal present that includes our past, present and future that he knows who of us will choose to accept His grace that He has offered to everyone.

So how do we recognize God's will for us? Some understand it through prayer (a two way communication when we're not too busy telling God what He already knows). Some have had visions. Some have known God's will through dreams, but this can be tricky, as there are certainly some pretty weird dreams that I'm sure don't come from God. We sometimes understand God's will through contemplation and often through Bible study and discussions with other Christians. Most of us are made aware of God's will by a growing awareness that seems beyond what we would have thought of on our own.

I recall that when I was a youngster how much I enjoyed hearing my Mother play the piano. Mother was a double music and art major in college, and some of my very dear memories are about our family gathered in our living room and singing together. Well, that isn't quite the whole story. Dad could whistle very well, but he couldn't carry a tune while singing. I've never quite understood that. Perhaps the music he was destined to make was just different than the rest of us. I thought it would be nice to play the piano too, so Mother and Dad arranged for me to take music lessons. I soon found out that liking music wasn't all that was involved in playing the piano. Becoming a pianist involves more than enjoyment of the instrument. It involves the discipline of practice. A remarkable discovery indeed: whatever is worth accomplishing involves not only attraction and interest, but it also involves effort, sacrifice on some level, and discipline. Looking back I've often commented that whatever my folks paid my music teacher, Mr. Arnold Beckman, in those monetarily tight times of the recovery phase of the depression, he certainly more than earned it to compensate for the frustration I must have given him. I didn't practice with regularity or discipline. After probably nine months I learned enough to make it through one recital. I can still pick out the treble notes in a piece of music, but I never became an accomplished musician. The point is that I had a fine instrument on which to learn; I had a well-qualified instructor. My parents were willing to pay for my lessons. I enjoyed music. Presumably I had the ability as well as the opportunity to learn the piano. Had I learned to play well, I'm sure I would still enjoy it, but I blew it. If I was destined to become an accomplished pianist, I thwarted my destiny.

Well, just how does this little story fit into a discussion of Christian answers to tough questions? I think there are several parallels. We must have a realization that there is a God to seek Him. We must have a love of God and a conviction that a relationship to God is in our best interest to want that relationship, or it will never happen. The Bible suggests that that desire must grow to be so great that it's actually like an all-consuming hunger and thirst. We must commit ourselves to the relationship as we come to understand the commitment God and His Christ made to it. And we must be willing to practice for the prize – Paul suggested it's like practicing for an athletic event. We must discipline ourselves, or we're likely to miss the goal of that relationship that many of us believe was the destiny planned by God for every person. Just as I thwarted my destiny to be a fine pianist, it's possible for those that God predestined to be a part of the Kingdom to thwart their destiny. God will not drag us by the ear to get us to become what he hopes for us, but, O my, how He will delight in even our first fumbling steps to be a part of those who perform his music. God is easy to please, but He hopes for so much more that He is difficult to satisfy. With practice some day we can expect to hear the loveliest words imaginable from our God: "Well done, thou good and faithful servant."[246]

---

[246] Matthew 25:21 (KJV)

174

# What can I do with my life to please God?
How do we know what God wants us to do with our lives or in a specific situation?

*(Jack Clark's answer)*

God speaks to different people in different ways. In the Bible it seems that some hear an audible voice. Some have visions, and to some God reveals Himself in dreams. God meets people where they are and in ways most significant or understandable to them. I have not personally talked with anyone who has heard God's audible voice. I know one person who is convinced that God sent her a vision to warn her of being in a congregation that, according to the vision, was on the edge of slipping into an abyss of dangerous error in relationship to their beliefs. I personally have had dreams that have given insights about God that seemed beyond my own understanding and could only have been a gift of the Holy Spirit. Most of the time other Christians I have talked with and I become aware of something God wants us to do by a developing awareness. If I try to ignore these urgings that seem to be from the Holy Spirit, the awareness becomes more intense. God doesn't command me to do something, but He has been known to bring more pressure to bear to get me to see things His way.

There are ways to judge an awareness that we may have to be sure it is from God rather than the result of some desire of our own or even from an evil source. The Apostle John suggested: "Dear friends, do not believe every spirit, but test the spirits to see whether they are from God, because many false prophets have gone out into the world. This is how you can recognize the Spirit of God: Every spirit that acknowledges that Jesus Christ has come in the flesh is from God, but every spirit that does not acknowledge Jesus in not from God."[247] Other aids in judging the source of an awareness include that it will not be counter to scripture. Some people have been deluded to the extent that they have even killed another person being convinced the source of their direction was from God. This is not in accordance with Jesus' teachings, and while it may be from an evil spiritual source or from their own twisted mind, it is not from God. Second the impulse will not be contrary to tradition, so the impulse of Thomas Jefferson to rewrite the Bible, leaving out those parts that he did not understand or agree with would not be something God directed. Thirdly the direction will not be contrary to good judgment or reason, so an

---

[247] First John 4:1-3 (TNIV)

impulse to do something physically harmful without overwhelming reason would not come from God. A fourth way to judge these things is by experience. These guidelines are known as the Wesley quadrilateral – scripture, tradition, experience and reason.

On one occasion one of my children was involved with a church group that seemed to have some mistaken ideas. My wife Carol and I had accommodated their ideas about trusting totally to God for all their needs including avoiding medical care. This wasn't easy, since I'm a physician. We knew of others in our area who had confronted family members in the same congregation about their beliefs only to result in a disruption of the family relationships. The Holy Spirit had given me a sense that, "You have other people in your family who take good care of their physical needs but who neglect spiritual matters, and you can accept them." After several years of accommodation, I developed a progressively insistent sense that the Holy Spirit wanted me to present the reasons to them that seemed to indicate they were wrong in this area of their faith. I didn't want to do this. Even though I was concerned that some of their congregation had gotten into health problems and a few had even died due to their belief, I wasn't anxious to risk our relationship. God seemed to ratchet up the urging. I felt a sense of gentle nudging becoming gentle pushing and then increasingly intense pressure. Still I resisted. Ultimately I was made progressively aware of the meaning of a well-known verse of the Bible. The awareness was very distinct and was in the third person – not presented as a thought that just happened to occur to me: "If you love these more than me, you're not worthy of me."[248] Perhaps if I had continued to resist, the direction would have gone from a thought in the third person to the audible voice that some have experienced. Hesitantly and with anxiety, I gave in to the direction. It all turned out well. I've noticed that when I do what God wants, it seems to be that way. This shouldn't surprise me, but it still can.

In my own experience of God giving me a direction to do something, it seems like it is usually something I haven't been thinking of doing – it comes out of the blue. If I have been thinking about a problem and get a directional inspiration from God, I may have been mulling over two or three options that had occurred to me when, again out of the blue, there is a much better solution or option that I hadn't been thinking about. Often when God has inspired me it is with something I wasn't thinking about doing – sometimes

---

[248] Compare to Matthew 10:37

something I wasn't anxious to do at all. I've even been reminded by my responses to the response Moses gave when God told him to go back to Egypt or the response Jonah gave when he was directed to preach in Nineveh. I too have had "reasons" that I shouldn't do what God wanted. I too have had times when I've run from God. Surprise! There's nothing new under the sun. God still doesn't accept excuses. There's no place to go where we can hide from God's presence.

Some people expect God to direct every one of their actions and fervently pray for God's directions in every life decision – where to live, where to work, who to marry – I'm sure God feels honored when we seek His guidance, but it seems to me that in most things He is pleased with our decisions as long as they are honorable and as long as they bring Him glory and joy for others and ourselves. There are certainly some times when God has a specific need or purpose to be filled, but in many things He seems to give us a great deal of latitude. I recall that when our four children were considering what to do with their life work, I was pleased when they asked my opinion, but I also remember saying that I wanted them to do what pleased them as long as it was honest work. It seems that fits in with how God usually works too. As a young man, I thought I would like to be an attorney and go into politics to make the world a better place. As a little older young man, I had taken a geology course and found it very interesting and considered being a geologist. My Dad, who was a family physician, kept encouraging me to think about becoming a physician. I took an undergraduate course in comparative anatomy and found it really interesting. I applied to medical school and was accepted, and the rest is history – perhaps at age 75 almost ancient history. Anyhow if there was any guidance from the Holy Spirit in my career choice, I wasn't aware of it. While a subliminal suggestion may have played a role, it seems to me that God would have been pleased and could have used me in any one of these choices.

Once in awhile there is an emergency situation that shows up. There really isn't any time to think about what we should do or to let the Holy Spirit make us consciously aware. If we've been open to God's direction in our life, we may have occasions when we must be guided by reflex.

In 1972, I was scheduled to be a speaker at a two-day seminar on death and dying in Rapid City, South Dakota. I had written a medical journal article on the subject of helping our patients and their families in the dying process, and was pleased to be a presenter. The famous psychiatrist Elizabeth Kubler Ross gave her presentation the first day.

My talk was to be included on the second day; I didn't get to give it. Part of the evening's entertainment included a drive into the Black Hills to see the famous Black Hills Passion Play and enjoy a very nice dinner. While we were at dinner, an extremely heavy rain started. Before dessert, we were advised that there was a concern that a dam in the mountains might burst and that we should leave. Carol and I drove the car we had been loaned by the program committee with three passengers, persons attending the seminar, a priest and a psychiatrist whose husband was with her. As I followed the bus carrying most of the participants across a bridge, the water rapidly rose to the car doors. We got across, but later learned that the car behind us carrying the organizer of the event stalled. They abandoned their car, wading to safety, as the car was washed off the bridge.

Strangely, gas lines burst in the buildings of the city inundated by the flash flood, and buildings surrounded by water went up in flame. We parked on high ground in a filling station. A police car came by and checked to see if we were all right. I offered to go with the officer to do what I could to help. We gave what comfort we could to those who escaped from the floodwaters, treating cuts and scrapes, advising tetanus shots when they could get to medical attention.

Later, as the waters subsided, the policeman took me to the hospital. I sutured cuts, tried to restore body temperature to an elderly lady who had spent three or four hours trapped in the cold water with a tree pressing her head against a shed and her face almost in the swirling water. I wrote prescriptions for medication to help the anxiety of those who couldn't find their loved ones, and wept with a young father that had his children torn from his grasp by the raging flood.

I spent the night and well into the next day dealing with a first hand experience on death and dying instead of a theoretical lecture which had been planned.

Communication had been restored by that afternoon, and I called our motel. A very relieved Carol who had gotten back to the motel and helped list survivors through the night was glad to hear from me. As I arrived at the motel, there was concern another dam might break and endanger this area. Happily this didn't occur. Over three hundred people were killed or were never found.

As we discussed the events, Carol told me of the reaction of the psychiatrist and the priest. These were people who had dedicated their lives to helping others. They were people who had taken time to learn more about dealing with death to be better able to help, but their reaction when I went with the policeman was very strange indeed. They repeatedly expressed to Carol that I was foolish to go with the policeman and that it was beyond the call of duty. At the time, what I did didn't seem to be any more than what just came naturally. Only in looking back, did I feel a sense of gratitude that I had been in the right place at the right time to help. Only in retrospect did I have a sense that anything I did was done for the "Least of these, my brethren,"[249] and in doing it that I had been serving my savior.

I hadn't felt like a hero; I actually did very little except lose a night's sleep, give my dear wife a good deal of anxiety, and share the loss and pain of the people who passed my way.

Fear does strange things to people and priests and psychiatrists certainly can know fear as well as anyone, but certainly these trained professionals could have helped in a very desperate situation.

It was only in 1998 that our granddaughter, Karen Ummel, gave the following perspective she had gained from attending a college Youth for Christ convention in Indianapolis during her Christmas break from Purdue University: In a way, day to day life is much like this. There are people all around us drowning in sin. There are people so overcome by their situation that they can't take logical action to save themselves. We have to be ready to help. We can't save them, but we can point them to Christ who can.

We have to be ready to jump into exhausting and sometimes even dangerous situations, to risk ourselves, to forget about our fears, to give them the help they need.

---

[249] Matthew 25:40 (NIV)

Otherwise some will perish who could have been saved. We have to be ready to be the Good Samaritan,[250] because the priest may go by on the other side of the road and the 'Levite' may be too frightened or absorbed in his own concerns to take a hand. Jesus told us we must do this. When I think of all he has done for me, I can do no less."[251]

One of the important considerations is to be open to change. God has different needs to be filled at different times. We have different needs, skills, and abilities at different times, and we need to be open to God's leading and resist the stifling and even potentially corrupting changes that tend to be imposed on us if we're not alert. There is some good advice in the scriptures to help us in this area: "Do not conform any longer to the pattern of this world, but be transformed by the renewing of your mind."[252] We are changing day by day. The objective must be that we are changing in ways that bring us closer to God's great plans for us and closer to the example Jesus has set for our lives. Along with Paul, we must recognize that we haven't arrived yet, but that we must strain for the goal with arms outstretched. If we wait until we are fully perfected, we will never do anything; we will never accomplish anything for the Kingdom of God, and we will be like the servant who was given one talent and hid it making no return for the master.[253]

Perhaps the best thing we can consider doing is to follow Jesus' lead. Instead of giving God my detailed plans, I can share the problem or concern with Him. I can even ask for the Holy Spirit to pray for me if I don't have any idea what to do in a particular situation.[254] Then I can turn it over to the one who loves us more than any other being possibly can with the phrase, "Thy will be done."

*(An answer by Betty Berger)*

His commission to us was to share the Good News.[255] If we study and learn His Word, He gives us discernment, and we can hear from the Holy Spirit the answers we need as well as help for others. The Lord gives me scriptures for many family and friends that are going through trials.

---

[250] Luke 10:25-37 (NIV)
[251] *The Reason for the Hope, A Spiritual Journey*, Jack prow Clark, M. D., copyright © 1998, pp. 200-261 (Copies available at the Indiana State Library in Indianapolis, IN.)
[252] Romans 12:2
[253] Matthew 25:14-28
[254] Romans 8:26
[255] Mark 16:15

The Holy Spirit tells us that prayer and Bible study are pleasing to God.

Challenge 25

# The problem of burn out

As a Christian how can I keep from burning out and getting discouraged and wanting to give up working for the church?

*(Thoughts of Jack Clark)*

Psychologically, it's good to recognize that everyone has limits and not push ourselves to exhaustion. A worn our worker is a dangerous worker. This applies to any regular job – bricklayer, truck driver, mother, doctor, and any other situation. It also applies to working for God in the Kingdom. Time to relax and renew is important. Several times the Bible tells of Jesus withdrawing to a quiet place to pray and to rest from pressing situations. This is one of the reasons God decreed a day of rest and worship. In Christ's observation, the Sabbath was made for man not the other way around. Too much exhaustion can lead to spiritual battle fatigue. Paul saw this happen to some Christians and wrote: "Let us not give up meeting together, as some are in the habit of doing, but let us encourage one another."[256] Burned out people drop out.

It's important to be aware that we individually are not carrying the total weight of the work of the Kingdom. Jesus is there to help carry the load: "Take my yoke upon you and learn from me, for I am gentle and humble in heart, and you will find rest for your souls. For my yoke is easy and my burden is light."[257]

Service needs to be deeply rooted in other spiritual disciplines such as solitude and Bible study so we can encounter the heart of God and see how the neediness of people breaks God's heart, and in turn let our hearts be broken too. By helping others we become the body of Christ, doing his work and experiencing his power on earth.

One problem with service is that we can become wrapped up in ourselves or in the service. This is what can easily result in burn out. Another danger in giving service is that we can burn out when doing overshadows the sense of serving with Christ. When we run on empty we can wear ourselves out. But when we stay connected to God through solitude, prayer, worship, and community our inner self can be filled and alert. We can pour out our hearts to God when we are troubled or fearful and our service remains

---

[256] Hebrews 10:25 (NIV)
[257] Matthew 11:29-30 (NIV)

passionate allowing us to serve with a full heart filled with the love of God himself.

Our Christ is speaking in Matthew (with some comments he might have noted speaking to our home congregation):

- "I was hungry, and you gave me something to eat." (Hungry not only for food, but hungry for acceptance and love. When some of you brought food for the food pantry and when some of you served food to the Hope Rescue Mission, I was there. When you've helped others feed themselves through Heifer International you've helped my brothers and sisters. When some of you donated to the Gideons for a Bible that will feed the soul of someone who has never heard of me or someone who can see no purpose in their life, you gave to me. Bread is essential, but remember "man does not live by bread alone."[258] )
- "I was thirsty and you gave me something to drink." (Some of you sent donations after the Tsunami and after Hurricane Katrina that brought pure water to those who needed it. Some have supported Indian Mission work that dug wells where they were needed. Some of you share the water of life in the good news of salvation with others.)
- "I was a stranger, and you invited me in." (Some of you invite new neighbors to share your friendship or over for a meal or to share fellowship in your congregation. Did you realize that I am with those you invite when you do these things?)
- "I needed clothes, and you clothed me." (Some of you donate clothes to Red Bird Mission in Kentucky or to the Salvation Army or to your congregation's thrift shop, and some of you sort the clothes and tend the shop where those who need the items can come and have their needs met while preserving their dignity. When you clothe them, you clothe me. When you give them dignity, you give me dignity.)
- "I was sick and you looked after me." (Some of you visit or send cards to your sick friends or visit people in nursing homes. When you do this you refresh their weary spirits and remind them that they are important to you and to God. By doing this you tell me also that I am important to you. It is like sending me a note that expresses, "I love you.")

---

[258] Deuteronomy 8:3, Matthew 4:4, & Luke 4:4

- "I was in prison, and you came to visit me."[259] (Some of you have shared with Prison Ministries or through the Angel Tree with those in prison or their families bringing awareness that if Christians think they and their families are important, then Christ must feel they are important too. When you do this, you're telling me, "I hear your message, Lord, I receive your love, and with boundless joy I share your love to those you love.")
- (Some of you have gone with work camps or raised funds for Habitat for Humanity to build shelter for individuals and congregations who can't do the job themselves. Can you see now that along with them, that you are also sheltering me?)

Did you ever wonder why God would choose you to do a task? I certainly have. The only reason I can think of is that God can see beyond our shortcomings and see our potential to return His love, accept Him, and accept the blessing He offers. In turn He can see in each of us the potential not to hoard the blessing for ourselves but to pass it on to others around us. Remember the reason that Abram was chosen for blessings? It was to pass them on to others. We're chosen for the same reason. Human nature being what it is there are times when the kingdom needs our efforts, but we don't want to do the job. Read about God offering Moses the job of going to Egypt to free the enslaved Israelites. He certainly was less than an enthusiastic participant. When we recognize or are made aware of an important job to be done for the Kingdom, we too often come up with a lot of reasons why it just should be someone else's task. I've been there, and I suspect almost every Follower of the Way has been there too at some time or another.

Are there things that inhibit you in your responses to Christ's call in your life? Are there things that threaten to block your effectiveness? Scriptures suggest, "Do not fear or be dismayed because of this great multitude, for the battle is not yours, but God's."[260]

God chose you because of His immeasurable love of you. He has faith in you, and He wants you to have faith in Him. He chose you to bless you in order that you could be a blessing to others. He chose you that your joy might be complete and so that His joy might rest with you.

---

[259] Matthew 25:35-36 (NIV)
[260] Second Chronicles 20:15 (NAS)

God and his son, Jesus, love us with an everlasting love.  We can never repay that love, but I think we must ask ourselves if we are going to respond to that love by doing what he asks of us.  It's uncomfortable to tell someone else about Jesus' love and salvation.  I can't fully explain why.  If I knew of a sure-prevention for the common cold, I'd be telling everyone about it, but here I am knowing about the prevention of spending eternity separated from God, and I hesitate.  Perhaps it's because I know that I'm no better than the person, I'm talking with, and I'm concerned that they will think that I feel that I am.  Whatever my reasons, I need to get over my hesitancy.  I hope that we Christians can all get beyond this hang up.

We have to learn to pace ourselves.  God wants us to be effective, cheerful workers.  This would only in very rare instances involve our working ourselves into exhaustion or loss of joy.  Take heart!  "Those who hope in the Lord will renew their strength.  They will soar on wings like eagles; they will run and not grow weary, they will walk and not be faint."[261]

*(An answer from Betty Byers)*

Continue to read the Bible and study it.  Have time each day to talk to God.  Have devotions.

---

[261] Isaiah 40:31 (NIV)

Challenge 27
# Why do bad things happen to people?

*(Jack Clark's views)*

There have been multiple complete books written on this subject. The writers of several psalms and proverbs and millions of every day people have asked this same question for thousands of years. People don't enjoy failure, acute or chronic illness, betrayal by friends, their own suffering, the suffering and death of loved ones or friends, financial reversals, poverty, loss of one's dreams, or any form of natural, man-made, or self-made disaster.

Jesus said, "Blessed are those who mourn, for they will be comforted...; blessed are those who are persecuted because of righteousness, for theirs is the kingdom of heaven. Blessed are you when people insult you, persecute you and falsely say all kinds of evil against you because of me. Rejoice and be glad, because great is your reward in heaven, for in the same way they persecuted the prophets who were before you."[262] Probably if the vast majority of us were to be asked to sign up to go through any of these events and to receive these blessings, very few would respond, yet Jesus did. I've dealt with why Jesus volunteered to face the heartache of rejection, betrayal, physical and emotional abuse and a hideous death in answering the question was the crucifixion of Jesus necessary. Of course the answer as to why Jesus would volunteer for this is the depth of his love for us and to keep us from our personal disasters that would have resulted if he hadn't taken these things on himself.

Well, if it's put that way, perhaps most of us love someone enough to take on some personal disaster to avoid a worse disaster in their life. But that rather avoids the original question – why are bad things in life necessary in the first place?

Mary, Queen of Scots, went through a lot of heartache. She was, by arranged marriage at a very young age, Queen of France, but her young husband died. She married again after becoming Queen of Scotland in her own right. Her husband was unfaithful to her and seems to have had syphilis. The next man in her life murdered her husband. She was accused of being complicit in the murder; although, extensive

---

[262] Matthew 5:4-12 (NIV)

research makes this doubtful. She was opposed by many of her subjects for her personal Roman Catholic faith; although, she made no effort to make her Protestant subjects conform to her views. She was betrayed by her nobles, fled Scotland, and asked for sanctuary from her cousin, Queen Elizabeth I of England. Instead Elizabeth kept her in prison for many years and finally had her beheaded. She certainly had a life filled with "bad things." Interestingly something she wrote near the end of her life indicated that she found some good in what had happened to her: "Tribulation has been to them as a furnace to fine gold – a means of proving their virtue, of opening their so-long blinded eyes, and of teaching them to know themselves and their own feelings."[263]

One of the most difficult things for me in which to see any benefit is prolonged, chronic suffering. I once took care of a lovely family of three, an elderly farmer, his wife and their disabled son in his thirties. The son was a bright child but had been afflicted with very crippling juvenile rheumatoid arthritis. He had barely been able to complete high school, graduating as valedictorian of his class. He wasn't able to go on to college and spent his shortened adult life in chronic uncontrollable pain that could not be relieved even with narcotics. His mother died first. The son eventually became bedridden and was faithfully cared for by his father for several years before the son died in his late thirties of pneumonia. The father lived alone for several years – too old to farm anymore – his only joy a hutch of rabbits that he cared for. The person who was farming his land tricked him into signing it over and then attempted to evict him from his home. He befriended a young lady who was a single parent and who cheated him out of considerable money. Long-term suffering such as this is certainly beyond my ability to understand as having good aspects, but Mother Teresa of Calcutta said that when we suffer, we share in Christ's suffering. I haven't achieved this degree of spiritual perception, but I certainly greatly admire her and trust her perspective. This being so, these three certainly will certainly receive great rewards in heaven.

There are three verses of scripture that I find helpful in dealing with why bad things happen and how we should deal with them. "My brethren, count it all joy when you fall into various trials, knowing that the testing of your faith produces patience." [264] The

---

[263] Mary Queen of Scots, *On the lives of rulers,* Essay on Adversity, 1580. Quoted by Antonia Fraser, *Mary Queen of Scots,* p. 432, ©1969 by Antonia Fraser, Published in England by Weidenfeld & Nicolson
[264] James 1:2-3 (NKJV)

second verse is "Giving thanks always for all things."[265] The first suggests God working through the event to a beneficial outcome. The second is often very hard for me to accomplish. I find it relatively easy to give thanks <u>in</u> all things, because I can realize that God is with me or others through these tough times, but I must admit there are some events in my life and the life of others that I find it very difficult to be thankful <u>for</u>. I have to remind myself that nothing happens that doesn't pass through the mind and heart of God. There are times this truly stretches my understanding and my faith. The third verse is: "Can anyone ever separate us from Christ's love? Does it mean he no longer loves us if we have trouble or calamity, or are persecuted, or are hungry or cold or in danger or threatened with death? (Even the Scriptures say, 'For your sake we are being killed every day; we are being slaughtered like sheep).'"[266]

Perhaps I've sidestepped the question until now. It would seem that God, when He decided to make human-kind with a free will had to accept bad, even evil events as a price to pay. Some bad things happen as a result of our own actions and choices. If I am allowed to make bad choices and at times to sin and do evil things, this is going to result in heartache for those against whom I have acted (including God) and often for me too. If others have the free will choice to do evil against me or those I love, that too can result in terrible pain for me. My wife Carol has very aptly observed that choices have consequences. This applies both to good choices and bad choices. Good choices result in joy, salvation, fabulous relationships, and a great deal of personal satisfaction. It also relates to bad choices that can disrupt relationships, bring sadness and ultimately the possibility of missing out on salvation. The more radical the goodness, the more radical the result. The good choice of accepting Jesus' gift of redemption and salvation results is an eternity of communion with God. The more radical the evil choice, the more radical the consequences. Even forgiven sin has bad consequences. This illustrates bad things happening due to willful actions – ours or someone else's.

God when He created the universe not only set up moral laws, He also established physical laws. So if I choose to step off the top rung of a ladder or if my tire is blown out by hitting a sharp object when I'm driving 70 miles an hour causing my car to roll over several times, it's very likely that something bad is going to happen in my life. Financial

---

[265] Ephesians 5:20 (KJV)
[266] Romans 8:35-36 (NLT)

loss will occur from my wrecked car, if nothing more personal. If I'm walking through a woods and a large limb happens to fall on top of me, something bad is certainly going to result. Thus bad things can occur in our lives by happenstance (unless one is so convinced of predestination that they believe there is no such thing as happenstance).

It seems that such unpleasant and sometimes random events are an unavoidable result of God having given humankind free will to make choices. This in turn was necessary to allow each person the opportunity to choose to love God and to choose to be a part of God's plans. Without this freedom we would have been compelled to follow God's rules and compelled to essentially be unwilling slaves to God. This is not the relationship God wants from us. It's not the relationship I would choose either. It is possible to choose voluntarily to be a servant or some might say a slave to God, and this can be a loving, desirable relationship because of its voluntary nature.

If we believe there is a fallen angel that we call Satan or the Devil, it would seem that sometimes he is allowed to cause disastrous things to happen (read the book of Job in the Bible and also read of how Satan plotted against Jesus). I certainly have seen plenty of evidence of Satan to believe he exists. Peter warns us, "Be self-controlled and alert. Your enemy the devil prowls around like a roaring lion looking for someone to devour."[267] Some people even have a strange attraction to Satan. For those who do, there is scripture that tells us that in the end he will destroy even those who serve him.[268] I'm not sure why God created him in the first place. I understand where Satan went wrong in the Bible accounts – like we often do, he decided he was going to put himself first as being more important than God. This is making an idol of oneself, and results in major disasters if it is done by Satan or if it is done by a person.

Rarely, if we believe the accounts in the Bible, God Himself may inflict some very unpleasant events on some of us. This seems to happen when we have wandered so far away from Him that we are in danger of never finding our way back. It can happen when we have ignored the built in moral law in our consciences, or the word of God given to those who recorded our scriptures, or by the good advice of Godly people. When this happens God may have to design some unpleasant events that we likely would classify as

---

[267] First Peter 5:8 (NIV)
[268] Revelation 18:6

something unwanted or bad from our perspective to get us back on track. Scripture talks about the effects of not applying discipline[269] when needed, and it even talks of turning over a person who simply will not listen to Satan himself to bring about an ultimate return to God.[270]

C. S. Lewis in his book *The Problem of Pain* suggests that when everything is going well, few if any will turn their lives over to God. He suggests that some of the reason for making things less than agreeable on earth is that we will be directed away from false happiness to God, the ultimate source of true joy.

Strangely when disasters hit – circumstantial, self-made, made by others, devised by Satan, or in rare instances imposed as discipline from God – they often result in our turning to God. This turning may result from our disgust with what we have done, or it may represent our desperate grasping hold of God's ever-ready hand offered in love when we can't see any other place to get help. This is certainly an example of God working for good in all things[271] - even the bad things!

Another example of God working for good in all things is the understanding given to us after something bad has happened. With this understanding we can more easily comfort someone who has had a similar tragedy. I can comfort someone who has experienced the death of a loved one, but if I have experienced a death of one of my loved ones, I can do a much better job. I can, in theory, explain to another that Jesus Christ can forgive their sins, but I can do it so much more effectively when I have been convicted of my sins and realized the joy of Jesus' redemption and salvation in my own life. I notice it's even more effective when my sin was along the same line as the person I'm comforting.

Life contains misfortunes for us all. There are no worldly cushions to ease the pain of a great loss, disillusionment with an unfaithful friend, or an ideal gone sour. Without the spiritual growth that comes from overcoming misfortune, great faith would cease to exist, courage would have no place, and life would be an intolerable succession of sweet experiences with nothing sour to make the sweetness pleasant. Greatness is the child of

---

[269] Proverbs 13:24
[270] First Corinthians 5:5
[271] Romans 8:28

adversity, not that of complacency or tranquility. The ability to face adversity as a Christian can lead to a vital, giving, growing peace of mind never known by those sedated by easy living.

The above is a theoretical discussion of the subject. Below I'm copying a letter to friends (names changed) to put the problem of the pain of bad things happening on a personal level – where people live and feel the pain.

---

*(A second thought by Jack Clark)*

"Dear Jim and Martha,

"A short time ago Martha visited Carol and me sharing a deep hurt. We count you both among our dear friends and a brother and sister in Christ. Paul says that when one part of the body of Christ rejoices, we all rejoice, and when one part of the body hurts, we all hurt.

"There was sadness in Martha's face and voice, much different from her usual quietly vivacious manner. The two of you had been visited by an old friend who had come to your home with another member of his congregation to seek forgiveness for a sin of betrayal of your trust that had occurred years earlier. The sin had obviously been eating on his spirit as sin is so capable of doing. He had confessed it to his pastor. They had determined that a part of its resolution needed to be for him to seek your forgiveness. Like an old abscess that has smoldered for a long time, the sin still needed to be incised and drained for him to find healing, and also like an old abscess, its drainage was very unpleasant for all involved (pus stinks!). It was a sin like so many that couldn't be taken back once committed, and a sin for which no earthly reparation could be made. Later Jim spoke to me. The twinkle wasn't in his eye; his usual quick smile wasn't evident. He voiced the same question I and many other Christians have for some two thousand years and which was voiced before this by the nation Israel: "Why does there have to be evil in the world, or why can't God get rid of Satan now?" Not being too quick in our thinking through such situations, Carol and I initially could only share the pain, hug you, and pray with you that God would hold you very tenderly in His mercy and ease your pain and our pain. Perhaps such a simple reaction is the best initial response. Deep pain does not lend itself to deep

192

philosophy – only to sharing.

"Later I thought of the promised time Satan will be bound for a thousand years, or the ultimate solution when he will be cast into the lake of fire for eternity. I thought of the time that Zechariah had a vision of wickedness, personified as a woman in a basket. In the vision, wickedness was pushed back into the basket with a lead cover being pushed down on the mouth of the container. Then two women with the wind (God's Holy Spirit) in their wings, lifted up the basket to carry it away for a permanent place of confinement. I longed for this to occur. I longed for it to have occurred before the unfaithful friend perpetrated his sin.

"I was reminded of a great truth: When a man of God fails, nothing of God fails.

"I looked at a pin I had purchased that proclaims, "Life is tough, but God is Faithful." There was no great comfort there, but at least there was the realization that oftentimes the problems and even the disasters bring us closer to God. It would seem that God is able to turn the actions even of Satan to God's advantage. I thought of how Nebuchadnezzar, king of Babylon led off the nation Israel to seventy years of exile and slavery. I thought of how Assyria had led off King Manasseh of Judah to prison with a hook in his nose and bronze shackles. God used these evil nations to mold God's people and to get them to want to be in relationship to God again.

"Even though some evil events seem to fit in with God's plans, and some can be seen as the destructive covert plans of Satan, some appear to be totally random events. Some of the things we perceive as quite unpleasant in life are not even evil at all, but are God's pruning away unproductive things in our lives so we can accomplish more – also referred to as bearing more fruit.

"It often seems strange, but in response to disastrous accidents, mankind's sins and Satan's designs, we can grow closer in our relationship to God. When we contrast the filthy, joy-destroying effect of sin imposed by or on others or ourselves with the beauty of God's love, that love is seen to be so much more desirable.

"I think of each individual fresh from the hand of God – newborn. They are like a fresh unpainted canvas or a lump of clay waiting to be turned into something unique by God's efforts and plan. But unlike an artist's painting or a potter's clay, the individuals have will and a mind of their own. A canvas or a piece of pottery must accept whatever the artist does. On the other hand, we as God's works participate in our development and even have the ability to accept or reject the great plans He has for us. To further complicate the situation God's antithesis, Satan, is forever skulking around the corner. In his jealously over God's position and power in the universe, Satan wants to destroy God. Unable to accomplish this, he wants to destroy God's plans and those things He has created thereby destroying God's joy. Satan's ready to dash in at any opportunity to try to convince us to reject God's creative artistry.

"God looks on, compassionate but also amused. He smiles and in effect says, 'Well, Satan, you really put your foot in it this time, and it certainly looks like a real mess, but I think I can take this mess and fix it up just fine. I even think I can make it into a greater work of art, because it's been through some special refining that gives it more character and makes it tougher. On top of all that, these special efforts make my creation dearer to me and make me dearer to my creation.

"At this point Satan glowers, gnashes his teeth, and waits for his next chance. He doesn't realize that his next attempt will also play right into God's hands. After each event, the reshaped clay or the redone painting has more depth and better perspective, and the reshaped child of God is closer to God's image. The only chance for calamity is that the artwork may rebel itself.

"All these observations give only a glimmer of understanding about why the lead lid hasn't been pushed down on wickedness and why Satan hasn't been bound yet. God is using even the unlikely tool of Satan's destructive efforts to bring us to Himself. Satan's ultimate defeat has already happened in the mind and will of God, so it is a completed act. We await the manifestation of this act with eagerness. The effects of evil, sins, accidents, and Satan's schemes are often exquisitely painful. It isn't easy, but we need to be patient, God isn't finished with us yet!"

Bad things happen because there is a devil seeking who he can destroy,[272] but we have a God who is able to bring good from it.[273] The thief (devil) comes only in order to steal, kill and destroy. Jesus came that people may have life in abundance (to the full until it overflows). Draw a couple lines on a paper and make a list—

Kill, steal, destroy                                                    Abundant life

On which side do the bad things belong?

*(Betty Byers' understanding)*

Bad things happen because this is not a perfect world. God did not say being a Christian would be easy or a perfect life.

*(Answer by David Berger)*

If it's good – it's God. If it's bad – it's the Devil.[274]

*(Some thoughts of Matt Gunter)*

## Suffering and Belief in God

Scriptures: Exodus 3:1-15, Psalm 103:1-11, 1Cor 10:1-13, Luke 13:1-9

Why do you believe in God? Why *do* you believe in God? Maybe you've had some mystical, burning-bush experience like Moses. Maybe you've had a dramatic conversion experience and you can point to the difference God has made in your life. Maybe you are struck by the beauty and grandeur of creation. Or maybe, you were just raised that way and it makes sense to you. All of these reasons are fine and good, as well as whatever other reasons you might have. But for me, when it gets right down to it, I think I believe in God mostly because of the suffering and injustice in the world.

I know that the suffering and injustice in the world is supposed to be the great stumbling block to faith in God. But, I'm just backwards enough to find that to be the

---

[272] I Peter 5:8
[273] Romans 8:28
[274] John 10:10

reason to believe. Let me explain. Every time I tried to be an atheist (and I have tried) I kept running up against the reality that an atheist is forced to live a contradiction. I was forced into living a contradiction between my mind and my heart. Either I went with my mind and I followed logic to its utmost conclusions, or I followed my heart. But the two could not be followed together.

When I tried to be an atheist and followed the logic of my mind I was forced to admit that the beginning of all that is, and the beginning of all that I am, was an accident. The end of all that is and all that I am will also be, more or less, an accident. Everything in between is a meaningless event suspended between two accidents. Nothing, ultimately, has any meaning. Nothing, ultimately, has any purpose. All we are left with is our personal preferences and prejudices as to what is good and what is not so good. I was forced to agree with Albert Camus who wrote that if we believe in nothing, then it does not matter ultimately if we stoke the fires of the crematorium, as did the Nazis, or if we serve the lepers in Africa, as did Albert Schweitzer. It all comes to the same thing. Right and wrong, good and evil are just matters of personal prejudice and preference. The flipside of the question "How can there be a good God when there is so much suffering in the world?" is the question, "If there is no God and no meaning, why do I care about the suffering in the world?" Why should I? If you follow the logic to its end, the slaughter of cattle in England because of Hoof and Mouth Disease is a matter of indifference. But, then, so is the slaughter of teenagers in a suburban high school. It's all the same. There is no logical reason to give the lives of children priority over the lives of cattle. They are both just the accidental byproducts of evolution and history. Our inclination otherwise is only conditioned sentimentalism.

But, that is a dry and weary land where no water is and humans cannot live there. According to a recent book, even so honest and courageous an atheist as Camus could not live there. However much our minds might say that there is no meaning, our hearts cry out in contradiction, "No!" Our hearts insist that there is meaning. It's not a matter of indifference. When a child is abused, tortured and killed, my response is not just a matter of my own personal preference. The response of my heart is in tune with the response at the heart of the universe. The offense I take at the slaughter of innocents, or for that matter the accidental deaths along the way, is not just an offense against my preferences, but is an offense against the very fabric of reality. That offense, the offense we take in the

196

face of suffering and injustice does not prove that there is a God, but it at least points us towards God.

In the gospel referred to, some people come to Jesus, and ask, "What about the people who were murdered by Pilate and whose blood was mingled with their sacrifices? Were they killed because of their sins?" Jesus responded, "No." "What about the people who were killed in the accident in Siloam when the tower fell on them? Did they die because of their sins?" Again, Jesus answers, "No." Jesus does not offer a nice and neat answer to why there is such suffering. His response in this gospel is uncomfortably blunt. In essence he says, "The suffering of others, the tragic deaths of others, might well give us pause to remind ourselves that our time also is short and we have no guarantees of how long we will be around. Therefore, today is the day to repent. Today is the day to turn and seek God." He also suggests in the parable that, as the bumper sticker used to say, "'manure' happens". But manure is fertilizer. If you look at your own life, often it is the hurts and the sufferings that cause spiritual growth. Still, that does not explain *why* there is suffering. It's not much comfort when you're in the midst of pain, or when you look at things as horrific as the holocaust. For better or for worse, Jesus does not give us a clear, nice and neat answer to why there is suffering. Neither does the rest of the Bible or Christian tradition. In the book of Job in the Old Testament, God's ultimate response to Job's query about why he is suffering is to say, "It's beyond you. It is hidden in the mystery of God's own being." Not the answer Job was looking for. Not the answer we want. We don't like it because we want to have answers. We have been bred to believe that we have the right, and the capacity, to understand anything if we just put our minds to it.

And so, we create answers. To bring it under control, we invent reasons for the suffering that befalls us. Surely the people who died in that accident at Siloam were worse sinners and that was just God's way of getting back at them for their sins. Everybody suffers. The reason you suffer is because of what you have done in your life or perhaps because of what your parents did. It's all payback. Jesus says, "No. That's not how it works."

The idea of reincarnation is a related way of addressing the reality of suffering. You

197

get what you deserve, if not in this life, in the next. Whatever you get in this life, good or bad, is the result of what you earned in lives before. Everything that happens to you is karmic payback. The karmic ledger, sooner or later, will be balanced. We all get what we deserve. You may remember Shirley McClain's book *Out on a Limb* where she writes about her spiritual explorations and espouses the idea of reincarnation. In that book she recounts a journey she made, a pilgrimage to Macchu Picchu, the Inca ruins in the Andes. Traveling with one of her teachers along a winding mountain road, they came across a place where a bus had driven off the road, rolled down the ravine, and crashed – most likely killing everyone in it. Shirley McClain's response was; "How tragic, how terrible." Her teacher said, "Actually, nobody got anything they didn't deserve." It's all karmic payback. Reincarnation is a nice and neat and tidy answer to why there is suffering. But Jesus says, "No."

The best Christian approach to the existence of evil and suffering is to suggest that God has this thing about freedom. God makes space for us and for all creation. That means he also makes space for us to make a mess of it, to make a mess of one another, to make a mess of ourselves. But even that doesn't really satisfy. Does God have to make so much space for freedom? Why does God tolerate so much suffering and injustice? Why has God created such a world? If God is at the heart of it all, the creator and sustainer, he is not off the hook.

Which is, of course, the point of the Gospel? On the cross, God puts himself on the hook. God, in Christ, enters in to the mess that we have made of the world. God, in Christ, on the cross, enfolds and absorbs the pain and suffering of the world. He transforms it into resurrection. There is the promise that we too will be transformed, our pain, our suffering, will be transformed. By his wounds, we will be healed. As we read in the above psalm, "He will forgive all our sins and heal all of our infirmities." We live in a world of great suffering, of great injustices. It can be a hard place. It can be a hard place to believe in God, especially the generic God of human imagination. But the God we know in Jesus Christ is not a God of our own imagining. He is the God of the cross. Karl Barth wrote, "God earns the right to be God in this world on the cross." God earns the right to be God in *this* world - with all its pain, suffering, and injustice - on the cross

Elie Wiesel, a Jewish writer who survived Auschwitz, wrote about his experiences in a book called *Night*. He relates a tragedy within the tragedy that occurred during his time at Auschwitz. Four Jews, including a young boy, were accused of some breach of the concentration camp's rules. They were hung in front of all the other prisoners. Elie Wiesel recounts that somebody in the assembly watching the hanging, asked, "Where is God now? Where is God?" And another voice responded, "There is God . . . hanging, dead." I suggest, with some trepidation, that that was exactly the right response. Indeed, God was there, hanging, as God is there always hanging, hanging on the cross. God earns the right to be God in this world . . . on the cross. He does not explain the suffering, but he comes to fill it with his presence and promises to transform it. French poet, Paul Caudel, wrote that Jesus did not come to end suffering (at least not immediately). Jesus did not even come to explain suffering. Jesus came to fill suffering with his presence.

In the Gospel of John (9:1-5), there is a story similar to the one we have this morning from the Gospel of Luke. There, Jesus is asked if a man who was born blind was born so because of his sin or because of the sins of his parents. Again, Jesus' response is, "No." But then he says, "This man was born blind to reveal the works of my Father." Where are the works of the Father revealed? On the cross. In the resurrection. In Jesus' presence by the power of the Holy Spirit. There, heart and mind meet. There we see the works and the glory of God. And *that's* a God you can believe in.

# Challenge 28
## What happens when believers sin?

*(A shared experience of Bruce Clark)*

(To fully understand Bruce's situation I would suggest that the reader see his biography before reading his contribution.  Jack Clark)

A few weeks back, my wife Eliza's great Uncle (the husband of the Glaucoma-blinded Aunt Rosie) felt so very bad.  They had little to no money and so HIS decision was to avoid racking up bills and remain home and "tough it out" regarding his illness.  Rosie lives in the poorest of poor areas our Philippine family lives in called ENGLIS (NO H).  I can NOT visit them as the cement steps are narrow and no railing and I almost fell on the past visits.  THEN the house steps are weak and rickety.  I have, on occasion sent small food gifts, BUT I don't often think about them.  I have NEVER said a word to him although we exchanged pleasant smiles and I feel touched that this man is (and has been) a good husband and father.  NEVER a complaint heard about him from the family.  He is ONE OF THE FEW who received a Social Pension.  It was Eliza's grandfather who helped him get a job and then he paid to Philippine Social Security.

A few days ago, I sat up, panicked, and felt like Tevia in Fiddler on the Roof for real, as I had dreamed about Rosie's husband and felt GOD, through the Holy Spirit ASKED STRONGLY for me to send MONEY to help.  Feeling I might just be having my normal FEVER (I had one), I could rationalize my dream.  I had to ask Eliza what Rosie's husband's name was; as I said, only pleasant smiles had EVER been exchanged.  A name, Fernando was given to my "dream" subject.

I told Eliza very distinctly and exactly that I had felt called by the Holy Spirit to help (in my mind about $100.00), BUT, with assurance he was doing Okay, and the instructions and soothing of my wife, I was convinced to reevaluate the dream and situation.

Rationalizing, I purchased some food for them the next day and sent it to their home.  He (Fernando) and Rosie thanked Eliza through a third party family member telephone call almost immediately.  The next day, it was reported that Fernando went outside and was walking around the "family compound" area, enjoyed talking to Eliza's cousin, Eric, and enjoyed the fresh air.  A while later, he died.

I hurt so bad, not because he died, but because I did NOT listen to God. I am so sorry I didn't listen to Him... How I betray my God. I hang him minutely on the cross. How can I ask for forgiveness for my continued sins? This is truly a sin of omission where I have no indication and NO CARE if a million U.S. dollars would have helped this man breathe one more breath. God spoke; I heard; I CHOSE to ignore. Now I show my true side. I am more Satan's Angel then God's blessing.

I have found new meanings to less then new thoughts about pain. Pain of the physical kind MUST go, but the spiritual... Perhaps there is a reason "ghosts and spirits" cannot find peace. By the way, I have begun a new questioning on a phrase "rest in Peace" ... Why? I don't want to REST but to do God's glorious work (I hope anyway). I HOPE that part of a "thin healthy spirit" means I DON'T HAVE to be in bed anymore! NO REST in PEACE for me as my spirit is, somehow, more the messenger of Satan... AND IF by Grace (as the song says), a "spiritual lobotomy" can cast this evil out, then I want to do Glorious "Deeds" for the one who made it possible.

I guess my loss and low feelings come from the understanding that forgiveness comes from repentance, and repentance means to "go and sin no more" yet I never stop sinning even in the middle of a prayer to stop sinning... God knows this yet, he hasn't char broiled my evil spirit; there must be a chance somewhere.

Give to me your Evil ways for they surely can find refuge in my black spirit....

I didn't let Rosie or Fernando DOWN... I let God Down. Fernando was an opportunity to act upon a direct instruction from Christ. I understood (Often I don't), REFUSED and rejected.

One time, I remember asking about judgment on those from areas where a messenger of God had not been (parts of South America, Pigmies, Etc.). My Dad said, as I remember, that he was convinced the Holy Spirit still teaches and therefore accountability still exists even in these places. Yes, I think he is correct. Worse for those who Know God has chosen and called them then THEY rejected. We don't DESERVE Hell. It seems we deserve even worse: God's "Unthinking us from existence."

We are warned of Satan and Judas... God forgot to warn of – Bruce. The truth hurts.

I would close with love, but I think I don't understand it, and I wonder if I even deserve to use it in any sentence or even a thought.

*(A response from Jack Clark)*

"All have sinned and fallen short of the glory of God."[275] That includes everyone – you, dear reader, me, and Bruce as he so deeply felt in the above event. God certainly knows of our sins – they may be sins of thought, action, or omission of an action desired by God. Christians have sometimes referred to some sins being worse than others – mortal sins, but it seems that in God's mind there is only one unforgivable sin, blasphemy against the Holy Spirit.[276] Other sins, if ignored, can certainly lead to our spiritual death, but they don't have to. Paul wrote that he often found himself not doing the things he wanted to do and doing those things that he didn't want to do.[277] It's helpful to know that he suffered the same problem that Bruce and all the rest of us have.

It's even more helpful that God, His Son and His Holy Spirit know about our problem and have devised a solution. The solution is that God's son took onto himself all the sins of the world that could have led to our spiritual death. He chose to do it. No one forced him to. All we have to do is accept the gift and be decent enough to acknowledge it and make sure others know it's available to them. God promised that if we do He will blot out our sins – totally forget them[278] – remove them from us as far as the east is from the west. [279] While the Scriptures say that God will forget, they don't say we will forget them. If we totally forgot them how would we try to avoid them in the future?

On our end of the problem of sinning there are several aspects to our dealing with it. First is conviction – recognizing that something we have done or not done or even thought leads to separation from God or others. Then comes contrition or remorse – feeling sorry. The next step in the management of our sins is confession. Some find it helpful to confess to a priest or other confidant, and there is certainly nothing wrong with this, but if we prefer we can go directly to Jesus who will take it to God. "There is one God and one mediator between God and man, the man Christ Jesus."[280] The next step in dealing with

---

[275] Romans 3:23 (NIV)
[276] Matthew 12:31, Mark 3:29, and Luke 12:10
[277] Romans 7:18-19
[278] Isaiah 43:25
[279] Psalm 103:12
[280] First Timothy 2:5 (NIV)

our sin is restitution – making it right for the one who was sinned against – if this is possible. Then comes repentance. Repentance is a lot more than being sorry. It involves turning away from the sin with a resolve that we will do our best and ask God's help in trying to avoid the sin in the future. The final action is accepting sanctification – the restoring of rightness offered by Jesus.

In trying to avoid future sins, we can pray for God's help. We can ask brothers and sisters to pray for us. (Having a friend ask me to pray that he could avoid going back to smoking was a special honor for me.) We can make a conscious effort to avoid things that might lead us to sin. (As a man "thinketh in his heart, so he is."[281]) Paul gives some good advice in this area too: "Whatever is true, whatever is noble, whatever is right, whatever is pure, whatever is lovely, whatever is admirable - if anything is excellent or praiseworthy - think about such things."[282]

A couple Bible verses are a real comfort when we feel the weight of our sin and feel the pain it brings to God, Jesus, and the Holy Spirit. "There is now no condemnation for those who are in Christ Jesus."[283] "If God is for us, who can be against us?" "Who shall separate us from the love of Christ? Shall trouble or hardship or persecution or famine or nakedness or danger or sword? No, in all these things we are more than conquerors through him who loved us. For I am convinced that neither death nor life, neither angels nor demons, neither the present nor the future, nor any powers, neither height nor depth, nor anything else in all creation, will be able to separate us from the love of God that is in Christ Jesus, our Lord."[284]

(A response for Bruce from Betty Berger)

Hi,

After reading what Bruce wrote, my heart hurt for him. Surely he knows that our loving God does not consider him the way he thinks. God is love, and would want Bruce to know that He stands beside him with His loving arms around Him saying, "So, you missed it this time. Just do better next time; it's ok."

Think about this, Bruce: when the devil came to Adam and Eve in the Garden, he came to steal the righteousness, dominion, wholeness, freedom, peace, and joy that God had given them.

---

[281] Proverbs 23:6 (KJV)
[282] Philippians 4:8 (NIV)
[283] Romans 8:1 (NIV)
[284] Romans 8:31, 35, & 37-39 (NIV)

When they sinned, they lost their relationship with God. At that very moment, God put into action a plan to restore what the devil had stolen. That plan was for His Son, Jesus Christ, to come and get back what had been taken from them and also from us. That included a renewed relationship with God, but also it takes into account everything that has been stolen from us.

In Joel we find a situation where Israel had sinned against God, and sin opened the door for the enemy to come in, steal, kill, and destroy. God told Israel through his prophet, "Rend your heart and not your garments; return to the Lord your God, for He is gracious and merciful, slow to anger and of great kindness and relents from sending harm."[285]

You have had your peace and joy stolen from you. This is the time to open your heart to God and get into position to rise up and say, "I'm taking it back." Go after it with your faith. Nothing is too hard for the Lord.

I have six simple words for you, Bruce: God is not mad at you! He IS mad about you.

The willingness of God not to let what we do, say feel, or think break His relationship with us is a model to help us forgive and keep on loving one another with no strings attached.

God is good. His Word is true, and it works in my life…. Yours too.

---

[285] Joel 2:13 (TNIV)

## Challenge 29
# How can my individuality continue to exist after the death of my physical brain?

*(Jack Clark's answer)*

Sometimes we can find signs of life unexpectedly. It can be when a flower blooms in the middle of a construction site, or in a dry desert, or poking out of a rocky cliff.

On the first resurrection morning no one was expecting to find any sign of life when Mary and the other women and later when Peter and John went to the grave. To their bewildered surprise, life in the resurrected, living savior of the world was exactly what they found.

Earlier Jesus had commented to a group of Sadducees who were questioning him about the resurrection of the dead. He had said, "You do not know the Scriptures or the power of God... Have you not read what God said to you? 'I am the God of Abraham, the God of Isaac, and the God of Jacob.'[286] He is not the God of the dead but of the living."[287] God had used the present tense verb – not the past tense. God in the original quotation and Jesus in his explanation indicated that Abraham, Isaac, and Jacob were still alive!

I've thought a lot about the reasons for the cross and the resurrection. Obviously the main reason was to show to us that Jesus, God's Christ had paid the ransom for our sins. Christ himself said that another very important reason was that it would draw all men to him.[288] This may seem really strange. I think he was saying that if he could show the unfathomable depth of his love and the mind-blowing ability to continue his life after his physical death that many would be convinced that he has the power not only to forgive our sins but also to offer us eternal life.

Understanding how I could exist forever as an individual after my physical death has always been extremely difficult for me. Other things about God are easier for me to grasp. I can see the created universe testifying all around me to the fact that God exists. I can see the absolute goodness manifest in Jesus Christ and recognize him as the Son of God

[286] Exodus 3:6 (TNIV)
[287] Matthew 22:29-32 (TNIV)
[288] John 12:32

and see his part in God's plan from the very beginning. I have felt the thrill of insights beyond my ability that could have only been a gift of the Holy Spirit "blowing where he wills." But the existence of my mind (myself) apart from my physical brain has, at times, seemed beyond the realm of possibility.

Finally a sense of peace flowed over me when once again the Holy Spirit gave me an understanding beyond my own abilities. I fully understood the significance of Jesus Christ's saying that he was going to the Father to prepare a place for me and for everyone who has faith in him. I accepted the affirmation inherent in Jesus' speaking about our future in Heaven. You may remember that he said, "If it were not so, I would have told you."[289]

There it is. It's just that simple. Jesus is one with the Father. There is no way he would break the commandment about lying. I still don't understand how it can be. I only understand that since Jesus Christ said it, that it most certainly is so.

Just as God's gift of the sun and the rain gives new life in places we wouldn't expect it, God's son gives new life now and eternal life in the future!

*(Sherry Doherty's thoughts)*

The person I am continues in the design of my life that God made. He is and always will be. By His design I am a part of His life. I also feel that in some small way I will also be in those people whose lives I have touched. Maybe not in their memory as a whole person, but in the minute changes I made by being with them, working with them. Am I a different person because of the checkout person at our local mega mart? Of course I am. Their smile or kind word leads me in the direction of happiness. By the same token, if I look at all the people in one day who have affected me, then have I not in some small, small way affected them? If I don't believe that I have made an impact on others' lives, then I would have to wonder why God put me here. Our life is but a brief flash of time, and I truly feel that God put me here to make a difference in the people I meet.

---

[289] John 14:2 (NIV)

208

[Bracketed items have been added by Jack Clark. The following gives insights from the book of Job 19:25-28. The material comes from study of the passage shared by David Schramm in a Hebrew language class he taught in the spring of 2008 at St. Andrew's United Methodist Church in Syracuse, Indiana. In addition to affirming the expectation of life after physical death, several other interesting observations can be made. Bible scholars agree that the book of Job was not written about a Hebrew person. This affirms the acceptance of interaction between the Holy Spirit and all people – not only between God and the people Israel, or between God and Christians. This of course is also affirmed by the Old Testament's acceptance of interaction between Abram and the non-Hebrew priest Melchizedek.[290] The New Testament indicates the validity of Melchizedek in importance by relating him as being in the same order of the priesthood as Jesus Christ.[291] It explains why it was necessary for Jesus to be born as a human. It predicts a redeemer who will live, die, and arise. It affirms that Job is assured of his own personal resurrection, return of sensory function and personal knowledge after his physical death. Some people suggest that life after death was introduced in the New Testament and not referred to in the Old Testament, but here in what many feel was the first recorded book in the Old Testament, there is a clear reference to resurrection and continued individual life after physical death.]

The passage from Job is: "I know that my redeemer lives. And that in the end he will stand on the earth. And after my skin has been destroyed, yet in my flesh I will see God. I myself will see him with my own eyes – I, and not another. How my heart yearns within me!"[292]

The Hebrew text starts with "I, I know." The pronoun I is followed by the verb know. In Hebrew verbs can have a pronoun attached as occurs here. When this is the case and the pronoun is doubled, it serves to emphasize the pronoun or to make the expression intense. The effect is to express, "I, even I myself know." The Hebrew word used for "know" in this passage implies intimate knowledge – it expresses certainty; it was the word used when the Scriptures said that Adam knew his wife Eve and she bore a child.

---

[290] Genesis 14:18 and Psalm 110:4
[291] Hebrews 5:6
[292] Job 19:25-28 (TNIV)

The word redeemer actually means my kinsman redeemer. This is the word used in the Book of Ruth where Boaz as the relative of Ruth's deceased husband claims her as his wife. In the nations of the near east, only a blood relative could serve as such a redeemer. A stranger could not redeem someone. Even a person from another tribe of Israel could not be the redeemer of someone. This is why Jesus, God's Christ, had to become a physical human being born into the human family – a flesh and blood man. He could not have otherwise been our kinsman redeemer to purchase us back from our slavery to our sin.

The Scriptures go on: "I know that my redeemer lives," or is alive. The term is in the present tense. The passage does not refer to a future event or a past event. Before Job was created his kinsman redeemer, who we now know was Jesus, was alive. This was known to Job by divine revelation from God through the Holy Spirit. To us, it is significant that Jesus himself confirmed our relationship to him by calling us his brothers. This gave him the opportunity to serve as our kinsman redeemer.

The passage continues: "and in the end he will stand on the earth." Some translators translate this "in the end (or after or afterward or at last) he will stand on my grave." "He will stand" could also be translated "arise." This is the same word Jesus used when he raised the daughter of Jairus from the dead.[293] It is a word that expresses an active process rather than a state of being. It would seem that it is the kinsman redeemer (Jesus) who has died and will rise from the dust (referring to his dead body as dust, as in the quotation, "Dust thou art, and to dust thou shall return.")

The passage continues: "and after my skin has been destroyed." Job had among his multiple afflictions a severe skin disorder that he would scrape with a broken piece of pottery. Many presume that this severe skin disease had convinced Job that he was going to die, but the term skin has been destroyed comes from a root word meaning "skin surround." Skin surround seems to refer to the wrapping with a burial shroud done after a person has died. So it would seem that the meaning of this sentence just as well could be that Job was referring to his own death shroud.

Going on: "yet in my flesh I will see God." Thus Job affirms that despite the fact that he

---

[293] Mark 5:22-24 and 35-46

has died that he personally will see God with eyes that were dead but now restored to functioning. The double I as a free standing pronoun and as a part of the verb is used again for emphasis. The verb see is the word used for intensely gazing upon. It is a word from which the word seer as referring to a prophet is derived. The looking involved in such an instance totally captivates the person who does the seeing. The anticipation of seeing God with his own eyes anticipates Job's resurrection as a physical body such as Moses and Elijah had on the Mount of Transfiguration. It is interesting that the Hebrew word for God used here is Eloha; this is the singular form of the word. In most Bible verses, when this word is used for God, the word is Elohim, the plural form of the word. This section could be also translated: I myself will see him with my own eyes – I, and not another." Job again confirms that it will be him who will personally see God using his own resurrected eyes with no intermediary, and that seeing God he will know God without the need of another human to act as an intermediary.

"How my heart yearns within me!" The Hebrew word used here is kidneys instead of heart. Ancient people in the near east understood kidneys to be the seat of emotions. We may chuckle, but in fact when we in the western world refer to heart as the seat of the emotions, it is no more accurate. Job is eager for the fulfillment of his understanding.

# What if you Christians are wrong?

In the final analysis, what if you are wrong?  What if there is no God?  What if there is no eternal life?

*(Jack Clark's thoughts)*

First of all, I would say that my conviction is that God Is.  That is to say that God exists and that everything else derives its existence from God.  I feel as certain of this as I am of anything else.  It would be easier for me to concede that my own existence is in question – a dream – than to doubt God's existence.

Paul observes that if there is no resurrection of Christ and no resurrection of the dead, our faith is futile, we are still in our sins, and we are to be pitied more than all men.[294]  Of course the atheist would respond, "For once Paul is right on."

I would take a little different view of the matter than Paul.  I am convinced of the truth of the testimony about Christ and the great gift he has offered us, but conceding that there is a theoretical possibility that I could be wrong, I would say that my life has already been vastly enriched by what I have believed and the change my belief has made in me.  If this enrichment would be the sum total of the benefit of my belief, then I wouldn't have it any other way.

Some people have argued that even if there is a God, the idea of eternal life was a late one with almost no indication in the Old Testament.  In some way, they seem to think this negates the possibility that there is eternal life.  This in their thinking would make relating to God or serving God unnecessary, as there would be no eternal life or eternal existence apart from God (Hell).  Certainly Jesus gives our most complete understanding of the possibility of the blessings of Heaven, but I would point to a couple earlier references.  Probably the most well known is from the Twenty-Third Psalm where the claim is made that "I will dwell in the house of the Lord forever."  Less frequently thought of are verses from the book of Job.  It's not certain when Job (that translates where is my Father?) was written, but most authorities suggest about 1500 BC which would make it the oldest written book in the Bible.  It seems unlikely that Job, an undisputed model of virtue, was even an Israelite.  The verses that obviously refer to life after death are: "I know that my

---

[294] I Corinthians 15:4-19 (NIV)

redeemer lives, and that in the end he will stand on earth (or on my grave). And after my skin has been destroyed, yet in my flesh I will see God. I myself will see him with my own eyes – I and not another. How my heart yearns within me!"[295] At this time of history, many people were convinced that either good or bad things in life resulted form one's actions. Job, who could not give a satisfactory answer to his friends about what he had done to cause all his misfortune, anticipates being saved by a redeemer – God. He is convinced that the awful disease from which he suffers that has covered his body with sores, made his breath so foul that his wife can't stand to be near him is going to be fatal. But despite this, even after he has died, he is convinced that he will see God with his very own eyes. This could only happen through life after death.

Going on to the argument that there is no God, I would say that if God doesn't exist and if there is no eternal life, it would seem that I would never have an opportunity to realize it, as I would pass from this life into oblivion. Three years before I was born there was a world-wide economic depression. Although it was a terrible problem for people trying to make a living then, and it had a severe effect on my parents and grandparents, it had no direct effect on me. If our sum total is that we are a collection of complex organic molecules that developed by spontaneous accident in a universe that developed by spontaneous accident and we have no purpose or plan, then oblivion is the source from which we came and oblivion is our destination. I don't think this will be the case, but that's not terrifying. At the very worst we will be no worse off than we were in our non-existent state before our birth.

On the other hand, if I and a lot of other believers are right, contemplate the result for those who hold this premise when they complete this life. I've said that I consider a relationship with Christ and through him with the Father to be more life assurance than fire insurance, but there is that aspect to consider too. "We have this hope as an anchor for the soul, firm and secure."[296]

*(Another view- from Cathy Ann Turner)*

I was talking with my brother-in-law whose wife had just died. He suggested that he just really doesn't know if there is anything after the "here and now" and he says that it doesn't really bother him to think that there might not be anything else.

---

[295] Job 19:25-27 (TNIV)
[296] Hebrews 6:19

Sometimes I think conversion is easier with a younger person – they've not lived long enough to have so many deep thoughts about "what ifs" and "what if nots" nor have they been so self reliant for an extensive period of time.  Faith is easier when you don't know some of the questions to ask.

*(A view of Betty Berger)*

If you live a Christian life anyway, this is the only hell you will know.  For the unbeliever's life, this life will be the best he will ever know.  Walking in love has its own rewards.  Paul said, "Love never fails."[297]

*(Dean Culbertson's answer)*

What if there is no God or eternal life?  Then I have been spared sexually-transmitted diseases, alcoholism, worship of stone "gods" (who would have no actual existence for the purposes of this question), and many other things that would only hurt my short life.

(I love this part!)  Having answered that, it's my turn.  What if there really is a God who would have you saved?  What if He really <u>does</u> judge disbelief?  Honestly, if one or the other proved to be wrong, I think it would hurt the one who asked this question worse than it would hurt the believer.

*(Betty Byers' answer)*

I know Christians are right!  There is a God.  Jesus said he will come again.  The Bible mentions Heaven and Hell.

*(Mark Eastway's understanding)*

Questions regarding ultimate reality are very important for all of us to ask, since the answers may impact our eternal destiny:  Is there a God?  If so, what is God like?  Is He the Christian God or the god of some other religion?  Contrary to the opinion of many secularists, it is possible to think objectively regarding God, and to decide what we believe

---

[297] I Corinthians 13:8 (AB)

based on the evidence.

Probability studies on the formation of the human eye or on our incredibly complex DNA through natural selection appear to demonstrate that it is nearly mathematically impossible for their development without the intervention of an intelligent designer. Studies of Biblical prophecies and their fulfillment in Christ provide strong evidence that the Bible must have been written by someone who is all-knowing. And the logical necessity of a perfect Savior to die for our sins to meet the standard of a perfect God, as described in the Bible, is intellectually satisfying; so much so, that it would only be wise and prudent to conclude that the Biblical message is trustworthy and true.

However, this does not mean we will not have doubts. For example, one could speculate that God could be something far more mischievous than the God portrayed in the Bible. What if wrong is right and right is wrong? What if God decided to save from hell only those who did not believe in the God of the Bible? What if God intends that all of us will be excluded from heaven, no matter what we believe? Since, as human beings, our knowledge is so very limited, such reasoning can only be speculative, and, as a result, unhelpful.

Of much less concern is the possibility that God does not exist. The consequence of facing eternal annihilation is far less worrisome than finding oneself eternally in the hands of a wrathful God. Only the insane would chose never-ending torment over soul sleep.

On a practical level, nothing is lost if Christians, in spite of our best reasoning, prove to be wrong and there is no God. Research has demonstrated that people who live by Christian values are some of the happiest people in the world. For example, according to a 2006 Pew Research Study, *People who attend religious services weekly or more are happier (43% very happy) than those who attend monthly or less (31%); or seldom or never (26%)*. And they conclude *this correlation between happiness and frequency of church attendance has been a consistent finding in the General Social Surveys taken over the years.*

In other words, if there is no God, the only meaning one can find is in the temporal here-and-now. However, if the Christian lifestyle brings the greatest pleasure, it would seem to be the most appealing lifestyle, even for the practicing hedonist.

Of much greater concern is if atheists are wrong and there is a God? The potential negative consequences of their decision will be much greater than for Christians; more specifically, eternal torment. This may be the only natural explanation of behavior that is inconsistent with their held views. For example, there is logically no reason why so many atheists should be as passionate as they are about extinguishing any vestiges of Christianity in the public arena, except for the fear that they are wrong and can't bear being reminded of the possible consequences of their decisions.

So in answer to the question, it would seem Christians have the best of both worlds: We live the most happy and fulfilling lives in the here-and-now, and we have good reason to believe that eternity will bring us a greatly improved quality of life. In contrast, atheists are at risk of living unhappy and unfulfilled lives, only to be faced with the possible terrible consequences of rejecting God.

## Challenge 31
# What did Jesus mean when He said his followers would do greater things than he did?

What was Jesus talking about when he said anyone who has faith in me will do what I have been doing? He will do even greater things than these, because I am going to the Father, and I will do whatever you ask in my name, so that the Son may bring glory to the Father."[298] (Submitted by Betty Berger)

*(An answer from Jack Clark)*

First let me say what I don't think he was saying. Some people interpret this to mean that there has been a loss or a partial loss of the gifts of the Holy Spirit given at Pentecost, because in modern times only a few speak in tongues or interpret tongues and the frequency of classical miracles seems to be less. They imply that if we had more faith we would exceed Jesus and the early church both individually and as the modern church in these areas.

It seems to me that Jesus was indicating that his followers would be able to multiply the telling of the good news and the making of disciples because we would be able to branch out and contact more people with our testimony than Jesus could during His time on earth. After all these are the two special assignments he gave us.[299] Of course, the Holy Spirit can and does contact all people, so Jesus certainly wasn't indicating we would be able to accomplish more that God could in this area. I think it's also significant that Jesus very clearly informs us that we won't be doing this under our own power, but that we will be doing it through Him and in answer to our prayers given in His name.

---

*(An observation by Joyce Schramm)*[300]

Throughout the New Testament followers of Jesus receive the challenge to become Christ-like in thought, word, and deed. That seems like a daunting task, considering our many failures and inadequacies. How can we think only pure thoughts and speak words of forgiveness and life? How can we heal the sick, raise the dead, or calm the seas? That may have been possible for the Son of God, but we are merely human. And yet Jesus proclaimed that anyone who has faith in Him will do what He did while here on earth (John 14:12). Surely He would not have issued this prophetic word if He knew it were impossible.

---

[298] John 14:12-13 (NIV)
[299] Matthew 28:1920
[300] This article is copyrighted © 2008 by Joyce Schramm, used with permission.

The baptism of Jesus gives us a clue to the divine provision to overcome our human failings and to enable us to fulfill our miraculous calling. In Philippians we discover the master plan that Jesus set before us: "Let this mind be in you, which was also in Christ Jesus: Who, being in the form of God, thought it not robbery to be equal with God, but made himself of no reputation and took upon him the form of a servant and was made in the likeness of man. And being found in fashion as a man, he humbled himself, and became obedient unto death, even the death of the cross.[301]

Although he was a co-equal part of the God-head, Jesus submitted to the divine plan of salvation by becoming like a man, dying daily to Himself, and submitting to the voice of the Father. The phrase "made himself of no reputation" literally means "he emptied himself." Although He was still divine, He became like man by emptying Himself of His divine powers. All Jesus did, including His miracles, were done in the power of the Holy Spirit as He followed the Father's direction. Jesus said, "I tell you the truth, the Son can do nothing by himself; he can do only what he sees his Father doing, because whatever the Father does the Son also does."[302]

As we study Jesus' pattern of dying to His own will by submitting to the will of the Father in the act of baptism and then receiving the infilling of the Holy Spirit, the truth that we too can do the same transforms our understanding of walking in His footsteps. Everything that Jesus did on earth, He did as a man, guided by the Heavenly Father and empowered by the Holy Spirit. In baptism by water and by the Spirit we can die to our rebellious egos and be empowered by the Holy Spirit to hear the voice of the Father and act on His directives. Then we can become like Christ. We can do His work of preaching good news to the poor, proclaiming freedom to the prisoners and recovery of sight to the blind, to release the oppressed, and to proclaim a visitation of the Lord's favor.[303] We are without excuse. Jesus said we would do as He did and in His baptism He clearly showed us the way.

---

[301] Philippians 2: 4 (KJV)
[302] John 5:19 (NIV)
[303] Luke 4:18

# Why spend so much time analyzing what we believe and dissecting it instead of just having faith in God through Jesus?

(An observation of Judy Hardy)

It seems we often spend too much time on small details such as trying to figure out how miracles might have happened or exactly what a given sentence of scripture means instead of simply taking the scriptures at face value and placing our faith in the salvation of Christ, declaring our faith to others, and trying to follow His plan for our lives.

(From Harlan Steffen)

To be very honest with you, I do not get excited about many of the questions proposed for this book. I guess I see nothing wrong with theorizing and voicing speculative answers to these questions. Many of them could be very debatable. Hopefully you would make very clear at the very beginning of the book that there is one main focus in the Christian faith – and that is Jesus. Hopefully, these issues would not lead to doubt and uncertainty in the faith.

I'm sorry but my plate already is more than full. Our community and our county have a very serious drug and alcohol problem. I am devoting a lot of my time to helping with this issue. I'm told that 90% of the inmates in our county jail are there due to drug and alcohol involvement. Every week I visit at the jails and prisons throughout the state. I've received many calls from people who want me to visit family and friends and try to help them find a new direction in life – Jesus. Also, for that reason, I became instrumental in helping to put together the Rose Home on the north edge of Syracuse, which is a halfway house for women with drug and alcohol problems.

Very honestly, I would like to see a lot more effort put towards the solving of this problem. Your program (writing this book) certainly can become very fascinating, but I'm not sure that it would do much for the real problems of our community and world. For that reason, I will not be more involved with your project, but I do wish you God's blessing and guidance as you seek to do His will.

The above two Christians were among the one hundred thirty five people I contacted to invite them to contribute to this book. Although all were friends, not everyone including these two had a strong urge from the Holy Spirit to be a part of this. They and some others didn't see much need for such a book. Several were too busy. Others like my long-time friend Dale Allen said these were some of the questions he has and didn't feel he had the answers. If some like Dale had questions but no answers, then the book seems to have some potential for use by brothers and sisters in Christ.

Will the book contribute to some readers accepting Christ as their personal savior? I have no idea, but I feel the urge was there from the Holy Spirit to accomplish something in the life of someone. Perhaps it was to bolster the faith of a brother or sister in Christ by resolving some questions. Perhaps it was to help me or those who did contribute to explore our own faith more deeply and to grow spiritually. Perhaps it was to help lead someone toward accepting the salvation of the Holy Spirit in their own lives. If any of these ends result, it's worth while.

It seems that God's Holy Spirit relates to each person differently as their different personalities require. So for some a faith with little questioning can result in a great relationship with Christ; whereas, for others deep questioning can increase our understanding of and faith in God. I'm reminded of Paul's statement that he became all things to all people so that by all possible means some might be saved.[304]

There are many people in our society who see Christianity and the Church as totally irrelevant. I've mentioned this in the question about Christianity and science, but it goes much deeper. The people Rev. Steffen is working with who are committing slow suicide by their addictions are doing so because they haven't found meaning in life – they have lost their way – a few never found their way in the first place. There are others who place their total importance in life in their own desires – this self-worship is idolatry. There are those who have no idea at all about what Christianity is. You don't have to go to some far-off, out-of-the-way place to find these people. One of the teachers in the day care center right next to our congregation asked one of our members, "What goes on over there?" She had never been to a worship service anywhere and really had no idea of what was going on. For those who don't have an understanding about what we do in the church, we

---

[304] First Corinthians 9:19-22

need to get out the message that we meet together to worship the living God who created everything – including us – and to give Him our praises for the great gifts He has given us. We meet together to study the word of God in the Bible and to understand that most of the challenges of living we have today have been shared by people in Bible times. We meet together to pray to God for the needs of others and for our needs. We meet together to help each other grow to be more like Jesus in our thoughts, concerns, and actions. We meet together to help others grow spiritually and to be helped to grow spiritually by others. We meet together to give love and support to each other. We meet together to have fun and enjoy each others' company. We meet together help others who have special needs and problems – not only those in our congregations. We meet together to work toward helping our communities be better places for everyone. Seemingly we hadn't done a very good job of getting the message out, especially since our congregation had donated the land on which the Day Care Center was built and where this lady worked.

To some people Christianity is as relevant to living as Santa Claus, the tooth fairy, or a Disney character. We aren't doing what our savior required of us when he said that we are to go into all the world and spread the good news. Part of that world is right next door to us! What if we could give a reason for living to people before they give up and turn to an addiction or a false god? For those who overcome anything leading them away from God including an addiction, the book of Revelation suggests there will be great rewards.

Questions and challenges to faith do have the potential to lead to doubt and uncertainty in the faith as Rev. Steffen suggested, and that would be an unwanted result. It seems to me that an unanswered question or an unanswered challenge might be more likely to cause doubt and uncertainty than a thought-through response.

Paul speaks of putting on the full armor of God so that we can take our stand against the devil's schemes. He speaks of a struggle against the powers of this dark world and against the spiritual forces of evil in the heavens.[305] The armor of God (truth, righteousness, the gospel of peace, faith, salvation, prayer) is certainly of primary importance, but training oneself and being ready for the struggle, doubts, temptations, and challenges is important too. Only with this preparation can we be ready as this scripture tells us to stand our ground.

---

[305] Ephesians 6:13-18

The importance of faith compared to works is addressed in another question in this book and relates to the concerns noted above by Judy and Harlan. The conclusion, of course, is that both are important.

Peter wrote, "Always be prepared to give an answer to everyone who asks you to give the reason for the hope that you have."[306] For me, having thought through some of these tough questions and challenges before hand has been helpful. If I'm sharing the reason for my hope in the Bible study class with other believers, or standing off a challenge to my faith that Satan may sneak in like he did when he challenged Jesus,[307] such preparation has been helpful. One very minor challenge was given to me by a non-believing older patient who noticed the small cross on my jacket lapel and demanded, "Why do you wear that thing?" Being ready gave me a chance to tell him why my faith is important to me. (I wear the cross to remind me of how much the Father, the Son, and the Holy Spirit love me. I wear the cross to remind me of the terrible price they paid for my salvation. I wear the cross as a reminder to me that I have chosen to give my love and service to God and Jesus, and I wear the cross to let others know of my choice and as an invitation to become a follower of Christ and share in the joy.) A bigger challenge came when a patient had been expelled from his church's communion upon confessing a sexual sin that occurred years before. I have discussed this in the challenge titled "God save me from the Christians."

Not everyone has the same gifts, but everyone's gifts are important, so certainly not everyone is called on to be an author.[308] Like Rev. Steffen I too have worked in my medical practice with multiple people addicted to alcohol, tobacco, and drugs. He's right – it is a big and an important problem. It requires a great deal of time, love, and the ability to start over and to not be defeated by failures. I've been involved in rescuing a number of people trapped in these addictions. I've also been involved in some failures such as a co-dependant husband and wife whose careers and lives went down the drain of alcoholism and a patient who I was able to help escape a lifelong addiction to alcohol only to have his grandson who was also a patient die of the same problem. These works and others are an important part of our Christian lives. They represent to me the taking up of our crosses that Jesus advised we must do.[309]

---

[306] First Peter 3:15 (NIV)
[307] Matthew 4:1-11, Mark 1:12-13, and Luke 4:1-13
[308] First Corinthians 12:1-30
[309] Matthew 10:38-39 and 16:24-26; Mark 8:34-36; and Luke 9:23-26 and 14:27

# How can the Bible be trusted?

How can Christians claim the Bible is the inerrant word of God, when it has some conflicting accounts?

*(Observations of Jack Clark)*

(Much of the answer for this question was borrowed from another book I have written.[310])

There are two views held by believers about what is written in the Bible. Most Evangelistic Christians or Fundamentalists understand the Bible to be literally the Word of God completely without any error. The view of some other Christians is that the Bible was inspired by God, written under the guidance of God by great men of God, but colored by the understanding, knowledge, literary abilities, and occasionally the prejudices or failures of those who recorded the Scripture. The latter group and the former would agree totally on the vast majority of the Scripture as being true literally or written in allegorical terms.

The author of Hebrews states, "In the past God spoke to our forefathers through the prophets at many times and in various ways, but in these last days he has spoken to us by his Son."[311] To me this indicates there are differences in expression and understanding and communication as expressed by the writers of the Bible, but all recounting the truth of God in accordance with the grace they were given until the perfect expression of God's message in the person, life, and message of Jesus Christ. Many of the authors of the books of the Old Testament affirm the source of their message and authority with words such as, "Thus says the Lord," "The word of the Lord came to me," "The Lord called to Moses and spoke to him." There are many, many similar declarations in the Old Testament, each one indicating that the statements made by those who employ them are expressing the Word of God. Jesus confirmed the importance of the Old Testament when he affirmed that not the smallest part of the law will pass away until it is all fulfilled.[312] Also a considerable space in the New Testament is given to point out the many ways in which the life of Christ fulfilled the Old Testament prophesy. Paul stated, "All scripture is given by inspiration of God, and is profitable for doctrine, for reproof, for correction, for instruction in righteousness: That the man of God may be perfect, thoroughly furnished

---

[310] *The Reason for the Hope: A Spiritual Journey,* ©1998 by Jack P. Clark, M.D., pp. 106-111
[311] Hebrews 1:1-2 (NIV)
[312] Matthew 5:18 (NIV)

unto all good works."[313] It is important for modern readers to recall that when Paul wrote this, the word Scripture referred to what we now know as the Old Testament. The New Testament was just in the process of being authored, and no gathering together of the writings had begun as yet.

As often happens in my own spiritual journey, I find myself somewhere in between the understanding of my brothers and sisters in Christ who hold opposing views. This is not a comfortable position, as both sides can feel let down or even betrayed by one's views and lack of agreement with their fundamental beliefs. I struggle with this, because I know it will be a disappointment to some of my very dearest friends and fellow Christians who I greatly admire. I struggle with it even more because I passionately want to present the Bible in the perspective God wishes. I am constantly reminded of Paul's observation about theological error: "Each one should be careful how he builds. No one can lay any foundation other than the one already laid, which is Jesus Christ. If any man builds on this foundation using gold, silver, costly stones, wood, hay or straw, his work will be shown for what it is, because the Day will bring it to light. It will be revealed with fire, and the fire will test the quality of each man's work. If what he has built survives, he will receive his reward. If it is burned up, he will suffer loss; he himself will be saved, but only as one escaping through the flames."[314] I have prayed for guidance, but as sometimes happens God has sent many ideas to help in my understanding, but no perceptible universal revelation in answer to my prayers.

Benjamin Warfield has made the observation that, "Every word of the Scriptures, without exception, is the word of God, but alongside of that... every word is the word of man."[315] Perhaps finding this quotation is the answer to my prayers, as this seems to pretty well reflect my personal views.

There are some obvious contradictions and discrepancies in the Scripture. When these are pointed out, some Christians defend the Scripture with the observation that they were passed down by oral tradition for many years before being written in the case of the Old Testament. They point out that this process naturally brought about some differences

---

[313] Second Timothy 3:16-17 King James Version (KJV)
[314] First Corinthians 3:10-15 (NIV)
[315] The Inspiration and Authority of the Bible, Benjamin Warfield, Edited by Samuel G. Craig, Nutley, NJ, Presbyterian and Reformed, 1948, p. 421

such as the differences in the timing of the creation sequence recorded in Genesis. In the first account, man is one of the last things to be created. In the second account, man is one of the first things to be created.[316] I certainly understand this observation and agree with it. Bible scholars can even unravel some of the various accounts by referring to the name used for God in the different accounts. The names Elohim and El were generally used in the account as it was transmitted by the tribes that would make up the Northern Kingdom of Israel. Yahweh was the term generally used by the tribes of Judah and Benjamin that would constitute the southern kingdom of Judah. Of course there were Levites scattered throughout both kingdoms. Having agreed with the observation that explains the reason for the differences, we still come back to the fact that the accounts are different. The same process is evidently involved in the account of the number of animals Noah was to bring into the ark. One account says he was to bring two of every kind of living creature. The other says to take seven pairs of every kind of clean animal and seven pairs of every kind of bird with the one pair designation limited only to the unclean animals.[317]

I have difficulty correlating the recognized fact of these differences with the view of some of my dear and very respected Christian brothers and sisters who stoutly maintain that every word of the Bible is just as God said it and is an exact irrefutable rendition of how it happened according to God.

To me there is a discrepancy I cannot resolve. In my understanding, God inspired the Hebrew people to understand that He did indeed create the world. The order of creation is irrelevant, but the fact that He did create everything is extremely relevant. Likewise the number of the animals in the ark has no spiritual significance. We should not mistake a magnificent Hymn of creation for an historical or scientific document.

Another obvious discrepancy occurs in Exodus. It is recorded that as Moses was seeking to free the Israelites from Pharaoh that there was a terrible plague on the horses, donkeys, camels and cattle of the Egyptians. "All the livestock of the Egyptians died."[318] Later, when Pharaoh finally released the Hebrews, it is recorded that his heart was

---

[316] Compare Genesis 1:1-2:4 with Genesis 2:4-25
[317] Genesis 6:19 and Genesis 7:2
[318] Exodus 9:2-6 (NIV)

hardened again. Pharaoh "pursued them, and all Pharaoh's horses and chariots and horsemen followed them into the sea."[319] If all the horses had been killed in the plague, where did all these horses originate?

There is a great source of concern among some of my very dearest friends that the traditional view of how God accomplished the creation be accepted. I do not see anywhere in scripture a description of how he created those things He made. He could, in my understanding, if he had so wished, have created each thing, animal, and mankind from nothing in either of the orders listed and in a literal seven days' time. Recognizing that much of the Bible is allegorical and written in simile to facilitate a better understanding for the original readers' Eastern manner of thought, we who are used to thinking of things in a somewhat different way, must adapt our thinking in order to understand. Almost any of us would recognize that when Christ referred to his followers as the salt of the earth,[320] he was not indicating that we are literally a crystalline compound made of one atom of sodium and one atom of chlorine. He was, of course, referring to our having some of the properties of salt: adding flavor to the world, preserving what is good, cleansing. Likewise, we should be able to recognize that the Hebrew word *yowm* used in Genesis and traditionally translated day comes from a "root meaning to be hot; a day (as the warm hours), whether literally (from sunrise to sunset, or from one sunset to the next), or figuratively (a space of time defined by an associated term)."[321] It should be obvious that there is no fundamental conflict with changing the word day to some other rendition of a passage of time, even geological ages. It's also interesting that if we insist on the definition of a day as being what we now accept it to be that when the creation hymn in Genesis starts, there is no earth. Since a day as we now measure it is defined as the time it takes for the earth to make one complete rotation on its axis, it seems obvious that at least on that first "day" the time measurement must have been different than what we now recognize it to be.

Some things have obviously been added to material in the Bible at some date later in time than is indicated. For instance, Second Samuel could not have been written by

---

[319] Exodus 14:23 (NIV)
[320] Matthew 5:13 (NIV)
[321] <u>Strong's Exhaustive Concordance, Complete and Unabridged, Compact Edition with Dictionaries of Hebrew and Greek Words</u>, James Strong, S.T.D., L.L.D., Word Books Publisher, Waco, TX, Reprinted 1997, p. 48 of the Hebrew and Chaldee Dictionary

228

Samuel. He was dead before the time of the events recorded. Part of the book of John (7:53-8:11) seems to have been added at some time after the writing of the Gospel. We don't know who added it or just when, but the earliest existing manuscripts don't include this material. The earliest copy of John we have is the "Bodmer II" manuscript dated about AD 200.[322] Had the material been deleted from the earliest manuscripts and re-entered in later ones? Had some writing of John other than the Gospel disclosed these events, and some copier added the material later to the Gospel so that it wouldn't be lost? Could it have come from some other source and have been incorporated into this book? The fact is we don't know the answer. I for one am grateful the material is there. It certainly is one of the things I would have expected the Pharisees and Christ to have done. The actions are entirely consistent with Christ's dealing with people, and I am persuaded, whatever the source, that it is a true recounting of an event that took place. I've led you on to the point that I hope you're asking, "What is this passage?" It's the recounting of the events concerning the woman caught in adultery who the Pharisees tried to use to trap Jesus into saying she should be stoned or that the Law of Moses should be ignored. It tells of how Christ wrote with his finger on the ground and eventually responded, "If any one of you is without sin, let him be the first to throw a stone at her."

We all know who Jesus' Mother was–Mary. We all know that she was impregnated by the Holy Spirit, and that Joseph, Mary's betrothed, married her after he had a vision from God's angel. The world counted Joseph as being Christ's father. There are two accountings of the genealogy of Christ in the New Testament. One is in Matthew[323] that starts with Abraham and goes to Jesus thereby relating Jesus to the Nation of Israel. The other account is in Luke[324] that starts with Jesus and goes back to Adam and God. This is designed to be more significant to the Gentile Christians. Both these accounts state they are the genealogy of Jesus through Joseph; however, the Matthew account names Joseph's father as Jacob while the Luke account names Joseph's father as Heli. Joseph's paternal grandfather in Matthew is Matthan; in Luke it is Matthat. The preceding generation lists Eleazar in Matthew and Levi in Luke. So it is that there is a difference between Jesus and his ancestor David in every generation when the two accounts are compared. The son of David who is listed as the ancestor of Jesus in Matthew is

---

[322] The Bible Almanac, J. I. Packer, Merrill C. Tenney, and William White, Jr., Guideposts, Carmel, NY 10512, 1978, p. 70
[323] Matthew 1:1-16 (NIV)
[324] Luke 3:23-37 (NIV)

Solomon, while the son of David in the Luke account is Nathan, one of Solomon's brothers. Obviously there is a discrepancy here. Every extant copy of the Scriptures and every translation we have available contain this discrepancy. Obviously both accounts cannot be correct; as the genealogies are now stated, one is in error. This is a case where there can be no doubt that our Scripture as we have it does not totally contain the inerrant word of God. My friends who maintain that the Scripture is totally the inerrant word of God, would assert that the original was correct, and some later date scribe made an error. I would agree that this is probably right, and speculate, as do many Bible scholars, that one of these genealogies is presumably Joseph's and one Mary's. We have no way of determining which belongs to what person, but this would certainly seem persuasively likely. It's important to note that if this is the case Jesus still descended from David. We can speculate that it may be more likely that the account in Luke is Mary's genealogy, because we know that Luke spent more time with Mary than Matthew did. The fact still remains that we cannot say in this area that everything in our Bible as it is presently written constitutes the word of God, as there is an obvious error here. Likewise there are some differences in the synoptic Gospel accounts of some of the events recounted by more than one author. If God had been dictating the events to the authors as one would to a secretary, I feel there would have been no differences in the material as recorded.

As another possibility, which seems most likely to me, the material can be considered as the inspired word of God as revealed to men of great faith, great dedication, and a passion to share it at God's behest and because of their concern for others. In this view, God reveals an infallible truth and understanding to those he elected and selected guaranteeing the basic truth of the things they expressed under His prompting and direction. The truths are infallible. The expressions of the truths can include the perspective of the individual. Minor differences in understanding, perception, errors in copying or other unimportant discrepancies in no way detract from God's truth or His power. They only confirm that our Great God can and does use imperfect people to accomplish His ends. If we as His people were perfect or even almost perfect, there would be a terrible temptation to become proud. This seems to have been the awful fate that befell Satan. I for one don't mind being reminded of the multiple reasons I have to feel my humility. I doubt those who wrote the scriptures would feel any differently.

Some people point out that Christ is presented as accepting incorrect views of things. For instance, when a person had an epileptic convulsion they were presumed by the people of the time in which the Bible was written to be demon possessed. When Christ cured epileptics, the Bible describes the event as casting out demons. We now know that epilepsy results from some injury or abnormality to the physical brain that intermittently allows an abnormal discharge of electrical activity. Jesus met the people of the time where they were in their understanding. It wouldn't have helped the situation or increased the peoples' understanding to have entered into a scientific explanation of brain function or electricity. Having no understanding of brain function or electricity on which to base the understanding, it would have been meaningless. In addition to this, it wouldn't have solved the epileptic's problem. No, Jesus solved the problem and gave the glory to God. The Holy Spirit still meets us where we are in our understanding. This also explains why different people today can read the same passage of scripture and get different understanding. For that matter, I may read a passage that I've read many times before and now gain a different understanding; my situation is different, and God meets me where I am at the time.

One of my very favorite people often holds up the Bible and observes that it is the Word of God. I am absolutely certain that it contains the Word of God. I am certain that is the best source and basis of understanding of the Word of God. I am convinced that nothing that is the Word of God will be in conflict or negate what is found in the Bible. I am absolutely certain that everything Jesus said, as it was originally stated, was indeed the Word of God, but I have some doubts that every word in the Bible is the Word of God. This can be a dangerous area, because there is the temptation, if we accept this viewpoint, to say those things that we don't understand or those things in the Bible that seem counter to the understanding God has given us about His nature are not the Word of God. For instance, it is my understanding that Martin Luther felt the book of Revelation should be removed from the Scripture, dismissing it with the comment that, "It finds the author mad and leaves the reader mad." I once heard that Thomas Jefferson who was a professed Christian literally blocked out those parts of the Bible he did not feel were from God. This is a very hazardous mindset. I would encourage no one to contemplate this. I would certainly be much more at ease with those who accept every word in the Bible as being the word of God than I would be with the second type of person.

I certainly don't understand everything in Revelation, but as time goes by and as I study more and as God opens my mind more, I'm able to understand ever-greater themes and truths. For me, it is enough to understand that Jesus is very interested that we as the church constantly re-examine ourselves and strive on toward perfection. It's comforting and important to accept that Jesus stands at the door and knocks in the hope that people will invite him in, and that Satan loses and God wins along with those who love and serve Him. If I could gain no more understanding from Revelation than this, it is more than worthwhile.

Understanding my limitations, I do feel there are some things in the Bible that are not the word of God. Some are historically important; some are interesting insights into the life of the people God made his chosen people, so they certainly have value. I would never suggest that any of the recorded material be deleted. The first chapter of the book of Numbers seems to be a civil record of the nation. It is recorded that this census was ordered by God. The nation was important to God; the nation was a treasure of God, and as such the people who constituted the nation were important, and if God wanted their names recorded, who am I to argue? But I still cannot see that these records, as important as they are, constitute the Word of God. If someday God looks me in the eye, and says, "Jack, you were wrong," I'll certainly defer to that, because I don't understand all of God's ways.

Paul would seem to indicate that, on occasion, what he is writing and what has become part of the Bible is based on his views, and does not constitute God's Word. On other occasions he is very definite that what he is saying does constitute the Word of God. Both positions are expressed in First Corinthians. "To the married I give this command (not I but the Lord): A wife must not separate from her husband. But if she does, she must remain unmarried or else be reconciled to her husband. And a husband must not divorce his wife. To the rest I say this (I, not the Lord): If any brother has a wife who is not a believer and she is willing to live with him, he must not divorce her... for the unbelieving wife has been sanctified through her believing husband... Now about virgins: I have no command from the Lord, but I give a judgment as one who by the Lord's mercy is trustworthy. Because of the present crisis, I think it is good for you to remain as you are."[325] It would seem that while most of the material Paul contributed to what would become the Bible would be recognized by Paul himself as being God inspired and therefore the Word of God, that some of what he wrote was not recognized as such even by the author.

There are unresolved areas in the Bible. On one hand, we read, "No Ammonite or Moabite or any of his descendants may enter the assembly of the Lord even down to the tenth generation. For they did not come to meet you with bread and water on your way when you came out of Egypt, and they hired Balaam son of Beor from Pethor in Aram Naharaim to pronounce a curse on you."[326] Going on to a later time in the history of Israel, we read of the tender relationship between Ruth and Naomi. Ruth, the widowed, loving, and faithful daughter-in-law, returned to Judah with her Jewish widowed mother-in-law Naomi when the famine which had driven Naomi's family out of Israel was over. Her pledge of faithfulness brings admiration from all that hear it. Ruth was a Moabite.[327] Naomi had encouraged her to stay in Moab and go back to her people. Ruth's response was, "Where so ever you go, I will go. Where so ever you stay, I will stay. Your people will be my people and your God my God. Where you die, I will die, and there I will be buried."[328] Ruth remarried Naomi's kinsman after their return to Judah and ultimately was to become the great grandmother of David who became the King of Israel. Nowhere in the scriptures do I detect that David, Solomon or the other descendants of David were excluded from the Tent of the Tabernacle or its successor the Temple; although this obviously was not in conformity with the rule noted in Deuteronomy.

Taking all the above into consideration, the Bible is the best source there is of information about God and His aspirations and provisions for us. I do not understand that any of these observations detract from its importance and its spiritual guidance.

---

*(Comments of George Shaffer)*

Over the years when I was teaching a Bible study class at Trinity United Methodist Church in Warsaw, Indiana I was always careful to neither add anything to the Bible nor

---

[325] First Corinthians 7:10-14 and 7:25-28 (NIV)
[326] Deuteronomy 23:3-4 (NIV)
[327] Ruth 1:4 (NIV)
[328] Ruth 1:16-17 (NIV)

take anything away from the Bible. You will recall that the end of the last chapter of the last book of the Bible reads: "I warn everyone who hears the words of the prophecy of this scroll: If any one of you adds anything to them, God will add to you the plagues described in this scroll. And if any one of you takes words away from this scroll of prophecy, God will take away from you your share in the tree of life and in the Holy City."[329]

I remember a Mennonite preacher who worked on the night shift at Endicott Church Furniture Company where I worked most of my professional life. I'd asked him a question about something in the Bible that seemed doubtful to me. He responded, "Do you believe in the Bible?" To my answer of, "Yes," he advised, "Believe it cover to cover."

*(An observation of Dean Culbertson)*

Show me one conflicting account – I'll show you where the real conflict is!

*(An answer from Betty Byers)*

I understand the Bible to be the inspired word of God written by Godly, holy men.

*(Some insights of David Schramm)*

[Bracketed items have been added by Jack Clark. The following gives insights into probably the best known of the Scriptures – Psalm 23. This Psalm has probably caused more people to trust in the Bible and in God than any other single selection. The material comes first from a sermon by David Schramm in late 2007, and from insights to the Psalm in a Hebrew language class he taught in the winter and spring of 2008. Both were at St. Andrew's United Methodist Church in Syracuse, Indiana.]

The twenty third Psalm starts with the words "A psalm (*mizmowr* in Hebrew) of David" as it is usually translated. The very first word that we translate as "A psalm" indicates "to pluck with the fingers." This suggests a couple things: the psalm was designed to be sung while accompanied by a harp or some similar stringed instrument. The stem word also means to prune, so this is a hymn of pruning or removing the dead and useless things from us that will result in an increase in our ability to produce (as in the pruning of a grape vine). Probably a better translation going on from this point would be "A psalm <u>to</u> David." You might ask yourself if this is of any significance. To me it seems that it is. The first translation would suggest that the song was written and originally sung by David. The

---

[329] Revelation 22:18-19 (TNIV)

second translation suggests to me that the song was sung to David by God (that is God put the song into David's mind to pass on to the rest of us). It is a song of David only in the sense that it was a gift to him that he chose to share. The meaning of the Hebrew word "David" is beloved of God.

The first verse starts ADONAI meaning The LORD. This uses the same original Hebrew letters as YHWH (God's personal name). In the original Hebrew only consonants were used. About 1500 AD vowel points were added. The Jewish people were very hesitant to use YHWH verbally due to the fear that it might accidentally be used in a way that would not glorify God and violate the commandment not to take the Lord's name in vain. Then comes the phrase "is my shepherd" (the word shepherd can also be translated friend. This would indicate the relationship is not that of a ruler and a subject). "I shall not want" (or lack or fail; that is I am not a failure through the intervention of God. This would refer to failure in a spiritual sense. One might very well fail in a worldly sense. In fact I knew of a lady who was aware that God wanted her to do something special for Him. She indicated that she would be pleased to. Then came the understanding that, "Even though you're doing it for me, from the standpoint of the world your efforts will be a failure." She responded, "Well I don't know about that." This was followed by an understanding from God, "All right, I'll get someone else to do it for me." At that point, she responded, "Oh no. I'll be happy to do it." Upon the completion of the task there was no obvious positive result. It was, from the world's standpoint, as predicted, a failure. But there was a sense that she was given of, "Well done you good and faithful servant." C. S. Lewis observed in *The Screwtape Letters,* "If the will to walk is there, God is pleased even with our stumbles." Being able to recognize a spiritual success when the world judges our efforts a failure is part of the pruning process in this psalm. Failure has no place in the mentality of this psalm.)

It's interesting that John 10:11-16 is the only place that I know of in scripture where Jesus calls himself good. If you remember, there was a time when a rich young man came to Jesus and said, "Good teacher, what must I do to inherit eternal life?" And Jesus said, "Why do you call me good, there is only one good and that is God."[330] But here (in John), He says "I am the Good Shepherd," and I want to spend a few minutes looking at

---

[330] Mark 10:17-18 (NIV)

ways in which when we allow Jesus to be our shepherd that there are some very interesting things that begin to happen in our lives.

The twenty-third Psalm is another description of the Good Shepherd, and let me use that as kind of an outline for what I want to say. So "the Lord is my Shepherd, I shall not be in want." I think there ought to be an "if" in front of it: if the Lord is my shepherd, I will not be in want. When we let Jesus be the Shepherd, when I allow Jesus to call the shots in my life, when I allow Jesus to open doors, when I allow Jesus to present the opportunities to me, then the blessings begin to come.

Verse two in the Psalm talks about some of those blessings; it says, "He makes me lie down (this in relationship to the sheep refers to lying down with all four legs under the sheep. From this position the sheep is ready to get up and ready for action. It is not the helpless passive position that the sheep would be in if it were on it's back. This second position is taken advantage of at the time the sheep are sheared. Then they are turned on their back, and they are helpless). "In green" (this is fresh, nourishing grass – not old winter killed, withered grass) "pastures." (Pastures in this sense represents home.) Now, I am not a shepherd, but I have read from shepherds that sheep will not lie down until their belly is full. If their bellies are not full, they keep wandering around. That is the way sheep get lost, they just nibble; they don't run away from the shepherd, they just nibble their way away from the shepherd. (This by the way is how we usually fall into sin. Not many people get up in the morning thinking, "I'm going to sin today." We just nibble our way away from God, and before we recognize what's happening, we've sinned.) But, if the sheep are lying down in the middle of green pastures it means that they have had all that they want. In the original language it says, "He leads me beside the still waters." The word "beside" really means "over" still waters. The image is the sheep getting a drink. So his belly is full; you have had plenty of food and you have the nourishment of the water. And it is still water; it has to be still water because a sheep, I'm told, instinctively is concerned about any rapidly moving water. It knows with that heavy coat of wool, if he falls into a rapidly moving stream, he is very likely to drown. And so, if the only thing that is happening in this particular valley is a rapidly moving stream, the good shepherd has to dam it up, has to find the rocks, the sticks, and whatever else in order to make a quiet pool, because without a quiet, safe pool, the sheep are not going to drink.

God provides for us when we follow the Good Shepherd. Let me give you an example. Our daughter, Jeannie, has been trying desperately to find a teaching position for months and months. Nothing has opened and every time there is a possibility and she does the interview, it is always somebody else who is selected. First of all, she has much too much experience, and some of you are nodding your head, right? The dollar figure for most school systems is designed to get somebody immediately out of school because they don't have the experience, so we don't have to pay for experience. We can get a cheap teacher. Jeannie ran into that time after time. And, she was banging on doors; I mean to tell you, that girl is determined. If I am ever in a fight, I want Jeannie on my side. Okay. She would go online, and evidently in the State of Indiana it is mandatory that you post the openings. She would check the night before, check the openings, and the next day, she would be in the office of that school principal. She wasn't going to wait for him or her to come around and respond to her email, because she responded to all the emails that she wanted to apply for the position. So, Jeannie would just go and park there in the office until the principal would come out. As soon as he or she would come out, she would introduce herself, say she was interested in the position, and, if the principal seemed to indicate that he or she had something else to do, Jeannie would sit back down in the office. But, she wasn't going; she was there. She wanted the position, and time after time even though she got the interview, by arm-twisting or whatever; she never got the job. She was ready to do that one other day and she listened to the Shepherd, and she heard in the still small voice, God, say to her, "Do you want to do it your way or do you want to do it my way?" Do you want to keep nibbling here and there, or do you want to wait until... Do you want me to provide green pastures? Now Jeannie is no dope, and she said, "I think I'll take your way." She did not do all of the knocking on doors that day; she went and did something fun with her family. When she got back from that, there was a message on her answering machine from a principal who said, "I want to talk with you about a position." She did the interview the next day, passed it with flying colors, and she is now doing what she yearned to do. Besides being a wife and mother, she has yearned to be a teacher and she is able to do that now because she followed the Shepherd. She did it the Shepherd's way. This was not something you looked for. It was something I suggest that was provided by the Shepherd. When we follow the Shepherd, there are things, there are ways, in which the Shepherd can provide for us in ways that we cannot begin to imagine. That is verse two.

(Verse 3) "He restores" (or refreshes or revives) "my soul" (breath, wind, the Hebrew word for soul usually is *ruwakh*. Here the Hebrew word translated as soul is *nephesh* meaning a breathing creature. The picture is bringing back one's breath after having been hit hard in the upper abdomen and having one's breath "knocked out." [Anyone who has ever had that happen to them can recall the struggle to get their diaphragm to work again. Just when you think you may never get another breath there comes a deep gasp and relief.] "He guides" (could be also translated leads, drives, or impels) "me in paths of righteousness" (or along the right paths; this refers to a path laid our by a wheeled cart that would be fairly straight and involve some rutting making it difficult to get out of the path; it would not represent a wandering path made by animals on their own. The shepherd has to herd or force us into this path because we are prone to wander. This rutted path includes long-used anchors of our faith: the Lord's Prayer, the Apostles' Creed, hymns and praise songs that have touched our souls. In Jeremiah it is suggested that we should seek the ancient paths and not bypaths.[331]) "for His name's sake." (Note that God's reason for doing this is for His name's or His presence's sake. That means He does this because He wants to. It is His nature to do so. He isn't obligated to do it or forced to, nor does He do it because we've earned His actions.)

This is a little different aspect about following the shepherd. It's called restoring the soul and walking in the paths of righteousness. This is where the Shepherd fixes the sheep, not just provides for them. How many of you know that God accepts you just the way that you are, but He never leaves you that way? So we begin to follow the Shepherd, and the Shepherd begins to meddle. Some of you know something about the Shepherd that meddles. The Shepherd begins to meddle and begins to try to set things right in your life. For example, I know a pastor who I know really intimately well, who even though he is now 68 years old is still pushing the envelope in terms of the speed limit. Now I just know that this particular pastor, who will remain nameless, doesn't have the reactions that he had when he was twenty years old. And the fact that he is pushing the speed limit an extra five miles an hour, when he is not in a really big hurry, is probably not smart. Well, it took this particular pastor a conversation with a police officer last Thursday night. You know when you come out of Warsaw and you take the old Lincoln highway across? Do you know right out of Warsaw it is still only 35 miles per hour? Well this particular pastor

---

[331] Jeremiah 6:16 and 18:15

had FORGOTTEN that and it was brought to this pastor's attention that he was going 56 miles per hour in a 35 miles per hour zone. It was not a really comfortable experience for the pastor. Now I suggest that that was the work of the Shepherd fixing one of his sheep.

(Verse 4) "Even though" (or when or if) "I walk" (the word for this type of walk is not what would be used for a short afternoon stroll or a short trip. It infers a lifelong walk) "through the darkest valley" (This word for valley is not the one used for a gentle rolling valley. It is a gorge. There would be no easy escape from this valley. As we walk through it, it would become more and more pressing. This section could also be translated "the valley of the shadow of death." This indicates circumstances of greatest peril – note this is not the valley of death, but the valley of the <u>shadow</u> of death. Something will die in this valley. It will not be the person in the valley, but it will likely be a part of the personality that is keeping them – us, me - from a full relationship with God. This is more pruning that is suggested in the earliest part of the psalm.) "I will fear no evil (the words would probably be best rendered "I will not fear evil." In other words no matter what the Devil throws at me, he who is in me is greater than he who is in the world.[332]), "for you" (are – this word is not in the original Hebrew) "with me. Your rod" (an instrument of authority and even correction, punishment or discipline – still more pruning – used for shepherds to guide their sheep) "and your staff" (an instrument of rescue or support. Staff is a feminine word suggesting a mother's role of nurturing, whereas rod is a masculine word suggesting a father's role in correcting), "they comfort" (reassure. The word comfort comes from two parts: com- indicates together and –fort indicates strength. Here is both the pruning and the product of pruning. Something dies, and the result is that what remains becomes stronger) "me."

(Verse 6) "You prepare" (set in order. This is in future tense) "a table" (this is not the word for a dining table, but the word for the table of sacrifice – additional pruning is going on, but this would not be pruning by the shepherd. The individual determines if he will make a sacrifice and what the sacrifice will be.) "before me in the presence of my enemies" (This would be a close encounter. The root word for enemies means to cramp, so these would not be passive enemies. They would be those who wish to actively do harm. God takes the evil the enemies would do and makes it result in good. Under God's

---

[332] Adapted from I John 4:4

protection none can destroy us). "You anoint my head with oil" (An anointing involved pouring a large container of oil on the head, so that it ran down their face and well onto their garments. There was no mistaking the extravagance of the blessing, or that it had significance. It was a sign the person so treated was an honored guest); "my cup overflows." (Overflows indicates to have one's thirst fully satisfied – to have everything needed and much more. Significantly this overflowing comes after the anointing. Here we find that our best gift comes to us in our process of giving. More blessings than one could possibly have anticipated are received. We find out why there is the evil and why we need not fear it, why the sacrifice, why it is happening to us. Here is a chance for each one to place things on the sacrificial table or not – we are not compelled – at this point of pruning it is our choice. We choose what to place there.)

(Verse 7) "Surely goodness and mercy" (Also translated your goodness and love. This, however, is not the mercy of protection. It is the tough mercy of covenant love in which God is willing to be tough when necessary for our good). "will follow" (literally pursue or run after. There is no escaping this love. God has been characterized as the hound of heaven. In this relationship there is more pruning or cutting away – this time what is removed is self-pity) "me all the days of my life, and I will dwell" (or am dwelling – not a finished action - as God's welcome guest) "in the house (in this sense house includes family. Another use of house in this sense would be when Jesus was said to be of the house of David.) "of ADONAI, the LORD, forever." (This "forever" is not a static situation. This "forever" involves change, movement, and newness. Although this verse has been a source of comfort at many funerals, it should actually be understood as an understanding that God has seen the hearer and the one who shares this psalm through so much that he has become confidant that with each new day God will be there going through the same process. In effect the singer of the psalm indicates, "You have seen me through so very much that I am confident that with each new day you will be there with me." This too is another pruning. Because of this understanding and conviction, we have to forget about giving up. I am reminded of Winston Churchill's famous speech to Eaton College during World War II. They were expecting a major address by this master of English prose and this master of inspiring thoughts. He stood before this body of Englishmen. His total speech was, "Never give up! Never, never, never give up." With that, he sat down. In this final pruning God shared with David and David shares with us this same spirit and admonition.)

So the twenty-third psalm is a passage of being – not of dying. It speaks of the hard ways God deals with us and prepares us to yield more for ourselves and for others by pruning away what is not productive, and by tenderly tending us to preserve and enhance us.

[Below is this Twenty-Third Psalm in the King James Version. This is probably how most of us learned it. It is part of the rutted paths discussed above that guide us toward fellowship with God.

> "A Psalm of David. The Lord is my shepherd; I shall not want. He maketh me to lie down in green pastures; he leadeth me beside the still waters. He restoreth my soul; he leadeth me in the paths of righteousness for his name's sake. Yea, though I walk through the valley of the shadow of death, I will fear no evil, for thou art with me; thy rod and thy staff they comfort me. Thou preparest a table before me in the presence of mine enemies; thou anointest my head with oil; my cup runneth over. Surely goodness and mercy shall follow me all the days of my life, and I will dwell in the house of the Lord forever."

Now there is recorded what might be called an expanded version of the Psalm taking into account the above discussion.

> "A Psalm from God to David, God's beloved. The Lord is my shepherd, my friend. I shall not want or lack anything or fail. After I am filled, He makes me to lie down in green nourishing pastures at rest but alert and ready to act. He leads me to drink over the safe still waters (He gives me everything I need). He restores my very breath, my soul. He makes right those things in me that are wrong. He guides me into paths of righteousness because this is what He wants for us. Even though my life's journey is through a gorge of dark danger and peril, I will not fear evil for you are with me. Your correcting authority and your means and eagerness to rescue me reassure and comfort me. You set in order a table of sacrifice on which I can let go of those things that keep me from you even in the close up presence of those who would do me harm. You publicly declare your love, protection, and acceptance of me by anointing me. I am overwhelmed by the overflowing blessings with which you have showered me. Surely goodness and

your covenant love mercy will pursue and track me down all the days I live, and I will live in your house and as a part of your family at your invitation for every day of my life."]

Challenge 34

# Bible versus personal experience as the basis for faith

Which is more important in our growth in faith – our study of the Bible or our personal experience with the Holy Spirit?

*(Jack Clark's answer)*

Carol and I were delegates to our church's North Indiana Annual Conference in 2007. One of the delegates raised this exact point expressing his concern that our members are relying more on personal spiritual experience and less on Biblical guidance than had been traditional for us, so this is not only a theoretical concern.

Some very meaningful personal experiences in my own spiritual life have involved understandings that I have felt are from the Holy Spirit. These have been ideas or understandings that seemed beyond my abilities. These usually occur in quiet times as an awareness of something I hadn't been thinking about or as a course of action that was something I wasn't even considering. Sometimes it may be a course of action that I am not anxious to undertake, and I may resist it. The Holy Spirit has been known to apply increasingly more pressure to get me to see things His way when this occurs. On one occasion it even came down to the understanding that if I persisted in doing things my way that I wasn't worthy of Christ. Notice I still had the free choice to accept or reject the assignment, but this was certainly more than a little nudge. I did what I had been asked, and everything worked out all right, but I understood how Jacob felt after he had wrestled with God.[333] These times of interaction with the Holy Spirit have been growing experiences significant in my spiritual life.

One of the reasons for the concern about relying on personal spiritual experiences is the fact that it's hard for any of us to be sure which things are valid experiences. There are ways to evaluate an awareness that we may have to be sure it is from God rather than the result of some desire of our own or even from an evil source. The Apostle John wrote: "Dear friends, do not believe every spirit, but test the spirits to see whether they are from God, because many false prophets have gone out into the world. This is how you can recognize the Spirit of God: Every spirit that acknowledges that Jesus Christ has come in the flesh is from God, but every spirit that does not acknowledge Jesus in not from

---

[333] Genesis 32:24-32

God."[334]  Other helps in evaluating such ideas to see if they are actually from the Holy Spirit were suggested by John Wesley and are known as the Wesley quadrilateral.

Some psychotic people have been convinced that they are directed to destroy someone or something and believe the direction is from the Holy Spirit. Some have wanted something so much that they have confused their wants with directions from the Holy Spirit. Those of us who believe in the existence of Satan believe that this master of deceit, this great liar, can and does fool people at times into thinking something he plants in some people's mind actually came from God. The things we can use to judge such situations include: scripture, tradition, experience and reason.

Any understanding actually from the Holy Spirit will not be counter to scripture. If the understanding is not in accordance with Jesus' teachings, it may be from an evil spiritual source or from the person's own twisted mind, but it is not from God's Holy Spirit. Second the impulse will not be contrary to tradition, so the impulse of Thomas Jefferson to rewrite the Bible, leaving out those parts that he did not understand or agree with would not be something God directed. Thirdly the direction will not be contrary to good judgment or reason, so an impulse to do something physically harmful to oneself without overwhelming reason would not come from God. A fourth way to judge these things is by experience. From this short discussion, we can understand that such matters can be tricky to evaluate.

Although such personal spiritual experiences can be enlightening and even exciting to those of us that have them, we need to recognize that God meets different people differently. There are Christians who don't have such experiences. Satan could try to use even these experiences against us as a source of false pride. Just as some Christians have not been given the gift of speaking in tongues and some have, that too can become a source of false pride or a source of suspicion. Paul observed that there are various gifts and no one has them all.

Going to the Bible as a basis of our spiritual beliefs and the source of our growth in spiritual understanding, it seems that this is a long-used, thoroughly evaluated and found to be valid basis. This source is available and an important asset for any Christian.

---

[334] First John 4:1-3 (TNIV)

Studying the Bible avoids the concerns of mistaken ideas. I recently had a paranoid schizophrenic patient in my practice. He was convinced that he was the Messiah, but with some very twisted ideas. When I asked him how he related some of his ideas with the Bible, he told me he had never read it.

The scriptures are God-given and reliable. For this discussion, it's important to remember they <u>were given</u>. This understanding requires a source: the Holy Spirit. It also requires a recipient, the person who originally understood and recorded the material that now is found in the Bible. With this understanding, anything we study in our Bible went through the process of originally being the personal experience with the Holy Spirit interacting with Moses, Isaiah, Hosea, or one of the other authors of the Bible. The exception to this would be the recording of the words of Jesus by those who actually heard them or by those who collected the material from those who heard him first-hand. Since we Christians understand Jesus as being one with the Father and one with the Holy Spirit, this would have the same validity as the other Bible verses given by interaction with the Holy Spirit.

With the above understanding, it seems logical to conclude that any spiritual growth including the basis of our faith results from the interaction of the Holy Spirit or Jesus with those who wrote the Bible or with personal interaction with the Holy Spirit. Other than the need to be careful about validity of the experience, it would seem that Bible study is very similar to personal experience – we're only using the personal experience of others or the personal experience of ourselves. Both seem valid. Both seem important.

---

*(Betty Berger's understanding)*

Both are important, but studying the word should come first, so we know how to walk in Jesus' will. The more word we know, the more we can hear from the Holy Spirit, and be the witness He wants us to be.

---

*(Betty Byers' answer)*

They are both and equally important. See Second Timothy 2:15.

---

Challenge 35
# What's this business about taking up one's cross?
Just what did Jesus mean when he said, "Anyone who does not take his cross and follow me is not worthy of me."[335]

*(Understanding of Jack Clark)*

For a few he literally meant that they would meet a martyr's death. This applied to ten of the disciples. According to church history and tradition, John was the only disciple who died a natural death, but he too suffered persecution and heartache, so he certainly wasn't immune from suffering. There were many other early Followers of the Way who were martyred too, and even today there are those in many countries where to be a Christian is to risk the scorn, injury by, and sometimes death by non-believers. This can include missionaries or simply any follower of Christ. It can especially involve those who convert from another religion

For most of us there will be no facing of physical injury or death because of our belief, and even scorn or biting remarks are few and far between. What most Christians have to face in this generation is being ignored as irrelevant and the pain of knowing the joy we could share if others were willing. That certainly was a "cross" that our savior bore too.

For most Christians taking up our cross involves taking on the burden of those Jesus Christ said he was especially concerned with – the downtrodden, the poor, the widows, the orphans and those with problems that they didn't ask for and can't overcome. For some taking up our cross may involve visiting on a regular basis in a nursing home and spending time with lonely folks. For some it may involve being a volunteer in a camp for disabled or disadvantaged children. For me as a physician it may involve telling a young family that their child has a cancer, or telling an anxious wife that we couldn't save her husband's life after his cardiac arrest. It may involve visiting in jail a young adult who had been in the youth fellowship I taught when he was a teen and who has messed up his life and the lives of his Mom and Dad who are my friends. It involves telling him that I know Jesus Christ still wants him to be a part of the family, because I too have fouled up in other ways, and Jesus still wants me to be a part of the family. It may involve telling a young woman that she's pregnant and comforting her after she advises me that the young man who had pledged to love her forever doesn't want anything to do with her any more.

---

[335] Matthew 10:38, & 16:24, Mark 8:34, & Luke 9:23 (NIV)

It may involve telling a woman in her forties that had a stroke a year ago and can still not speak or help herself to live a normal life that we have reached the end of our ability to rehabilitate her. All that is involved in being a loved wife and the mother of her young children had been wrenched from her grasp.

These are those who mourn. These are those who are poor in spirit. These are those who Christ said we should bless and comfort. These are those who Mother Teresa of Calcutta said in them we meet and serve Jesus Christ. Many times the only comfort is to share their pain and to let them know we care. I recall the lady with the stroke I mentioned. As I explained her situation I held her hand. Tears rolled down both our cheeks. She knew I cared. Much more importantly, I shared with her that I knew that God cared too. There were still tears for both of us, but her expression changed from total discouragement to a smile. I wonder how many people in the year of her struggle had told her that they cared and more importantly that God cares? I think these burdens, for most of us, are what Christ meant when he said to take up our cross and follow him.

Sharing in Christ's mission by taking up our crosses can seem to be tough work. Being a cross bearer is painful; it involves sacrifice. To love is to give. We cannot give without sacrifice, but to love is to obey Christ's command. To love and to sacrifice is to share in Christ's mission. What an honor, and through the shared mission what a privilege and a joy. Christ said, "Take my yoke upon you and learn from me, for I am gentle and humble in heart and you will find rest for your souls. For my yoke is easy, and my burden is light."[336]

For some taking up their cross involves taking a difficult situation of their own and working with God to make something positive out of it that will bring God glory. I'm reminded that Christ said: "You are the light of the world. A city on a hill cannot be hidden. Neither do people light a lamp and put it under a bowl. Instead they put it on its stand, and it gives light to everyone in the house. In the same way, let your light shine before men, that they may see your good deeds and praise your Father in heaven."[337] I'll tell you about doing something the person didn't think was anything unusual. It's about a lady who made her whole life style a cause of sharing

---

[336] Matthew 11:29-30 (NIV)
[337] Matthew 5:15-16 (NIV)

Mary was a lovely lady who graced our community and our congregation with her presence. She was born in the Dominican Republic. Her father sent her to the United States to escape the turmoil of revolutionary activity and for education when she was very young. She never was able to return to her beloved family. Mary recounted how heart broken she was on that great lonely ship in the darkness of night coming to America. As she stood at the railing thinking about her loss of family, she has told her friends that she contemplated jumping over and ending her life. Happily she did not do this, as she was such an inspiration to so many.

Mary married, stayed in America, moved to Syracuse, raised a daughter, sang in our choir, and became widowed. Widowhood can destroy the joy of life for some, but not for Mary. She continued very active in study clubs, choir, and church. The joy of her lilting, slight accent brightened the gatherings of our congregation for many years.

Late in life, she studied painting locally and with prominent artists in the east. She painted many lovely works of art that she gave as gifts to friends and donated to our church bazaars to help raise money for worthy projects. As she became more proficient, she shared her talents with others; several fellow artists met with her in her home to share her abilities and theirs with each other.

After my father's death, my mother tended to withdraw from life--not in all aspects but in many. My wife Carol made the apt observation that it's a shame some people quit living before they die. Mary remained mother's close friend and booster.

Mary chose to blossom and expand her horizons. She and mother both remained active in choir. Mary developed a hearing loss that became progressively profound. Mother would stand beside her trying to help Mary keep her place and carry the tune. Eventually she became completely deaf. She continued to wear her hearing aid, probably more as a symbol of her problem for those who might not know her. She went to multiple clinics and even considered cochlear implants only to be told there was no hope to restore her hearing. As she could no longer hear herself sing, she had to give up her beloved choir. She could no longer hear the service. She could lip read, but struggled to comprehend what others were saying.

Many would have given up coming to church in such a situation, but Mary attended consistently. She would often come to the choir room after the service to say how much she had enjoyed the anthem even though she couldn't hear a single note or word. Mary also had painful osteoporosis of the spine that often caused discomfort and sometimes-severe pain. She treated it medically, but also chose to work through the pain with daily exercises and gardening. She inspired others and me with her tenacity and her faithfulness. She encouraged me in my weaknesses and in my occasional minimal maladies. She spread joy wherever she went and in all the activities in which she participated.

She could not hear the sermon, but she participated in the worship and built up her fellow worshipers. She was a personification of what Paul wrote to the Romans: "We know that in all things God works for the good of those who love him, who have been called according to his purpose."[338] The interesting thought also occurred to me that in a world which so often seems to have a superabundance of those who "have ears but hear not,"[339] that there are also those who demonstrate the positive side of this observation. Mary had no ears that functioned, but she heard! She heard the call of Jesus Christ in her life; she glorified God with her talents and her weaknesses. She manifested what God revealed to Paul and Paul's response when he spoke of the thorn in the flesh that Satan had placed there and which God declined to remove despite Paul's pleading three times for its removal: "'My grace is sufficient for you for my power is made perfect in weakness.' Therefore I will boast all the more gladly about my weaknesses, so that Christ's power may rest on me."[340] Mary Bushong had faith and shared her faith in very practical ways. She stands tall in the great cloud of witnesses singing forth the Glory of God!

*(An answer by Betty Byers)*

Jesus was talking about the cost and compensations of discipleship.

---

[338] Romans 8:28 (NIV)
[339] Isaiah 42:18-20, Jeremiah 5:21, Ezekiel 12:2, Matthew 13:15, Mark 8:18, and Acts 28:27 (NIV)
[340] Second Corinthians 12:7-9 (NIV)

## Challenge 36
# What about prayers that don't get answered?
"Whatever you ask for in prayer, believe that you have received it, and it will be yours."[341]
In spite of this everyone who is a Christian knows someone who has very specifically
asked for some blessing and did not receive it. How do you explain this?

*(Jack Clark's understanding)*

Perhaps implied in the question is another question: does God even hear prayers? My answer would be yes. He most certainly does. Even as I heard my children's requests when they were small, God hears all our requests and delights in our times of sharing with Him. There's good scriptural basis for this answer too: "And it shall come to pass, that before they call, I will answer; and while they are yet speaking, I will hear."[342]

Prayer isn't an order catalogue! There are things that may seem good to me but God knows would be detrimental. I often pray for an ill friend's restoration to health. Nothing at all wrong with such a prayer, but what if God's granting my friend's recovery from a heart attack would result in his having a stroke next month. And what if the stroke resulted in years of the friend being confined to a wheel chair, unable to express himself and having to be fed by a tube because he can't swallow without choking? I might not see that result from my prayer, but God can.

Some things I might pray for could seem good, but could be in conflict with another's prayer. I might pray for a sunny week in order that my family and I could enjoy a pleasant, relaxing few days of canoeing and camping. At the same time a farmer might be praying for rain so that his crops won't wither and die and result in the loss of a year's work and needed income to send his child to college. There seems to be no way that both prayers could be answered even though there is no right or wrong involved with answering either prayer.

There are prayers that God declines to answer, because He has better things in mind for the seeker. Paul had experience with such a prayer. Paul had a problem that he couldn't shake. He referred to it as his thorn in the flesh. He asked that it be removed – not once – not twice – but three times. God's response was, "No." So often when God's

---

[341] Mark 11:24 (NIV)
[342] Isaiah 65:24 (KJV)

response to a prayer is no, we're left to figure out the reason on our own. In this instance, after the third turn-down, God made his reason clear to Paul: "My grace is sufficient for you, for my power is made perfect in weakness."[343] God has a plan for our lives, and there are times the things we ask for would interfere with our ability to best be a part of His plan.

In view of these observations, someone could make a valid point by repeating the tough question with which this discussion started. The Bible says, "Ask and it shall be given to you,"[344] and "Whatever you ask for in prayer, believe that you have received it, and it will be yours."[345] In spite of this everyone who is a Christian knows someone who has very specifically asked for some blessing and didn't receive it. How do you explain this? The answer seems to be found in reading a little farther. These words of Christ are found in two books of the New Testament. Both go on to say that if our children ask for good gifts we won't give them something hurtful, and that if we, as imperfect as we are know how to give good gifts to our children, we can expect God to give good gifts in response to our requests.[346] Luke goes one step farther and even indicates what the good gifts will consist of: the Holy Spirit.[347] This then is the answer to prayer and the power of prayer – the Holy Spirit. I might say no to my teen age child's request for a new sport car to drive to school for various reasons (cost, too many other places to put our money, concerns about not spoiling him or her, concerns about too much power for them to handle safely, etc.). But I might answer their request with seeing in-so-far as I could that they had a safe way to get to school. So it is with our heavenly Father. For reasons sometimes known only to Him, He may say yes, or He may say wait, or He may say no, but He will always give us good gifts and the presence of the Holy Spirit in response to our requests.

Too many of my prayers are self-centered. I suspect this applies to a lot of other peoples' prayers also. Don't get me wrong. There's nothing wrong with asking God's help in overcoming my problem or the problem of a friend, but it seems that more of our prayers should focus on what we can do for God. What can I do to glorify you God in the

---

[343] Second Corinthians 12:9 (NIV)
[344] Matthew 7:7, Luke 11:9, and John 15:7 (NIV)
[345] Mark 11:24 (NIV)
[346] Matthew 7:7-11
[347] Luke 11:9-12

pain I feel due to my loss? What can I do to let others see you through me and want to share a relationship with you? Perhaps the best prayer is one that asks God to help us be one with Him, to help us follow Christ and through the Holy Spirit to use us in God's service. It seems the objective should be to be in relationship with Him. When I pray that God accepts me and uses my service to advance the Kingdom, I think that prayer most certainly will be answered. When I hunger and thirst for God's presence in my life, I'm sure that God is going to do a new thing. When I pray this kind of a prayer, when I long to see and taste God's goodness then my life will be changed as will the lives He and I together will touch. I must decide if I consider God as a handyman to fix those things that I would like made good, or as a lover whose presence is sufficient to make any situation better.

*(Betty Berger's answer)*

The person whose prayers aren't answered didn't really believe, or they asked for something outside of God's will. Look up the word ask in a concordance. Jesus is pretty clear how He will answer. Believe in your heart and say with your mouth, 'Jesus is Lord[348] - that's the way we receive everything from Him. Believe He wants us to have it, and then (very important) <u>speak</u> the result – not the circumstance. The power of life and death are in our words.[349] God says "yes" when He has promised.[350]

*(Betty Byers' answer)*

God knows what the answers should be.

*(An answer from Sherry Doherty)*

I completely believe in prayer. Does God always answer my prayer the way I think it should be answered? No. I also believe that God in His writing of my life knows the best for me and for those I pray for. I feel He answers all my prayers great and small but with the answer He knows is best.

I must tell you this story about my answered prayers. I hope you find it as funny as we did in my family. Our daughters both moved out of state, and I was feeling a little distant

---

[348] Romans 10:10
[349] Proverbs 18:21
[350] I Corinthians 1:20

from one of them. So in my prayers I asked God to help me find a common ground to talk about with her. I said this prayer almost nightly for some time. Then she called and told her Dad and me that her car was broken, and that it could not be repaired. She had figured her finances and started looking for a used car. Days, then weeks passed with no luck – we talked very often with a common ground of "cars." Finally, in the end, I drove down to help her look for a car. Ironic – two women buying a used car hundreds of miles away from her Dad, Bob, who designs cars. One evening after a day of car shopping, I told her about my prayer. She laughed, and we decided next time I make a prayer like that I should be more specific. Are prayers answered? You bet. Did God break her car? Heavens no, but He showed me that I am still a parent, that my child and I are still bound in love and devotion to each other. Bob and I have been married just over twenty-seven years with three amazing children. I am in awe each day of God's gifts and praise Him for those gifts. Some days I know I get frustrated thinking I know best what I need, and yet in the end God does know best, and when I release myself to Him all works out by His design.

---

Challenge 37

# How can a man be born again?

(Submitted by Nicodemus)

*(Jack Clark's answer)*

When Nicodemus the Pharisee and a member of the ruling council came to Jesus under cover of darkness to avoid being noticed by the other Pharisees, he sincerely expressed his belief that Jesus had come from God because of what he had done. Jesus responded in a rather unusual manner. He didn't respond as he did when Peter confessed his faith by telling him that this knowledge had to have come from God. He didn't invite him to become a disciple. He didn't ask him to keep it to himself, as he did a number of people who received miracles. He didn't ask him to go back to the other leaders of Israel to share his understanding with them. He just seemed to go to another subject entirely and responded: "I tell you the truth; no one can see the kingdom of God unless he is born again." Rather taken aback and amazed Nicodemus then asked, "How can a man be born when he is old? Surely he cannot enter a second time into his mother's womb to be born!" To this Jesus answered, "I tell you the truth, no one can enter the kingdom of God unless he is born of water and the Spirit. Flesh gives birth to flesh, but the Spirit gives birth to spirit." You should not be surprised at my saying, 'You must be born again.' The wind blows wherever it pleases. You hear its sound, but you cannot tell where it comes from or where it is going. So it is with everyone born of the Spirit. 'How can this be?' Nicodemus asked."[351]

Of course Nicodemus was thinking of something entirely different than Jesus was during this conversation. Even though he didn't seem to fully understand, Nicodemus later spoke in Jesus' defense when the Sanhedrin was almost entirely against him. He also honored Jesus after his death.

What Jesus was speaking about when he spoke of being born again was the life-altering experience of being so totally changed by the action of the Holy Spirit that in many respects we're totally different people spiritually than what we were before. Spiritually, he was talking about a new beginning with a personality so totally different in so many ways that it was like being a new person!

---

[351] John 3:3-9 (NIV)

Sometimes those of us who have been born again narrowly feel that the way we're reborn is so meaningful to us that it is the only way to be born again, or at least if it isn't the only way it must be the best or most significant. When we're tempted to think in this way, it's important to keep in mind that God chooses to meet each person where they are and in the way in which they can relate. There are forty-eight presentations from which a person may be physically born in a normal delivery. This does not include some presentations from which a normal delivery cannot be effected. Even these can result in a live birth through surgical intervention. It is not unreasonable to expect that there may be multiple ways in which one may be spiritually reborn with the Holy Spirit acting as our obstetrician. Just as some physical births are more dramatic and excite more conversation in the delivery room and some are relatively calm affairs, and just as some physical births are quick and some take quite a long time, the characteristics of spiritual rebirth differ from person to person.

Some people will come to know God and be changed gradually through the example of someone else. Through God's effect in the life of this other person, we can come to want to be part of the great adventure of life lived with God and accept Him. Many of us know God through the lives of our parents or other great Christians such as Mother Teresa or Albert Schweitzer and can be reborn in response to wanting lives that glow like these for ourselves.

Others of us come to know God and be spiritually reborn because we see the power of goodness and want to be a part of what is good. We come to recognize that the source of goodness is God. We see that goodness, love and kindness have a lasting nature that can change lives of those who attempt to make them our guiding principles. We can see that these principles change others with whom we come in contact. We recognize that if we accept this life change, we have become a part of something that is uplifting, lasting, and something that makes us, others, and the world better. When we recognize the power of goodness, we can understand that this is a force that directs the universe, and when we are perceptive we will recognize this force as God. In contrast, we can see hate, selfishness, and pettiness and recognize that these bring people into blind alleys of living and determine to avoid these traits. This will lead some of us to our spiritual rebirth.

Unfortunately, some of us come to know God through the pain we have given someone else. When we have betrayed or misused someone for our own advantage or become separated from someone we loved, our sense of disgust with ourselves, our selfishness, our indifference, our weakness, our hostility, and our lack of association with the positive, lasting things of life can lead us to turn to something better. This something is God. We cannot make our lives whole without Him as the central focus. Our desire to be rid of the old shallow life and acknowledge the depth of existence can lead us to God and being born again.

Some of us have come to know God through a loss or a tragedy or a period of danger to ourselves or to someone we love. In such a time of spiritual pain when despair destroys our joy and courage, some of us have found God. At these times reliance on ourselves and on the routine way of running our lives isn't enough. When we're caught in the quicksand of a disaster, we may throw up our hands for help, and finding that friends, our own efforts and the activities of the world cannot rescue us, we may grasp God who is always ready to give us spiritual support. The skeptics may say that this is merely a defense mechanism by which a grieving person protects his ego, but you could never convince the person who has known God's help at such a time and through the experience has become a new, born again follower.

The evidence that a person is born again is that their life has been totally changed in positive ways. The primary change that can be noticed is that an attitude of "me first and what I want above everything else" is changed to an attitude of "God first" and what His wishes are taking first priority and the realization that "only when God wins do I win."

Although how we're born is significant to each of us, and even though it sometimes makes a great story, the important thing really is not how we were born but simply the fact that we were born, and having been born chose to live life to the fullest, accepting with joy and with thanks the gifts of the spirit and the honor of being a part of God's kingdom.

I'm convinced our spiritual rebirth in no way proves how great we are, but how great God is, and I'm convinced that this rebirth is available as a free gift to anyone who will seek and accept it.

Spiritually we can be born again by accepting Christ as our personal savior.

# Which is more important in our Christian lives our faith or our good works?

*(Jack Clark's understanding)*

That's sort of like asking which is most important to our physical life: water or food. Both are vital.

Some people have the idea that God holds our lives on a cosmic balance or scale and decides if we're to be a part of heaven according to how our good deeds balance against our bad deeds. They are mistaken. In counting what would be considered good deeds Isaiah pointed out that, "All of us have become like one who is unclean, and all our righteous acts are like filthy rags; we all shrivel up like a leaf, and like the wind our sins sweep us away."[352] Jesus is reported to have answered a rich young man who wanted to know what good thing he had to do to get eternal life: "Why do you ask me about what is good...? There is only One who is good. If you want to enter life, obey the commandments."[353] This would seem to indicate there would never be any truly good things to put on the positive side of our balances in such a system of determining salvation when the things we do are compared to the absolute goodness of God's perfection, so this wouldn't seem a viable option on which to decide our salvation.

Jesus said, "I am the way and the truth and the life. No one comes to the Father except through me."[354] He also said, "Whoever acknowledges me before men, I will also acknowledge him before my Father in heaven.[355] On another occasion Jesus was being pressed: ""They asked him, 'What must we do to do the works God requires?' Jesus answered, 'The work of God is this: to believe in the one he has sent.'"[356] These passages would seem to make faith and acknowledgement (which would be a deed or a work) both pretty important, but the work referred to is a spiritual deed rather than some good work on a worldly level.

There was a heresy that carried the importance of faith as opposed to works to an extreme in the early Christian Church. This group in effect said confess Jesus as your

---

[352] Isaiah 64:6 (NIV)
[353] Matthew 19:17 (NIV)
[354] John 14:6 (NIV)
[355] Matthew 10:32 (NIV)
[356] John 6:29 (NIV)

savior and do whatever you want. They even suggested that they should try their best (or their worst) to be sinful so that they could more fully experience the joy of redemption and salvation.

Certainly every one of us who considers ourselves to be saved by faith continue to sin, but we must never accept our sins as a lifestyle. "It is impossible for those who have once been enlightened, who have tasted the heavenly gift, who have shared in the Holy Spirit, who have tasted the goodness of the word of God and the powers of the coming age, if they fall away, to be brought back to repentance, because to their loss they are crucifying the Son of God all over again and subjecting him to public disgrace."[357]

So faith is of primary importance. It is the key that unlocks the chains of sin and potential spiritual death. It is our faith and belief that result in eternal existence united with God the Father, the son and the Holy Spirit and the company of the saved in heaven. Faith is what transforms the fate of separation from these (which is hell) into life and Heaven.

So this raises the question can we make it on faith alone and forget about doing good works. It would seem that the answer is no. At the very least a person of faith must have the work Jesus mentioned above – belief in the one God has sent. There are, however, many people who never had an opportunity to know Jesus personally or through their faith and by name but have known him only spiritually such as the dozens of those listed in the "great cloud of witnesses"[358] from Old Testament times. There are also many people who have never had a chance to know Jesus personally but still have faith in God in-so-far as they can understand what God has put in their hearts. The Scriptures would seem to indicate that it is possible that their faith can still justify them.[359]

It seems that if faith is the source of our salvation that good works are the result of our faith. God and Jesus and the Holy Spirit so enrich our lives that we who have received the free gift of salvation will want to do those things that will please them. Carol's love in our marriage and my friends so enrich my life that I find a great joy in doing things that will

---

[357] Romans 6:4-6 (NIV)
[358] Hebrews 11-12:1
[359] Romans 2:12-16 (RSV)

enrich theirs. So Jesus' love and friendship enrich me so much that I want to do those things that will please him and those things that will help the people he loves and wants also to be a part of his kingdom. It seems a little strange to think that God, who possesses everything, can still desire something more: the voluntarily given love of as many as possible of those he has created. But it does seem that we who choose to love him do in fact enrich Him. There really isn't much that I can offer God in return for the fabulous gift He has given me, but encouraging others to seek and commit to Him is one thing. Serving those Jesus holds as dear to him is one more thing I can do. Jesus said, "Let your light shine before men, that they may see your good deeds and praise your Father in heaven."[360] He also said that simply calling on and claiming his name will not result in salvation. I can only conclude that if our faith doesn't produce action and works that that means we really didn't have faith.[361] These good works are certainly the result of the fruit of the spirit: "Love, joy, peace, patience, kindness, goodness, faithfulness, gentleness, and self control. Against such things there is no law."[362]

One of our Methodist Bishops observed that faith without works is like a spirit without a body, and works without faith is like a body without a spirit. One is a ghost and one is a corpse. To be alive in Christ we must have both.

*(Betty Byers' answer)*

Both are important. When we receive Christ good works follow.

---

[360] Matthew 5:16 (NIV)
[361] Matthew 25:31-46
[362] Galations5:22-23 (NIV)

## Challenge 39
# Why is it necessary to forgive?

Someone has said, "Revenge is sweet." It isn't; it's bitter. It causes one's soul to wither. Carried to the extreme it can cause one's soul to die.

*(An answer by Jack Clark)*

If we want to pattern our lives after our savior, we need to recall that he forgave. He forgave and restored Peter for denying him three times. He forgave those who crucified him because they didn't know what they were doing. He forgave the sins of the crippled man restoring his spiritual health before he restored his physical health. He has forgiven your sins, and he has forgiven my sins.

Paul wrote, "Let all bitterness and wrath and anger and clamor and slander be put away from you."[363]

Jesus gave several good reasons that we need to forgive considering that those of us who are Christians view him as being in charge of the final judgment. His command was, "Love your enemies, and pray for those who persecute you, that you may be sons of your Father in heaven."[364] "Do to others as you would have them do to you."[365] "In the same way you judge others, and with the measure you use, it will be measured to you."[366] Little children understand this before they have even studied the Bible. They chant, "I'm rubber, and you're glue. Whatever you do bounces back and sticks on you!"

In the novel *The five People You Meet in Heaven* a great observation is made: "Holding anger is a poison. It eats you from inside. We think that hating is a weapon that attacks the person who harmed us. But hatred is a curved blade. And the harm we do, we do to ourselves."[367]

*(Betty Berger's answer)*

Most importantly for me, the Bible says if I'm unforgiving my prayers can't be answered.

---

[363] Ephesians 4:31 (NAS)
[364] Matthew 5:44-45 (NIV)
[365] Luke 6:31 (NIV)
[366] Matthew 7:2 (NIV)
[367] *The Five People You Meet in Heaven*, Mitch Albom, p. 141, © 2003 by Mitch Albom, Published by Hyperion, 77 West 66th Street, 11th Floor, New York, NY 10023-6298

God tells us to forgive.  We can't be forgiven unless we forgive.

Anger closes my heart – blocks my ability to be truly open to God's word.  The act of forgiveness opens my heart back up – keeping my body ready to receive and understand God's word,

# Challenge 40
## Why have Christians persecuted Jews?

*(Jack Clark's thoughts)*

Despite the recent efforts of the President of Iran to re-write history and claim that the Holocaust never happened, it did! Millions of Jews were exterminated during World War II – not just at the instigation of the major offender, Nazi Germany, but with the collusion of people in France, Italy, Poland, and with similar organized massacres in Russia and other European countries. Throughout the previous centuries there were organized massacres and oppressions against the Jews in most of these countries and even in England. Even the Christian Church as part of the Inquisition was responsible for persecution of Jews – even those who had converted to Christianity. In many of these, Christians were the instigators. In others they tried to ignore the event – individually or as the organized church.

I thank God for the many Individual Christians and officials who did their best to help the Jews in these times – people like the ten Boom family who lived in Amsterdam and hid Jews in their home because they knew they would be killed by the Germans. Eventually the family was discovered and sent to the Ravensbruk concentration camp where several of the family died. Corrie ten Boom lived through this horror and emerged an even more committed Christian. Two of her observations follow: "Forgiveness is the key that unlocks the door of resentment and the handcuffs of hatred." And, "There is no depth so deep that He is not deeper." Dietrich Bonhoeffer was a Lutheran clergyman active in the anti-Hitler resistance. He was offered a job and refuge in the United States in 1939, but declined as he was convinced that it was his duty to face the expected difficulties with the Christians and the anti-Nazi Pastors in the German "church struggle." He was arrested in 1943 for smuggling fourteen Jews to Switzerland and hanged by the Nazis at Flossenburg in April 1945. His papers published after World War II have had great influence in the need to resist war and oppressive political systems and in the need for ecumenism. These Christian heroes and others serve as inspiring tributes to Christian discipleship, martyrdom and heroism from a time when these were in short supply.

So what could have led to such terrible events? There is probably no one answer, but many underlying excuses. The nation of Israel always kept itself aloof from other people.

This was necessary in their early history, or they would have been swallowed up by their enemies or by false religions. When Israel returned from exile they found that many who had not been taken away by Nebuchadnezzar and his army had intermarried with foreigners. To re-purify the nation the people who had made these intermarriages were forced to divorce the foreigners. In Jesus' time the Samaritans who were reviled by the Jews were the descendants of Jews and foreigners who had intermarried. Such events and such actions on the part of the Jewish nation naturally resulted in resentment on the part of some of the people around the nation of Israel and its people. Many of these Samaritans' descendants were the gentiles who were open to the acceptance and affirmation of their value to God that the early Christian church offered them. There naturally would be pent up resentment on the part of these people that would churn inside and boil forth at times despite Christ's admonition to love one another.

In later years the Jewish people have found it necessary to impose segregation on themselves to avoid being absorbed into the communities in which they were living. A need for segregation can result in an appearance of superiority or actually in a sense of superiority. Such a situation will result in resentment by those excluded from the group even if they didn't want to be a part of the group in the first place.

Another factor in the causing of early resentments against the Jews was that wherever Paul went to establish a church, he was followed by a group of Jewish Christians telling the new Gentile converts that Paul was wrong – that they did in fact have to become Jews including following all the dietary and other laws and circumcision in order to be a follower of Christ. This would naturally cause a good deal of resentment among the Gentile Christians. No one likes to be told they are wrong and second class persons. This would cause bad feelings against Jewish people by some of the Christians who were involved even though an early Christian church council made up totally of Jewish Christians decided this was not a requirement.[368]

Another factor that would breed resentment in the early church was that the non-Christian portion of Judaism was determined to stamp out what to them was an apostate splinter group that in their mind threatened the true faith. So the Jewish faith persecuted

---

[368] Acts 15:1-35

the Christians – primarily the Jewish Christians, but they were happy to do everything they could to work against the believers as a whole. This would have led to resentment of Christians. When the persecution of Christians by the Roman emperors was added to this, there were many years of terrible suffering by Christians. The pain and resentment of these combined persecutions and the suffering that they brought about seems to have been more laid to the Jews than to Rome which actually was more responsible for the events.

As often seems to happen, sins against others often give birth later to even greater sins. One of the things that occurred in medieval times was that Jews were excluded from the guilds. This meant that they could not engage in trade or skilled jobs. There was also a legal prohibition at this time against Christians being money lenders, as the church interpreted this as being against the teaching of the Bible. Not being Christians, the Jews were allowed to be money lenders and played a very important role by filling this need of society. Kings, nobles and common people were very often dependant on this function. As often happens when one borrows money even today, people are pleased when they get the loan, but are less than eager when it comes time for repayment. If a money lender, happened to be driven out of the country or even killed by one of the periodic persecutions, the result for the debtor was that the debt was canceled. This resulted in one more risk of evil befalling the Jewish people during this time.

Some of the dominant characteristics of the Jewish people as a whole are that they are hard working and intelligent and industrious. These characteristics were probably an important part of why God chose Israel to be the chosen people to receive His blessing and to pass it on to everyone. These same characteristics and their not wishing to mix with outsiders would lead to economic and political advancement wherever they might be living. Unfortunately these same characteristics and the resultant status that they produced could easily lead to covetous resentment among their neighbors including Christians who are less than perfect in our spiritual lives. Resentment and covetousness are a bad combination that has led to much of the persecution of the Jews.

Well, we've considered some of the natural results of resentment and some of the causes over the years. Now let's consider some of the inflammatory statements by early Gentile Christians. About A.D 100 a book titled *The Epistle of Barnabas* was attributed to

Justin Martyr. Although Stephen was the first martyred Christian according to the Bible and was followed by ten of the disciples giving their lives for their faith, Justin Martyr was such an important person in the early Christian church that his last name would be forever identified with the type of death he suffered for his beliefs. Martyr and martyred are terms now used for anyone killed for their belief. Justin Martyr in his book wrote, "Take heed now to yourselves, and not to be like some, and saying, 'The covenant is both theirs and ours.' But thus they (the Jews) finally lost it."[369]

Irenaeus has been called the founder of Christian theology. He was Bishop of Lyon in Gaul. He worked to correct the Gnostic heresies that threatened the early Christian church. About A.D. 180 Irenaeus wrote, "They who boast themselves as being the house of Jacob and the people of Israel, are disinherited from the grace of God."[370]

The much respected early church historian, Origen is said to have written six thousand books on religious subjects. He was born and educated in Alexandria, Egypt and died from torture at the order of the Roman Emperor Decius. Included in Origen's writings in about A.D. 250, was his understanding that when the scriptures referred to Jesus being sent to the lost sheep of Israel this was an allegorical reference to Christians who were the "heavenly" lost sheep rather than the Jews who were "carnal" lost sheep.[371]

John Chrysostom was one of the most highly regarded early Christian fathers. His preaching was so moving that he was given the title that became his last name and translates golden-mouthed. The collection of his sermons, the *Homilies* of St. John Chrysostom are considered among the best of ancient Christian writings. He was born at Antioch, Syria. He became the patriarch of Constantinople and was famous for his charity. In A.D. 387 he preached in Rome and is recorded as having said, "It is because you (the Jews) killed Christ... It is because you shed the precious blood that there is now no restoration, no mercy anymore, and no defense... You have committed the ultimate transgression. This is why you are being punished worse now than in the past... If this

---

[369] "The Roots of Replacement Theology," the magazine *Israel My Glory*, May/June 2007, p. 19 from "The Epistle of Barnabas," *The Anti-Nicene Fathers,* ed. A. Roberts and J. Donaldson, vol. 1 (1885; reprint Grand Rapids: Eerdmans, 1993) chapter 4.

[370] Ibid, p. 19, Irenaeus, "Against Heresies," *The Anti-Nicene Fathers,* op. cit., 3:21:1.

[371] Ibid, p. 19, from Origen, *"De Principiis,"* *The Anti-Nicene Fathers,* op. cit., vol. 4, 4.1.22.

were not the case God would not have turned his back on you so completely."[372] It would have been interesting in view of his conclusion to have asked his evaluation about why the Christian Church had itself been so cruelly persecuted. Would he have presumed it was because God had turned his back on them? Was it possible that this line of reasoning could have included Christ himself as personally guilty of sins rather than taking our sins on himself that resulted in his crucifixion and in God having forsaken him?

Well with such a background, it seems easy to understand the scene in the musical Fiddler on the Roof where the Christian Russian officer refers to the Jewish people as Jesus killers and justifies their persecution.

To me these views seem totally wrong. Our savior, Jesus Christ, was himself an observant Jew who made a great point of claiming that he had not come to change the law. All the Apostles were Jews. All the books of the Old Testament were brought to us initially in the oral tradition of Israel and then written down by Jewish scholars. Only two books of the New Testament (Luke and Acts) were written by anyone who was not a Jew. All the promises and covenants in the Old Testament were made by God with the people of Israel forever. There is nothing in the Bible about forever ending with Christ's crucifixion. Jesus is quoted speaking to his disciples: "I tell you the truth, at the renewal of all things, when the Son of Man sits on his glorious throne, you who have followed me will also sit on twelve thrones, judging the twelve tribes of Israel. And everyone who has left houses or brothers or sisters or father or mother or children or fields for my sake will receive a hundred times as much and will inherit eternal life."[373] Interesting to observe that even though only the tribes of Levi, Benjamin, and Judah had kept knowledge of their identity at that time that God knows the whereabouts of the lost tribes of Israel and even more to the point of this discussion that there will be no loss of their standing with God at the last judgment. Again in the Book of Revelation, the tribes of Israel are there.[374]

There is only thing recorded in the Bible that seems to me to be possibly useful to justify contempt for Jews. It occurred during the trial of Jesus before Pilate. Pilate is trying to release Jesus because he has found no fault with him. The Jewish leaders have

---

[372] Ibid, p. 19, Quoted in Rosemary Ruether, *Faith and Fratricide: The Theological Roots of Anti-Semitism,* Eugene, OR, Wipf & Stock, 1995, pp. 146-147.
[373] Matthew 19: 28-29 (NIV)
[374] Revelation 7:1-8

blackmailed Pilate: "Pilate tried to set Jesus free, but the Jews kept shouting, 'If you let this man go, you are no friend of Caesar. Anyone who claims to be a king opposes Caesar.'"[375] Pilate finally gave in. No Roman wanted to be accused of being an enemy of Caesar. He washed his hands, declaring, "'I am innocent of this man's blood... It's your responsibility.' All the people answered, 'Let his blood be on us and on our children.'"[376] While this conceivably could be used by those who would through the years blame the Jewish people for Christ's death, I don't believe God would let a blood thirsty mob revoke the promises He had made to His chosen people forever, nor do I believe that God would allow these few people to condemn the entire nation for all time. Not when God Himself declared about this often rebellious people: "I have loved you with an <u>everlasting</u> love; I have drawn you with loving-kindness. I will build you up again and you will be rebuilt, O Virgin Israel. Again you will take up your tambourine and go out to dance with the joyful."[377]

A very significant passage from the Bible that Martyr, Irenaeus, Origen, and John Chrysostom seemed to have missed was written by Paul: "I ask then, did God reject his people? By no means! I am an Israelite myself, a descendant of Abraham, from the tribe of Benjamin. God did not reject his people, whom he foreknew. Don't you know that the Scripture says in the passage about Elijah – how he appealed to God against Israel: 'Lord, they have killed your prophets and torn down your alters; I am the only one left, and they are trying to kill me.' And what was God's answer to him? 'I have reserved for myself seven thousand who have not bowed the knee to Baal.' So too at the present time there is a remnant chosen by grace. And if by grace, then it is no longer by works; if it were, grace would no longer be grace." Paul goes on to say that some of the branches of the house of Israel have been broken off and that we Gentiles have been grafted onto the tree and nourished by the tree of Israel. He also urges us, "Do not boast over those branches. If you do, consider this: You do not support the root, but the root supports you... Do not be arrogant, but be afraid. For if God did not spare the natural branches, he will not spare you either. Consider therefore the kindness and sternness of God: sternness to those who fell, but kindness to you, provided that you continue in his kindness... I do not want you to be ignorant of this mystery, brothers, so that you may not be conceited: Israel has

---

[375] John 19:12 (NIV)
[376] Matthew 27:24-25 (NIV)
[377] Jeremiah 31:3-4 (NIV)

270

experienced a hardening in part until the full number of the Gentiles has come in. And so all Israel will be saved, as it is written: 'The deliverer will come from Zion; he will turn godlessness away from Jacob. And this is my covenant with them when I take away their sins.'[378] As far as the gospel is concerned, they are enemies on your account, but as far as election is concerned, they are loved on account of the patriarchs, for God's gifts and his call are irrevocable."[379]

So why do Christians persecute Jews? Many reasons – some have to do with haughtiness of some Jews. Some have to do with persecutions of Christians (including Jewish Christians) by some of the Jews. Some have to do with the sin of Christians coveting what Jews have achieved, and some have to do with the terrible errors of some of the early Christian church Fathers ignoring scripture and ignoring Jesus' command that we love one another and that we go and make disciples. There are still Jewish Christians, but it is a wonder after all they have been through in the past. To me it still shows that they are very special people – indeed God's chosen. It is certainly difficult to understand how they could face the persecutions by other Christians that they have faced over the years and still choose to follow Christ. The Holy Spirit truly must be active in their souls.

Forgive us Father in heaven, for we have sinned!

*(Betty Byers answer)*

Ignorance!

---

[378] Isaiah 59:20, 21; 27:9
[379] Romans 11:1-29 (NIV)

271

# Challenge 41
## How does a Christian view war?
(Question submitted by John Munson)

*(Jack Clark's thoughts)*

Here there is a question that will certainly not result in uniform answers by every Christian. The Friends (Quakers), Mennonites, Amish, and Brethren among us would answer that no war is justified. And they have good scriptural support for their stand. Consider the following Bible verses. "You have heard that it was said, 'Love your neighbor and hate your enemy.' But I tell you: Love your enemies and pray for those who persecute you, that you may be sons of your Father in heaven. He causes the sun to rise on the evil and the good, and sends rain on the righteous and the unrighteous."[380] In the Beatitudes Christ tells us, "Blessed are the peacemakers, for they will be called sons of God."[381] In another verse Jesus is speaking to Peter at the time of Jesus' arrest and following Peter's cutting off the ear of the servant of the high priest: "Put your sword back in its place... for all who draw the sword will die by the sword."[382] Significantly Christ illustrates his admonition to love our enemies by healing the damaged ear. One of the most potent evangelistic tools the early Christians had was their non-violent response to the evils thrust upon them by Rome and other authorities.

Many Christians feel strongly that wars of self-defense are justified. World War II could be cited as an example of this type of event. Some would say that wars are justifiable as a last resort to correct grievous wrongs – such as the American Revolution (although there certainly were also other less worthy motives by some who promoted this war).

Even more Christians could probably be convinced that wars to protect other innocent people being subjected to persecution are justified. In addition to World War II they might suggest peace-keeping efforts in African conflicts or in Bosnia as examples. The problem of course is that any of these events result in some atrocities by both sides that are sickening to any Christian. Even the Civil War in the United States that resulted in the very laudable freeing of the slaves didn't start out with such a high purpose, and quite frankly this objective was not supported by a large minority of the northerners who considered themselves Christian. In considering the motives of so many, it would seem

---

[380] Matthew 5:43-45 (NIV)
[381] Matthew 5:9 (NIV)
[382] Matthew 26:52 (NIV)

that the laudable results of such conflicts can be cited as examples of the observation in scripture that "In all things God works for the good of those who love him, who have been called according to his purpose."[383]

There are other wars, wars of aggression such as the Indian Wars that many Christians would not be able to support. Although even such wars as these were supported by many who saw themselves as Christians at the time.

Historically it would seem from Jesus' viewpoint some of the saddest wars of aggression have been fought claiming they were for the glory of Christ. These would include the Crusades that may have had a laudable objective, but developed into wars of plunder and atrocities – not only against Moslem people but also against the Jews and even other Christians. Programs of persecution of the Jews have been carried out in many Christian countries – not just 20th century Germany, but Russia, France, Spain, and even England in the middle ages. These were based on the excuse that the Jews crucified Jesus. What a flimsy excuse that is. The reasoning bypasses the fact that the Romans had the final legal right to crucify or to not crucify, but thankfully no one has ever persecuted the Italians. This misdirected hatred ignores the fact that Jesus himself was a Jew and that all the disciples were Jews, and that all the books of the New Testament except Luke and Acts were written by Jews. It also ignores the promises of God that were made to the Jewish people for all time. No wonder that the Messianic Jewish Christian movement is so small! Of course in the 1700s we can find French or Spanish Christians killing English Christians and English Christians returning the favor. Very recently we have had Catholics killing Protestants and Protestants killing Catholics in Northern Ireland. If there are any tears of sadness in heaven by God or Christ, these kinds of warfare must certainly be one of the causes!

From the standpoint of scripture, there certainly are many wars in the Old Testament. Some of these are clearly wars of self defense, but some of the wars by Israel are clearly wars of aggression such as the taking of the Promised Land. This kind of a war would be hard for most of us to justify, but the leaders of Israel understood this was God's will, and the nation even got into trouble with God when they didn't fully prosecute the war. Joshua

---

[383] Romans 8:28 (NIV)

even understood that an angelic army fought with them in battle: "When Joshua was near Jericho, he looked up and saw a man standing in front of him with a drawn sword in his hand. Joshua went up to him and asked, 'Are you for us or for our enemies?' 'Neither' he replied, 'but as commander of the army of the Lord I have now come.' Then Joshua fell facedown to the ground in reverence, and asked him, 'What message does my Lord have for his servant?' The commander of the Lord's army replied, 'Take off your sandals, for the place where you are standing is holy.' And Joshua did so."[384] I have discussed this elsewhere in the area of how could the God of the Old Testament be the God of the New Testament?

The Bible even mentions spiritual warfare between God and the forces of evil. I suppose that every Christian would feel this type of warfare is justified. "Our struggle is not against flesh and blood, but against the rulers, against the authorities, against the powers of this dark world and against the spiritual forces of evil in the heavenly realms. Therefore put on the full armor of God, so that when the day of evil comes, you may be able to stand your ground, and after you have done everything, to stand. Stand firm then, with the belt of truth buckled around your waist, with the breastplate of righteousness in place, and with your feet fitted with the readiness that comes from the gospel of peace. In addition to all this, take up the shield of faith with which you can extinguish all the flaming arrows of the evil one. Take the helmet of salvation and the sword of the Spirit, which is the word of God, and pray in the Spirit on all occasions with all kinds of prayers and requests."[385] Certainly this seems to be making us ready to do spiritual battle.

However, in the book of Revelation it certainly sounds like a spiritual battle will be fought in physical terms with Jesus Christ as commander of the Armies of God: "I saw heaven open wide, and before my eyes appeared a white horse, whose rider is called faithful and true, for his judgment and warfare are just. His eyes are a flame of fire, and there are many diadems on his head. There is a name written upon him known only to himself. He is dressed in a cloak dipped in blood, and the name by which he is known is the Word of God. The armies of Heaven follow him, riding upon white horses and clad in white spotless linen. Out of his mouth there comes a sharp sword with which to strike the nations. He will shepherd them with a 'rod of iron.'" The account goes on, "I saw the

---

[384] Joshua 5:13-15
[385] Ephesians 6:12-18 (NIV) also see Revelation 12:7-17 (NIV)

animal with the kings of the earth and their armies massed together for battle against the rider upon the horse and his army." [386] It seems obvious Jesus Christ is going to do battle against evil, and that evil is prepared to do battle against good. Some would affirm that this is an allegory, a story in which symbols are used to illustrate truths, but many Christians anticipate a literal battle. Fortunately for us we know the end of the episode whether a literal or an allegorical event is being reported. God wins! Satan loses! And it's by far better to be on the winning team!

Dr. Timothy Johnson who is well-known for his health advice on television suggests: "Jesus reveals a God who weeps over the loss of life, even when justified by earthly necessity, because it represents a failure of the gift of free choice. In other words, war is always a failure of some humans to choose life over death, to choose love over hatred, to choose inclusion over exclusion. Although I believe war sometimes becomes necessary to correct the results of our human sinfulness, I can't believe that is ever God's hope for humankind."[387]

In the Broadway Musical *Jesus Christ Superstar*, one of the disciples asks a question. Jesus responds, but the response really doesn't satisfy. The disciple complains, "But you didn't answer the question." The character playing Jesus says, "I never said I would give you all the answers." This is seemingly one of the questions to which we haven't been given all the answers. It would seem that generally war should be avoided, but that there are obviously some wars that are justified and have God's blessing and participation.

*(Betty Byers' thoughts)*

We Christians do not like war; however, we support our troops that serve and pray for them. We send care packages and letters to let them know we care.

---

[386] Revelation 19:11-21 (JBP)

[387] Dr. G. Timothy Johnson, *Finding God in the Questions,* p. 174, Intervarsity Press, ©2004 by Timothy Johnson

Challenge 42

# What about homosexuality?

One of the great challenges of the church today is the problem of how to deal with homosexuality. How do you understand this?
1. Did God say Homosexual relations are a sin?
2. Can the church declare a sin to no longer be a sin?
3. Can a practicing homosexual be a part of the Kingdom of God?
4. What do those who have defended a change in attitude have to say?
5. What significance does this have for church leaders?
6. What should be the attitude of church members?

*(Jack Clark's thoughts)*

This question requires consideration of several points listed above.

In 1998 our denomination of the church, the United Methodists, faced the wrenching prospect of becoming the disunited Methodists. Many of the universal church's splits in the past have been on minor matters such as form of worship, how ministers are selected to serve local congregations, or other non-basic issues, but this seemed to be based on a much deeper perception of values. There was a national church trial held in Kearney, Nebraska that acquitted an ordained minister of the United Methodist Church of defying the Book of Discipline of the United Methodist Church and his Bishop by performing a covenanting ceremony to bless the union of two lesbians. While this was not actually a marriage ceremony, its effect and public perception were the same. Suspension of the minister's pastoral duties was lifted after the decision. The jury voted eight to five in favor of conviction on the charges with nine votes in favor of the charges required for conviction. The observation had been made that such a ceremony recognized the importance of the couple in God's sight, gave them a sense of personal worth and acceptance, and recognized their resolve to lead responsible lives committed to each other. In addition to the United Methodists, the Episcopalians and the Presbyterians have been struggling with this issue.

In thinking about this question and the facets of the answer, it is important to consider what a sin is. A sin is anything that leads a person away from God. Usually sins also separate us from other God-seeking people. Since Christians accept God as our creator and the example on which we are to build our behavioral morality, it follows that if God has indicated that a particular action is sinful that is the case. The Bible contains many records of what Christians affirm is God-given revelation of moral values to various God-seeking people. Probably the most basic of these revelations is in the Ten

Commandments given through Moses, but many other prophets were also given such revelations. Jesus Christ considerably expanded our understanding of the nature of sin by including our thoughts that tend to lead us away from God and negative passions as well as actions as being sinful. He also talked about the need for positive thoughts and actions that lead us closer to God and benefit others that should replace the negative constraints[388]

There are sins into which we fall by accident or deception. There are also sins that involve a person or a group deliberately turning their back on God and embracing evil. This latter act is also known as a transgression. Either can ultimately lead to spiritual death.[389] It would seem the sin that involves deliberate choice should be avoided at all cost because each act of such defiance makes it easier to willfully grow ever farther away from God with future choices. It seemed to many that this is the type of sin with which our denomination was being presented. This was a calculated move on the part of the minister defying denominational rules established by our General Conference, the specific directions of his Bishop, and most importantly what was felt by many to be the authority of scripture in order to advance his agenda and the agenda of the homosexual community.

The church is filled with sinners. I am one of them. It's to announce God's redemption of our sins through Jesus Christ that He devised the sacrifice that was made on the cross. If the church should ever fail to embrace the sinner, offering Christ's salvation and grace, we would cease to be the church. On the other hand, whenever the church embraces or sanctifies the sin, it also risks ceasing to be the church of Jesus Christ. This is a narrow path and one that isn't easy to follow. It would seem that, in this instance, the church was being asked to sanctify the sin.

On the other side of this question is the statement attributed to Christ: "You are Peter, and on this rock I will build my church, and the gates of Hades will not overcome it. I will give you the keys of heaven; whatever you bind on earth will be bound in heaven, and whatever you loose on earth will be loosed in heaven."[390] Some Christians understand this power to have been given only to Peter. Roman Catholic Christians understand that

---

[388] Matthew 5:17-48
[389] First John 5:16-17 (JBP)
[390] Matthew 16:18-19 (NIV)

the power was given to the office that Peter filled as the first Pope, and some Christians understand that it had been given to the church as a whole. In theory it would seem that Peter, or the Pope, or the Church as a whole (according to one's view of the verse) might be able to declare what had been a sin to no longer be a sin! There is no record that Peter ever declared homosexuality not to be a sin. I am pretty sure that no Pope has ever declared homosexuality not to be a sin despite the tragically sad transgressions of some individual priests. To get the total church to make a declaration of anything certainly would be impossible.

From a personal standpoint, I am old enough to have had a homosexual man in my early medical practice who served a prison sentence for homosexual solicitation. He was never obnoxious to me or in my office. He cared for his aged mother with tenderness (more than some people in my practice who attended church did). Two of my dear church friends have daughters who are lesbians. Another couple who are church friends had a son who was a homosexual. I am a personal friend of one of the lesbian women, having known her since she was a child. One of the women is HIV infected. I was the physician of the man until the time of his death from AIDS. I did surgery to drain the abscessed malignant skin tumors due to the Kaposi's sarcoma and personally treated him through multiple bouts of pneumonia, infectious uncontrollable diarrhea, and developing dementia that complicate the last part of the lives of AIDS patients. I held his hand to let him know of my concern and compassion when this was the only comfort left I could give him. I hope I was able to convey to him how precious he was in God's eyes. They had and have my deepest sympathy for the horrible illness that has destroyed one and is destroying the second one. They and their families have my compassion and love for the heartaches and lost dreams that their lifestyles have inflicted on the three children and their parents. They have my hope and prayers for their salvation through the cleansing of their sins by the love, grace, blood, and sacrifice of Jesus Christ just as he saved me from my own sins. I would not classify myself as a homophobic.

Jesus said to the woman caught in adultery and saved from stoning by the Pharisees, that he did not condemn her and that she should go and sin no more.[391] He didn't instruct her to forget the incident, go on sinning if she wished, nor to assume that sin has no price.

---

[391] John 8:3-11 (NIV)

Sin does indeed have a price. Jesus Christ paid a terrible price for the forgiveness of the sins of any of us who will accept that forgiveness. As far as God is concerned, when we have accepted that forgiveness, he removes our sins from us "as far as the east is from the west."[392] However, part of that acceptance is that we become convicted in our own understanding of our sin and repent of it. Repentance involves a genuine sorrow for what we have done, making amends when possible, and a determination to do whatever we can to turn our lives around avoiding the sin in the future in-so-far as we are capable with God's help. Even though God forgives our sins and forgets them, they still have consequences in our lives and the lives of those the sin has affected.

To maneuver the church into performing a covenanting ceremony and thereby placing its stamp of approval on the sin of homosexual union, does not speak of conviction. To go on living in a homosexual union does not represent repentance.

Some would have us believe that homosexuality is not a sin. They speak of a gene that makes some people inclined to become homosexuals. They indicate that, if it is proven to be present, it cannot be resisted and nullifies homosexuality as a sin. Although this genetic theory is not proven, there may in fact be such a gene that does predispose some people to this sin. Likewise there are genes that predispose some people to being violent, but so far the church has not approved the violent lifestyle of a wanton murderer or a wife beater because of their genetic make up. One of the genes that is certainly associated with violence is the gene that makes men male. There are many more violent males in our society than violent females, yet we expect males to cultivate their tender, compassionate side and resist their tendency to be violent. Additionally there are other recognized genes that cause even a greater tendency to be violent, but our society expects those who carry these genes to control their genetic tendencies. Certainly not every person with the possible "homosexual" gene is a practicing homosexual. Although identical twins carry all the same genetic material, not all identical twins of a homosexual person are themselves homosexual.

There can be no mistaking the Bible's stance on homosexuality. It is an abomination to God and is detestable.[393] God caused the destruction of Sodom and Gomorrah in the Old

---

[392] Psalm 103:10-14 (NIV)
[393] Leviticus 18:22 (NIV)

Testament because of this sin.[394] The tribe of Benjamin was practically wiped out by the rest of Israel because they refused to give up for punishment some of their members who by choice would have sodomized the Levite who was visiting their town but who traded this desire to become bisexual rapists and murderers.[395] Christ himself referred to the sins of Sodom and Gomorrah and their resultant destruction in the New Testament.[396] There can be no doubt, if we believe the Bible accounts, that God considered this a sin and that God abhors this sin, as he abhors any sin. We can also rest assured that any new revelation of God only amplifies or clarifies previous revelation. It never changes it.

I strongly doubt that any Methodist minister would honor a request for a marriage ceremony that would result in polyandry or polygamy. Certainly there is very little scriptural basis for denying marriage to multiple partners, but there is scriptural recording of the heartache and jealousies that go with such an arrangement. All the pain, bad feeling, and jostling for position between the sisters Leah and Rachel would hardly recommend such a marriage.[397] Such a request would almost assuredly be turned down even if the group expressed that they felt they were very suited and wished to have such a ceremony to have the church's blessing on their predetermined living arrangement. Even if they would say that such a sanction was highly desired as it recognized the importance of the group in God's sight, gave them a sense of personal worth and acceptance, and recognized their resolve to lead responsible lives committed to each other. Even if they pled genetic necessity because there is a God-given genetic urge for a man or a woman to have more than one mate, I doubt that this would bring compliance.

The poignant tragedy of the homosexuals who do wish to avoid a wild and irresponsible lifestyle with a committed relationship is that they long to be assured God loves them and that Christ's redemption is for them just as I and every other person do at some level of our soul. We, as members of the church, must assure them of God's love and Christ's redemption. Christ longs for each of them to be a son or daughter of the King, just as he longs for this blessing for every one of us.

Christ and his disciples had a discussion indicating that for some persons it "is better

---

[394] Genesis 13:13, Genesis 19:1-29, and Jeremiah 23:14 (NIV)
[395] Judges 19:1 through 21:25 (NIV)
[396] Matthew 10:15 through 11:24, Luke 17:29, and Jude 7-8 (NIV)
[397] Genesis 29:1 through 35:26 (NIV)

not to marry." The disciples were referring to the demands of Christ that we not divorce except for unfaithfulness. Christ responded that it is appropriate for some to "renounce marriage because of the Kingdom of heaven."[398] The modern priests of the Roman Catholic Church and Christ himself chose to renounce marriage because of the pressing needs of their responsibilities.[399] Some should renounce marriage because they cannot make the required commitment. Some renounce marriage because of health problems that cannot be overcome and out of love for the person who would be their caregiver. I think Christ might say to the homosexuals who cannot be helped to a heterosexual orientation that they should join the ranks of those who should renounce marriage because of the Kingdom. Because we all long for tender, deeply committed human companionship, this is a difficult thing. It is no less difficult than the person who knows he has the gene for Huntington's chorea renouncing marriage to avoid passing the physically and mentally destroying disease on to future children and to avoid the years of despair and care that marriage would impose on the person they love. For some, the most loving thing is not to marry and to direct their love to God and into agape and brotherly love rather than erotic love.

Am I saying that there is no place in the Kingdom of God for the practicing homosexual who continues in a monogamous relationship? No. Not at all. I am convinced that Jesus Christ is the only judge of who will be in the Kingdom of Heaven. He has said, "No one comes to the Father except through me."[400] I am also convinced that there will be absolutely no one in the Kingdom who was not a sinner, because, "All have sinned and fall short of the glory of God."[401] The determining factor for inclusion is the redemption of our sins by Jesus Christ and the individual's acceptance of that redemption. A very pertinent point is made by the Apostle Paul. He has spoken of wanting to do good but finding evil ever a problem to avoid. He speaks of the law of sin at work in his body waging war against the law of his mind. He finally comes to the conclusion: "What a wretched man I am! Who will rescue me from this body of death? Thanks be to God—through Jesus Christ, our Lord! So then, I myself in my mind am a slave to God's law, but in the sinful nature to the law of sin. Therefore there is now no condemnation for those who are in

---

[398] Matthew 19:9-12 (NIV)

[399] It is interesting to note that this requirement was not originally made for a person to be a Roman Catholic Priest. We know that Peter who is counted as the first Pope was married, as the Bible speaks of his mother-in-law (see Matthew 8:14-15)

[400] John 14:6 (NIV)

[401] Romans 3:23 (NIV)

Christ Jesus."[402]

In case some might mistakenly infer that a homosexual life style is the worst sin, it isn't. Remember there is only one unforgivable sin: blasphemy against the Holy Spirit.[403] All sins are an abomination to God. We just must be especially committed not to sanctify any of them. Placing power or money or even family above God is a great sin and an abomination. Lusting after someone else's spouse in our heart is as great a sin as adultery and an abomination to God. Being angry with our brother is the same as murder.[404] Jesus said that to divorce one's wife except for marital unfaithfulness constitutes the sin of adultery.[405] I divorced my first wife and was therefore guilty of this sin regardless of all the circumstances that seemed to justify the action at the time. I believe Christ cleansed me from this sin when I accepted his redemption and salvation. I believe he will also cleanse people from the sin of homosexuality, but we have to confess our sins and repent of our sins, or we can't receive the free gift of forgiveness. Putting extra time on our work record is stealing. A little white lie or even avoidance of telling the whole truth is still false witness. Yearning to be able to do the things my neighbor does is coveting. All these are sins. All these are an abomination to God. None of these sins can be totally avoided by any of us, but we must not sanctify them. We must not embrace them. We especially must not embrace them in a way that represents them as approved by the church, as this risks becoming a stumbling block to others that could destroy their salvation.[406]

The present failure of the befuddled church is not the first time we have embraced or even sanctified sin rather than reserving our embrace and grace for the sinner. In the middle ages, the church embraced the horrible sin of the Inquisition in the name of keeping the church pure. More recently the church in Bosnia embraced the sin of ethnic cleansing as being justified by past atrocities on the other side. Part of the German church embraced the sin of the Holocaust, and the church in Rome tried to ignore it. Thank God for some brave Christians such as Dietrich Bonhoeffer and Corrie Ten Boom's family who defied the state and ignored the church's embracing of the sin to fight against this atrocity. Great Britain has been rife with both the Protestant church and the Roman Catholic Church embracing the sin of persecuting, hating, and killing one another in years past. This sin most recently plagued Northern Ireland. Christ must weep! Our own Methodist denomination had a previous break in the fellowship before and during the Civil War, because Methodism in the south embraced the sin of slavery. They justified this by declaring that blacks were the descendants of Cain,

[402] Romans 7:1-25 & 8:1-2 (NIV)
[403] Matthew 12:31-32 and Luke 12:8-10
[404] Matthew 5:17-31
[405] Matthew 5:32
[406] First Corinthians 8:10-13

and the pigment of their skin was the mark that God had put on Cain. In their thinking, they declared that the descendants of Cain should have to serve the descendants of Abel throughout all time. There is no indication in Scripture of what constituted the mark of Cain. Wouldn't it be ironic if it turned out to be the removing of pigment from the initially dark skin? Most of us recognize these as false teachings with horrible cost to many individuals and to society and to the church itself. Let us not slip into the heresy of approving homosexual unions. Let us stand firm in facing this sin, ever ready to love the sinner, but always determined to hate the sin – whatever the sin may be.

On March 30, 1998, I happened to tune into a public broadcasting radio station as I was driving to Chicago. I believe the program was Talk of the Nation. The discussion group featured Rev. Jimmy Creech, the United Methodist pastor who was the subject of the church trial in Nebraska that I have already mentioned, with a retired Methodist Bishop and a third person. Mr. Creech's statements that certainly are at variance with established religious beliefs of our denomination and my comments on his observations included the following:

1. Mr. Creech stated that Fundamentalist lay persons have not been instructed in how Scripture was selected and therefore falsely believe all Scripture is without error. He faulted the clergy including himself for this lack of instruction. There are certainly many of us who characterize ourselves as Fundamentalist who understand the way the Scripture was selected. We recognize that large parts of the Bible were passed in oral tradition resulting in some inconsequential differences in the accounts. The Bible unabashedly presents these differing versions. We recognize that there were numerous writings that were excluded by the early church. Another thing that we recognize that Mr. Creech does not seem to recognize is that the writings that were selected to become scripture were chosen by the acceptance of the church as a whole through general agreement of the congregations and through ratification of the whole church often gathered in great church councils. We believe that the Holy Spirit directed these church fathers in their choice even as he had directed the writers of the various books of the Bible. In no instance did a single person decide what would or would not be accepted as canon. Even Luther who did not feel that the book of Revelation deserved to be included in the Bible succeeded in having it removed.

2. Mr. Creech maintained that the Old Testament rules are not relevant to today's society, as they were for an entirely different time and circumstance. Specifically they were for a desert people surrounded by antagonistic neighbors who were anxious to destroy them. In such a setting, it was important that they maximize the number of births in order to have future fighting men. For this reason it was important to those people at that time that only heterosexual relations be allowed. Mr. Creech disregards the Old

Testament concept of the remnant.[407] God repeatedly chose only a small part of the people to be left to do His work and even specifically chose to reduce fighting force numbers under Gideon to seemingly ridiculously small numbers when more were available in order to impress on Israel that it was basically by the strength of God that they were saved rather than by their own power.[408] We Fundamentalists do recognize that there are things in the Bible that only had significance to the people at that time such as not eating pork to avoid the frequent parasite infections that went with its eating. We also recognize that such things as ritually cleaning pots[409] and not cooking a kid in its mother's milk[410] were practices that had significance to the Hebrew people but hold no place in our religious practices. However, these things are not fundamental rules of morality. Certainly Christ himself talked about laws of man versus the laws of God such as when he spoke against the practice of making one's possessions Corban or dedicated to God in order to avoid God's directions that each person is to care for their father and mother.[411] Also Jesus got into trouble on multiple occasions with the Pharisees because he healed on the Sabbath. His response was: "The Sabbath was made for man, not man for the Sabbath."[412] Christ also cautions us, "Do not think that I have come to abolish the Law or the Prophets; I have not come to abolish them but to fulfill them. I tell you the truth, until heaven and earth disappear, not the smallest letter, not the least stroke of a pen will by any means disappear from the Law until everything is accomplished. Anyone who breaks one of the least of these commandments and teaches others to do the same will be called least in the kingdom of heaven, but whoever practices and teaches these commands will be called great in the kingdom of heaven."[413] He teaches that helping others on the Sabbath is in fact keeping it Holy. He teaches that our thoughts and desires are as important as our actions in the obeying of the Law.[414] If we deny the Old Testament's values because they were set up in a different time, as Rev. Creech suggests, we could just as validly deny the teachings of the New Testament on the same basis. If we deny part of the Old Testament on this basis, there is no basis for accepting anything in the Old Testament. This includes the existence of God, the validity of the Ten Commandments, and prophesies about Christ's predicted coming and redemption.

3. Mr. Creech made the statement that even if some totally accept the Old Testament, it only speaks against male homosexuality, not female homosexuality. Paul asserts, "You are all sons of God through

---

[407] Genesis 45:7, Second Kings 19:4-31, Second Chronicles 36:20-23, Ezra 9:8-14, Nehemiah 1:2-11. Isaiah 11:1-16, Isaiah 28:5-6, Isaiah 37:30-32, Jeremiah 6:6-9, Jeremiah 23:1-7, Jeremiah 42, Jeremiah 50:20, Micah 2:12-13, Micah 4:6-7, Micah 5:7-9, Micah 7:18-20, Zephaniah 2:6-7, Zephaniah 3:12-20, Zechariah 8:4-17, and Romans 11:1-10
[408] Judges 6:1-7:23
[409] Leviticus 6:28
[410] Deuteronomy 14:21
[411] Mark 7:9-13
[412] Mark 2:27
[413] Matthew 5:17-20
[414] Matthew 5:21-48

faith in Christ Jesus, for all of you who were baptized into Christ have been clothed with Christ. There is neither Jew nor Greek, slave nor free, <u>male nor female</u>, for you are all one in Christ Jesus."[415]  My understanding of this is that all the blessings of Christ are fully available to every believer, and that the flip side of this is that all believers carry the same obligations and responsibilities. It is a thinly veiled fallacy to suggest that men are subject to a religious responsibility to which women are exempt. It is interesting to note that, Mr. Creech does not mention that the New Testament does specifically deal with the subject of both female and male homosexuality as follows: "God gave them over in the sinful desires of their hearts to sexual impurity for the degrading of their bodies with one another. They exchanged the truth of God for a lie, and worshipped and served created things rather than the Creator-who is forever praised. Amen. Because of this, God gave them over to shameful lusts. Even their women exchanged natural relations for unnatural ones. In the same way the men also abandoned natural relations with women and were inflamed with lust for one another. Men committed indecent acts with other men, and received in themselves the due penalty for their perversion.[416]

4. Mr. Creech suggested that animals demonstrate homosexual behavior, suggesting that if God made animals this way, it must have been part of God's plan. One can only draw the logical conclusion that if one action of animals indicates an action is all right for a Christian then any action of an animal would equally prove it is all right for a Christian. Some animals will mate outside their own species. Does this make bestiality all right for a Christian? I think not. I have seen a mother animal eat its newborn offspring, and a father cat will kill its kittens. Does this make cannibalism of newborns or infanticide by a father acceptable? I don't think so!

5. Mr. Creech stated that God would have not made people homosexuals if this were not acceptable to Him. By the same fuzzy illogical process, one could conclude that since God made people who are prone to violence, killing, hate, stealing, adultery, lying, sexual abusers, pedophiles, and those who put other things in importance before God (idolatry) that all these practices are also acceptable to God. I don't think so, and neither do most other Christians.

The final point that I recall Mr. Creech making was that Jesus never spoke against homosexuality. If one goes by such a narrow criterion, it could be noted that Jesus never spoke against bestiality or gang rape, and I strongly doubt he was for any of these deviant practices. There are multiple references in the Old Testament on the subject and especially on the consequences of such sin in the towns of Sodom and Gomorrah. Of course, Mr. Creech discounts these references. By inference, it seems to me that Christ

---

[415] Galatians 3:26-28
[416] Romans 1:24-27

did speak against homosexuality. After some of the towns of Israel had rejected him, he said, "I tell you the truth, it will be more bearable for Sodom and Gomorrah on the day of judgment than for that town."[417] Certainly this was an instance of holding up a bad example. Christ was not saying that everything would be all right for Sodom and Gomorrah on the Day of Judgment. What he was saying was that as great as their sins were and as great as their guilt and punishment were to be, that the sins, guilt, and punishment of those who reject Christ will be even greater. If one accepts the words in the Revelation of John as having been spoken by Christ, then he did have something negative to say about sexual sins even though the exact nature of the sins are not specified: "To the angel of the church in Thyatira write... I have this against you: You tolerate that woman Jezebel, who calls herself a prophetess. By her teaching she misleads my servants into sexual immorality and the eating of food sacrificed to idols. I have given her time to repent of her immorality, but she is unwilling. So I will cast her on a bed of suffering, and I will make those who commit adultery with her suffer intensely, unless they repent of her ways."[418] It should be noted that the reference to adultery can refer to any unfaithfulness of God's people to God and does not necessarily define the specific nature of her sexual immorality.

It seems to me that Rev. Creech's theological problem arises from his understandable compassion for those caught in the sin of practicing homosexuality. Certainly Christ taught that it is proper for us to feel compassion for sinners. In the words of the comic strip character Pogo, "We have met the enemy, and he is us!" We are all sinners, and Christ directed us to work to bring God's grace to other sinners, just as we have been given that grace for our sins. The problem is that redemption, forgiveness, and grace do not come by redefining the action as not being sin. There are reports of one hundred twenty other ministers and even some Bishops and the California/Nevada and Troy (New York) Conferences who are ready to embrace this sin.[419] The majority of United Methodists have indicated in our Discipline and in our meetings that we do not agree with this approach. More importantly God has indicated that He does not agree with this approach.

The Bible has something to say about this situation: "'Woe to the shepherds who are destroying and scattering the sheep of my pasture!' declares the Lord. Therefore this is what the Lord, the God of Israel, says to the shepherds who tend my people; 'Because you have scattered my flock and driven them away and have not bestowed care on them, I will bestow punishment on you for the evil you have

---

[417] Matthew 10:15
[418] Revelation 2:18-22 (NIV)
[419] Good News, A Forum For Scriptural Christianity Within the United Methodist Church, 308 E. Main Street, Box 150, Wilmore, KY 40390, May-June 1998 issue, p. 13

done."[420]  Another quotation from Jesus is, "If anyone causes one of these little ones who believe in me to sin, it would be better for him to have a large millstone hung around his neck and to be drowned in the depths of the sea."[421]  Even if those of us who are convinced that this minority is wrong would one day become the minority ourselves, we would be obliged and privileged to borrow the statement Joshua used when facing the apostasy of Israel: "As for me and my house, we will serve the Lord."[422]  Paul wrote to Timothy advising him to hold "on to faith and a good conscience.  Some have rejected these and so have shipwrecked their faith."[423]  Christ tells us how to deal with a brother who sins: "Go and show him his fault, just between the two of you.  If he listens to you, you have won your brother over.  But if he will not listen, take one or two others along, so that 'every matter may be established by the testimony of two or three witnesses.'  If he refuses to listen to them, tell it to the church; and if he refuses to listen even to the church, treat him as you would a pagan or a tax collector."[424]  Sadly Rev. Creech was spoken to by some of the members of his congregation and by his Bishop in private and in small groups.  He was spoken to by eight out of thirteen of the church jury.  In spite of their good council, he persists in his heresy.

Paul explained what must be done with those who obstinately embrace evil despite the best efforts of their brothers and sisters in Christ to point them in the right direction.  "Hand this man over to Satan, so that the sinful nature may be destroyed and his spirit saved on the Day of the Lord."[425]  This is a sad and painful thing to do, but it is for the benefit of the person who is in error when all else fails.  To not do everything possible to bring someone back after wandering from the truth is itself a sin.  "Remember this: Whoever turns a sinner away from his error will save him from death and cover over a multitude of sins."[426]  Paul also instructs us to be ready for reconciliation if the person changes: "You ought to forgive and comfort him, so that he will not be overwhelmed by excessive sorrow.  I urge you, therefore, to reaffirm your love for him... in order that Satan might not outwit us, for we are not unaware of his schemes."[427]  Unpleasant as this is to contemplate and unpleasant as this is to go through, it is effective.  There was a time when I had disregarded God and had really messed up my life.  I feel that I had been turned over to Satan.  God hunted me down in my self-imposed state of hell, forced me to see there had to be something better, drove me to read the Bible avidly, led me to know that despite my sins He loves me, and led me to be born again.  It's radical therapy, but it works.  Pray that it will work for Rev. Creech and these others who have wandered

---

[420] Jeremiah 23:1-2 (NIV)
[421] Matthew 18:6 (NIV)
[422] Joshua 24:15 (NIV)
[423] First Timothy 1:20 (NIV)
[424] Matthew 18:15-17 (NIV)
[425] First Corinthians 5:5 (NIV)
[426] James 5:19-20 (NIV)
[427] Second Corinthians 2:5-11 (NOV)

off the Way.  Our motto and prayer must be to embrace the sinner, not the sin; win our brothers and sisters if possible; do not compromise; avoid this heresy at all costs, overcome our weaknesses and temptations, and keep the faith!

Through the good times and the difficult times, we must love Christ and his holy bride, the church. Choose to be an active part of the Body of Christ as he directed, even if at times being part of this body can cause conflict and pain and suffering and discouragement.  It can also bring conflict resolution, rapprochement, reunion, deep commitment, deep love, and great accomplishment.  The author of Hebrews recognized and addressed the discouragement that can come to Christians through outside pressures or from friends who let us down, or our letting others down, or exhaustion from being over extended.  He urges, "Do not give up meeting together as some are prone to do."[428]  I really enjoy a campfire.  Significantly when three or more logs are burning together in a campfire, the heat generated will keep the fire burning brightly and the light and warmth generated will be a joy for everyone sitting around the circle.  If the logs are moved apart, the fire rapidly decreases and is soon nothing but glowing embers and goes out.  There is still plenty of fuel and oxygen, but the heat has decreased enough to douse the fire. It's very much the same with Christians.  I find I cannot burn with the flame of the Holy Spirit without contact with other Christians which Christ promised would bring his presence and the presence of God's Spirit. Paul suggested the same thing, "Do not be weary in well-doing."[429]  Discipleship is not a spectator sport; we are a part of the body of Christ.  The work we do, the faith we proclaim, and the life we live must be parts of what we are.  We cannot be a part of Christ's plan and sit on the sidelines.

---

*(The understanding of Betty Berger)*

God hates the act, but loves the people.  We don't condone it, but we love them too.

---

*(Betty Byers' observation)*

God said Adam and Eve, not Adam and Steve.  In the Bible message it's always a man and woman.

---

*(Dean Culbertson's answer)*

Honestly, I think there are two principles that best answer the problem.  First, we must show love and compassion to everyone.  Jesus died on the cross for murderers, rapists,

---

[428] Hebrews 10:25 (NIV)
[429] Galatians 6:9 (KJV)

liars, idol-worshipers, foul-mouthed people, and yes homosexuals. He loved with every fiber of His being – and He still does. We must show homosexuals love and concern the way we should everyone else. Second, although we are to act in love, we must still look at the act as sin. This means we love the brother or sister caught in sin, but we do <u>not</u> condone the behavior. Certainly we are not to accept the practice of homosexuality. It simply boils down to the attitude of Jesus. We love the sinner even though we hate the sin.

---

(Sherry Doherty thoughts)

Wow, I'm a little hesitant to answer this one; this is such a volatile subject. A subject though that I feel very strongly about. I do not believe homosexuality is in God's plan. I feel it is a sin. With that said, I also believe that God told us to love our neighbor. And yet am I saying that I accept the sin by loving my neighbor without judging him or her. If I accept the sin, isn't this sinning too?

My choice is to love my neighbor, as I would want my neighbor to love me. I am not completely without sin. I do my best to learn from my sin and not commit that sin again. This leads me to my second dilemma – to me a homosexual continues their sin. From their perspective, I would say that they may not see this as a sin (which by the way does not exclude it as a sin). So I have chosen to love a person who commits sin regularly, and I pray that God does not see me as weak but as a person who follows His lead of loving those who commit sin, such as me.

---

## Challenge 42
# Who is going to be in heaven?

Universalists think that all people who believe in God are striving toward the same goal and that God wants all of them in heaven and will see they get there. Christians seem to say only Christians will be saved and all the rest are destined for Hell. How do you answer this?

*(Jack Clark's answer)*

First it is absolutely true that God and His Christ want all people to be saved and share the joy of being a part of the Kingdom with them. "Turn to me and be saved all you ends of the earth; for I am God, and there is no other."[430] "I urge, then first of all, that requests, prayers, intercession and thanksgiving be made for everyone... This is good and pleases God our Savior, who wants all men to be saved and come to a knowledge of the truth. For there is one God and one mediator between God and men, the man Christ Jesus who gave himself as a ransom for all men."[431] How important did Christ feel about people achieving salvation through the free gift he offered? He mourned over those who rejected it.[432] How does God feel about someone who has willfully left Him but eventually returns? Read the story of the prodigal son.[433] Jesus reports there is rejoicing in heaven over every person who is saved.[434]

It seems that some people probably have the idea that only professing Christians will be saved based on a couple things Jesus is quoted as having said in the scriptures: "Jesus answered, 'I am the way and the truth, and the life. No one comes to the Father except through me.'"[435] Also the following might come to mind: "Whoever acknowledges me before men, I will also acknowledge him before my Father in heaven. But whoever disowns me before men, I will disown him before my Father in heaven."[436]

On the surface this might seem pretty cut and dried. It's easy to see how someone could come to the conclusion that Jesus is saying that for him to be acknowledged is the only possible way to achieve salvation and eternal life, but this doesn't account for Jesus talking about Abraham being in heaven and Paul talking about the "great cloud of witnesses"[437] surrounding us. Certainly Abraham nor the great cloud of witnesses from

---

[430] Psalm 45:22 (RSV)
[431] First Timothy 2:1-6 (NIV)
[432] Matthew 23:37
[433] Luke 15:11-32
[434] Luke 15:7
[435] John 14:6 (NIV)
[436] Matthew 10:32-33 (NIV)
[437] Hebrews 12:1 (NIV)

the Old Testament ever heard of Jesus, so they couldn't have confessed him by name. One might reason that since Jesus existed from the very beginning[438] that Abraham and the others could have known him and had faith in him in spite of not knowing his name. One might even consider that since the Father and the Son are one, that Abraham's faith in God and the faith of the many other witnesses qualified them to be included in the Kingdom.

Certainly if we are to accept what Jesus has said, it is obvious that acknowledging Jesus before man, and having Jesus acknowledge the individual before the Father goes a long way toward gaining a place in the heavenly Kingdom. However, it seems that there are some people who aren't covered between those who acknowledge Christ and those who deny him. There certainly even today are many people who have never heard of Christ (not to mention the many who did not hear of him in past years).

There are also many who have been presented with such a distorted picture of Christ that they never really had a chance to come to know him and accept him. Consider an example of the conquest of Cuba by Diego Velásquez in 1511. Despite an inspired resistance by the Indian cacique Hatuey, Velásquez defeated him. When he was captured, Hatuey was offered a chance to convert to Christianity before being burned at the stake, so that his soul would go to heaven. The chief asked, "And to heaven the Christians also go?" On receiving the answer of, "Yes, if they are good and die in the grace of God, they go to heaven," Hatuey answered, "If Christians go to heaven, I do not want to go to heaven. I do not wish ever again to meet such cruel and wicked people as Christians who kill and make slaves of the Indians."[439] Few would suggest that such a relationship was what Jesus had in mind when he said, "Go and make disciples." It's been said that forced worship stinks in the nostrils of God. Few would have responded otherwise than Hatuey, the Indian, did in this circumstance.

Paul seems to have addressed this situation: "All who have sinned without the law will also perish without the law, and all who have sinned under the law will be judged by the law. For it is not the hearers of the law who are righteous before God, but the doers of the

---

[438] John 1:1
[439] As reported in the book *Humboldt's Cosmos*, Gerard Helferich, p.193, Gotham Books, Penguin Group (USA), Inc., © Gerard Helferich, 2004

law who will be justified. When Gentiles who have not the law do by nature what the law requires, they are a law to themselves, even though they do not have the law. They show that what the law requires is written on their hearts, while their conscience also bears witness and their conflicting thoughts accuse or perhaps excuse them on that day when, according to my gospel, God judges the secrets of men by Christ Jesus."[440]

It seems very significant to consider a couple non-Christians and even non-Hebrews that from Bible descriptions would be expected to be among the great cloud of witnesses that one would anticipate finding in heaven. The first was Melchizedek. He is described as being the King of Salem and priest of God Most High. He was not a Hebrew, yet he is recorded as proclaiming, "Blessed be Abram by God Most High, creator of Heaven and earth and blessed be God Most High who delivered your enemies into your hand." Then Abram gave Melchizedek a tithe of everything he had just captured.[441] Perhaps even more significant the Psalms state "You are a priest forever in the order of Melchizedek,"[442] and of even more importance to Christians the New Testament declares that Jesus Christ himself, because he was not a Levite or a descendant of Aaron is himself a priest in the order of Melchizedek.[443] If Melchizedek is a priest forever, could anyone deny that he is alive right now? And where can he be alive forever and performing his priestly duties but in heaven?

Another interesting person to consider is Reuel also known as Jethro. He was a priest of Midian. Midian was not an Israelite. The ancestor of this people was the son of Abraham and Keturah who he married after Sarah's death. Jethro was not a Hebrew, but it was he who gave his daughter to Moses in marriage. It was he with whom Moses lived for years and tended his sheep. He must have had many discussions with Moses about matters of faith before Moses met God at the burning bush. It was Jethro's daughter Zipporah who ritually circumcised their first son Gershom in Moses' place when Moses was in danger of dying in order to save Moses' life as they went back to Egypt to free the Israelites. It was the priest Jethro who gave sacrifice to God to celebrate God's greatness and the deliverance of Israel from slavery in Egypt. It was Jethro who helped Moses organize the administration of the Israelite people into a manageable system of judges in

---

[440] Romans 2:12-16 (RSV)
[441] Genesis 14:18-20
[442] Psalms 110:4 (RSV)
[443] Hebrews 6;20-8:7

order to prevent Moses being overwhelmed by his workload as they were returning from Egypt.[444] It would certainly be surprising not to find Jethro among the cloud of witnesses in heaven. These two men certainly point to those outside the professing Christians and even outside the Israelite people as being saved through the intervention of Jesus Christ even though they could have not known him by name.

C. S. Lewis had considered that it seemed unfair that salvation and eternal life should only be available to people who have heard of Christ and believed in him. As he thought this through, he came to this conclusion: "We do know that no man can be saved except through Christ; we do not know that only those who know Him can be saved through Him." Lewis goes on to suggest, "If you are worried about the people outside (the faith), the most unreasonable thing you can do is to remain outside yourself. Christians are Christ's body, the organism through which He works. Every addition to that body enables Him to do more. If you want to help those outside you must add your own little cell to the body of Christ who alone can help them. Cutting off a man's fingers would be an odd way of getting him to do more work."[445] Lewis also says in his book *The Problem of Pain* that he would be pleased to do away with the understanding that there are those who will not be saved. He then observes that if we say that everyone will be saved, the only logical question to follow is, "Without their will or with it?" The next question would be if everyone will be saved without their will, how can this be the voluntary act of surrender that Jesus says is necessary for our salvation? If the question is answered, "With their will," how can this be if the individual won't give in?

So does acknowledging Christ before man provide an automatic pass into heaven? It would seem that something else is involved. What really seems to be needed to achieve salvation is that the person has to want a deep committed relationship with Christ, or lacking first hand knowledge of Christ with goodness which Christ represents. If a person wants this relationship with Christ it will make an observable difference in our lives. Christ says that such a relationship will bear fruit; that is the relationship will produce results that Christ and others can recognize. The good works do not earn our salvation, they are the observable results of our salvation that are done out of our love.

---

[444] See Exodus 2:18, 3:1, and 18:1. Also Numbers 10:29
[445] *Mere Christianity,* C. S. Lewis, p. 65, © 1943, 1945, 1952 by Macmillan Publishing Company, © renewed 1980 by Arthur Owen Barfield

Christ warned that only claiming him (even before others) does not result in our salvation: "Every tree that does not bear good fruit is cut down and thrown into the fire. Thus by their fruit you will recognize them. Not everyone who says to me, 'Lord, Lord,' will enter the kingdom of heaven, but only he who does the will of my Father who is in heaven. Many will say to me on that day, 'Lord, Lord, did we not prophesy in your name and in your name drive out demons and perform many miracles?' Then I will tell them plainly, 'I never knew you. Away from me, you evildoers!'"[446] What a staggering concept to realize that God, who knows everything, would indicate that He never knew some of us! Even prophesy and miracles without love and relationship won't earn salvation.

Even though God wants everyone to be a part of the Kingdom and works to help people accept His love and choose to be a part of the kingdom, the Bible clearly indicates that it simply isn't going to happen for everyone. God will not force us to love Him. He offers us His love. If we at first reject that love, He will ardently pursue us; He will pursue us to the point of having been called the hound of heaven by one who tried to avoid Him.[447] But He will not compel us to love him. Ultimately each person must come to the place that we accept or reject that love. C. S. Lewis in his book *The Great Divorce: A Dream* asks if everyone is given the choice of accepting God or not. The answer given is: "There are only two kinds of people in the end: those who say to God, 'Thy will be done.' And those to whom God says in the end '*Thy* will be done.' All that are in Hell choose it. Without that self-choice there would be no Hell. No soul that seriously and constantly desires joy will ever miss it. Those who seek find. To those who knock it is opened."[448]

---

*(Betty Byers' answer)*

Only those who have accepted Christ as their personal savior will go to heaven.

---

*(Another answer – from Cathy Ann Turner)*

I was talking with my brother-in-law. His wife, my husband Tom's sister, had recently died from a recurrent brain tumor many years after it was first diagnosed. She had become progressively disabled over many months despite repeat chemotherapy before her death. Mike has some pretty deep questions that are along the following lines:

---

[446] Matthew 7:19-23 (NIV)
[447] This was how Francis Thorsson, a nineteenth century poet who had almost destroyed himself with alcohol and drug abuse, referred to the persistent unrelenting pursuit God engaged in to literally save Thorsson's life and his soul.
[448] *The Great Divorce,* C. S. Lewis, copyright © 1946 by C. S. Lewis, Harper Collins Publishers, Ltd.

Everyone who follows a belief system thinks/is taught that theirs is the best/the only right (real) one. How can you be sure that being a Christian is the right choice?

We can't, of course, do more than have Faith that the Holy Spirit within us has brought us to "the right, the only choice". If in the end, we were wrong and there is another "path" that leads to Salvation then we will still be judged by God (no matter what the religion – we all pretty much believe in "God" and His judgment – even if by some other name) and we must Trust that He will judge our hearts for what they were. If we were totally wrong and there is nothing behind any of the belief systems but man's attempt to give an eternal purpose and picture to life on earth – as well as to have an established set of "spiritual" regulations to guide a culture, well, then we've lived a life striving to be good and serve others and something other than ourselves, which most think is more satisfying than living a life of total self-service.

Mike's second question: What happens to all of those who've followed their non-Christian belief systems in a committed and honorable way? Mike can't believe that a "just God" would condemn all who are not Christian to eternal Hell – especially if they have followed the teachings of their own Faith. What happens to all of the people that never had the chance to make the choice to be Christian – those who lived before Christ was on earth or in a time/place where the spread of Christianity didn't reach?

My answer to that isn't as fundamental as church teachings and even the Bible state – my personal belief is that God judges the heart of man and only holds him accountable for choices that he could reasonably be expected to make. If a man never is exposed to the teachings of Jesus, nor hears His name then he can't reasonably proclaim Jesus his Savior. God will judge what man knows and what he's done/the choices he has made with that knowledge – and there is always "end time" opportunity for those who've not known Christ or proclaimed Him Savior while on earth to do so at final judgment. (That's assuming that there is a final judgment and an eternal existence)

*(An answer from Betty Berger)*

If we believe in our heart and confess with our lips Jesus is Lord, and rely on the truth that Jesus was raised from the dead – we are saved.[449]

---

[449] Romans 10:9-10

Challenge 44

# What can we do for the unsaved?

What can we do about those who haven't given their lives to Christ or those who seem hung up only part way to such a commitment?

*(An answer by Jack Clark)*

It might be good so that we don't get hung up with the speck in our brother's eye while ignoring the log in our own eye to recognize that every Christian is on the way or a path toward being one with Christ as he prayed.[450] Jesus said, he is the Way, but so far, I've only met those who are on the way. None has arrived in this lifetime (most certainly including me).

It might also be good to reinforce what we know about the source of salvation. It is through the gift of our Lord Jesus Christ and during this time is given by the Holy Spirit. You cannot give salvation, nor can I as much as we may want it – for ourselves or for others.

This should never lead us to be complacent and suggest that since it's up to the Holy Spirit, it's all taken care of and we can go on to the next concern. Jesus himself said we as followers do have an obligatory role in the salvation of others. He commanded, "Go and make disciples of all nations, baptizing them in the name of the Father and of the Son, and of the Holy Spirit, and teaching them to obey everything I have commanded you." He added a very important encouragement: "And surely I am with you always, to the very end of the age."[451] So we do have an important job – introducing Christ to those who don't know him as we do, telling them of what he has done for us and what we're sure he can do for them, and teaching them as much as we can about Christ. From there on, the Holy Spirit takes over.

I should point out that some of the world we're to present Christ to is right next door and even in our own families. This doesn't exclude far away places, but we need to be aware of all areas of opportunity. I should also point out that Christ suggested that we may not see quick results. In fact, it would be welcome but unusual to see anything close to immediate acceptance. It's our job to plant. It's our job to water. Sometimes we may see the hoped for harvest, but sometimes that joy may be far down the line for someone else to witness.

---

[450] John 17:20-26
[451] Matthew 28:20 (NIV)

I have prayed for family members and friends in the past that seemed to need a deeper relationship and commitment to Christ. Incidentally, I have prayed for the same thing for myself. I've seen these prayers answered. I made a friendship with a Jewish attorney on one of the cruises to Central America on which I was the ship's doctor. We were enjoying a Mayan city and the museum that contained their intricate carvings and expressed their life and religious practices. Their accomplishments were great. Their pyramids and temples and carvings and the stelae on which they carved their history were inspiring, but their religious practices included human sacrifice by cutting out the still beating hearts form the chests of their victims. As we toured the museum, my attorney friend asked, "Jack, what sense of spiritual values do you get from this place? I recognize their great achievements, but the sense I get is one of evil. I've been to the Basilica in Rome, and there I get a spiritual sense of goodness even though this is different from my own faith." We had several good discussions. I felt that we had a good deal of mutual understanding and shared values. He disclosed that one of his children wanted nothing to do with religion and one was seeking his place and considering Christianity. I asked my new friend if he would be offended if I sent him a book that I had just written about my faith. The book is *The Reason for the Hope: A Spiritual Journey.* He invited me to send it, and I did. Several months later, he wrote thanking me for the book and expressing his feeling that I was sincere in my faith, but he could never go against his own tradition. I have no idea if there will be any more results from the planting that his son had done and the watering I was allowed to do, and the efforts of the Holy Spirit, but I have prayed that there will be. I would love to be assured there is one more Messianic Jew in the Kingdom, and that I had some small role in the process.

In our congregation we have been recently having a set aside prayer time outside our worship service for those who haven't accepted Jesus as their savior. Mark Eastway, our pastor, asked that the congregation put names on slips of paper and turn them in for those of us who gather once a week and also pray at home for their commitment to God. Our congregation of about a hundred on that day turned in well over a hundred names. Most were just first names – Mary, John, and so forth. Some were only identified as Mom and Dad. A few included last names. It doesn't make any difference. God knows who they are. My wife Carol hesitated to join the effort, because she didn't feel that we can possibly know the status of another's salvation, and it seemed presumptive to pray because it seemed to hold us up as some way better than they are. Of course the assurance of our salvation certainly doesn't reflect on our goodness or that we are special; it reflects on the goodness of God as shown us by his Holy Son. Also if some of these are in fact already saved, I doubt that God is offended by prayers for them. I certainly know that I still need the prayers of others and wouldn't in any way resent that someone prayed for my salvation even now.

Knowing how the Holy Spirit pursued me before I gave my life to Christ, I don't think my prayers or the prayers of the group will increase the intensity of God's efforts on behalf of these people. It seems to me that prayer more often changes those who pray than bringing about a change in God; although, the Bible records occasions when the latter effect has taken place. Much of my prayer time in this effort asks that I can be changed to be a better witness. I also ask that our congregation and the church as a whole can be changed to be better witnesses to these people, and especially that those who have loved the people and were concerned enough to ask for prayers be the most effective witnesses possible.

I'll share, as nearly as I can recall one of my recent prayers with this group from our congregation: "Lord, you know those on our list who have committed to you and are saved by the redemption of your son and the power of your Holy Spirit. For those of us who have been saved, I ask that you protect and strengthen us and use us to lead others toward you. You are the beginning and the end and all points in between right now. You know our hearts. You know the hearts of each person on this list. You know our love of you, and we know your love of every person. We pray that you will use us and that you will use those whose concern led them to put these names on our list and more importantly on our heart, and most importantly on your heart. You know those who only need to hear your son's gentle knock in order to respond by opening the door wide to let him come in. Some have had their ears plugged so they haven't heard the knock; for these please clear their ears so that they can hear and respond. Some are stiff-necked. Gently bend their necks if this is possible; wrench their necks if this is necessary. Some of them are very stubborn like some of us were. They may kick against the sharp goad,[452] as some of us have done. If this is what is necessary, let the goad be sharp enough to get their attention and lead them to want your salvation, as you did with us. Then gently heal the hurt of their injury. Go to what extent is necessary to achieve the result that we know is so dear to your will and so necessary for them. Break a leg if this is needed to get their attention. Pursue them as the hound of heaven that some have found you to be;[453] even

---

[452] Acts 26:14 (NIV). A goad is a sharp pointed stick used in herding cattle.
[453] This was how Francis Thorsson, a nineteenth century poet who had almost destroyed himself with alcohol and drug abuse, referred to the persistent unrelenting pursuit God engaged in to literally save Thorsson's life and his soul.

nip their heels if necessary!  Some may even have to be temporarily turned over to Satan, as some of us have needed.  In such a case, as we've gasped for life and held out our hands in desperation, you were there ready to rescue us.  This is a scary, painful cure, but so much better than missing your salvation would have been.  We thank you for your gift and your mercy to us and we ask it for all those on this list.  We claim salvation for them even as you said we could ask and receive."

One of the people on our list recently died.  In my heart I want to believe that our prayers, the Holy Spirit's response, and the individual's knowledge of God had led him to the salvation that God, his family and we had wanted for him.  I was struck once again with the urgency of the needs of people who may have not accepted Christ's redemption and salvation.  I recalled that when the ship Titanic sank there were lists posted outside the shipping office of the company.  One list read "SAVED."  One was headed with the stark word "LOST."  There was no in between list.  There was no list headed "status unknown," or "status pending."  When we come to the end of our lives, then too, there will be only the same two lists.  The sad truth is that many more of the people on the Titanic could have been saved except there were too few life boats, because the engineers had assured that the ship was unsinkable.  For our eternal lives you, God, have provided the life boat, your son, and there is plenty space for everyone.  You have shown the way to the life boats, and you have provided loving friends and family to help us find the path you have given us.  You have come in the Holy Spirit to guide and urge people on the right path, and you have given us the opportunity to share our stories and point the way to the eternal life you have offered and promised.

Many years ago Matty Jones, one of my patients, lingered a long time with his terminal carcinoma of the larynx.  He often visited with me over wide-ranging topics including plans for his dog, missing Edna, his wife, who had died several years earlier, and his relationship with God.  He enjoyed talking with me about his experiences as one of the very first airplane pilots in Indiana (recognized as such at our Fort Wayne, Indiana regional airport).  He told of how Edna's parents had opposed their marriage, so they had eloped and hid in some woods to avoid her father.  He liked to talk about his work as a gunsmith and the fun he and my Dad had skeet shooting and hunting together.  His mother had been a Bible reader who emphasized how important it was to stay away from all sin.  He confided that he couldn't bring himself to believe in miracles including the resurrection of the body.  Worst of all, he found so much fault with church members that his faith in God was badly shaken.  Matty had been Township Trustee for many years and had helped many needy families. He wasn't much impressed with church peoples' level of concern for the needy. He wanted to believe, it was clear, but found too many people standing between him and God. The answer to his problem didn't come easily. Late in his illness, he had to be admitted to the hospital for pain relief and because he was too weak to care for himself. He grew weaker, more restless, demanding, and antagonistic (a very unusual thing for one of the nicest people I've known). Then one day a very simple truth occurred to me. I sat quietly at his bedside and said. "You know, Matty, I believe that this whole universe is governed by an intelligent power that for want of a better name we call God. I don t know much about Him, and I don't think anyone else knows a great deal, but I'm convinced that whatever happens works out for the best because He has something to do with it." He smiled, squeezed my hand, and whispered a hoarse, "Thanks, Doc." The rest of the day he was calm, rested well, and was pleasant to the nurses. He died peacefully the following day. My simple words seemed to have helped more than an injection of sedative or pain killer, and made our relationship a far more rewarding experience for both of us. We have to be genuinely concerned and interested with those who haven't accepted Christ's salvation, and we have to tailor our efforts at evangelism to meet people where they are.[454]

"God our Savior... wants all men to be saved and to come to a knowledge of the truth."[455] We can't give salvation, but we can be the tools the Holy Spirit uses to help get the job done.

*(Another view from Betty Berger)*

Keep living Christ in front of them.[456] Love never fails! Walk in love. Pray for their eyes to be opened.

*(Suggestions from Betty Byers)*

We need to pray for the unsaved, and tell them about the love of Jesus. Be committed to testify to the saving knowledge of the Lord, Jesus Christ. Memorize the scriptures so you can lead sinners to Christ.

---

[454] Including the account about Matty and identifying him by name was approved by his two grandchildren, Jean Havens and David Jones.

[455] First Timothy 2:4 (NIV)

[456] For some people the lives we lead may be the first glimpse of Christ they see.

# What about the tribulation?

Why are there different understandings about when the followers of God and Christ will be gathered (referring to the timing known as Pre-tribulation, Tribulation itself, and Post-tribulation)? (Submitted by Cathy Ann Turner)

*(An answer by Jack Clark)*

I'm glad the question asks why are there misunderstandings instead of which one is correct, because I wouldn't have an answer to the second question. There are a lot of people very interested in not only what will happen in the end times surrounding Jesus' return but especially when that's going to happen. Jesus' disciples questioned him about this, and his only answer was, "Soon." Obviously, since close to 2000 years have passed, the word soon has a different meaning for God and his Son than it has for the people who asked the question then and the people who still ask the question today. Jesus indicated that that even he didn't know when it was to be – only the Father knows. The important thing for his followers is that we be ready[457] and realize that it will come when no one is expecting it. He did say that there will be no mistaking the fact when it happens and that it will be obvious to everyone.[458]

I've often said that even though there are interesting observations about these times in the Books of Daniel and Revelation and in Matthew Chapter 24, that I too am confused about the timing and all the details. In the words of a recent praise song, "I know not what the future holds, but I know who holds the future." I figure that if we concern ourselves with faith in Jesus, our Father in Heaven, and the Holy Spirit and work to become as close to being one with them as we can, that they are going to take care of what's coming, and that whatever it is, it will be for the best because they love us. It's sort of like going on a trip with our family when we were youngsters. We didn't know exactly where we were going, where we would sleep each night, where or what we would eat, or what we would do or see. But we did know we would be all right, because our parents would take care of us. We knew that we would be better off for having gone, and we knew we would have some great adventures and be closer to our parents for having made the trip. I think the same perspective applies to the end times – whether they are the end times of the earth that individually we may possibly experience or our individual end time when our bodies wear out and we depart to be with Jesus.

---

[457] Matthew 25:1-13
[458] Matthew 24:4-51

I think we can safely say that there are going to be some very unpleasant rough times at the end of the age. At some point Jesus will take the church (the Followers of the Way) to be with him. Some understand this will happen before all the difficult times (the pre-tribulation). Some people understand it will happen part way through the tribulation, and some after the difficult times (post-tribulation). There are things in the various prophesies to support all three understandings. I would say that the prophesy in Revelation is clear that some of those John saw in heaven while the tribulation was going on were identified as those "who have come out of the great tribulation,"[459] so it wouldn't seem that there is total support for the pre-tribulation viewpoint. Whatever one understands we're assured that in the end God, Christ and the legions of heaven will win. Satan and his henchmen will lose. And it's a whole lot better to be on the winning side. A very clear synopsis of the events was given by Jesus: "I have overcome the world."[460]

Now back to the question. Why is there confusion? There are several factors. First a single prophesy often applies to events that will happen at different times, so the events talked about in Revelation, for example, apply both to the Roman Army destroying Jerusalem in AD 70 and to the total overcoming of all evil and making of everything new at the end of the age. This itself tends to be confusing. Part of the prophesy has already been fulfilled, and part is yet to come.

Another confusing factor is that when John dictated the Revelation to his scribe he was in a prison work colony on the Island of Patmos now owned by Greece. He was under Roman guards. He was a prisoner of Nero who was the Roman Caesar at the time. Nero was well known for such pastimes as feeding Christians to the lions in the arena, having them killed by gladiators, and soaking them in tar and lighting them to make living torches to light his gardens. This was not exactly the type of fellow that you would want to get angry with you or your friends to whom you had sent your letters. Most people think the secret code 666 referring to the beast that would reap the wrath of God was a common code that worked out to indicate that Nero himself was the beast who was part of the trinity of evil along with the antichrist and the false prophet.[461] (Many also think that others, including Adolph Hitler, have fulfilled that role over the years and that there will be

---

[459] Revelation 7:14-17
[460] John 16:33 (NIV)
[461] Revelation 13:11-18

another final antichrist, beast and false prophet at the end of time.) So this is another reason for confusion. It was deliberate to confuse the authorities. The outcome is already decided. It is only waiting to be manifest. God wins!

*(Matt Gunter's thoughts)*

The Who of History - Scriptures: Zechariah 14:4-9, Psalm 50, 1 Thessalonians 3:9-13, Luke 21:25-31

In the religious circles I grew up in, passages like today's gospel lesson were among the most important in the Bible. The world was going to end very soon. Our imaginations were inspired by apocalyptic images: nation against nation, great earthquakes, famines, plagues, dreadful portents, and great signs from heaven. We were sure all the signs indicated we were living in the end times. No one ever said, "Sell everything you own and go wait on a hill." No one ever actually predicted an exact date for the end. But, just about everyone agreed that it would be sooner rather than later. And, once it began, we were pretty sure we knew how it was going to play out. I remember seeing wall charts that had the chronology of the Last Days with descriptions of the events leading up to and immediately following Jesus' return. And it was clear that you were in trouble if you weren't ready. We talked about the mark of the Beast, the number 666, and sang a song called "I Wish We'd All Been Ready." What we tended to miss was that it is not the when, the what, or the how of the world's future that matters. What matters is the Who of the world's future.

The church Luke belonged to was also fascinated and concerned with the when, the what, and the how of the world's last days. They also had reason to believe it was going to be soon. They remembered that Jesus had said something about the destruction of the Temple. Now the Temple had been destroyed. In fact, Jerusalem itself had been destroyed and the Jewish people, still God's people, had been scattered. Members of the church were getting their first taste of persecution at the hands of their neighbors and the authorities. To top it all off, it's possible Luke wrote around the time Mt. Vesuvius erupted and buried the city of Pompeii. That's a pretty dreadful portent. The when, the what, and the how were all there. It must be the end of time. Either that, or maybe God wasn't really in control, and the world was just lurching aimlessly through time.

As it turned out, even though all the signs were there, it wasn't the end of time. In the larger passage from which our lesson is taken, Jesus tells the Lucian church, and us, to beware of putting too much stock in such signs and in people who claim to see the end coming.  This is good for us to hear because there is a cottage industry built around such predictions.  Best sellers abound describing in detail the final days of the "late great planet earth" and foretelling its early demise.  In every generation, there have been those who were sure that the when, what and how of the world's end were upon us.  So far, every generation has been wrong.

Most of us don't think too much about the end of time.  We leave that to the fringe groups.  We are much more likely to wonder if time has any point in the first place.  It's hard not to look around at world or national events and become discouraged.  Sometimes it feels like we are trapped by history.  Maybe history, as one wag has it, really is "just one damn thing after another" headed nowhere.

The problems are many and overwhelming.  The forces of darkness appear to have the upper hand.  The tears in our social fabric continue to widen.  Our moral confusion becomes more profound.  Our will to risk compassion is more constrained.  The when, the what, and the how of futility, despair, and cynicism are evident and the constraints of history bind us.  But, it is not the when, the what, and the how of history that are important.  It is the Who of history that matters.  Jesus in his resurrection presence is the Who of history.  He has promised to be present with us in the midst of our public and private struggles for peace, justice, and joy.  It is his presence that gives us the patience and the power of endurance.  It is his power that gives us hope.  It is a sober hope, because we know that the powers of sin, evil, and death are still very real and they still exact some casualties.  But we also trust that those powers do not control Tomorrow.  Tomorrow is in Christ's control and all of our little tomorrows will be caught up in his Tomorrow.  Jesus Christ has torn down the "No Exit" sign at the end of history and at the end of each of our lives.  Our future is open.  Our struggles for love and truth and joy are not in vain. Jesus will come on that final day.  But, Jesus comes to us now inviting us to enter into his grace and his future.

The apocalyptic imagery of today's Gospel, like all things apocalyptic, is fascinating.  But, if we are not careful, we can get lost in the imagery of the when, the what, and the how and forget that it is the Who, Jesus Christ, whom we trust as Lord of all history.  He will surely come on the Last Day to set things right and catch all up into the embrace of the Trinity.  But, let us be ready now to receive him in the myriad ways he comes to us day by day as Lord of the history of our own lives.

Challenge 46

# What is heaven like?

*(Jack Clark's thoughts)*

I feel that those of us who have chosen to live our lives in relationship to God through Jesus Christ have already experienced a sampling of heaven, but there is certainly more and better to come. In spite of my lack of personal experience with the after life part of heaven, the Scriptures tell us a good deal that I'll be pleased to share.

My first thought about understanding heaven involved a delightful short story by Mark Twain. In twenty-two lively, funny, tender pages titled *The Diary of Adam and Eve* Samuel Clemens tells a tale of how God's first created couple related to each other, to God and to such problems as choosing suitable names for all the animals. In the story Eve picked the animals' names wanting to spare Adam embarrassment, because he wasn't adept at such things and just because the name went with that particular animal. The end of the story finds Adam standing beside Eve's grave and tenderly observing, "Where-so-ever she was, *there* was Eden."[462]

So my first suggestion was wherever God is, there is Heaven. Well that hardly works, because God is everywhere. My ultimate resolution was to recognize that wherever I am or other people are in a loving relationship with God, and Jesus, and the Holy Spirit, and the great cloud of witnesses talked about in the Scriptures – *there is heaven.* John the Baptist suggested that heaven isn't some far off place; "The kingdom of heaven is near."[463]

It's easy to get confused by overlapping terms. Kingdom of God, Kingdom of Heaven, paradise and heaven are referred to in the Bible, and they can cause some confusion.

The term Kingdom of God refers to a situation in which God is accepted as the ruler and ultimate authority. It can involve those who have decided God is number one in our lives during our earthly existence. It certainly involves all who are a part of God's plans for our eternal existence after our physical death. All those who are destined to be with God

---

[462] *Short Stories by Mark Twain,* Mark Twain, Airmont Publishing Company, Inc., 22 East 60th Street, New York , NY 10022, © 1968 Airmont Publishing Company, pp. 280-302
[463] Matthew 3:2 (NIV)

are in the Kingdom of God now and remain in the Kingdom when our bodies die. Jesus said, "I am the resurrection and the life. He who believes in me will live, even though he dies, and whoever lives and believes in me will never die."[464] This certainly promises that our existence continues unbroken by this transition from the earthly part of being in the Kingdom of God to the heavenly part of the Kingdom (also called the Kingdom of Heaven). It is the Kingdom of Heaven that Jesus said will be given to the poor in spirit and those who are persecuted for Christ.[465]

Paradise was originally a Persian word for a pleasure garden. In the Scriptures it signifies a situation in which God and believers are restored to a perfect relationship. The dictionary defines paradise as a place of bliss or complete happiness. As such it wouldn't necessarily require a relationship with God or a personal salvation or eternal life; however, it is hard to conceive of paradise in a situation not involving these attributes. Without them it's obvious that most concepts of paradise would be unachievable and only an illusion. Interestingly the term paradise is used only three times in Scripture – all in the New Testament. When Christ was being crucified and one of the thieves recognized who he truly was and begged that Jesus would remember him when he came into his kingdom. "Jesus answered him, 'I tell you the truth, today you will be with me in paradise.'"[466] This tells us of God's eagerness to save anyone. It tells us that faith, belief, acceptance, and a resolution – even a very late resolution – to live for Christ meets the requirement for our salvation. It indicates the timing of when we will be with Christ after our physical death – not at some distant future time after Christ's return, but now, today! Paul spoke of being caught up and visiting paradise (also referred to as third heaven) to gain in understanding and to return and carry on his earthly ministry.[467] The third reference is about the tree of life found in paradise.[468]

Heaven is the place where we will be in relationship with God after this physical life. It will be a relationship that will continue throughout eternity. As such, to the Christian this would also be Paradise. Although, the Bible says the old heaven and the old earth will at some point pass away and be replaced by a new heaven and a new earth no detail about

---

[464] John 11:25-26 (NIV)
[465] Matthew 5:3 & 10
[466] Luke 23:43 (NIV)
[467] Second Corinthians 12:2-4 (NIV)
[468] Revelation 2:7

what will happen to those in heaven at the time is given. This shouldn't be any source of concern, as we understand, despite changes in both earth and heaven at some point, that "Jesus Christ is the same yesterday and today and forever"[469] and will continue to care for His own.

Some confusion arises because the term heaven is also used in conversation, lay literature, and even the Bible to refer to the sky and the rest of the non-earthly universe.

The Bible contains 503 entries about heaven. One would expect a pretty good understanding of heaven from so many references. First it is explained that heaven was a creation of God. Heaven is God's dwelling place. In heaven there is the joy of giving constant praise and worship to God and his Son. Many find significance in the first chapter of the Book of Genesis that indicates God created heaven (mankind's permanent destination) before earth (our temporary home).[470]

Jesus used several comparisons to illustrate the nature of heaven. He said that it's like a person sowing good seed in his field only to have his enemy come and sow weeds among the good seeds. When the servants wanted to pull out the weeds, the owner refused because the wheat might be pulled up with the weeds, but plans were made at harvest time to collect the weeds first and destroy them and then gather the wheat into the barn. This illustrates the original plan of the kingdom and how handling the situation of unrepentant sinners would be taken care of.

He likened heaven to a mustard seed, the smallest of seeds that would grow into a large garden plant in which birds could rest. This suggests that it is the ultimate home for those who choose that destiny.

Another parable likened heaven to yeast working through flour and transforming it illustrating how the Kingdom can spread its influence and be a transforming power through society.

---

[469] Hebrews 13:8 (NIV)
[470] From a discussion in 2008 by Rev. David Schramm at a Hebrew Bible study at St. Andrew's United Methodist Church, Syracuse, Indiana

Jesus suggested that heaven is like a treasure hidden in a field or the most glorious pearl that ever was. When it was found, the finder was filled with joy and sold all he had to buy the field or in the other case to buy the pearl in order to have the treasure. Of course this illustrates that there is absolutely nothing worth more to any of us than being a part of the Kingdom of Heaven, and that it is worth giving up things of lesser value to get its blessings. What it does not suggest is that we should jealously desire heaven for ourselves and exclude everyone else. The more we share the blessings with others, the greater the blessings we receive.

Jesus suggested that heaven is like a fishing net let down and brought up full of all kinds of fish. When the net was pulled in, the good fish were selected and kept and the bad fish were discarded. This, of course, indicates the separation and salvation of the redeemed from the lost that is to occur on the Day of Judgment.[471]

Another time Jesus emphasized that heaven is in the business of forgiving unless the person involved has been unforgiving.[472] This of course goes along with Jesus' warning that "In the same way you judge others, you will be judged, and with the measure you use, it will be measured to you."[473]

On another occasion Jesus said the Kingdom of Heaven is like a king who prepared a wedding banquet for his son. Although personal messengers were sent to invite the honored guests, they refused to come. Messengers were sent again to the invited guests who ignored the invitation and went about their own business. Some even mistreated and killed the king's messengers. The king then sent more messengers to invite anyone – the bad as well as the good. Unfortunately one of these guests showed disrespect by coming improperly dressed and he was thrown out. The parable ends with the warning, "Many are invited, but few are chosen."[474] At first thought, this seems harsh. After all, just showing up in the wrong clothes seems a poor basis for throwing someone out of heaven. There are some other verses in the Bible that give more understanding about what was lacking. Two verses advise us to clothe ourselves with Jesus Christ.[475] Another verse

---

[471] These parables about the nature of heaven are found in Matthew 13:24-52
[472] Matthew 19:21-35
[473] Matthew 7:2 (NIV)
[474] Matthew 22:1-14
[475] Romans 13:14 and Galatians 3:27 (TNIV)

advises that we clothe ourselves with compassion, humility, gentleness, and patience.[476] It's even more understandable to realize how lacking these things could exclude a person from heaven when we realize that scripture indicates that all those who are there - "a great multitude that no one could count from every nation, tribe, people, and language" - will be given white robes. In other words, the proper dress will be supplied.[477] All that is necessary to be acceptable is to take what is freely given.

People who didn't believe in resurrection were trying to corner Jesus. They asked him about the rule of Moses that if a man dies without children his brother is obligated to marry the widow to have children for the deceased brother. They presented a scenario in which seven brothers eventually died after successively marrying the same woman. They wanted to know whose wife she would be at the time of the resurrection. Jesus' answer tells us a good deal about heaven: "At the resurrection people will neither marry nor be given in marriage. They will be like the angels in heaven. But about the resurrection of the dead – have you not read what God said to you: 'I am the God of Abraham, the God of Isaac, and the God of Jacob?' He is not the God of the dead but of the living."[478] This is why Jesus could say that whoever believes in him will never die.[479]

The above Bible verse was somewhat discouraging to my widowed Grandfather Prow. When I was sixteen and living with him during my senior year of high school, he commented to me that if he couldn't be with Hallie, his wife, in heaven, it didn't hold much attraction for him. Their relationship had been one of deep tenderness, support through terrible financial losses in our country's great depression of the 1920s, being involved in each other's interests – painting, gardening, public service, and church work. I can still recall my answer. I suggested that God certainly wouldn't want to separate people who already had such a good idea of what love is. Even though we won't be married in heaven, we're told that we'll be in a great cloud of witnesses. The apostle Paul indicated that he was torn between his desires to stay in this life where he was needed by his friends or to departing to be with Christ.[480] This would certainly indicate that he anticipated knowing Christ when he got to heaven, and by implication suggests that we

---

[476] Colossians 3:12 (TNIV)
[477] Revelation 7:9 (TNIV)
[478] Matthew 22:23-33 (TNIV)
[479] John 11:26
[480] Philippians 1:23-24

will recognize others. I suggest that we will love everyone in heaven more fully than we were ever capable of loving anyone in this life. I anticipate everyone will be dearer in heaven than the ones who were most dear to us now in this life. Far from having no relationship with Grandmother, I'm convinced that Grandfather's relationship with her surpasses the great love they shared in this life. There is a difference. The love is a giving love (Agape love), even the love of brother and sister (Philos love); it goes beyond the erotic love they had shared in their marriage (Eros).

Jesus suggested that the kingdom of God will come unexpectedly, and that only those who are prepared will get to be a part of it.[481] He also suggested that the Kingdom will give assets to servants in accordance with our abilities, but that a multiplication of the assets entrusted is expected, and that God doesn't expect us to be do-nothing citizens of the Kingdom.[482]

An understanding of what will happen at the return of Christ "in his glory with all the angels with him" is given in Matthew. This involves who will be a part of the Heavenly Kingdom. He will separate the people like a shepherd would separate goats from sheep placing the sheep on the right and the goats on the left. "Then the King will say to those on his right, 'Come, you who are blessed by my Father; take your inheritance, the kingdom prepared for you since the creation of the world. For I was hungry and you gave me something to eat. I was thirsty and you gave me something to drink. I was a stranger and you invited me in. I needed clothes and you clothed me.'" The chosen ones were certainly surprised. Jesus had to explain, "Whatever you did for one of the least of these brothers and sisters of mine you did for me." Then the King turned to those on his left advising they had to depart from him, because they had not done these things. Needless to say they were even more surprised and asked when they had seen Christ in need. The obvious answer was whenever they had failed to do it for one of the least ones they had failed to do if for Jesus![483] This would seem to leave an impression that we are saved by works instead of by the free gift of God's grace. This also seems to tie into another verse: Christ says we will be known by our fruit. "Not everyone who says to me, 'Lord, Lord will enter the kingdom of heaven, but only he who does the will of my Father who is in heaven.

---

481 Matthew 25:1-13
482 Matthew 25:14-30
483 Matthew 25:31-36 (TNIV) Also compare with Isaiah 58:5-6 (NIV)

Many will say to me on that day, 'Lord, Lord, did we not prophesy in your name, and in your name drive out demons, and perform many miracles?' Then I will tell them plainly, 'I never knew you. Away from me, you evildoers!'"[484] What this indicates is, that even though it is by faith that we are saved, if we truly have faith, it's going to make a change in our lives that is obvious – usually to other people and certainly to Jesus Christ. Without those changes – those fruits – it will indicate that there wasn't really the changing faith that is necessary for our salvation.

Jesus says there are rewards and joy to be experienced in heaven.[485] He says our names are written in heaven.[486] We're told that there is great joy in heaven over a sinner who repents.[487] We're told that there is a great cloud of witnesses that testify to God and His Messiah in heaven.[488]

We're told of treasures in heaven that we should lay up for ourselves. These include doing good, and generosity.[489] Certainly one of the greatest rewards that can be imagined and offered is the possibility that if God is pleased with the lives we have led and the things we have accomplished: we can stand before Him and hear the loveliest words imaginable, "Well done!"[490]

Some popular ideas about heaven include eternal rest and relaxation – perhaps with praise on harps and by singing. Certainly praise will be a joyful part of our heavenly experience, but Scriptures don't indicate eternal leisure. They do indicate that we will be given full knowledge of the nature of God and His plans: "Now we see but a poor reflection as in a mirror; then we shall see face to face. Now I know in part; then I shall know fully, even as I am fully known."[491] In addition to a lot of instruction and imparted knowledge there are going to be other assignments. Jesus speaks of at least some, the victorious in the struggles against the temptations of the world, being given authority over the nations when he returns.[492] In the parable of the talents – also known as the parable of the bags

---

[484] Matthew 7:20-23 (NIV)
[485] Luke 6:20-23
[486] Luke 10:20
[487] Luke 15:7
[488] Hebrews 11:1 through 12::3
[489] First Timothy 6:18-19 (NIV)
[490] Matthew 25:21 (TNIV)
[491] First Corinthians 13:12 (NIV)
[492] Revelation 2:26

of gold – the master entrusts his servants with his assets according to their abilities. Two servants use the talents to gain a return while one hides it away for fear of losing it. To those who make the profit, the master expresses his pleasure on his return with, "Well done, good and faithful servant! You have been faithful with a few things; I will put you in charge of many things. Come and share your master's happiness!"[493] To me this says productive work completed will be rewarded with more productive work to be done – even in heaven. Incidental to this discussion, but of importance, the one who makes no return earns the great displeasure of the master. Since he had been given according to his abilities, he could have made a return with an effort. I've often thought that this parable could have used a fourth servant – one who did his best but for whom things went wrong resulting in loss of the master's assets. The Bible doesn't indicate how the master would deal with this, but I suspect that he would have been pleased because of the effort. Whereas earthly standards seem to indicate that the end justifies the means, it seems that by Godly standards that the means justify the end.

One of the visions of heaven from Revelation has given comfort to countless grieving families. In the vision God, "He who sits on the throne, will spread his tent over them. Never again will they hunger; never again will they thirst. The sun will not beat down on them, nor any scorching heat. For the Lamb at the center of the throne will be their shepherd; he will lead them to springs of living water. And God will wipe away every tear from their eyes."[494]

There's a fictional story that, while it is imaginary, does illustrate a lot about heaven: A certain physician had his office in his home. He was being visited by an anxious patient who was terminally ill. The patient asked his doctor, "What's it like on the other side of this life?" The doctor answered that he didn't know. The response was, "You mean that a man with all of your learning doesn't know what it's like in heaven?" Just then there was a scratching and whining at the door separating the office from the home. The doctor opened the door, and his dog bounded in ecstatically wagging his tail. The doctor explained that the dog had never been through that door before and never in the office. Even though the dog didn't know what was in the office or what went on in the office, the dog knew that his master was there and that his master loved him, so everything would be

---

[493] Matthew 25:21 (TNIV)
[494] Revelation 7:14-17 and 21:4 (TNIV)

all right if he got in. The physician went on to explain that he thought heaven was like that.

Is there any more? There sure is. God has declared that, "I have loved you with an everlasting love."[495] The apostle Paul assures us, "No eye has seen, no ear has heard, no mind has conceived what God has prepared for those who love him."[496] Whatever else heaven may be, I am convinced that it is a place filled with ecstasy, delight, pleasure, and joy beyond our present ability to grasp.

*(An answer from Dean Culbertson)*

Jesus told us that we will be made like Him… We will be individuals, but the beauty of the Gospel is that we will be with Him!

*(Betty Byers' understanding)*

Heaven is the dwelling place of God. Angels will be there. There will be no death, sorrow, crying or pain. It's beautiful!

*(Gary Lewis' thoughts)*

As much as we talk about heaven in the Church, you don't hear that many sermons about heaven. There aren't that many resources dedicated to describing it.

In Revelation 21, there are these familiar, wonderful words: "God himself will be with them… He will wipe every tear from their eyes. There will be no more death or mourning or crying or pain, for the old order of things has passed away."

Hallelujah! John tells us He who sits on the throne says, "I'm making everything new." Heaven is a real, eternal place.

What's it like? What is heaven like? Heaven is like nothing you've ever seen! "Eye has not seen and ear has not heard all that God prepared for those who love Him."[497]

---

[495] Jeremiah 31:3 (NIV)
[496] First Corinthians 2:9 (NIV)
[497] First Corinthians 2:9

You take the best day you've ever had, the greatest things that have happened to you on this earth, and multiply it by a million times… and you still aren't even close to what it's going to be like. We can't even imagine how great it's going to be. That's what heaven is like.

God is love. God is the author of love. God is the creator of love. And when we are in God's presence, we experience that love. You see, it's the same love that brings family together. We just get a glimpse of it on earth.

In heaven we get the full experience. It's like a family party every day – without the clean-up. The love we experience on earth is magnified and perfected in heaven when our loved ones stand in God's presence.

The Bible gives us some practical pictures about heaven. It's God's city where everything is perfect. It's God's throne where He reigns; He rules everything. Everything complies with God's standards.

The Bible talks about it being filled with jewels and we walk on streets of gold. That means everything in heaven is valuable – it drips with value! Significance! Importance! Revelation 21 says, "Heaven is where God is." God is everywhere, but Heaven is where God is! What lights up everything in heaven is God's presence. That's what we look forward to. That's what heaven is like.

But what will people be like there? What am I going to be like? The Bible says we are going to have a body, but it's going to be a perfect one. I don't know how old or young it's going to be, but it will be however old or young God wants it to be.

The Bible uses a word to describe our lifestyle in heaven – glory. It's going to be glorious, everything about it. That's what we look forward to. Our character will be holy. That means perfect or set apart or different than anything we've ever experienced before.

What about our circumstances? What are my days going to be like? The word the Bible uses is perfect. No more death or crying or pain or any such thing. Perfect! Every moment of it! That's what we look forward to.

What will we do in heaven?  Heaven is a place of real significance.  We are all kings and queens with significance and importance and responsibility for eternity.  We work – it's not a boring place.  We celebrate.  The party in heaven is for all eternity.  Imagine the fun things we get to enjoy in heaven.  We'll enjoy true fellowship.  We'll worship.  We have relationships with God and with other people.  We rest in heaven.  And somehow we rest and work with significance at the same time, eternally.

Do we play harps in heaven?  I don't think so.  The Bible says there are some ruling elders that do, but nowhere does it say we all play harps in heaven.  If you wanted to you could, because it's heaven.  But you don't have to – you can play a trumpet if you want!

The striking message about getting to heaven is that it is not a matter of how good you are.  It doesn't depend on how good or bad we are.  It's because of a choice we make about God's son, Jesus Christ.

And that choice gives us not only HOPE for tomorrow, but HOPE for today.

Challenge 47

# Why are Christians sad when one of you dies?

If you Christians really look forward to being in Heaven why is there so much sadness when one of you dies?

*(Jack Clark's thoughts)*

Carol and I were recently waiting for our turn to take communion in our congregation. My thoughts wandered from the event itself to the brothers and sisters sharing the experience with us and then to those who have been a part of it in the past but who have departed to be with Christ. I missed the friends, my parents and my grandparents who had shared in my past communion services. I missed the joy of their greetings, their smiles, and our shared discussions.

Most Christians feel that Jesus is a pretty good example for us to follow. I recall that when his friend Lazarus of Bethany died "Jesus wept."[498] The Bible says that Jesus loved Lazarus and his two sisters, Martha and Mary. When Jesus got to their home four days after Lazarus had died and Martha and Mary came out to be with him, he wept. It seems to me that the reason he wept was because of his compassion for his friends' grief. It must not have been due to sorrow for Lazarus; as a friend and follower of Christ, his spirit was in heaven. (I've often thought that it must have been a come down for Lazarus to have to return to this life after tasting life in heaven. Not only that, but he would have to live under threat of the chief priests of Israel who would have liked to have killed him to stop his testimony to the power of Jesus,[499] and even beyond that, he would have to go through the dying process again.) Anyhow Jesus certainly felt the grief of his friends and the pain they had gone through during those four days when their brother was in the tomb.

When Martin Luther's daughter died in her childhood, Martin wept for the loss even though he expressed his conviction that her soul was in heaven. When loved ones of mine have died, I have cried for them. Because our friends and our family are so very much a part of our life, it tears our life into shreds when they can no longer fill the important place that contributed so much to our joy. Although we believe in heaven, and although we are convinced that they don't suffer any more, they are still sorely missed.

The only similar thing would have been to have lived in Europe in the eighteenth and

---

[498] John 11:35 (NIV)
[499] John 12:10

early nineteenth centuries and to have had a part of our family immigrate to North America leaving us behind.  There would have been much unknown to us who were left behind, but the greatest problem would have been to give up their being with us and interacting from day to day.

Grief is associated with any loss, and no loss is greater than the death of a loved one or the facing our own death.  This is true even when we have belief in much better things to come.  Few of us are able to copy Paul's great faith that allowed him to state: "To me, to live is Christ, and to die is gain."[500]

It helps to understand the phases of grief everyone goes through in facing one's own death or the death of a loved one.  I've borrowed from a medical journal article I wrote to help understand what happens in the grieving process.

"What usually comes first is the shock of disbelief, which may be carried to the extreme of an actual denial of the death. Especially in accident cases, it may also be manifested in such fantasies as "It was only an hour (or day or week) ago that he was alive, and if we could just turn the cock back his death could have been prevented.

"This phase is commonly followed by a sense of guilt 'If I had only done (or not done) such and such he wouldn't have died.'  Or 'if I had only been kinder...' I try to assuage such guilt by mentioning the impossibility of foreseeing most events, or by stressing the care and concern that the relative did give the deceased.

"Self-blame may pass quickly to a third phase of blaming others – the other driver in auto accidents, the police for lax enforcement, and the physician for lack of skill or concern. Every doctor should be prepared for this, and be ready with a simple recital of what he and others have done, and perhaps some regretful mention of the limitations of medical science.

---

[500] Philippians 1:21 (NIV)

"Often God gets the blame. ('Why does it always happen to the good ones?' or 'It was God's will.') Here it may help to point out that if God actually caused all the events of our lives, instead of giving us freedom to decide things for ourselves, we would become mere puppets.

"Still a third expression of such grief is to blame the deceased: 'I told Billy a thousand times not to run out in the streets.' Usually such outbursts require only sympathy and such common sense as talk about the nature of children or of human beings. But when this phase is expressed in a flat denial of loss such as an elderly man's delusion that his wife had been unfaithful to him years ago and is therefore not worth mourning, psychiatric help may be required.

"The final phase of grief is a gradual return to normal life patterns, interspersed with temporary regressions to one of the former stages. I advise two or three weeks of inactivity while shock and grief subside. But except in unusual circumstances, I advise strongly against such escapes as quitting a job, going immediately to live with the children, or moving just to get out of the house. Running away is usually a poor method of adapting to a new situation.

"Few pains are as great as that caused by the loss of a loved one,"[501]

I have felt that when someone dies, we should look at it as going on a trip with our parents when we were children. We only had a fuzzy idea of where we were going, what we would do when we got there, where we would stay, how we would be cared for and the exciting new experiences we would have. But we did know this – we would be with those who loved us. We would have good times and experience things we couldn't have even dreamed of. It seems that it will be much like that when we die – Abba, our loving Father will be with us.

Jesus who has called us his friends has promised that he will be with us too: "Surely I am with you always, to the very end of the age."[502] This promise will certainly include the time our loved ones have made this journey, and it will include the time that you and I will

---

[501] "Helpful Words When Your Patient is Dying," Jack P. Clark, M. D., *Medical Economics,* September 28, 1970.
[502] Matthew 28:20 (TNIV)

make this journey. I can't think of anyone else better to be with. Jesus talked about this with the disciples in the New Testament, and the same understanding is for all of us who are his disciples today: "'Do not let your hearts be troubled. Trust in God and also trust in me. My Father's house has plenty of room; if that were not so, would I have told you that I am going there to prepare a place for you? And if I go and prepare a place for you, I will come back and take you to be with me that you also may be where I am. You know the way to the place where I am going.' 'Thomas said to him, 'Lord, we don't know where you are going, so how can we know the way?' Jesus answered, 'I am the way and the truth and the life. No one comes to the Father except through me.'"[503]

It is tough to be separated from those we love, but it is an everlasting comfort to know that they are with Jesus, God's Messiah. As much as we love someone, God and Christ loved them first and love them more than we're capable of loving. That's a pretty great company with which to leave them until Jesus returns to take us also to be with him and with them.

I thank our great God for the gift of life and for the magnificent, majestic, glorious world that He gave us to live in. As great as these blessings are, He has promised even more. He has promised that He will love us with an everlasting love – through all eternity. He's promised that He will always be with us – that includes the pain we might suffer during the process of our own death. It includes the pain we suffer in the dying process of those we love or in the pain of temporary separation due to the death of those we love. He's promised that whatever great things we've experienced in this life – the love of our God as we can understand it now, the love of our wife or husband and family, the friendship of brothers and sisters in Christ, the most beautiful place we've ever seen – that all of this will be ever-so-much surpassed in the things He has planned for those of us who love Him in the life to come. Death certainly brings sadness, but it also promises better things than we can imagine.

*(An answer from Betty Byers)*

We're sad because we will miss the person; however, we know we will see them again in Heaven. This is our blessed hope.

---

[503] John 14:1-6 (TNIV)

The sadness comes because there is a void left by a loved one's death. We are sad for ourselves, not the loved one in heaven. But a true believer can grieve without having a spirit of grief[504] which is bondage.

---

[504] Spirit of grief would signify being totally consumed by grief.

## Challenge 48
# When do our souls go to be in heaven?

Do Christians go to Heaven at the time of their death or at the end of the age when Christ will raise all believers into the Heavens? If believers go directly to heaven at the time of their physical death, then who are the Dead in Christ that will be gathered and raised? (Submitted by Cathy Ann Turner)

*(An answer by Jack Clark)*

Some Christians have suggested that when our earthly body dies our soul goes into a soul sleep until Christ comes again and raises the dead. The Bible certainly indicates that the dead in Christ will rise when he returns.[505] The scriptures suggest that we will be given an imperishable body with none of the flaws of our earthly body when Christ returns.[506] So it seems that those who wrote the New Testament indicated there will be a great event and a joyous transformation of our existence when Christ returns, but it doesn't seem to me to indicate that we must wait for that day to enjoy heaven and a relationship with God and other redeemed believers.

Jesus said, "In my Father's house are many rooms; if it were not so, I would have told you. I am going there to prepare a place for you. And if I go and prepare a place for you, I will come back and take you to be with me that you also may be where I am."[507] Of course, although this is his indication that we will share heaven with him, it doesn't directly refer to the timing of the event.

When Jesus' friend Lazarus had died and his sisters Martha and Mary were in grief, Jesus asked Martha if she believed that her brother would rise. "Martha answered, 'I know he will rise again in the resurrection at the last day.' Jesus said to her, 'I am the resurrection and the life. He who believes in me will live, even though he dies, and whoever lives and believes in me will never die. Do you believe this?'"[508] This doesn't seem to suggest a time of waiting for Jesus' return for continuing our lives. It doesn't suggest to me an interruption of our existence. It sounds like an ongoing, never-ending, uninterrupted life. Another reference that suggests this uninterrupted communion with Christ is: "Jesus Christ has abolished death."[509]

---

[505] First Thessalonians 4:16
[506] First Corinthians 15:35-44
[507] John 14:1-4 (NIV)
[508] John 11:24-26 (NIV)
[509] Second Timothy 1:10 (NIV)

In case we become too concerned about the details, it is suggested: "Seek first his kingdom and his righteousness, and all these things will be given to you as well. Therefore do not worry about tomorrow, for tomorrow will worry about itself."[510] To me this suggests that if I concern myself with living in relationship with Jesus Christ in this lifetime, that he will take care of what is coming. I can't think of better hands in which to leave our destiny.

The Bible does speak of departing to be with Christ[511] and falling asleep in Christ.[512]

Paul suggested that the dead in Christ will be raised first on Christ's return, and after that those who are left alive will join them to meet the Lord and be with him forever.[513] Later in life, after Paul had faced many hardships and had many friends in the congregations he had established and felt the enthusiasm to do more and the weariness of age he commented in one of his letters, "I eagerly expect and hope that I will in no way be ashamed, but will have sufficient courage so that now as always Christ will be exalted in my body, whether by life or by death. For to me, to live is Christ, and to die is gain. If I am to go on living in the body, this will mean fruitful labor for me. Yet what shall I choose? I do not know! I am torn between the two: I desire to depart and be with Christ, which is better by far, but it is more necessary for you that I remain in the body."[514] This certainly sounds like Paul was convinced there would be no wait to be with Christ after the death of his physical body.

I place great stock in the recounting of the thief's experience on the cross next to Jesus. He had the perception to realize who Christ is – a perception that had escaped the Chief Priests and the Sanhedrin. He had the temerity to imagine that this "God with us" would be interested in him, an outcast. Jesus Christ looked on this sweating, tortured, scum of the earth with compassion and love and redeemed him and made him pure and acceptable to God. Christ's response to the justified former thief was strikingly clear: "I tell you the truth. Today you will be with me in paradise."[515] Notice the timing. It wasn't on my return in glory you will be with me in paradise. It wasn't someday you will be with me

---

[510] Matthew 6:27 & 33-34 (NIV)
[511] Philippians 1:23 (NIV)
[512] First Corinthians 11:30 &15:18
[513] First Thessalonians 4:16-17
[514] Philippians1:20-24 (TNIV)
[515] Luke 23:42-43 (NIV)

in paradise, but <u>today</u> you will be with me in paradise. Jesus didn't say the man who believes in me will die and later live again, but that the man who believes in me will never die.

For me an even tougher question involves those whose bodily functions continue, but have no awareness of their surroundings. When does the soul of a person in an irreversible coma go to heaven? When does the soul of one who has lost the evidence of their personhood to irreversible brain damage due to Alzheimer's disease or some similar problem go to heaven? I don't know the answer. I find no discussion in the scriptures and have had no indication from the Holy Spirit on the subject. The only thing that I can observe is that God remains totally in charge of the universe and is involved in everything that happens in it. He is also the total lover of these people and every other person, and He works for good in all things – even such difficult situations. I can only, through faith, leave these loved ones in the hands of God who knew each one of us before He formed us, who counts every hair on our head, and who never falters in the great plans He has for us.

I am persuaded that life goes on from the moment of our physical death – no time lapse, no waiting, no holding area. I am also convinced that some great change will happen to us – the living then and those who have been spiritually with Christ in paradise when Christ returns, but this seems to be a separate event.

*(Dean Culbertson's answer)*

Jesus told the thief on the cross, "This day, you will be with me in Paradise."[516] He also said, "I go to prepare a place for you."[517]

The terms Paradise and Heaven are considered by some scholars to be the same – yet, I would encourage us to look more closely at the previous passages. Jesus taught that he would come back for us.

This is my personal belief; although, I will always respect those who disagree: Paradise and Hades are referred to in Scripture. They are both related to Sheol, the place of the

---

[516] Luke 23:43 (NIV)
[517] John 14:2-5

dead. Jesus went, with the thief on the cross, to Paradise. He later walked on the earth, after the resurrection. Recall that after the resurrection Jesus told Mary, that he had not ascended yet to his Father. I believe that at first, people go to Paradise or Hades to await the final judgment. Sheol will be replaced permanently by Heaven and Hell.

*(Betty Byers' answer)*

My understanding is that our souls go to heaven when we die. The dead in Christ will get new glorified bodies when Christ comes to earth the second time.[518]

---

[518] First John 3:2, and First Corinthians 15:42-49 (KJV)

## Challenge 49
# God save me from the Christians

Look at all the strife that has characterized the Christian Church throughout the past and even recently. For example, consider the horrors of the Inquisition, the excesses of the Crusades where Muslims and Jews and even other Christians were slaughtered by the crusaders, the sectarian killings between Catholics and Protestants in Medieval England and modern Northern Ireland. When I consider these things, I think: God save me from the Christians. (Submitted by Robert Craig, MD)

*(A discussion by Jack Clark)*

It's impossible to consider these charges and not confirm the imperfections of the church and Christians. It's easy to look at others who have done such things – not to mention burning of "witches" and haughty attitudes that certainly would have been condemned by God's Son who commanded us not only to love one another[519] but to love our enemies.[520] In case we tend to spend too much time looking at others' sins, we need to spend some time looking at our own. These aren't easy precepts to follow. Probably there is not a one of us who on occasion hasn't shown prejudice in one form or another. There is probably not a single congregation that hasn't been unfeeling and unkind on occasions when a pastor was left "hanging out to dry." Every one of us has missed opportunities to show compassion for a brother or sister in Christ who needed our support. There are times when each of us have not comforted the mourning or looked after the poor, or failed to share our faith when it was desperately needed. These are the roots of such actions. Bitter disagreements can mar many church governing bodies' meetings.

I can recall more than one occasion when a member of the body of Christ has expounded that such and such is "never going to happen in our church." We must occasionally be reminded that it is not our church. It is the church of Jesus Christ, or it is no church at all!

The problem was historically made worse when the church as a whole became respectable and achieved power. Power does corrupt – including power in church members or church organizations. Satan loves to use such human failings to direct us away from God's plans and progressively away from our Christ-assigned tasks. When we as a church were all poor – when we were all downtrodden – when the only thing we could all be was humble – we were concerned for each other and for those outside our

---

[519] John 13:34-35, Romans 12:10 and 13:8, Galatians 5:13, Ephesians 4:2, I Peter 1:22 & 3:8, I John 3:11 & 3:23 & 4:7 &11
[520] Matthew 5:43-44 & Luke 6:27 & 35

circle who were as needy as we were but hadn't been introduced to Christ, or hadn't given themselves to His salvation.

Another major stumbling block is to assume that because I understand God through Jesus Christ in one way, everyone else should too. I am sorely tempted to think that someone else's understanding has to be just like mine, or it's wrong. Then comes the temptation to correct the other person. Then comes the temptation to try to force my views and understanding on the other person. I can easily forget that God meets people where they are, and not all of us are in the same place. I have often wondered when I consider such things why God doesn't give up on us; why doesn't He give up on me. The answer must lie in His unfathomable love.

John Wesley learned to accept other's differences and eventually could come to the place where he would greet others with, "If your heart is as my heart, give me your hand." Of course John had been subjected to some of the troubles I've mentioned and he viewed himself as one plucked from a fire, so he could eventually come to the place where he could sympathize with others rather than persecute them.

Queen Elizabeth I was a powerful politician and had come through a see-saw of persecution of Catholics by Protestants and Protestants by Catholics as well as a frighteningly unstable childhood. She understood the terrible political price of such conflicts and wanted to avoid them, but on a deeper level this lady who had some very real personal shortcomings had some understandings that many of us would do well to follow. Her half-sister, bloody Mary, who had been queen of England before Elizabeth, had been responsible for burning hundreds of English Protestants. Elizabeth observed that, "Consciences are not to be forced." On another occasion she answered the French ambassador who was intent on converting Elizabeth from her Protestant faith to Catholicism, that, "There is only one Jesus Christ. The rest is a dispute over trifles." She at one time characterized arguments of theologians and churchmen as "ropes of sand or sea-slime leading to the moon." She tried to avoid the backlash against Catholics following Mary's reign and commented that, "If I were not certain that mine were the true way to God's will, God forbid that I should live to prescribe it to you."[521]

---

[521] *The Life of Elizabeth I*, Alison Weir, pp. 54-59, A Ballantine Book, Published by The Random House Publishing Group, Reading Group, copyright © 2003 by Alison Weir and The Random House Publishing Group, a division of Random House, Inc., Copyright © 1998 by Alison Weir

Just in case we're tempted to think that the really major problems along these lines of persecution happened either long ago or far away, I'll share something that happened in my small town family medicine practice.

One autumn a lady called early one day to advise me that her elderly father-in-law had tried to commit suicide by cutting his wrist. A recent heart problem had required a pacemaker implant. He had been too weak to work on his beloved farm, and to top everything off, he had a stroke, which, although it was mild, had left some additional weakness. As I drove to the office to meet them and care for him, I assumed despondency over his multiple physical problems had driven him to this act of desperation. However, on my arrival, the daughter-in-law explained that in order to clear his conscience, he had gone to his preacher to confess a sexual sin that had occurred many years ago. His church was very important in his life. Instead of receiving the release from guilt he had needed, the minister advised him that, according to the precepts of their congregation, he had no choice other than reporting the sin to the whole congregation and removing him from fellowship. This meant that he could no longer take communion. I knew this isn't how God's Holy Spirit has dealt with my sins, and I knew, through this Spirit, that I was to share this with my patient.

One of the great benefits of Bible reading is having some good guidelines available in tough situations. As I was examining his wrist, I was moved to ask him if he had accepted Jesus as his savior, and if he was sorry for his sins. On his answering, "Yes," I told him that Jesus Christ "By one sacrifice has made perfect forever those who are being made Holy."[522] Also that, "God so loved the world that He gave his only son, that whoever believes in him should not perish but have everlasting life,"[523] and "As far as the east is from the west, so far has he removed our transgressions from us,"[524] and "The sacrifices of God are a broken spirit; a broken and contrite heart, O God, you will not despise."[525] As these verses poured out, I advised him that I wasn't speaking for only myself, but at the direction of the Holy Spirit. With great tears in his eyes, he looked down at his poor cut wrist and asked, "But how can God forgive this? This is murder!" I rejoined with great sadness for his suffering and great sadness for the violence which is sometimes done in the name of religion, "Yes, this is murder, but Jesus Christ's sacrifice

[522] Hebrews 10:14 (NIV)
[523] John 3:16 (NIV)
[524] Psalms 103:12 (NIV)
[525] Psalms 51:17 (NIV)

covers any sin, even this one." In my heart, I wasn't sure who had done the murder, but I felt it wasn't my patient.

Happily he had not done great physical harm to himself. I bandage his arm. He seemed somewhat relieved, but still was hurt and confused. I saw him several times and each time reinforced that Christ loves him, not because I said so, but because Christ said so, and I was sure of it because I know that I am loved, and if I am loved, anyone who accepts Jesus Christ as savior is loved and is saved. He never seemed fully convinced.

A few weeks later, I attended our Elkhart District Spiritual Growth Retreat at Oakwood Park in Syracuse. It was a great event. One of the things asked of us was to write down our spiritual journey. One of the significant things on mine was this man's recent problems. All night long, like Jacob, I wrestled with the Holy Spirit.[526] It was one of the most restless nights I have ever endured! I knew there was something God wanted me to do, and, on this occasion, there wasn't time for the usual slowly growing awareness with which He has usually prompted me to do things. In the early hours of the morning, a scripture verse came to my mind that until then had held little if any meaning for me: "Whatever you bind on earth will be bound in heaven, and whatever you loose on earth will be loosed in heaven."[527] I knew what it was the Holy Spirit wanted me to do.

To this Spirit-filled group of brothers and sisters in Christ, I presented this man's story without identifying him. I asked them to consider his problem and consider the scripture which the Holy Spirit had given me. I asked them if it was their understanding that this man's sins are forgiven, to join with me in loosing him from them. They agreed with me, and we prayed as a group that this would be accomplished. The next time I saw my patient, I was able to tell him what we had done, stressing that I had not revealed his name, just the facts. He was able to accept his forgiveness because we had loosed him from his sins. There were no more suicide attempts; he would come to the office with a happy smile and enjoyed life. To me, it was a great joy to be a part of God's plan of action and great to work with the Holy Spirit in relieving this man's heartache and returning him to the love of God where he belonged.

---

[526] Genesis 32:22-31 (NIV)
[527] Matthew 16:19 (NIV)

Praise God! I must confess that when I was talking to the patient, I wanted to bring up such scripture as, "Let him who is without sin cast the first stone,"[528] and that the leaders of the church should judge not lest they be judged,[529] as no one is without sin.[530] I wanted to point out that if any of these leaders had ever lusted after someone other than their spouse, they were guilty of adultery because Jesus said so.[531] I wanted to say these things, but the Holy Spirit held me back. What my patient needed was an expression of God's love, not an expression of my anger.

Early Christian church history recorded that when the Apostle John had grown very old and it was recognized that his feeble status indicated that he was soon to leave this life and depart to be with Jesus, the Christian brothers gathered around him and asked if he had any final instructions for the church. It was reported that he responded, "Love one another." Rather taken aback, the gathered friends asked, "Is that all?" He answered, "Christ commanded it. It's enough." If we, the church, if I, a Follower of the Way, will keep this advice and this command uppermost in our heart and mind, we and the world will be better off for it and Satan will grind his teeth in defeat. The Apostle John wrote: "No one has ever seen God, but if we love one another, God lives in us and His love is made complete in us."[532]

It's important to remember that when a follower of Jesus fails that this is not a failure of Jesus or God.

I find it interesting that Dr. Craig, who submitted this challenge to our faith, accurately diagnosed an illness that has plagued our Christian Fellowship. Jesus Christ has already prescribed the medicine and the Apostle John has already given an affirming second opinion about the remedy.

---

[528] John 8:7 (NIV)
[529] Adapted from Matthew 7:1 (NIV)
[530] First John 1:8 (NIV)
[531] Matthew 5:28
[532] I John 4:12

## Challenge 50
# What should we do when we disagree with another Christian?
(One of the answers focuses on the issue of abortion)

Most of us have occasionally disagreed with someone in our congregation on a political, social, or religious view. (Submitted by Fairplain Presbyterian Adult Church School class in Benton Harbor, Michigan)

*(Jack Clark's answer)*

To focus attention on a specific instance of such a disagreement, I'll visit the disagreement that various Christians have over the issue of abortion. It's no secret that for many years the law of the land allowed abortions to be done to save the life or health of the expectant mother or in cases where there was a major likelihood of severely deformed fetus. It's also no secret that the law of the land was changed through the action of our supreme court in the case of Rowe versus Wade to allow abortion for any reason that the pregnant woman chooses.

On one side of this controversial issue were those who had great sympathy for young women caught in tragic, personal, physical, emotional, or even financial traps due to an unexpected or unwanted pregnancy. Illegal abortions done in poor conditions and by technically poorly qualified operators had destroyed the health and in some cases killed the pregnant women. Recent statistics have shown the number of abortions is about the same where they are legal or where they are illegal. (Yes there are still places where this is the case).

Another view is held by those who focus on the protection of the pregnant woman's privacy and emotional interests as excluding the interests of the unborn child. It seems indeed strange that if I carelessly drive my car in such a manner that an accident causes the death of an unborn child, that the unborn child's rights were violated and I can be sued by the parents, or charged with criminal neglect. But the law recognizes no rights for an unborn child if I as a physician agree to do a requested abortion on an expectant 14 year old girl because of her wish even if her parents don't know of her pregnancy and were not able to give their advice. Likewise consider the case of a 26-year old woman who decides on an abortion without the wishes of the father being considered (whether married or single) or the "rights" of the child playing a role. Legally this is not a problem. Even stranger yet if a woman is at term and in labor but does not want the child she can request that her doctor kill the child in the process of delivery (known as a partial birth abortion). This usually involves cutting through the top of the infant's head (without anesthetic) and removing the baby's brain. For this there is no legal liability. However if the child has been delivered in a time frame only minutes after the previously described event could have happened and is noted to have a severe spina bifida that will result in paralysis of the lower limbs but not affect the child's intellectual potential (or some other major deformity) and the father in the delivery room chooses to bash the child's head against the delivery room wall, then the father can be charged with murder. In case you suspect that this is only a theoretical possibility, it has actually occurred. Another factor in the present legal situation is that many women who feel very uncomfortable in considering abortion are pressured to choose that by the father of the child or the parents. So much for free choice in that setting.

There are devout Christians on both sides of this question. I have literally cried for the pain of some pregnant patients who have been convinced by their boyfriend's promise that they would love them forever only to give themselves away sexually before marriage and discover after they were pregnant that the young man is no longer interested in them. I have felt the hopelessness of a woman whose husband was disabled and could no longer work and who found herself pregnant and not able to support the children they already had. I have had patients with abusive husbands who were broken hearted to find themselves in a morass of an impossible situation made worse by another expected child. I have known those impregnated by the incestuous lechery of a family member. These women often feel they have no place to turn.

On the other hand I have had patients who could not have a pregnancy of their own and could not find a child to adopt because most of the unwanted pregnancies are now aborted. And I have known pregnant mothers who have given their child for adoption or chose to raise it on their own instead of aborting it. I must say that I admire the bravery of such a mother.

Part of the problem comes from defining when human life begins. The Roman Catholic Church has said that life begins at the moment of conception. The Jewish view, as I understand it, is that life begins when there is quickening (the feeling of movement of the unborn child by the pregnant woman). Interestingly scriptures seem to suggest an even earlier time than either of these views. God has indicated that he knew us before he formed us in our mother's womb.[533] This would seem to indicate that we are conceived in the mind of God even before the joining of the ovum and sperm of our parents.

Well, I've talked long enough about the situation without saying how I feel about it. The way I would assess the problem of abortion is that it is a poor way to deal with tragic situations. As a Christian I can't solve my hunger by stealing from someone who has less than I have. The vast majority of abortions in our country are abortions of convenience. Looking at the results of abortions from the maternal perspective, complications are in fact uncommon, but they do occur. In my family practice of medicine, I have seen women who had legal abortions and became infected or bleed and had to have hysterectomies because of the complications. I have seen women who were rendered infertile due to infection plugging the fallopian tubes; when later in life they wanted to have children, they could not become pregnant. There are emotional complications associated with abortion. I have had women confide in me the pain they feel when they think of their aborted children, wondering what they would have been doing at the age they would have now been. I have wondered how many more have the thoughts and don't confide them to me. There are spiritual problems associated with abortion. Will God accept these innocents into heaven? Of course. Can the mothers who give their permission to the destroying of these innocents be forgiven; can those who perform the abortions be forgiven? Of course they can. Any sin except blasphemy against the Holy Spirit can be forgiven. One problem is that for a sin to be forgiven one must be convicted that it is a sin. Our society has brought many people to believe that abortion is not a sin. Even some of our denominations have avoided declaring abortion to be a sin. Without conviction, there cannot be repentance. Without repentance, there cannot be forgiveness. Without forgiveness, there cannot be redemption, and without redemption, there cannot be salvation.

The sin of the deception is even a greater sin than the killing of the innocent lives. God help our society for not protecting the helpless. One of the distinguishing things about early Christians in Rome was the way they treated their newborns. The old Roman society view was that children who were inconvenient or imperfect could be killed at birth. One of the observations about the early Christians that the pagan society made was,

---

[533] Jeremiah 1:5

337

"They are the ones who do not kill their children."

Jesus made it very clear that, whatever we do or don't do for the "least of these" we have done or not done for our Messiah.[534] The "least of these" involves those unable to protect themselves or deal with their own problems. If I include the unborn as a human, then certainly they are among the least of the least. As I understand it, abortion preys on individuals who are completely helpless and cannot protect themselves or even speak for themselves. It preys on those who have been created by God in His image. Those who would sanitize the procedure with euphemisms and platitudes argue that the fetus is not yet a human, but God declares, "I knew you before I formed you in your mother's womb."[535] These lives that are being destroyed are holy, set aside for God's glory. He has planned great things for each of these lives. Not all would have achieved their destiny, but all were precious to God.

I certainly believe we humans must take an active role in limiting our population to a level that can be sustained by our earth's resources without privation. We also have an obligation to leave adequate resources for the other life forms God has created that share this planet with us. We also need to strive to try to assure every child that it is wanted, loved, will be cared for, and can develop its capacities to the utmost, but abortion is not the route to go to achieve these goals. Those who would conclude that abortion should be acceptable, talk of the fetus as a blob of protoplasm to be terminated if it's inconvenient. They ignore pictures of a twelve-week-old fetus in its mother's uterus sucking its thumb. They ignore its beating heart, and the fact that if it is touched it will withdraw from pain. A toddler can look at the picture of a fetus and respond with the pronouncement, "Baby!" In their innocence, they declare its status, a fact that tragically escapes our courts, Planned Parenthood, and thousands of misled women who find themselves in embarrassing, tragic, betrayed, forced, and lifestyle-threatening situations due to their pregnancies.

There are support groups and counselors who deal with the problems of women who have had abortions. One of their favorite scriptures that gives hope for the children and the mothers is from Jeremiah. It is also quoted in the New Testament relating to King

---

[534] See Matthew 26:31-46
[535] Jeremiah 1:5 (NIV)

338

Herod's killing of all the young babies in his attempt to kill Jesus. "This is what the Lord says, 'A voice is heard in Ramah, mourning and great weeping. Rachel weeping for her children and refusing to be comforted, because they are no more.' This is what the Lord says: 'Restrain your voice from weeping and your eyes from tears, for your work will be rewarded,' declares the Lord. 'They will return from the land of the enemy. So there is hope for your descendants,' declares the Lord. Your children will return to their own land."[536]

Early in my practice of medicine I had a patient who was single and pregnant. The father had been committed to a hospital for the insane. I had written the hospital enquiring about the father's problem to determine if it was inherited. They advised it wasn't, and I shared this with the expectant mother. She started having vaginal bleeding (confirmed over several weeks in office visits). Finally her aunt who was a licensed practical nurse and had been a trusted co-worker of my father advised that she had seen tissue passed. This was in the days before ultrasound and blood hormone levels to help us confirm the status of a pregnancy. I made the very logical diagnosis of an inevitable spontaneous abortion, got the required consultation from another hospital staff member and scheduled a dilation and curettage (D & C) to remove the remaining products of conception and avoid the complications of a "missed abortion." The cervix dilated easily, and I introduced the small ring forceps to remove any remaining tissue. To my horror, I soon realized I had been hoodwinked. The first tissue I removed was the right shoulder blade, arm, forearm, and tiny hand – it showed no evidence of degeneration that would be expected if the fetus had been dead. The whole limb was just a little over two inches long. The tiny hand was palm up with the five perfect little fingers slightly curled as if in supplication. I was heart sick. I felt a tightness in my chest and even found it difficult to breathe. I had been fooled into destroying a creation of God.

Do I think abortion on demand is in God's plan? No. Are there Christians who

---

[536] Jeremiah 31:15-17 (TNIV). An explanation of these verses is in order here. Ramah was a small town located about five miles north of Jerusalem. It was a town through which the citizens of Jerusalem passed on their way to exile in Babylonia. Many of the Jewish people had been killed in the battles leading up to this exile. This, of course, resulted in much sorrow for the parents who had lost children. Rachel represented all the mothers who wept for their lost children at the time of the exile. Rachel was the favorite wife of Jacob (who had been renamed Israel) and the mother of Benjamin and Joseph who was the ancestor of Ephraim and Manasseh (two of the most powerful of the tribes of Israel). In the New Testament (Matthew 2:16), the verse is applied to the heartache of the mothers whose children were killed on the order of Herod in his attempt to kill the newborn Christ after the visit by the wise men. The abortion support groups relate the mourning to the feelings of the women who have had abortions. Additionally they relate the land of the enemy to Satan and "their own land" to heaven. They anticipate a reunion with their aborted children in heaven.

sincerely believe that abortion is justified to avoid tragic things permanently damaging the lives of some pregnant women? Yes. Can I give assurance that my views represent the correct answer? No. What's the answer? I think it is to recognize that there are different understandings and conclusions even in such fundamental situations. I think we must, in love, try to see each other's viewpoint, pray to our God for His insight, and work without rancor for the understanding He gives us. For me this would be trying to go back to the status our country had before abortion on demand became the law of the land. Meanwhile we can all cooperate in efforts to decrease the things that would make a desperate woman contemplate such a solution. The same process could be used when we have other conflicts of understanding between ourselves and other brothers and sisters in Christ.

When there are honest, considered differences of any issue and the potential for conflict between Christians, Christ has advised: "A new command I give you: Love one another. As I have loved you, so you must love one another. By this all men will know that you are my disciples, if you love one another."[537] Christ didn't say such an approach would be easy. It's just a whole lot better than any other solution.

*(An answer by Betty Byers)*

Agree to disagree, and go on!

*(Some ideas of Mike Neff)[538]*

**Overcoming separation - Focus:** Romans 15:7: *Accept one another, then, just as Christ accepted you, in order to bring praise to God.*

I don't know how many of you have seen the Friar Tuck cartoons that often appear in church publications. I received one this week and it caught my attention.

The cartoon shows Friar Tuck coming inside a building. These words appear above his head representing what he is thinking: "Maybe I best start by being a missionary to those inside the church." At bottom of the cartoon are these words: "Death, taxes, and unlovable people are always with us. May we learn to love them anyway!" While this

---

[537] John 13:34-35 (NIV)
[538] From part of Mike Neff's sermon at St. Andrew's United Methodist Church in Syracuse, Indiana on 3/30/2008.

gave me a chuckle, I also realize that there is a lot of truth in this cartoon. I suspect that most of us have encountered people that we are uncomfortable to be around and have difficulty loving. Sadly, sometimes we find these unlovable people in the church. Sometimes we are uncomfortable because these unlovable people think differently and have different ideas than we do. Quite often our pride gets in the way and we think that our ideas are better than their ideas. Pride can cause us to think that we do not need to hear the ideas of people who disagree with us. This leads to bickering and separation in the body of Christ here on earth. Since we are the body of Christ, God's message of love, hope, and salvation is considerably weakened or worse yet is destroyed completely. A person, who is separated from others by bickering, usually does not see the need or sense the importance of being a member of the body of Christ. Thus any possibility of being an effective witness of God's love to those who are outside the church is both null and void. In fact over the many years since the resurrection, minor differences have led to many separations and, in some cases, the formation of a new denomination or a new church.

Differences between people have always led to difficulties in the church. The differences between people in the early church were often greater than the differences that exist today. In the early church there were great differences between Jewish Christians and non-Jewish or gentile Christians. They had differences about whether Christians needed to be circumcised, about what foods could be eaten and what made certain foods unclean, and which Jewish holy days should be celebrated as Christian holy days. They disagreed on just about everything.

I appreciate the way that the Apostle Paul addresses these problems in the fourteenth chapter of his letter to the Romans. I like what Eugene Peterson does with the fourteenth chapter of Romans in the paraphrase that he has named *The Message*. Rev. Peterson paraphrases the Greek text. He uses situations and words that are familiar to us. You may want to read Chapter 14 in your Bible to see if Rev. Peterson did capture the true meaning of Romans 14. Here is Romans 14: 1-14 from *The Message:*[539]

"Welcome with open arms fellow believers who don't see things the way you do. And don't jump all over them every time they do or say something you don't

---

[539] *The Message,* Eugene H. Peterson, © 2002. Scripture taken from *THE MESSAGE, copyright* © 1993, 1994, 1995, 1996, 2000, 2002. Used with permission of NavPres Publishing Group.

agree with—even when it seems that they are strong on opinions but weak in the faith department. Remember, they have their own history to deal with. Treat them gently.

"For instance, a person who has been around for a while might well be convinced that he can eat anything on the table, while another, with a different background, might assume all Christians should be vegetarians and eat accordingly. But since both are guests at Christ's table, wouldn't it be terribly rude if they fell to criticizing what the other ate or didn't eat? God, after all, invited them both to the table. Do you have any business crossing people off the guest list or interfering with God's welcome? If there are corrections to be made or manners to be learned, God can handle that without your help.

"Or, say, one person thinks that some days should be set aside as holy and another thinks that each day is pretty much like any other. There are good reasons either way. So, each person is free to follow the convictions of conscience.

"What's important in all this is that if you keep a holy day, keep it for God's sake; if you eat meat, eat it to the glory of God and thank God for prime rib; if you're a vegetarian, eat vegetables to the glory of God and thank God for broccoli. None of us are permitted to insist on our own way in these matters. It's God we are answerable to—all the way from life to death and everything in between—not each other. That's why Jesus lived and died and then lived again: so that he could be our Master across the entire range of life and death, and free us from the petty tyrannies of each other.

"So where does that leave you when you criticize a brother? And where does that leave you when you condescend to a sister? I'd say it leaves you looking pretty silly—or worse. Eventually, we're all going to end up kneeling side by side in the place of judgment, facing God. Your critical and condescending ways aren't going to improve your position there one bit. Read it for yourself in Scripture:

"'As I live and breathe,' God says,

'every knee will bow before me;

Every tongue will tell the honest truth

that I and only I am God.'

"So tend to your knitting. You've got your hands full just taking care of your own life before God.

"Forget about deciding what's right for each other. Here's what you need to be concerned about: that you don't get in the way of someone else, making life more difficult than it already is.  I'm convinced—Jesus convinced me!—that everything as it is in itself is holy.  We, of course, by the way we treat it or talk about it, can contaminate it."

So what should we do? First we should remember the words of Jesus in John 13:34-35: "A new command I give you: Love one another. As I have loved you, so you must love one another. By this all men will know that you are my disciples, if you love one another."

Learning to love one another is our primary task!  Romans 15:7 says, "Accept one another, then, just as Christ accepted you, in order to bring praise to God."  Unity with other Christians is often realized as a byproduct of humility.

The Apostle Paul says in Ephesians 4:11-13: "It was he who gave some to be apostles, some to be prophets, some to be evangelists, and some to be pastors and teachers, to prepare God's people for works of service, so that the body of Christ may be built up until we all reach unity in the faith and in the knowledge of the Son of God and become mature, attaining to the whole measure of the fullness of Christ."

We need to realize that God gives gifts and a vision to each of His people and it is only when the people love and accept each other that God's people can reach out to the community in a powerful way and bring a powerful revival to a community.  Thus one of our top priorities as Christians is to overcome the differences that separate us from loving other Christians.  True unity is a revelation of the Spirit of God that only

together can we see the results that we desire.

_____

# What are communion and baptism, and what do they do?

*(Jack Clark's thoughts)*

Communion is also known as the Lord's Supper and the Eucharist. This is a formal religious act of Christian congregations. It is referred to as one of the sacraments. In the Eastern Orthodox Churches and the Roman Catholic Church there are seven sacraments (Baptism, Confirmation, Holy Eucharist, Penance, Anointing of the Sick – or Extreme Unction, Holy Orders and Matrimony). Most Protestant churches recognize only two of these events as being sacraments (Baptism and Communion). Of course the other events are important in the life of the Protestant congregations; they just aren't considered sacraments.

Communion was something Jesus told his followers to do in remembrance of him.[540] It involves taking of bread and wine, as the disciples did during the last supper before Christ's crucifixion.

"While they were eating, Jesus took bread, gave thanks and broke it, and gave it to his disciples, saying, 'Take and eat; this is my body.' Then he took the cup, gave thanks and offered it to them saying, 'Drink from it, all of you. This is my blood of the covenant, which is poured out for many for the forgiveness of sins.'"[541]

The idea, as I understand it is that by this act we are declaring ourselves to be one with Christ. Many people have heard an old saying "we are what we eat." This would indicate that our physical bodies are one with the food we have at our meals. The act of communion indicates that we are reminding ourselves and others that we are spiritually one with Christ and one with the people who share the communion.

The early Christian church got into trouble and some of the early Christians were martyred because of this practice. Non-Christians heard about it and understood that they were eating human flesh (the body of Christ) and drinking human blood (the blood of Christ). In other words they understood that Christians were practicing cannibalism. Although the Christians denied it, a number of those who took communion were burned to

---

[540] Luke 22:19
[541] Matthew 26:26-28

death because of this. This practice would have been especially revolting to the Jewish nation that had strict rules about not even drinking the blood of animals – let alone human blood.

Some modern congregations understand that in the blessing of the elements (bread and juice or wine) that they are literally changed becoming the substance of Christ's body and blood (transubstantiation). Many of us feel that they figuratively represent the body and blood of Christ and represent our wish to be spiritually one with him.

Because the typical service of communion asks that we confess our sins and be in harmony with our brothers, and ask God to accept us as living sacrifices (as opposed to the old killed sacrifices), many people think this is the mechanism to make us right with God, but the Scriptures declare that Jesus, God's Messiah and priest, offered for all time one sacrifice (himself) for sins. It would seem that the living sacrifice being offered in the communion service is not a sin sacrifice but a sacrifice of worship. Confession comes after one is first convinced of his sin (conviction) and determines to make every effort to avoid it in the future (repentance). Confession need not be limited to the time of communion, but that is a time when we are especially aware of the price Jesus has paid for our redemption. Conviction, repentance, and confession to God are the necessary acts that open the door to the already given redemption and resulting salvation.

There are some quirky things that are associated with our religious practices including communion. Some denominations practice a closed communion. If the person is not a member of that particular community of faith, he or she cannot participate. Some practice an open communion. Anyone who declares they are followers of Christ and that they have asked that their sins be forgiven and is at peace with others is welcome. Some feel that it is essential that communion be from a common cup with shared bread (preferably unleavened), as this was what Jesus did in the first celebration. Some are comfortable only with separate cups of wine or juice and separate wafers for each communicant. Some share from a common loaf and dip pieces of the bread into the wine (in tincture). I've even seen the bread not only be yeast bread but be rye bread. Some feel that real wine must be used, and some feel that there is no problem with substituting grape juice.

One of the most stirring communions in which I have participated involved pouring the unfermented grape juice over a small wooden cross and collecting it in a cup to remind us of what price Christ paid for our redemption.

I remember a thought provoking event from the time I delivered babies. A Roman Catholic couple who were also friends had a living child and had lost two children due to prematurely. They had asked me to deliver their fourth pregnancy. Again the labor was very early, and the tiny premature baby was giving only intermittent labored gasps. Resuscitation attempts were not successful. Their priest had been sent for and was on his way, but it was obvious that the child was not going to live. It was also obvious that their priest could not arrive in time to baptize the baby. My friend asked me to baptize the child, and I did so with a great sense of humility and a sense of being honored. Their denomination views baptism as essential to salvation and accepts a sacrament of baptism done by any professing Christian as being valid. One happy result of this otherwise sad event was that I was able to determine the cause of the problem and correct it, so they could go on and have more children.

A few weeks later, I happened to be attending a Roman Catholic Mass. At the time of communion, I could not partake because I'm not Roman Catholic. I knew of this rule of closed communion in their denomination and certainly respect it, but it struck me as strange that they would accept the baptism that I had done as valid, but would not be comfortable with accepting me at their communion table. On the other hand, my denomination would have no trouble accepting my friend at communion but would not have accepted my baptism of the child as valid.

The apostle Paul wrote to Christians who were divided over leaders. While this challenge doesn't involve leadership, it does involve divisions. Paul's question is still appropriate here: "Is Christ divided?"[542] Sometimes I suspect Christ must look at his followers, sigh, and ask himself, "What are they thinking about?" He might even wish that we would recall what he said: "A new command I give you: Love one another. As I have loved you, so you must love one another. By this all men will know that you are my disciples, if you love one another."[543] Seems like pretty good advice.

---

[542] First Corinthians 1:13 (TNIV)
[543] John 13:34-35 (NIV)

A few of our family members have inquired as to why we had our infant son Ethan baptized. Both my wife Jennifer and I were raised with a "Believers' Baptism" understanding of baptism. We were both surprised and concerned when we found out that our church practices infant baptism, so we both spent a fair amount of time reading various works about the matter and reading the Bible to better understand this doctrine. Here is a brief summary of the understanding God has brought us to regarding infant baptism. The question of who is to receive the sign (or sacrament) of baptism is one that has been much debated since the appearance of the Anabaptists in the early 1500's. We do not pretend to think that this response will be able to answer all questions on the topic. We do hope however to give you some of the Biblical basis behind baptizing the children of believing parents. Others have dealt with the topic in depth and we would be glad to refer you to their works should you be interested in further study.

**God's Sovereignty**

We think this is important to discuss up front because God's sovereignty and our view of His sovereignty is the starting point of our theology. Ps. 115:3 – "Our God is in the heavens; He does whatever He pleases". Perhaps we see and experience God's sovereignty most clearly in the area of our personal salvation.

Baptism is not about what we have done or believed. It is about God's choosing a people for Himself, setting them apart, and marking them as belonging to Himself. Psalm 14 teaches us that no one seeks after God or chooses God. It is God's grace and the work of the Spirit in our hearts that even gives us the faith to believe; He is the potter, we are the clay (Rom. 9).

**Covenant Theology and Dispensational Theology**

There are two main frameworks that are used to understand the Bible: covenant theology and dispensational theology. The framework used greatly impacts the way much of the Bible is understood, including the issue of the nature of baptism and the question of who is to receive it. Dispensational theology fundamentally sees a discontinuity between God's people and His covenants – most importantly between the Old and New Testaments and between the church and physical literal Israel. It claims that Christ's coming completely did away with the previous covenants, ushering in their replacement:

> According to this view, while the New Testament often draws from principles in the Old Testament, it is nevertheless a complete replacement of the Old Testament, thus rendering the old covenant invalid.[544]

Covenant theology sees the continuity in the work of God, the people of God (children of Abraham) and covenants of God. The new covenant inaugurated by Christ did not do away with the old covenant, but expanded upon it. As Jesus says:

> "Do not think that I came to abolish the Law or the Prophets; I did not come to abolish but to fulfill. For truly I say to you, until heaven and earth pass away, not the smallest letter or stroke shall pass from the Law until all is accomplished. Whoever then annuls one of the least of these commandments, and teaches others to do the same, shall be called the least in the kingdom of heaven ..." (Matthew 5:17-19).

The commands and practices given under previous covenants remain intact except where something has been fulfilled in Christ or abrogated by Him. When we look at the Bible this way, we understand that unless something has been specifically set aside or done away with (such as the ceremonial part of Temple worship, see Hebrews) we are still to follow it (such as the 10 Commandments). Only God can set aside what He has first set in place. We also understand that just as God does not change (Hebrews 13:8), so the way He saves people does not change either. Under older covenants, people were saved by grace through faith in the salvation that God would provide; under the new covenant, people are saved by grace through faith in the salvation that God has provided. All of it is based on the substitutionary atonement of Christ.

## God's Dealings with Households

Throughout the Old Testament we see that God deals with families. God commanded Abraham to circumcise his entire household, sons and servants alike. Repeatedly in Scripture the head of the household speaks for the entire household, or parents represent

---

[544] Robert R. Booth, *Children of the Promise: the Biblical case for infant baptism*, p. 19, P&R Publishing, 1995.

their children (see Joshua 24:15 and Genesis 17:14). We see also that blessings or curses accrue to children based on the action of their parents (see Exodus 34:6-7 and Proverbs 20:7). In the New Testament, at the beginning of the spreading of the Gospel God shows that He will continue to deal with families (see Acts 2:37-41 (particularly v. 39) and 1 Corinthians 7:14, which speaks of children being holy – set apart – based on the faith of a believing parent).

We live in a very individualistic society where we tend to do everything for ourselves and always want to speak for ourselves. The individual is over-emphasized and we forget that God generally deals with families, communities, and even whole nations. If we read the Bible with our individualistic mindset (which is very much a product of our culture) it is harder to understand God's dealings with households.

As we look through Acts there are a number of household baptisms (Acts 10, 16, 18). Although it could be claimed that all members of each of those households believed, it cannot be shown in every case. Furthermore, it seems highly unlikely that in each household, *all* members were old enough to believe. Instead of arguing from silence (which can be done by both those who hold to believer's baptism and those who hold to infant baptism) it is important to see that it is whole households that are baptized rather than trying to show that each member of the house without exception believed. In light of God's dealing with whole households in the Old Testament regardless of the standing of each individual, it is not unreasonable to assume a similar dealing in these household baptisms.

**Circumcision in the Old Testament**

In the Old Testament, circumcision was the sign given to those included in the outward, visible people of God – those who were in covenant relationship with God ("I will be their God, and they shall be My people" – Jer. 31:33, Exodus 6:7 and numerous other places). When an infant was circumcised, it did NOT mean that he was saved. It meant that he was part of a family which was in covenant with God. As such, he would receive certain privileges (instruction in the ways of the Lord, and all the advantages that come with being in covenant with God) as well as certain obligations (obeying the commands of the Lord). This sign was also given to anyone who willingly joined themselves to Israel as adults. Some children who had received the sign of the covenant (circumcision) proved to be covenant keepers (Isaac, Jacob, Moses, Joshua, David ...), while others showed themselves to be covenant breakers (Esau, Jeroboam, Judas ...). All along, circumcision was supposed to indicate the need for circumcision of the heart (Deut. 10:16 and 30:6, Romans 2:28-29, and other places). Salvation, even in the Old Testament, was not a matter of an outward sign, but of an inward faith in God.

## Baptism in the New Testament

With the coming of the new covenant, there is a change in the sign of inclusion in the people of God. That sign is baptism (see Colossians 2:11-13 where circumcision and baptism are linked). Like circumcision, baptism does NOT equal salvation. Baptism signifies legal standing among the people of God, the need for cleansing, being united to Christ, and points to saving faith (in Christ). Like circumcision, the sign is given to the offspring of parents who themselves are in covenant with God, or adults who have made a confession of faith.

So why did God bother with a new sign at all? There are two sacraments in the Old Testament: Circumcision and the Passover. Both were accompanied with the shedding of blood, as both pointed to Christ who was yet to come. In the new covenant, these sacraments are changed to Baptism and the Lord's Supper (Communion). They both point back to Christ, and do not require the shedding of blood, as Christ's blood has already been shed.

## What About Keeping the Church Pure?

Sometimes it is argued that only administering baptism to believers helps to keep the church pure and from being filled with those who are baptized but are still dead in their trespasses and sins. God alone knows and discerns the heart of man. Those who seek to administer baptism only to those who give a believable profession of faith are still not able to discern the heart and can still end up baptizing those who are not truly circumcised of heart. We must examine ourselves to see if we ourselves are believers (2 Peter 1:10) and, with God's grace, seek to keep His church pure by not allowing into membership those who do not bear fruit in keeping with repentance (Matt. 3:8). At some point Ethan will have to make a profession of faith or his life will demonstrate that he has not believed. He will not be permitted to take communion or be admitted into church membership until he does profess his faith in Christ. We fervently pray that Ethan has been set apart by

God before the foundations of the world as one of His sheep.

### Why Not Dedication Instead of Baptism?

Those who hold to believer's baptism understand the importance of setting our children apart from the rest of the unbelieving world. This is evidenced by the infant dedications that many churches practice. Although the name given to the practice is different, the hopes of the parents and the vows they take to bring up their children, instructing them in the fear and the knowledge of the Lord are virtually identical. However, there is no instance of baby dedication in the Bible. There is the inclusion of infants in the people of God in the Old Testament, and household baptisms in the New Testament.

### Conclusion

Without an explicit command for parents to no longer include their children among the people of God (i.e., by giving to them the sign of belonging to the people of God), would it not seem strange for the people in the apostolic age to suddenly exclude their children? Historical records of the practice of the early church indicate that the people understood the continuation of giving the covenant sign to children of believing parents.

In baptizing Ethan we are not saying that he is saved. This is our hope: that God's Spirit will do a work of grace in his heart so that the inward reality will be united with the outward sign of belonging to the people of God.

Circumcision was administered to an infant without his input. It is the sign given *by God* that he is set apart. So it is also with baptism. It is not about our choosing God, but about His choosing us.

# Faith versus science

(A two-part question about faith and science.) Some scientists say DNA studies produce proof that all living things are related, so this shows life developed spontaneously, that evolution occurred by natural selection, and there can be no God. How can we answer? How do other areas of science fit into Christians' understanding and belief?

*(Thoughts of Jack Clark)*

Logically the above conclusion is faulty. If all living things are in fact related, it does not indicate in any way that life developed spontaneously. It only indicates that there is a common origin. That origin could just as well be the design of God as a spontaneous generation of life. Until fairly recently Christians felt no sense of controversy about this. The Bible very simply said that God created everything. It even gave the order in which the creation took place. Interestingly there are two accounts of the creation recorded in Genesis, and the order in which God did the creating is different in the two accounts.[545] Bible scholars hold that these represent two oral traditions of various groups of the Hebrew people. Both affirm that God did create the earth and everything in it. Both give the glory to God.

Let's think about what the Bible has to say about the creation: "In the beginning God created the heavens and the earth. Now the earth was formless and empty; darkness was over the surface of the deep, and the Spirit of God was hovering over the waters." It goes on to report a series of creative events that each start with, "And God said..."[546] Interestingly neither account gives the mechanism by which God did the creating.

Certainly the traditional Christian view has been that God created each sun, planet, moon, physical aspect of each created body, each form of plant life and each form of animal life and human life as an individual unrelated act. Probably many would presume that with each creative act, God's voice boomed out and the new creation existed. I personally see nothing in this account of creation that indicates that he could not have used other methods including a God-planned and God-directed evolution of species from previous forms of life for the creation process. God throughout the ages has met people where we are spiritually or intellectually – in whatever is our ability to understand Him. The people to whom God revealed that he did create the earth and everything in it in

---

[545] Compare the accounts in Genesis 1:1-2:4 with that in Genesis 2:4-25. In the first account, man is one of the last things to be created. In the second account, man is one of the first things to be created.
[546] Genesis 1:1-27 (NIV)

those early days of revealing himself to mankind could have never understood the concept of inheritance, DNA, or the other scientific understanding of today. In fact most of us have a good deal of difficulty in really understanding it even now. Additionally even the most advanced scientists in the various areas are still a long way from working out all the scientifically knowable aspects.

My understanding of Genesis is that it is a hymn of creation. It is an affirmation that God did create the universe, the world, and everything in it. It doesn't seem to be a scientific study of how creation took place or how God did the creating. This doesn't make this creation hymn any less valid, nor does it make science any less valid. Science is mankind's understanding of nature, and as such there is no real conflict between this hymn and science. Those who would demean God by scientific proofs might do well to realize that what was scientifically known 50 years ago has often little resemblance to what is scientifically known today. Genesis would seem to contain the essence of the truth in a form that could never be found in a scientific analysis. Can snow be better appreciated by reading a poem that describes its beauty or its fierce effects or by studying that snow is the solid crystalline form of water made of two atoms of hydrogen combined by atomic bonding to one atom of oxygen and subjected to a temperature of zero degrees Celsius? Both accounts are correct; both are important to know to fully understand snow, and a person who knows either one but not both lacks a full understanding.

Those who would pit scientists against a belief in God might do well to consider what a few pretty prominent scientists have had to say. Francis Bacon (1561-1626) who was one of the primary people to introduce the scientific method of study and understanding believed that the greater the understanding of the world, the greater the knowledge of the creator.[547]

Albert Einstein, the great theoretical genius who developed the theory of relativity, wasn't a Christian (although his son was a Serbian Orthodox Christian). Einstein was of Jewish heritage, but shunned organized religion. In spite of this, study of his life's records certainly indicate that he believed in God. He saw the cosmos as orderly and organized; in that orderliness and unity, he realized there was an organizer: God. He once posed the

---

[547] *Theories for Everything, An Illustrated History of Science*, p. 249, by John Langone, Bruce Stuz, and Andrea Gianopoulos, Copyright © 2006 National Geographic Society 1145 17th Street NW, Washington, D.C. 20036-4688

question: "How much choice did God have in constructing the universe?" Scientifically it has been determined that there is a very fine tolerance. If gravity were only slightly stronger, the stars wouldn't burn for billions of years; slightly weaker and they wouldn't burn at all. The total mass of the universe has to be within very precise limits. A few times less mass and matter would have dispersed from the "big bang" too rapidly to have formed the galaxies and the stars. A few times more mass and gravity would have long ago collapsed the universe. Similarly, the scientifically determined magnitudes of the strong, weak, and electromagnetic forces are poised on a razor's edge. If they were beyond the very narrow tolerances of their existence, subatomic particles could not have formed atoms, nor could atoms have formed molecules.[548] Seemingly some people can conceive that all these and thousands more equally critical delicate balances could have occurred randomly. I cannot.

Some scientists such as Richard Dawkins and Steven Pinker view religion as a relic of humanity's superstitious, pre-scientific past that should be abandoned. On the other hand, Francis Collins, one of the country's most prominent scientists comes to a very different conclusion. Dr. Collins is a physician who is the leader of the Human Genome Project aimed at a better understanding of mankind's problems by researching the variations in our genetic make up, He believes in God; he can even believe in miracles.[549] Einstein himself once said we can choose to live life either believing there are no miracles at all, or believing that everything is a miracle. Einstein wrote in one of his many letters to a friend, "A spirit is manifest in the laws of the universe – a spirit vastly superior to that of man, and one in the face of which we with our modest powers must feel humble."[550] Einstein also wrote that the cosmos follows laws that can be understood, and this signifies there is "God who reveals himself in the harmony of all that exists."[551] He shared also that he considered the mind of God when he conducted what he called his mind experiments: "When I am judging a theory, I ask myself whether, if I were God, I would have arranged the world in such a way."[552]

---

[548] *Why Aren't Black Holes Black? The Unanswered Questions at the Frontiers of Science*, by Robert M. Hazen with Maxine Singer, introduction by Stephen Jay Gould. Anchor Books Doubleday, pp.66-67

[549] *National Geographic magazine*, February 2007, pp. 33-39

[550] From the book *Einstein His Life and Universe*, Walter Isaacson, © 2007 Walter Isaacson, p.551, from a Letter from A. Einstein to Phyllis Wright, Jan. 24, 1936, Albert Einstein Archive 52-337

[551] *Ibid*. p. 551, Einstein from a letter to Herbert S. Goldstein, Apr. 25, 1929, Albert Einstein Archive 33-272. For a discussion of Maimonides and divine providence in Jewish thought.

[552] *Ibid*, p. 551, from Banish Hoffmann, in Harry Woof, Ed. *Some Strangeness in the Proposition,* Saddle River, N.J., Addison-Wesley, 1980, p. 476

Extensive observations especially on differences of finches and tortoises by Charles Darwin in the Galapagos Islands in 1835 led him to suggest that that species in fact evolve. Much more recent understanding of the genetic code of each living being by unraveling many of the secrets of inheritance through understanding the structure of deoxyribonucleic acid (DNA) strongly supports Darwin's field observations. Notice that his theory explains his understanding of how various <u>species</u> came to be through natural selection of favorable changes that give an advantage. It would seem that sexual preferences also play a role in this natural selection. I understand that certain birds will be ignored for mating if their feet are painted a different color. Obviously if an individual cannot mate, it cannot reproduce.

Darwin was a religious man and had a very religious wife. Probably based on this and some healthy skepticism about his conclusions, he reportedly struggled with his observations. Darwin finally was moved to publish his theory when a much less well known scientist, Alfred Wallace, independently came to the same conclusion and submitted his observations to Darwin. Darwin realized that his theory would cause an uproar in religious circles as great as when Copernicus proclaimed in the 16th century that the sun is the center of the solar system rather than the earth being at the center of a great celestial sphere. Galileo also became convinced of a universe that was not centered on earth. In 1616 he was forbidden by church officials to teach his findings, and in 1633 he was tried by the Holy Office of the Inquisition and found guilty of heresy. To save himself from imprisonment or even death, he had to renounce his findings. The church has since changed this ruling, but it took a very long time.

Interestingly Darwin developed a doubt about God's existence when his daughter died of a disease that the medical science of that day did not understand. It's always been hard for me to understand how some people are surprised by tragic events happening to believers. If we study what happened to Jesus himself and his early followers, it's clear God walks with us through our trials and helps us grow through our trials, but Jesus warned Peter himself that Satan is going to sift us.[553] Wallace, the other person who came to the same understanding about evolution, declared that it had to be guided by an

---

[553] Luke 22:31

"overruling Intelligence that watched over the action of natural laws, so directing variations and so determining their accumulation." A different understanding of how or why God has done something doesn't result in a change in God – only a change in our understanding of God's actions.

Darwin's theory has nothing to do with how life came to be – only how it evolved after it occurred.  Others have postulated that from a "soup" of organic chemicals, there was somehow a fortuitous coming together under just the right atmospheric circumstances to form organic molecules that could reproduce themselves, and that this was how life came to be.  I would suggest that even if this in fact occurred as the first life event that it is so complex that there is no way that it could have happened without the guiding plan of God. Even if humans could conceivably create laboratory conditions that would result in such a "soup" of non-living organic molecules becoming able to reproduce themselves (that is to become living simple organisms), that does not disprove God's role as some would imply. Can any person conceive of starting with nothing but the energy of their thought to produce the inorganic chemicals and ultimately have them transformed into organic chemicals and have them come together under just the right environmental circumstances to form both the recipe and the ingredients for the soup?

Each area of scientific advancement has contributed insights that are interesting to a person of faith.  For example consider the scientific field of archeology.  Digging through dusty ruins in Israel has confirmed time and again Bible accounts that had no other existing contemporary confirmation.  George Smith, a self-taught researcher in the British Museum, in 1872 pieced together and translated cuneiform wedge-shaped writing on shards of clay tablets that had been discovered in Nineveh (present day Iraq near Mosul – the former capital of the Assyrian Empire).  The efforts required the abilities of a jig saw puzzle worker with thousands of unrelated pieces mixed together with the puzzle parts.  It also required the ability to translate a language and to understand the recording of that language that was no longer in use.  These tablets confirmed, among other things names of Kings and prophets otherwise recorded only in the Bible.  Another very interesting find was the Mesopotamian Saga of *Gilgamesh* (one of the oldest literary works ever found.  It had been written 3200 years earlier and laid buried for 2500 years).  It spoke of a great flood, a bird sent out in search of dry land, and of a ship that ended on a mountain.  Smith later went to the site himself and remarkably found more of the missing story from an even earlier account than the *Gilgamesh*. This account had been written about 1800 B.C. It included the following: "Into the midst of it (the ship) (put) your grain, your furniture, your goods, your wealth, your woman servants, your female slaves... the animals of the field all, I will gather and send you, and they shall be enclosed in your door." Since then an account of a catastrophic flood has been found in multiple sources of Mesopotamian writings.[554] This interesting report can be tied in with reported geological findings and underwater archeology in the area of the Black Sea and the Bosporus, that narrow waterway that divides Europe from Turkey in Asia. National Geographic Magazine reported that underwater exploration showed evidence of multiple former sites of human habitation that are now deeply underwater in the Black Sea. Geological findings also reportedly strongly suggest that the Bosporus was very likely at one time not an open waterway, but consisted of a land area blocking the much higher waters of the Sea of Marmara, the Dardanelles, and the Aegean Sea from the lower Black Sea. At some point, it was suggested that the natural dam likely gave way allowing the higher water to rush into the Black Sea in a great engulfing flood. When modern natural or man-made earthen dams gave way, it is often after especially heavy rains, so the Bible's account of the heavy rain being associated with the flood certainly is also plausible. Geologists have determined that there never was enough water to have flooded the whole world. We know now that sea shells found on the tops of mountains come from former sea floors that were raised by tectonic activity instead of a world-wide universal flood, but in the days of this flood of the Black Sea shoreline the area involved would certainly have been the <u>known</u> world. Of course nothing in these scientific discoveries confirms the role in the Bible account of God interacting with Noah, but it certainly adds another aspect and understanding that takes nothing away from the Biblical version. Interesting isn't it?

While the genetic code and archeology are giving new insights that expand our understanding of the creation and historic events and thereby the understanding of the creator, other types of scientific efforts are also contributing to our understanding and often leave us standing practically as open-mouthed and as much in wonder as did our ancient ancestors when they first started to understand God's mighty works. The author of Deuteronomy well expressed his sense of wonder at the time he wrote: "O Sovereign Lord, you have begun to show to your servant your greatness and your strong hand. For

---

[554] *Epic Hero*, by David Damrosch, Smithsonian magazine, May 2007, pp. 94-103

what god is there in heaven or on earth who can do the deeds and mighty works you do?'[555] The same sense of wonder pervades the ever-expanding understanding of God's creation that is unfolding today in the changing and expanding scientific comprehension of the universe. I would suggest the following to Christians who feel that the changes in understanding of the creation somehow threaten our faith in the creator: "Everything God created is good, and nothing is to be rejected if it is received with thanksgiving."[556]

To those who would over-glorify the discoveries of scientists and accept them as unchangeable truths, I would suggest that new discoveries today often make the absolute knowledge of a few years ago seem quaint. It was the year 1900. One of the foremost physicists of the time, Lord Kelvin, was addressing the British Association for the Advancement of Science. Lord Kelvin had been president of the association in 1871. In this address of 1900, he made the profoundly inaccurate prediction that, "There is nothing new to be discovered in physics now." Well since that time it was discovered that the atom was not the ultimate building block of matter – there were electrons orbiting around a nucleus of the atom; the nucleus itself was composed of protons and neutrons that we knew about when I was in college in the mid-1950s. Certainly our knowledge then made previous "knowledge" seem primitive and incomplete. Well in case we're a little too smug, since then physicists have found positrons (the positively charged equivalent of the negative electron). They've also proven that the positively charged proton of the atomic nucleus is composed of even smaller ingredients – two up quarks and a down quark bound together. The neutron in the atomic nucleus has been found to be composed of two down quarks and one up quark. A quark is an elementary particle that is acted on by the strong force. There are multiple other particles and forces that have been discovered by particle physicists. All this is enough to make anyone's head swim – probably even Lord Kelvin's if he were still around. As I think of these things, a quotation from Shakespeare comes to mind: "There are more things in heaven and earth then are dreamt of in your philosophy."

Another fascinating example of a more recent change in our understanding is that when I took physics in college, one of the laws we learned was that two objects cannot occupy the same place at the same time. Seems logical enough – that's why my fender

[555] Deuteronomy 3:24 (NIV)
[556] First Timothy 4:4 (NIV)

gets bent when I run into a tree. Today we know that this applies only to certain objects that the physicists call fermions. There is another group of objects called bosons to which this does not apply. Probably the best known of the bosons are photons, particles without mass (that's another recent concept) that make up light itself. Probably the most familiar result of these particles being able to occupy the same place at the same time is their additive effect that we use to make lasers.

Consider Albert Einstein's famous theory of relativity. This has led to atomic power as well as atomic bombs. Also our ground positioning systems (GPS) couldn't function accurately without the knowledge gained from this.

Theoretical physicists have developed theories and models that <u>may</u> be represented in the real world. They look forward to being able very soon to test these theories using the Large Hadron Collider, a high-energy particle collider in Switzerland where the European Organization for Nuclear Research will circulate two beams of protons and collide them at previously unachievable energies.

Several of these recently developed theories and models involve what are known as string theories. In string theories all matter and all energy consist ultimately in tiny strings of material that may be open ended or closed into a circle or oval and oscillate. The theoretical size of these strings would be in the order of $10^{-23}$ centimeters – an object so small that it cannot be seen or measured with any instrument that is presently available. Different theories propose different numbers of dimensions – an independent direction in space or time – up to eleven. Some theoretical proposed dimensions are so small that they cannot be physically measured. Some are huge or even infinite and warped so that they cannot be directly sensed because the warping of the dimension concentrates the particles in such a manner that from our perspective they appear to all be in our familiar four dimensions (up/down, forward/backward, right/left and timespace).[557]

---

[557] For a very well written summary of recent developments in physics and various theories on strings, extra dimensions, warped dimensions, and the various recently discovered particles I would refer you to a fascinating book: *Warped Passages Unraveling the Mysteries of the Universe's Hidden Dimensions,* © 2005 by Lisa Randall, published by Harper Perennial in 2006. Ms. Randall is an expert in string theory, particle theory, cosmology, and theoretical physics, a member of the American Academy of Arts and Sciences, and has been a tenured professor at Princeton, MIT, and Harvard. Not only does she treat the subjects in scientific detail, but she also uses every day analogies and life experiences to make a confusing subject understandable.

To me as a Christian, one of the most interesting of these various new theories of physics is a theory that if an extra dimension was warped, the standard physical particles (and so all physical atoms, elements, and objects) would appear to be four dimensional from our perspective, but there could be an infinitely large fifth dimension.[558] While this possibility is only a theory awaiting experimental proof or disproof in soon to be conducted high-energy collider experiments, it in no way violates the findings in our standard model physical universe. In thinking about the possible implications of this fifth dimension, it occurs to me that this theoretical scenario could in some way be the mechanism God might use to allow transfigured bodies such as Jesus had after his resurrection. It could possibly be the mechanism to allow one's existence to go on after the demise of our physical bodies. Let me make it clear, this is my idea – nothing revealed to me by the Holy Spirit and not the idea of theoretical physicists who have enough trouble getting their ideas accepted among their own colleagues. Let me also be quick to point out that if the physicist's theory is a scenario awaiting proof or disproof as it applies to the real world, that my suggestion is only speculation about something that is itself only a possibility.

To those who feel in some way that scientific knowledge makes acceptance of God as creator out of date, I would suggest considering this: all creation testifies about the creator. When I see a tiny spring bud on a branch of the shaggy bark hickory tree in my back yard open in a few days to a compound leaf over a foot long, this observation from the science of botany testifies about the creator – God. For someone to look at a carved statue in a church in Belgium and comment, "Isn't this an interesting stone formation?" without recognizing that there was a creator would make no more sense than looking at the hickory leaf in my yard without recognizing there is a creator. A study of the science of geology would confirm that there are no natural marble formations that would look like this statue. The existence of the statue testifies that it had a creator. With a little investigation, it can be determined that the creator of the statue was Michelangelo. The creator of the leaf and everything else (including the marble stone from which the statue was carved and Michelangelo himself) is God! Years ago one of the writers of the Psalms made the same observation: "The heavens declare the glory of God; the skies proclaim the work of His hands. Day to day utters speech and night to night shows knowledge. There is no

---

[558] *Warped Passages Unraveling the Mysteries of the Universe's Hidden Dimensions,* p. 418-432, © 2005 by Lisa Randall, published by Harper Perennial in 2006.

speech nor language where their voice is not heard."[559]

Certainly the science of astronomy raises more questions with each new discovery. Dr. Hubble not so long ago made the observation that the universe is expanding at an ever increasing rate, and that the farther away from our local milky way galaxy one studies, the faster it is expanding. This is observed in all directions. The most recent scientific understanding of the universe understands the "Big Bang" not as an explosion but as a simultaneous unfolding or creation of matter, energy, time and space itself. The dominant concept is that a web of space was created and expanded with the matter that would form the galaxies being carried along for the ride. "Solid matter" is not expanding through space; space is expanding and dragging the matter with it. Initially the expansion was much faster; then it slowed; now the rate is increasing again. The universe is understood as being self-contained and expanding without expanding into something else.[560] Isn't it interesting to contemplate that at the time of the "big bang" estimated to have happened fourteen billion years ago that all the material and energy that now forms the universe was concentrated in a tiny dot? Science cannot tell us the origin of the tiny dot. Science cannot tell us of the source of the energy that released the "big bang." Science cannot explain what contained this tiny dot of everything. Science is awestruck to realize that space itself did not exist at the time of the 'big bang;" it was created at the same time as that initial event, and it expands even now with the expansion of the universe itself. What more testimony is needed that there is an intelligent guiding force in the universe that we call God, and in personal revelation of Himself to mankind gave His name as I AM WHO I AM?

Present scientific thought estimates that the visible universe consists of only fifteen to twenty percent of its total mass. Some of this invisible mass is probably in "black holes," those structures that pull in everything that gets close into them, and where gravity is so intense that nothing (even light) can get out. Still more of this invisible mass may be in what has been termed Weakly Interacting Massive Particles. These are conceived by the scientists as having huge size. They are not thought to either emit or reflect light, so they cannot be seen. Because of the fact that the vast majority of what makes up matter (even conventional atoms) is space, one of these structures can pass through the "solid" objects

[559] Psalm 19:1-3 (NIV)
[560] "Cosmology: 5 Things You need to know," Liz Kruesi, p. 28-33, *Astronomy* magazine, May 2007

that we can see. If this sounds pretty far out, think what people would have had to say for thousands of years if you tried to convince them that our voices could be carried for thousands of miles over wires or fiber glass cables or even through the air to satellites circling the earth and then back through solid walls to a device that would allow us to understand the speaker and reverse the process. Would this have sounded any less unusual to our great, great grandparents than Weakly Interactive Massive Particles that can pass through us unseen and unfelt, or for that matter a risen savior who could pass through a barred door to visit with his friends?

Science is still struggling to understand the physical universe. Quantum mechanics has made it clear that at the subatomic level, the distinctions between energy and matter vanish. Both energy and matter have the property of particles or quanta and waves. Space and time are actually one entity. A particle in one part of the universe responds instantly to a particle in another area. Physicists made the observation that electrons will jump from one orbit into another in abrupt, unpredictable, and discontinuous occurrences. In doing this they don't seem to travel through space or time/space. They simply suddenly appear in the new orbit with no trace of their path.

Niels Bohr suggested that particles exhibit "non-local influence" over other particles and over vast distances and at speeds that exceed the speed of light. This is far removed from the understanding of classical physics that taught that an object at rest tends to remain at rest, and an object in motion tends to remain in motion, that nothing is faster than the speed of light, and that for one object to react with another there must be contact (remember "for every action there is an equal and opposite reaction?"). Albert Einstein doubted this suggestion. He suggested that an experiment should someday be done to confirm or disprove the theory. In 1982 Alain Aspect conducted such an experiment showing that photons influenced the polarity of other photons instantly and without touching. Physicists call this relationship between distant particles or objects "entanglement." Christians believe that we too are invisibly connected to others, to the rest of the universe and to our creating God in this process of inter-relationship.

There is an area of scientific investigation called parapsychology that studies possible "supernatural phenomena" such as the invisible connection between others or between God and us. Recognized areas of such study include psycho kinesis (the influencing of movement or outcome by thought), precognition (knowing of events in advance), and mental telepathy (sending thoughts from far away).

In 1967 my brother Jerry who was an agnostic was getting ready for a mountain climbing trip to the highest mountain in North America, Mount McKinley also known as Denali in Alaska. One of those urges that seem to come from nowhere seemed to be directing me to write to Jerry in Oregon before he left telling him about the reason for my faith and the change it had made in my life. As often happens when the Holy Spirit sends these urges, I could think of several reasons why I didn't want to. Jerry was a very moral man, and I didn't want him to think that I saw myself as better than he was. Jerry knew of my struggles and shortcomings. I procrastinated. I sympathized with Moses trying to talk God out of returning to Egypt, but the urge didn't leave and grew in intensity. I finally wrote Jerry a multi-page letter. Several weeks later while they were on their climb, I woke one night in a drenching cold sweat. I had a dream where I visualized a black central area surrounded by blinding white. In my heart I felt the central area was Jerry and that he was in mortal danger. A couple days later the Park Service called to advise that his whole climbing party had been trapped in a white out storm after reaching the summit with winds of over 120 miles per hour. Jerry was an expert mountaineer who had made first assents and first route climbs not only in the United States but also in New Zealand and in Antarctica when he was there for two seasons as part of the International Geophysical Year. If anyone could survive the storm certainly Jerry could. A search party found no trace. The bodies of Jerry and his climbing group are still on the mountain in Alaska. Several weeks later while I was driving to see hospital patients I was very depressed. An awareness occurred that, "Jerry's better off than you are." Notice that this was in the third person. It wasn't my thought – that would have been Jerry's better off than I am. This thought was nothing on which I had been focused that morning. I'm convinced that the Holy Spirit could look into the future and see the danger toward which Jerry was heading, and that was the reason I had been directed to write the letter I didn't want to write. I'm convinced that Jerry got the letter, read it, and that at some point that it played some role in his accepting Jesus Christ as his savior. I'm convinced that at some future time I'll be meeting Jerry in Heaven and that this is why the Holy Spirit brought me the comfort of realizing Jerry was okay. I am convinced that I had been "connected" with the Holy Spirit when I was urged to write the letter, and that I had been "connected" to Jerry half way across the continent when I had the dream. So from my own experience it would appear that more than photons can influence other photons instantly and without touching; it would also appear that the scientific field of parapsychology would include awareness between different people across great distances – our own spiritual "entanglement."

Although this following paragraph has nothing directly to do with science, it gives me the chance to share some things I've learned from my brother's death. The people we love, those who are most closely attached to us in the web of life, are immeasurably important to God and to us. God takes a very personal interest and is totally involved in the lives of those He has created; He is anxious that every possible opportunity be given to every person to accept a saving relationship with Him, and since every created person is important to God, they should be important to us too. He knows our going out and our coming in and everything we plan and do. "Where can I flee from your presence? If I go up to the heavens, you are there; if I make my bed in the depths, you are there. If I rise on the wings of the dawn, if I settle on the far side of the sea, even there your hand will guide me; your right hand will hold me fast."[561] When God gives a nudge to do something, He has an important reason. It doesn't pay to resist His urgings; He'll get His way anyhow if we're committed to Him, and some important results may hinge on our following through. Just as Jesus wept at the pain of Martha and Mary after Lazarus' death,[562] God continues to feel and share in our pain and continues to comfort us.

Back to the subject of science, Barbara Brown Taylor has asked: "Where is God in this picture? All over the place. Up there; down here. Inside my skin and out. God is the web, the energy, the space, the light – not captured in them, as if any of those concepts were more real than what unites them, but revealed in that singular vast net of relationship that animates everything that is."[563]

Returning to the original point of dispute between the creationists and the evolutionists: do we Christians really need to be hung up on the origin of man as being an entirely separate act of creation by God, or can we see God's guiding hand in such an event no matter how it was accomplished? Certainly I for one am so in awe of God having created everything – including mankind – that His methods are not nearly as important as the fact

---

[561] Psalm 139:7-10 (NIV)
[562] John 11:35 (KJV)
[563] Barbara Brown Taylor, "Physics and Faith: The Luminous Web." Christian Century, June 2-9, 1999, pp. 617-618.

that He did it.  If He created each individual galaxy and star one by one, or if he started the process with his "speaking" or thought and it progressed as He planned and ordained and guided it, either is fantastic.

There certainly is ongoing evidence for evolution through natural selection.  The finches in the Galapagos have been observed at scientific stations there to evolve larger and then smaller beaks to adapt to difference in rainfall and difference in seed size over a mere 25-year time span.  Bacteria are known to evolve.  Antibiotics that wiped out many bacteria when I was a young doctor are no longer effective because the bacteria have evolved resistance.  Viruses certainly evolve.  Bird flu viruses can evolve to infect humans.  This is what brought on the disastrous 1919 pandemic.  The human immunodeficiency virus (HIV virus that causes AIDS) evolved in our life time from a virus that could infect monkeys to a virus that could also infect humans.  There is even observable evidence of human evolution.  Humans first appeared in northern Africa.  There the long days of intense sunshine would have burned and damaged the skin unless there was abundant dark protective pigment.  As the human race migrated northward, those of us with less pigmented skin evolved.  How did natural selection play a role in this?  It so happens that humans with dark skin and those with light skin have the same number of pigment producing cells; those with more pigment simply have more efficient cells.  One of the important biological events that take place in our skin is the interaction of skin cells and sunshine to produce vitamin D.  With the decreasing amount of sunlight exposure, people with dark skin living in northern areas could not produce enough of this substance that is essential to the formation of strong bones and the prevention of rickets.  The laws of natural selection in the tropics favored dark skin.  The laws of natural selection in the northern countries weeded out the families with efficient pigment production.  Now, of course, the vitamin D fortified milk makes this selection irrelevant, but there was a time when it was important.  A human evolution has also occurred much more recently.  When Europeans came to North America, they brought diseases such as measles and small pox with them.  These diseases were difficult and sometimes deadly to the Europeans, but they were devastating to the native people who had not been exposed to them and had no "natural resistance" (as opposed to individual resistance that develops after having the disease).  Whole nations of native people died when exposed to these diseases.  Eventually, through the laws of natural selection, the few who did have some natural resistance survived to reproduce, and those who didn't have any natural resistance died ending their reproductive lines. Today the remaining Native Americans are no worse off if infected with one of these diseases than those of us with European ancestors.

Development through natural selection in no way excludes God from the process. His guiding hand is behind the process itself. His ultimate goal was to lead to mankind, and to have mankind capable of existing in a consenting, loving communion with God. If someone might scoff at the possibility of guided natural selection, they should be aware that humans have utilized this process to breed different types of cattle and different breeds of dogs. Certainly if humans who are made in God's image can accomplish these results, it doesn't seem logical to believe it is beyond God's ability to also guide evolution. In case some might think God stands back and takes a hands-off approach, He has indicated this isn't the case. God in the scriptures has indicated that He even now has a hand in the creation of each individual person: "Before I formed you in the womb I knew you; before you were born, I set you apart."[564] Even though ninety percent of our genetic material is shared with lower life-forms, God still creates each individual so uniquely different that no two of us have the exact same DNA genetic code (unless they are the product of a multi-birth pregnancy of identical siblings) or even the exact same finger prints. God's role in the formation of each of us is affirmed even though the mechanism He chooses for each individual's creation involves heredity and the joining of the genetic material from the sperm of that person's father and their mother's ovum.

If He created each life form as an totally separate act, or if He created life and set in motion evolution guided by His ultimate plan eventually leading to mankind, is one any more astounding than the other, or is either one beyond the ability of God? When we add to either scenario the understanding that He still personally is involved in the creation of each individual creature that has ever been created (not only each person) this is more fabulous than ever.[565] We should avoid restricting the possibilities of God's actions by our limited ability to understand Him and how He works. Our Father God has created; He is creating even now, and He will continue to create. As God is reported to have suggested on a couple occasions to doubters in the Hebrew nation, why do you doubt my ability to do whatever I choose to do? "Is my arm too short?"[566]

---

[564] Jeremiah 1:5 (NIV)
[565] *Ibid*
[566] Numbers 11:23 and Isaiah 50:2 (NIV)

DNA similarity between species says no more about spontaneous development of life than the similarity between wristwatch components says about the end of time.

To suggest DNA is a constant in the fabric of life is both arrogant and shortsighted. DNA says more about common design than common origin. Since DNA makeup is so easily altered by outside factors like chemical and environmental influences, why wouldn't much of earth's creatures degenerate back to lower life forms in order to survive during the most horrific global catastrophes. The struggle toward advancement in nature supports ordered design rather than chaotic entropy. This evidence in creation says more about intention than accident.

With respect to the "comfortable" fit that true science can have with Christian belief, it might be illustrated well by remembering that science, that is indeed science, seeks to disprove its own theories and not every other understanding out there. Science is helpful in the realm of the natural order. However, when it attempts to challenge the realm of the supernatural, its tools and formulas become impotent. I believe Christian faith is the "science" of the inner man. It is interesting to note that honest Christian belief can provide answers to scientific questions but science cannot answer matters of faith.

*(An observation by Betty Berger)*

I read a book by Harold Hill, a scientist with NASA. When they had trouble determining the return of a space ship, he reminded them of the time in the Bible where prayer stopped the sun. When they included that in their calculations, the problem was solved.

*(An answer by Dean Culbertson)*

Well, if all things were created (oh, humor me), doesn't it stand to reason that they have similarities in their DNA? In fact, if a creator (not capitalized because it's a hypothetical discussion... for now) designed hundreds or thousands of things, would his handiwork not appear in all of them? For the believer creation is <u>not</u> a theory. Science is like anything else. Men of faith will maintain the creation story, while men of atheism will use whatever they find to create an advantage.

As a child I once argued with my grandmother that the caboose actually pushes the train over the tracks. I could tell her why the front of the train smoked, and I even knew how to give grandma cute, convincing arguments. I could tell anyone that the caboose did the work. These days, I don't always see the caboose. Science can work like my arguments. The key is to have the truth to begin with.

To be honest, I won't win an evolutionist this way, but I will say this. Any theory or explanation must be held accountable to the scripture. To make scripture answer to a theory like evolution is no different than a five-year-old who tries to make his parents defend their policies for discipline.

*(An answer by Don Impey)*

### CREATIONISM/EVOLUTION – WHAT'S THE BEEF?

So often in conflict, few advocates are found in the middle ground. Strong feelings of truth, of course, reside either up or down, right or left, but never will knowledgeable proponents be found wading around in the middle. And so it is with the nagging question of evolution versus creationism.

The theatre of battle is found less in academia then within organized religion around the world within which are found zealots on both sides. The creationists thump the Bible and chant age-old arguments about faith and God's inspired word. The evolutionists jump up and down and quote developing scientific facts that dispute and disprove much of the doctrine coming from the pulpit. Creationists and evolutionists, it seems, cannot exist on the same page.

I confess that for many years, I believed absolutely in the Adam and Eve plus creation stories as found in Genesis. Then, later in life, as I developed new pursuits in astronomy and particle physics, at an amateur level of course, I found myself vacillating in the middle alone and far from either pole. It's tough to turn away from years of religious teaching that goes back to early childhood. The conflict arose within me because it is also tough to ignore the undisputable scientific facts that are developing in rapid-fire sequence almost weekly.

Creationism likes to place much of its foundational arguments in the Adam and Eve story plus the one week creation story from Genesis; stories that are found under scrutiny to be flawed. First creation which will be touched on later, took considerably longer than a week to achieve. Period. Secondly, Genesis was written between 1450 and 1410 B.C. Who read and wrote in those days? Perhaps a highly placed government official or two, but mostly priests and religious scribes who were specially trained to read and write. Therefore, to get information across, an allegory worked much better than a list of rules that few could read in those days. Biblical authors had not a clue about modern astronomical observation. They could only guess about what they were seeing. They didn't know cosmos aging, so a week for creation was as good as 13.7 billion years. Better actually because the simple thinking peasant could grasp a week much better than the larger numbers.

The Adam and Eve story is a nice myth that crumbles under the glass. Language, cloth, farming tools we know were not part of the era of that story. It is important to remember that while this Adam and Eve story was very poignant, it was also able to adequately convey the simple truths of sin and obedience to worshipers of the time and through many generations of the Judeo-Christian ethic. Before I'm accused of heresy, I must explain that I have no problem with these stories being the inspired divine word of God. He knew that these stories would inspire, teach, and be meaningful to many generations of followers, so he planted the seeds. It does, however, beg the question to believe that the events described actually happened. Ask yourself where Cain's wife came from.

Evolutionists have had forty miles of bad road with the Christians ever since Charles R. Darwin, the naturalist from Shrewsbury, England, published *The Origin of the Species* in 1859. The book did not agree with the Scripture, so the church rose up and told him so. The fallout continued under God's watchful eye in such epochs as the famous 1925 trial of John T. Scopes, who was convicted and fined for teaching evolution in a public Tennessee school. The "Monkey Trial" was sensational news for months. Parenthetically, the sentence was set aside. This conflict continues today with many of the nation's school systems buying or not buying biology or science textbooks containing evolutionary content. The public continues to push for separation of church and state, but such topics as evolution provide rich ground irresistible to some creationists.

I recently heard a creationist equate evolution with the word accident, accusing that evolutionists believe that many species were an accident. Rubbish! God does not create accidents. The design of our world and all creatures therein is a well calculated and balanced process under God's complete control. Occasionally we mortals sweep in with our imperfect wisdom and cause such events as animal extinction and weather changes.

The words in the beginning open the Bible text. I'll borrow them here. In the beginning was the Big Bang. Creationists scoff at this also, but the science of this event is sound, studied, coherent, provable, and almost observed. Astronomers have observed to 13.7 billion years ago that is within 380,000 years of the Big Bang – a point in time when light photons began to form and become observable. Space telescopes such as the Hubble instrument have led the way to greater understanding of the universe and to more cohesive astronomical observations. The extreme reliability and efficiency of these telescopes is responsible for most of the recent advancement in this field.

In short, the Big Bang was born from a form roughly the size of a softball of unimaginable density. Everything – that is every thing – that now is mass within the universe was contained within this orb. Now before I explain what happened next, it is important to note that not one scientist or philosopher has ever been able to accurately identify how the orb came into existence. Postulate, yes. Identify, no. Much of our present laws of physics break down as the study tries to cross the line earlier than the creation moment. Christians who are familiar with the Big Bang process are generally quite comfortable in identifying God as the sole proprietor and manufacturer of the ball from which all things come.

Back to the beginning. Vexing questions haunted astronomers about how all of this material moved from the Big Bang singularity to today's universe, estimated to be about 40 billion light years across. (A light year is the distance that light travels in one year at 186,000 miles per second.) You do the math. Our telescope horizon is about fourteen billion light years, so there are objects that we will never see.

One major answer that astronomers found about three decades ago was the idea of an inflationary cosmos. This little ball in a rapid expansion of unimaginable heat and speed hurtled material into the cosmos at a rate never to be repeated. The Big Bang theory rests on the observation that the universe is expanding. Run this idea backwards, and you must conclude that the universe was smaller, denser, and hotter in the distant past. The further you take the idea, the closer you get to the creation epoch. The evidence is overwhelming.

As matter expands in the early inflation, we find only neutral hydrogen and helium. At this juncture, I could drive you into hapless boredom with long particle physics explanations that would not serve the purpose of this document. The point is that matter evolved from that Big Bang beginning to what we have today. The matter in your body was present in the first microsecond of creation. So was the matter in your car, your dog, your house, your computer – you get the idea. Timothy reports that, "This grace was given us before the beginning of time."[567] This is just one of many Biblical references to events prior to the beginning.

Over billions of years, everything that we know evolved into the structure that we now see in the universe: sun, stars, planets, and the life on this planet. The earliest evidence of life on our planet earth is 3.9 billion years old. The earliest fossils are 3.5 billion years old. Archeology is a formidable discipline that brings us the past by examining physical evidence. The first Homo sapiens appeared 200,000 years ago.

In conclusion, I observe that creationists and evolutionists are in a we-they relationship that is in fact out of step with reality. There is no need for two camps. If you are able to accept the fact that God created all matter, then it logically follows that He created the physical systems whereby that matter would evolve into intelligent humans that we have today. It is also necessary to recognize allegorical stories for what they were carefully designed by God to achieve and also to listen to the emerging scientific facts, and you will agree – What's the beef?

Jesus said to him, "I am the way, the truth, and the life. No one comes to the Father except by me."[568]

That's enough for me! Thank you for sharing a part of my journey.

---

[567] Second Timothy 1:9
[568] John 14:6 (RSV)

## Challenge 53
# Is going to church regularly really important?

I believe in God and Christ, but sometimes I'm just too busy to go to church. Some people are in college and need to spend their time studying. Some have children, and are so busy taking care of them that they have no energy for anything else. Sometimes I'm just too tired. Is going to church regularly really important?

*(Jack Clark's answer)*

Our daughter Cathy gave one of the most compelling reasons for attending church I've heard. Jonathan, our grandson, had asked his Aunt Cathy's opinion about the importance of his attending church while at college with all the demands on his time that went with being an engineering student. Cathy had responded that the way she looked at it from God's perspective, to miss church could be likened to having prepared your home for a visit from someone you deeply love and with whom you are longing to share your love and life experiences only to have them ignore you and not come to be with you. What a disappointment that would obviously be. It certainly would seem logical that God would feel this way when we ignore him and the family gathering.

It seems Cathy got her point across. Jonathan graduated as a multidisciplinary engineer with honors. He was active in Campus Crusade for Christ and church. He went on short term mission stints in Florida while he was in school, and after graduating he did missionary service in Chile and Turkey before becoming a civil engineer in the United States. His sisters, Karen, and Sharon, and his brother Steve followed his example in their college and religious lives and missionary service. Seems we never know what results our "planting" will produce.

God wants each of us in His church. It's a very imperfect place filled with imperfect people who at our very best are leaving the past behind and with arms outstretched are heading toward the goal–not perfect, but striving on toward perfection.[569] Christ said, "Wherever two or three of you are gathered together in my name, I will be there with you."[570] Knowing this, I'm encouraged to go to the gathering of fellow believers (the church) in order to experience the presence of Christ. This is a great time to follow the advice to encourage one another.[571] Christ said the world will know that we are his disciples if we love one another,[572] and we can love one another better when we get

---

[569] Adapted from Philippians 3:12-14
[570] Matthew 18:20 (NIV)
[571] First Thessalonians 5:11 (NIV)
[572] John 13:35 (NIV)

together and know each other's needs.  We are told that we have a job to do – sometimes we receive great blessings, but our job involves being part of the body of Christ, the church.[573]  Our job involves spreading the Good News of Christ's redemption for everyone who will accept it and going to make disciples of all people.[574]  This process happens one on one, but after telling the Good News and making the disciple, there has to be a place where that disciple is nurtured; that place is the church.  There are people in the church who can help us grow closer to God.  There are those in the church who we can help as they grow.  I have received God's salvation and other miracles.  Part of my job is to put myself in a place where I can use those miracles to God's glory.  From him who has much, much is required.[575]  We can never repay Christ, the Father, or the Holy Spirit for what we've received, but it is important that we become a blessing to others in response to what we have been given.  This response can and should occur in many places, but the place it occurs most often and most consistently is in the gathering together of the church in our congregations.

When we neglect our church attendance, our friends in the congregation miss us.  More importantly they and we miss some of the blessings we could have received.  Even more importantly we miss opportunities to grow and help others grow in faith and in our ability to serve.  More importantly yet, the body of Christ, the church, is missing some of its members (parts), and as any body does, it functions less well when parts are missing or not functioning to optimum capacity.  Most importantly God, our Father, Abba, misses any of us who are not there.

The church constitutes the body of Christ.  It is through the church that much of Christ's work is done in the world.  The church is destined to be in a deep, intimate, spiritual relationship with Christ.  It seems that we really need to be actively a part of the body.

*(Some thoughts of June C. Laudeman)*

As I sat and listened to the bride and groom say, "I take thee for better or worse, richer or poorer, in sickness or in health, until death we do part," I thought the parallel in our spiritual lives could be, "In holiness or in sin, when able to give or only able to take, filled with doubt or with faith, until we join in heaven."

We "take" our medicine, "take" out a loan, "take" a vacation, or "take" a nap.  In each instance "taking" implies that

---

[573] First Corinthians 12:1-31 (NIV)
[574] Matthew 28:19 (NIV)
[575] Luke 12:48 (NIV)

we did this and made it part of us. As the ceremony ended I rejoiced because the bride and groom had "taken" each other, to become primary, or most important in each other's lives. Have you "taken" your Lord lately? Have you claimed the church as your brothers and sisters in Christ?

The vows of church membership are also vows of love intended to bond you and God and fulfill what Jesus said was the first and most important commandment, "To love the Lord thy God with all thy heart, and with all thy soul, and with all thy mind."[576] Do you take Jesus Christ as your Lord and Savior and pledge your allegiance to His Kingdom? It does wonders for you.

When we "take" God it brings new strength to our lives.

*(Thoughts of Betty Berger)*

Jesus said we should assemble together, and He set the example by going to the temple. Also just like learning the manual to drive a car so it's second nature when you drive – knowing the Bible and spending time with other Christians before problems arise helps you know what Jesus wants us to do.

*(An answer from Betty Byers)*

Yes, going to church regularly is very important. Publicly we should unite with fellow believers in a local assembly to bring praise to God.

---

[576] Matthew 22:37-38 (KJV)

# What should be our attitude toward "governing authorities?"
(Submitted by Fairplain Presbyterian Adult Church School class in Benton Harbor, Michigan)

*(An answer by Jack Clark)*

"Let every person be subject to the governing authorities; for there is no authority except from God, and those authorities that exist have been instituted by God. Therefore whoever resists authority resists what God has appointed and those who resist will incur judgment. For rulers are not a terror to good conduct, but to bad. Do you wish to have no fear of the authority? Then do what is good, and you will receive its approval; for it is God's servant for your good. But if you do what is wrong, you should be afraid, for the authority does not bear the sword in vain! It is the servant of God to execute wrath on the wrongdoer. Therefore one must be subject, not only because of wrath but also because of conscience. For the same reason you also pay taxes, for the authorities are God's servants, busy with this very thing. Pay to all what is due them – taxes to whom taxes are due, revenue to whom revenue is due, respect to whom respect is due, honor to whom honor is due."[577]

It's important to put what the Apostle Paul wrote that is quoted above into a historical perspective. When he wrote this to the Christians in Rome, the Jewish authorities were intent on stamping out what they considered to be a cultic sect. They weren't above enlisting the power of the Roman state in accomplishing their objective. Because of this they were advising Rome that the Christians considered Christ as their King – a unilateral action that would very easily be viewed as subversive by Caesar who tolerated no challenge to his authority. One of Paul's objectives in writing this was try to be sure that the members of the church in Rome gave no cause to increase Caesar's suspicions that they were against Rome or himself. Another of Paul's objectives was to go on record to the Roman authorities to counter what they were hearing from the Jewish authorities.

These views in no way were counter to what Jesus had taught. Recall that when the Herodians tried to trap Jesus into saying it was right to pay taxes to Caesar that would have made him unpopular with the people or to say it was wrong to pay taxes to Caesar that would have made him an outlaw, he out foxed them. He said, "You hypocrites, why are you trying to trap me? Show me the coin used for paying the tax..." He asked them,

---

[577] Romans 13:1-7 (RSV)

"Whose portrait is this? And whose inscription?" "Caesar's," they replied. Then he said to them, "Give to Caesar what is Caesar's and to God what is God's."[578]

Throughout the Old Testament the prophets looked on the suffering of the nation Israel as being inflicted on them for turning away from following God. They looked on their rulers and even their conquers as being given by God in his mercy when they were good or as correction when that was necessary. That doesn't mean that the people of Israel were to fully cooperate with what these bad rulers wished when these wishes were counter to what God willed

Ahab was one of the evil kings of the Northern Kingdom of Israel. He married Jezebel who was intent on making a foreign god, Baal, be worshiped in the nation. Elijah, God's prophet, spent his ministry in opposition to the authorities even though their excesses were used by God to awaken the people.[579]

Even the rulers of Assyria and Babylon with all their cruelty were considered to be emplaced by God to meet His objective of bringing Israel back into a proper relationship with God. In spite of this the Jewess Esther worked to keep Haman from destroying the Israelites.[580] God ultimately even punished these rulers for their excesses used against Israel. While Daniel and his friends served their conquering king Nebuchadnezzar they passively resisted eating forbidden foods or bowing down to his golden god image.[581]

One of the psalmists observes, "Before I was afflicted I went astray, but now I obey your word. You are good, and what you do is good. Teach me your decrees... I know that your laws are righteous, and that in faithfulness you have afflicted me."[582] While it is not certain what his affliction was, it would seem that part of it involved opposition from those in authority.

Now back to the question. What should be our attitude toward those in authority? I would observe that in a democracy there would be some difference than in countries where there is some other form of government. I would suggest that in either form of government, we should cooperate with the authorities where the demands are not clearly

---

[578] Matthew 22:18-21, Mark 12:13-17, Luke 20:20-26 (NIV)
[579] I Kings 16:3-22:40
[580] Book of Esther
[581] Book of Daniel
[582] Psalm 119:67, 68, & 75 (TNIV)

against God's rules or instructions. In a democracy by our vote we can try to repeal or amend those laws that seem unjust or could be made better.

For those laws that degrade or endanger others I feel we should oppose them. An obvious example would be the laws in Nazi Germany that dispossessed and killed millions in the Holocaust. In case we spend too much time looking at those atrocities, we in the United States would do well to remember the laws that deprived Native Americans of their land, their livelihood, and often their lives. It would be well to recall that some such as the Cherokee Nation were leading lives of farming and were members of the Christian faith when Andrew Jackson's presidential policies drove them from their lands on the Trail of Tears where many died. This action is made even more deplorable when we realize the Cherokees had fought against the British with Jackson in the war of 1812 and one Cherokee man had actually defended General Jackson from an attack on his person in that war. Where were those who filled the later role of Corrie ten Boom's family[583] and Dietrich Bonhoeffer[584] in later sad events? Laws of discrimination against blacks, or Irish, or Poles, or Italians, or Chinese, or Japanese descendants, or women at various times in our history as a nation were and should have been opposed on Christian principals. When they were overtly threatening or counter to what Jesus has instructed we should do they often are and should be disobeyed by people of conscience – including Christians. There are still some laws that need to be defied if we are to render to God what is God's.


Jody Scarbeary demonstrates many important qualities of Christian discipleship. Her mother, Alice Nolan Scarbeary, and I went to grade school together. When I came back to Syracuse as a physician, I had cared for three of her grandparents, her mom, Jody herself, a maternal aunt, a paternal uncle, and the uncle's family. In their case, I was truly their family doctor. They were nice people, the kind anyone would be happy to have in their practice.

Jody's father had died when she was young making a difficult time for her family. I knew most of them had been church people. In so far as I knew, they were all fine people,

---

[583] Corrie ten Boom's Christian Dutch family hid Jews from the Nazis in World War II. They were discovered and sent to concentration camps where all but Corrie died. In one of her books she testified that there is no depth (of despair) so deep that does not find God as a deeper source of strength.
[584] Dietrich Bonhoeffer was a German Lutheran minister during World War II who opposed the Nazis and tried to shield the Jews.

but none of them seemed filled with unusual religious fervor.

Imagine my surprise and admiration when Jody visited my office one day as a young lady and advised me she had been smuggling. She had been active with a young adult Christian group and they had taken it upon themselves to smuggle Bibles into communist China. They had already made one trip and ultimately made two more. This was not smuggling for economic gain or as a lark as some do. It was smuggling because Jody and her friends were filled with love and compassion for the masses of people in China who had never had a chance to hear of the love of God and salvation of Jesus Christ. They were also concerned about the hunger of those few Chinese who had been evangelized by missionaries before China was taken over by the communists. Those few who clung to their faith in underground cells but could not have a Bible to call their own. They touched the hearts of these young smugglers.

The Chinese government's official position was to persecute Christians and imprison Christians. There was a specific prohibition against the importation of Bibles and religious literature. Those who harbored such literature or brought such literature into the country were subject to imprisonment. China was notorious for its intolerance of dissent. This was the country which imprisoned people for years at hard labor for daring to disagree with Mao, their leader. This was the country which impressed many hundreds and thousands into slave labor camps. This is the country where to write of democracy was a crime. This was a country where official policy declared they would control their overpopulation by enforcing a rule of one child per family and augment this policy with forced sterilization, forced abortion, and even infanticide. This was the country of the Tiananmen Square massacre where the military killed so many who sought freedom for themselves and their country. This was a country held in the grip of repression, subjugation, fear, thought control, regimentation, and evil. This was the country of darkness to which Jody and her friends determined they would bring light in the person of Jesus Christ.

This was an expensive thing for Jody to do; she had no sponsor and paid her own way. This was a scary thing to do; she was constantly concerned that she might be discovered or betrayed; her mother was understandably quite anxious. Jody couldn't solve the total problem of China; she couldn't give scripture even to a tiny fraction of the people living there, but she did determine that she would do her part of a great task. These young Christians took to heart that it is better to light one candle than to curse the darkness.

Jody and her friends remembered and acted on what Christ said, "You are the light of the world. A city on a hill cannot be hidden. Neither do people light a lamp and put it under a bowl. Instead they put it on its stand, and it gives light to everyone in the house. In the same way, let your light shine before men, that they may see your good deeds and praise your Father in heaven."[585] They obeyed Christ's command to, "Go and make disciples of all nations"[586] and "Go into all the world and preach the good news to all creation."[587] She believed the expressed reason for this command: "Whoever believes and is baptized will be saved, but whoever does not believe will be condemned."[588] Jody and her friends marched out into an evil empire to do spiritual battle. They prayed in the Spirit on all occasions. They chose to be strong. The word of God lives in them, and they have overcome the evil one.[589]

They recalled that Christ would have addressed the church in China as he did the churches in Smyrna and Pergamum: "I know your afflictions and your poverty--yet you are rich,"[590] and "I know where you live--where Satan has his throne, yet you remain true to my name. You did not renounce your faith in me."[591]

Jody and her friends chose to do something about the situation. They chose to "overcome evil with good."[592] Jody's sharing was purposeful and required careful, premeditated planning and preparation to be successful.

She came back home and took a job in her congregation--not as a leader, not as a missionary but in a supporting role. She didn't come home and receive accolades of the Christian Church, or a freedom medal, or write a book and become famous, or appear on talk shows or Christian TV. She resumed being an average young lady working in her church, but Jody changed lives. She changed lives in China where those she touched were blessed with the realization that others cared and were willing to risk. She changed her life. She changed the lives of those of us who admire the courage of this gutsy sister in Christ and are encouraged to take some lesser risks in our own lives. She brought joy

---

[585] Matthew 5:14-16 and Mark 4:21 (NIV)
[586] Matthew 28:19-20 (NIV)
[587] Mark 16:15 (NIV)
[588] Mark 16:16 (NIV)
[589] Adapted from First John 2:13
[590] Revelation 2:9 (NIV)
[591] Revelation 2:13 (NIV)
[592] Romans 12:21 (NIV)

to the Kingdom of God, and I'm convinced that one day Jody will stand before her God and hear the loveliest words imaginable: "Well done good and faithful servant."[593]

---

[593] Matthew 25:21 (NIV)

# Are politics and religion really separate parts of our lives?
(Submitted by Fairplain Presbyterian Adult Church School class in Benton Harbor, Michigan)

*(some thoughts by Jack Clark)*

Our coins declare "In God We Trust." Our pledge of Allegiance speaks of "One nation under God." Our Declaration of Independence speaks of God entitling us to a separate and equal station; it speaks of unalienable Rights endowed by our creator including Life, Liberty, and the pursuit of Happiness. The same document appeals to the Supreme Judge of the World to evaluate the moral integrity of the intentions of the colonies, and it relies on the protection of divine Providence.

The First Amendment of our Constitution prohibits Congress from making a law respecting the establishment of religion, or prohibiting the free exercise thereof. This has sometimes led to restrictions that seem to some religious adherents to be prohibited. So even though much of our legal system is based on Judeo-Christian ethics, the courts have ruled that the First Amendment makes display of the Ten Commandments illegal in the court houses of the nation or the states. This is the case even though Moses and the Ten Commandments are revered by Jews and Christians. To many of us allowing the display of such to be considered as establishing of a national religion seems to be a stretch of the imagination. Some argue that it does not take into account the atheist's view. To this many would respond that the Constitution establishes freedom *of* not *from* religion.

There are Christian religious fellowships (for example the Amish) that believe we should have nothing to do with government that we can avoid. Most of us feel that government like most everything else has the potential to be used for good or for bad. An analogy could be drawn using automotive vehicles as an example. A car can be used to rob a bank or to secrete a bomb that will kill hundreds, or it can be used as a vehicle to deliver help to an area devastated by a hurricane. So it seems it is with government. It can be used for good or selfish or even evil purposes, but it is not in itself good or bad.

Most of the governing laws and regulations are compromises between different groups and people with different convictions and perspectives. As such not many pieces of legislation or departmental rules satisfy everyone. I would say that it is the obligation of Christians in a self-governing country such as ours to attempt to pick officials who seem to best exemplify fairness, charity, and compassion – characteristics that Jesus exemplified. If one is so inclined and dedicated to such principles, he or she should be pleased and honored to serve in the government. It takes dedicated people in such an environment to not think too highly of themselves. It takes a lot of effort to be able to amicably differ, make constructive compromises and still maintain their own principles. In fact such difficulties face us in whatever work we do in this life. In working toward such a goal it helps to recall that "God is my strength and power."[594]

Quite another aspect to consider is that when Christ returns (the second coming), the government will be on his shoulders.[595] The Book of Revelation says that a group of martyrs will rule with Christ during Christ's thousand-year reign that will start at his second coming.[596] It certainly seems that these are political roles that will be a part of Jesus Christ's and his followers' work at that time. It would seem that if Christ and some of his followers will play a political role then, there should be no problem with those so inclined to play a political role now. To not do so could result in the government being in the hands of those we could regret having there.

[594] II Samuel 22:33 (KJV)
[595] Isaiah 9:6 (NIV)
[596] Revelation 20:1-6

# Challenge 56
# What role does commitment play in the life of believers?
What's the minimum effort we can give and still make it into heaven?

*(Jack Clark's answer)*

I recall a comic strip, Rose is Rose, that showed Rose on her knees beside her bed praying. In the comic she asked how much she had to do to get into heaven and indicated that it would be a shame to get there and find that she'd gone beyond what was required. The last frame of the comic shows Rose still on her knees asking, "Why do you always shake your head and sigh when I ask something like that?" Rose hadn't learned the meaning of commitment or the joy that it can bring. The word commitment means to pledge the parties of an agreement to a particular course of action.

First let's think of the role commitment plays from the perspective of God's relationship to humankind. If there wasn't great commitment of God on our behalf He would have dumped us a long time ago. Certainly mankind and every individual (including me) has given God enough grief and heartache through our foul-ups, thoughtlessness, and defiance to more than justify giving up on us multiple times and having nothing more to do with us. Of course if He did that would certainly have unpleasant consequences for us, as being absent from God is the best definition of Hell that I can understand. But God doesn't give up on us. He stands ready like the Father in the parable of the prodigal or lost son to welcome us home with open arms.

Jesus, God's Christ, shows his total commitment by unmistakably demonstrating his love. He proved it by voluntarily going to the cross for each of us. Then he showed that he has the authority to grant us forgiveness of our sins and the promise of eternal life by taking up his life again.

The Holy Spirit shows his total commitment to each of us by all the things this comforter does on our behalf. He's described in the scriptures as filling our hearts with God's love and joy. He will pray for us when we don't know for what we should pray (a promise that I've relied on over and over again). He will remind us of scripture to fill special needs (I should have included Him as a contributing author). He will give us power to accomplish great things and tell us what to say when we're in need of such help. The Holy Spirit is identified as the power of prayer and his presence is the answer to prayer.  He baptized Jesus and baptizes us.  He will make us aware of our sins and comfort us after he's convicted us.  He's the source of our ability to recognize and proclaim that Jesus is Lord.  He will counsel us.  He can be vexed, blasphemed against (the only unforgivable sin), and may sometimes withdraw from a person (a terrible disaster) in response to the person's repeatedly turning away from him.  In addition he gives the gifts of the Holy Spirit.  No one has all these gifts, but every Christian has some.  They include faith, hope and love with love being the greatest of these gifts.  (I think love is a universal gift to all Christians.)  He gives us an everlasting name, a new spirit, and a new heart.  Form him come knowledge, miraculous powers, prophesy (speaking in God's behalf), the ability to tell good from evil spirits, speaking in tongues and interpreting those who speak in this spiritual language.  There are fruits of the Holy Spirit (that is things resulting from the Spirit's effects in our lives).  These include joy, peace, love, patience, kindness, goodness, faithfulness, gentleness, and self-control.  It seems significant that love is listed both as a gift and a fruit.  From all this it is surely obvious that the Holy Spirit is committed to people.

Now let's consider the human side to commitment.  Commitment involves our making a pledge to do something and working to fulfill that pledge.  From a person to person standpoint it would include such things as being faithful to a friend, but being willing to confront that friend when he or she is off on a wrong course of action that has the potential to be harmful to them or to others.

An area in which people have become less willing to make a commitment is in the spousal/partner relationship.  Perhaps they hope they can avoid the trauma of a failed marriage by avoiding marriage all together by just living with one another.  Perhaps they have been so hurt by a previous relationship of their own or of someone they were close to that they cannot commit to a relationship without deep reservations.  I recently talked on the phone with a man who told me he was moving.  He had some things of my son's and made arrangements for me to pick them up at his house.  When I arrived at his home he wasn't there.  As I picked up what I had come for, I asked the lady how plans for the move were coming.  She advised that she was only the man's girlfriend and that they were not moving – only he was moving.  I didn't ask for additional explanations, but she repeated the information.  It must have had some significance to her, or she wouldn't have repeated it.  There was no evident bitterness, but a very evident sense of tenseness and regret.  No messy and costly court room involvement to dissolve a marriage that never was. I felt a sense of sadness not only for this couple but for so many others who have chosen this arrangement - cohabitation without commitment. Even though there was no obvious bitterness, there was a sense of loss because there had never been a commitment between the two that could have created a bond that with dissolution would have caused profound pain due to lost potential of what might have been. By avoiding a relationship that had the potential to cause pain they had also avoided a relationship that could have given profound joy. Jesus advised the church of Laodicea that being lukewarm - neither hot nor cold – was worse than being against him.[597] Essentially the message that comes across in such lukewarm arrangements is that one or both partners figure things probably won't work out anyway. Instead of being willing to commit to one another, learn to deal with differences, and grow together, the suggestion is that, "I'll live with you and share my bed with you as long as the arrangement is pleasurable. When I find that you don't please me, or if you find I don't please you any more, we're done with each other." Not much commitment there. No "for better or worse" or "in sickness and in health" clauses. Maybe there is some passion in the arrangement, but passion doesn't see one through the rough times that every relationship of a woman and man are bound to have. They've traded a deep, growing, committed, supportive and supporting relationship with another human for a pact of convenience – not to mention the effect on children that come along and the community. Tragically, a lot of marriages with a pledge of commitment do fail, but the good ones allow the development of deep, rewarding relationships not available to a bed partner of convenience. I know of some partnership without marriage relationships that have gone on for years, so it would seem that a level of commitment without a declaration vouched for by marriage vows is possible, but it would seem that even in these relationships there is always present the underlying reservation that "I can back out of this at any time if I don't like how things are going."

There are people who look on their relationship with God or their congregation very much as the cohabiting partners look on their relationship with each other. In their view the congregational relationship is OK as long as everyone believes and worships exactly as they do. Instead of a sense of commitment it almost seems that some seek separation – a reason not to be involved with the congregation and the work of the church. In fact we

---

[597] Revelation 3:14-19

very much need each other. There are people in the church who can share their vision and faith with me and help me grow. There are people in the church who will benefit from what I could give them in the same areas. The scriptures indicate that where two or three are gathered together in Jesus' name, that he will be there too. If for no other reason than that, we all need the church gathered in worship and fellowship and service.

There unfortunately are some who understand their relationship with God in the same casual way. God is there for their convenience and the emergencies. He's there to fix things when they're broken or when things go wrong. Maybe they occasionally pop into church for a Christmas program, someone else's' marriage, a funeral, or for some other special event, but there is no regular commitment or effort to grow closer to God and to share His promises and hopes with others. Their motive is to have an on-call repairman rather than a lover of their soul who they love in return and with whom there can be increasing closeness and growth.[598] Sad! When Carol and I visited England, we stayed in a lovely bed and breakfast. The owner was a widow. Despite what seemed to us a very beautiful and well-kept garden, she expressed her concern that it needed more care than she could give it. She suggested that perhaps she should advertise for a gardener – "marriage if necessary." I think she was joking, but it occurs to me that certainly such an arrangement for marriage partners wouldn't be very fulfilling. Just as having a marriage ceremony is only the initial declaration of an intention to work together and have a fully committed marriage, baptism or church membership is only the initial step, a declaration of one's intention to have a fully committed relationship with God. If the relationship goes no farther than these first steps, it will be as much a failed relationship as the marriage that goes no farther than the ceremony.

It doesn't have to be that way. God didn't plan for a shallow relationship with us. He loves us with an everlasting love. He has great plans for each of us, but a casual relationship won't do. God is a God of second, third and many more chances. Getting things wrong once doesn't prevent us from starting over with God and getting it right later. Just as a good marriage must involve physical passion, a good relationship with God must involve spiritual passion. But this can't be the extent of either relationship. Either

---

[598] This expression was used in a pamphlet prepared by Rev. Mark Eastway, pastor of St. Andrew's United Methodist Church in Syracuse, Indiana. The pamphlet was to help small group study and prayer in inviting God into our lives, churches, and communities.

relationship to be successful must involve commitment, dedicated effort, self-discipline, and time in getting to know each other, wanting to please each other, and wanting to promote the other's desires, dreams and objectives. In Carol and my marriage and in my relationship with God, I've found that when I place the other partner's wishes and needs ahead of mine, I'm ever so much better off than when I place my own needs first. I frequently pray that God will increase my love of my wife and my love of Him daily. When I do this, it makes the joys of a faithful relationship a special gift. Carol and I decided a long time ago to make our marriage a three-part union with Jesus Christ at the apex of this triangular partnership. This is the kind of a love triangle that really works with benefits for all involved. We've found out that when God wins, we win too. Frankly I don't see how any marriage between persons or between a person and God can prosper without such a priority commitment. Primary reliance on prosperity, financial security, health, societal position, fun activities, or misplaced objectives and motives instead of a passion-filled commitment to the relationship can only result in disillusionment and lack of fulfillment. This is the result in a relationship between marital partners or between a person and God. Sure a marriage or a relationship with God can survive without a thirsting and a hunger that leads to such commitment, but it's a poor substitute for the blessings that are otherwise available.

Such blessings between any person and God are available to anyone who is willing to dedicate the will and effort to seek them. Jesus Christ, God's own son, said so!

## A final challenge (submitted by Jesus Christ)

"Who do you say that I am?"[599]

"Do you love me?"[600]

"Tell... the good news"[601]

"Go and make disciples."[602]

The rest of the page is blank. Only you, the reader, can fill in the answers that are this final challenge!

---

[599] Matthew 16:15 (TNIV)

[600] John 21:15-17 (NIV)

[601] Mark 16:15 (NIV)

[602] Matthew 28:19 (TNIV)

# Contributing Authors' Biographies

Included are the biographies of the contributing authors. An attempt was made to have contributors from various backgrounds including Christians of various fellowships to serve as contributors and present a variety of views. Contributors include those with the following backgrounds: Agnostic, Anglican, Assembly of God, Baptist, Charismatic, Church of the Brethren, Episcopal of America, Evangelical (now United Methodist), Evangelical Covenant, Evangelical United Brethren (now United Methodist), Lutheran, Mennonite, Methodist Episcopal (now United Methodist), Missionary, Nazarene, Presbyterian, Reformed Presbyterian Church of North America, United Brethren (now United Methodist), and United Methodist. Representatives of several other backgrounds were invited to contribute but decided not to for various reasons.

Contributing authors include nine clergy and twenty-one lay people. The pastors are Two United Methodist Local Pastors, three United Methodist Elders (fully ordained pastors – one a retired district superintendent), an Episcopal Priest, a Presbyterian pastor, a Mennonite pastor, and one who has served as both Mennonite and Missionary churches as pastor. Eighteen contributors have been teachers (grade school, middle school, high school, special education, Bible and Sunday school classes, college, technical college, university, and adult education). One layman has served as a missionary with Campus Crusade for Christ. There is a certified lay speaker, two certified Christian counselors, two people who have worked with large publishing houses, a former journalist, three who have been lay delegates to their church's annual conferences, two who have been congregational lay leaders, and one who was a district lay leader in their denominations. Two now have their own businesses doing home repair work including a great deal of carpentry perhaps giving them a professional as well as a spiritual affinity with their Savoir. Three of the laypersons are wives or widows of pastors. One of the contributing authors has been a leader of Emmaus Walks and another has been a participant. One has been a presenter at Marriage Encounters and six others have participated in these events. Our views are our own; we do not presume to speak for our denominations in any official capacity.

Betty Berger was raised in the Presbyterian Church. Her Mother taught Sunday school and her Father sang in the choir. They attended church regularly. Her Dad read the Bible to the family nightly; however, she cannot recall ever hearing the "salvation message" as a child. In her twenties she drifted away from church for awhile until she married and had children. She and her husband wanted to raise the children in the church. Betty's oldest brother and his wife were saved early in their marriage, and had a burden to see all their family living for Jesus. Within a two year period and with a lot of perseverance, it happened. Her brother would take Betty's Bible and show her the scriptures – especially important were those telling of her need for salvation. With this conviction, Betty became saved by receiving Jesus into her life. Then she became hungry for more of God's Word. She has found that walking in the fullness of God's blessings is her best witness to others. Betty and her husband became Charismatic Christians nearly thirty five years ago, and twenty four years ago they joined New Life Christian Church in Warsaw, Indiana. Their love for Jesus and His Word grows stronger all the time. Betty and her husband, Dave, have worked in many areas of the church through the years. Presently she is head of hospitality, planning and serving meals for pastors and guests weekly and leads the prayer and healing school weekly.

David Berger is the husband of Betty, another contributor. He served in the U.S. Air Force in Japan from 1952 to 1956 with an early release to attend Indiana University School of Business. His Grandfather Herbst and his Mom and Dad saw that he was in church every Sunday from an early age until he entered the Air Force. On returning home he was a dashing figure in the area once being named one of the ten best-dressed men in Indiana. He and wife Betty became serious about their faith after having children. They both were involved in the Presbyterian Church in Warsaw,

Indiana. Both recommitted their lives to Christ in the 1970s, and became members of the charismatic New Life Christian Church in Warsaw in 1984 where they are still very active. David is retired from Donnelly's publishing in Warsaw, Indiana and also has worked since his retirement as a realtor and doing tax preparations. He has had many responsibilities in their congregation including being head usher ten years and head of the counters three years. Helping with their fellowship's homeless shelter program was one of his avenues of service to the Lord.

Arlene Berkey was born and raised in Northern Indiana and returned here in 1976 after a few years in Georgia and New York. Steve and she married just out of college, and she taught third grade and kindergarten until their children were born. She has been an active volunteer in local theater, schools, and church. She was the head of the adult literacy program in our community. She and Steve are members of St. Andrew's United Methodist Church in Syracuse, where she is a member of the choir, a Certified Lay Speaker, Sunday school teacher, Small Group leader, and member or chair of many of the standing committees. In 1996, Steve and she opened an online business, Extra-Mile, selling imprinted promotional products over the internet. They have three married children and six grandchildren. Nearing retirement, they are on the brink of a life-changing move, as they and two daughters and their families are building new houses next door to one another on 45 acres near Nashville, Tennessee. They are looking forward to the delights and challenges of this new phase of their lives.

Josephine Butler of Syracuse, Indiana is a retired first grade school teacher. She is a member of St. Andrew's United Methodist Church. She and husband Doyle are active participants in their congregation's Bible study class. Her first husband died in an auto accident. Her second marriage involved a blended family of nine children – four from each partner's first marriage and one from their second marriage to each other. Sometimes a mixture has seemed to better characterize the family, but a blending has been the goal.

Betty J. Byers was ten years old when her Dad took her to a revival meeting at the Puritan Avenue Baptist Church where she went forward to become a Christian. She was a member of Highland Park Baptist Church. She taught Sunday school and Bible school classes. She has been a United Methodist Women President, served on her church's Pastor Parish Committee, and enjoys being with other Christians. Betty was married to an ordained Elder (minister) of the United Methodist Church and has been a widow for twenty-one years during which God has taken care of her.

Becky Campbell is a member of St. Andrew's United Methodist Church in Syracuse, Indiana. She is very active in her congregation's prayer ministries especially seeking God's guidance for renewal in her congregation and her community. She also is active in her congregation's intercessory prayer ministry for those with illnesses and those who have yet to commit their lives to Christ. Becky is also active in her choir, has been a small group leader, and assisted in spiritual growth events in her congregation.

James Chupp was born in Goshen, Indiana in 1955. He graduated from Fairfield High School in 1974 and received a BA degree in Pastoral Ministries and Christian Education from Summit Christian College. He served in the Pastorate with the Missionary Church for twelve years in Hawaii and the Mennonite Church for seven years in Benton, Indiana. He presently lives in Benton with his wife Jennifer and three of their five children. The family is active in St. Andrew's Methodist Church in Syracuse, Indiana.

Bruce Clark, age 49, lives in Lapu Lapu City, Cebu Province in the Philippines. He went there about four years ago to marry a Philippine lady. They are still working to get a passport problem resolved so they could return to the United States. Bruce lives in their two bedroom home with his wife, his high school age step-son, his mother-in-law, and his wife's nephew. Their only income is from his disability Social Security check. Severe diabetes, sleep apnea, kidney failure, heart failure, and constant severe leg pain plague Bruce. He has recently been so disabled that he can hardly walk, and cannot even get out of bed without help. Before he was disabled, he worked with computers and taught computer classes at Ivy Tech College in Indiana. He would give free tutoring to students who had trouble with the classes. In the Philippines he has helped keep several students stay in high school and college with small monetary contributions and helped pay for his mother-in-law's broken hip repair.

Carolyn Clark has been a participant for years in Bible Study Fellowship. She is active in the Women's Society of St. Andrew's United Methodist Church in Syracuse, Indiana, volunteers in her congregation's thrift shop, and volunteers in her community food pantry. Carol leads a small group Bible study. She and her husband sing in the church choir. She grew up in the Evangelical Church which merged with the United Brethren Church to become the EUB church and then merged again with the Methodist Church to become the United Methodists. At present she is the lay leader of her congregation and a delegate to the North Indiana Annual Conference of the United Methodist Church. She is now a homemaker. In the past she was a policy writer for an insurance company, helped in the business office of her husband's medical practice, taught special needs children both as a volunteer and as a professional staff member at Cardinal Learning Center in Warsaw, Indiana, taught in an adult illiteracy program, and taught adult education quilting classes. Carolyn took the photo that is on the cover of this book and also has had fourteen of her photos published in the book *The Earth is the lord's and Everything in It*. She proof read this book as well as submitting questions. She is married to Jack Clark, another contributor.

Jack Clark is, through the intervention of the Holy Spirit in his life, a born again Christian member of St. Andrew's United Methodist Church in Syracuse, Indiana. He is a life-long Methodist. His Grandmother Prow, a Christian Scientist, asked him to always remember that "God is love." Jack has served as local and district lay leader and has served as delegate to the North Indiana Conference of the United Methodist Church. He has taught an adult Bible study class for many years and also taught Methodist Youth Fellowship Classes in his congregation in the past. Other teaching has been as a preceptor in Family Practice for Indiana University School of Medicine, a preceptor in Family Practice for Butler (Indiana) University Physicians' Assistant program, and an adjunct professor teaching human pathophysiology to junior nursing students at Goshen College in Goshen, Indiana. He retired from family medical practice late last year having filled in for ten years for other physicians in the area served by Goshen General Hospital in Goshen, Indiana. He also has served as a cruise ship doctor on fifteen high adventure cruises in Central America, Europe, the Sea of Cortez, the Azores, the Arctic and the Antarctic. He is the author of four other books, two on faith, one on his family history, and one on the history of medical practice in his home area. He is married to Carolyn Clark, another contributor.

Robert Craig, MD was an agnostic professional associate of Jack Clark who posed a challenge about Christianity to Jack a number of years ago. He had graduated from Indiana University School of Medicine during World War II and served in the Pacific Theater in that war primarily doing emergency surgery near the front lines. He participated in several invasion landings and witnessed the horrors of war and the inhumanity of man to man. He questioned why if God existed he would allow such atrocities. As an avid student of history later in life, he was struck by the evil often perpetrated on others by those who claimed to be Christians. Late in life he had a brain stem stroke from which he eventually recovered but which almost killed him. During the stroke he had an out of body experience. He was looking down on himself and the emergency room doctors. He realized his breathing had stopped and that an attempt was being made to place an endotracheal tube through his mouth and into his lungs to allow a machine to do his breathing for him. After his recovery he commented: "Now every day's a bonus. Every day is Sunday. Every day is beautiful. When something like this happens, you give thanks every day."

Dean Culbertson was born in 1962 in Kendallville, Indiana and moved to Syracuse, Indiana in a year. He was one of those kids who were signed up for T-ball, baseball and a few other things that weren't really his choice. He was a Life Scout and acted in a high school Christmas skit and a college play, "The Diary of Anne Frank." A childhood friend known since the third grade became his closest friend and was instrumental in his conversion experience. He notes that friends are a gift of God and can serve a great purpose in evangelism. His first youth group was not interesting, but another one involved guitar music and was more appealing. Dean graduated from Grace

College in Winona Lake, Indiana in 1985 with a BA in Spanish Education and a speech minor. He has served as a youth sponsor, a singles Bible study leader, and a poet for his church. He participated in eleven seasons of the Oakwood (Syracuse, Indiana) passion play (portraying Belial[603]), and is in his fourth season at Oakwood's Madrigal Dinner. Dean presently is active in St. Andrew's United Methodist Church where his wife Jamie is the organist. Aside from his relationship with Jesus Christ, he points out that his happiness comes from being married to a lady he met in a Christian Youth Group who stood him up for the senior prom, but married him later in life. He also attributes much joy to two precious teenagers at home who complete his family and notes that the joys of family confirm that God really is good. Dean commented that he was thrilled when asked to answer some of these tough questions.

Sherry Doherty is a registered nurse and a diabetic coach at Goshen (Indiana) General Hospital teaching patients about their condition and its management. She was born, baptized and raised in the Presbyterian Church and is now a member of St. Andrew's United Methodist Church. She comments that it's funny when someone asks her about how she became a believer in God, because as long as she can remember she has believed in His word. She comments that every day is a life-changing experience. She talks with God throughout the day, not always the long, formal greeting prayers, but many times just a "Please God help me teach this person today," or "God help me be a better parent of my adult children."

Mark Eastway is an elder (ordained minister) in the North Indiana Conference of the United Methodist Church. He is the senior pastor at St. Andrew's Church in Syracuse, Indiana. He originally attended college to become an engineer. He has been especially interested in the youth and personally leads the UMYF group at St. Andrew's. He is a leader in the Emmaus walk program, and has served multiple times as church camp counselor. He is helping to organize a Fellowship of Christian Athletes at the local high school. He is the president of the Habitat for Humanity program in Syracuse and president of the Syracuse-Wawasee Ministerial Association.

Fairplain Presbyterian Adult Church School class in Benton Harbor, Michigan took on as a project developing some of the questions and examining some of the questions to evaluate how the format could be used in a class setting. This group did not wish to have their individual names listed.

Gloria Frew is the head of the prayer chain ministry at St. Andrew's United Methodist Church in Syracuse, Indiana. She has been a discussion leader in spiritual growth events and is a certified Christian counselor. For years her primary function in the church was serving as her pastor husband, Phil's, confidant and sounding board. She has been a choir member and Women's Society president in the past. She has published a book of religious cartoons drawn by Phil.

Matthew Gunter is an Episcopal priest at Saint Barnabas Parish in Glen Ellyn, Illinois. He started in seminary in Massachusetts. He then shifted his interest and became a teacher of English as a second language in the California school system. He visited China with his father-in-law to give talks on this subject. Eventually he returned to seminary and finished his studies. He and his wife Leslie are parents of three daughters.

Judy Hardy is the leader of the worship team at St. Andrew's United Methodist Church in Syracuse, Indiana. She has been the Lay Delegate from her congregation to the North Indiana Conference of the United Methodist Church. She is also a prime mover in the congregation's intercessory prayer group and a participant in the weekly prayer group seeking the Holy Spirit's intervention in the lives of those friends and family members who have asked for prayer that others accept the salvation of Christ in their lives. Judy has contributed a photograph that was published in the book *The Earth is the Lord's and Everything in It*. After her first marriage ended in divorce, Judy had prayed for God to send her a Godly husband, or to give her the grace to accept a single life. She and her husband, Dan, who was God's answer to her prayer, were witnesses to God's changing power in

---

[603] Belial is a name used for Satan in II Corinthians 6:15

lives and were powerful evangels using their hospitality and concern for those with special needs to spread the good news of God's love as revealed in Jesus Christ. Judy is now a widow.

Donald Impey. At about 3:30 on a warm August morning in 1935, I popped into this world. I was a very healthy baby and to this day, the Lord has continued to bless me with excellent health. I'm very thankful to him each day for this health and His continued grace. I am fortunate and grateful to have been raised in a Christian home. My Sundays always included Sunday school and church – as far back as I can remember. I have responded from the very beginning to Christian principles as taught from the pulpit and at home. I graduated from Drake University in 1958 and promptly moved away from home to inspect new horizons. I have gained much from having worshipped with eight varied congregations in the six states where I have lived. I am in the 36th year of marriage to my lovely British bride, Rowena. I have four children and six grandchildren. All are dearly loved. I have had a varied work experience from publishing to sales and currently have a home improvement business. My wife and I have participated in Christian Marriage Encounter as presentation team members. Some of our most enjoyable weekends came from this endeavor. I am still working at 72 years of age. I divide spare time between cycling, skating, downhill skiing and church activities.

June Laudeman is a retired public school teacher. She is a member of St. Andrew's United Methodist Church in Syracuse, Indiana where she has been an inspiration with her energy and eagerness to pitch in on church projects. She is especially famous for her ability to sell tickets to the congregation and the community for church dinners, and fund raising events to help finance mission projects.

Gary Lewis is an Elder (ordained minister) in the United Methodist Church and is currently serving Cross-Wind congregation in Logansport, Indiana, a congregation that is the result of the merger of two small congregations. A former journalist, Gary worked at The Papers, Inc., Warsaw Times-Union and the Goshen News (all in Indiana) prior to entering seminary. Gary's home church was St. Andrew's United Methodist Church, Syracuse, Indiana. His current interests in ministry include pastoral care and church growth through small groups. Gary is married to Syracuse native Jennifer (Hughes) and they have one daughter, Sarah, a student at Purdue University.

John Munson is the pastor of the Fairplain Presbyterian Church in Benton Harbor Michigan. John contributed the title for this book. He submitted questions of his own and worked with one of his adult Church School classes to develop several of the challenging questions. He also reviewed how the material in the book could be used in group study. Their congregation recently added a large addition to the church including an area for the community food pantry. John enjoys beachcombing Lake Michigan's shore for bits of colored, wave-washed glass, walks in the woods, grouse, pheasant and deer hunting and trout fly-fishing. He also likes to buy, sell, and trade on E-Bay especially for fishing gear and fine pocket knives. John holds a doctorate degree, a Doctor of Ministry, from Pittsburg Theological Seminary. He and his wife enjoy flower gardening and showing their Scottie dogs that they raise.

Michael Neff is a Local Pastor in the United Methodist Church. As a young person, his family had no church affiliation. He was introduced to Christ by a Youth Fellowship affiliation when he was a senior in high school. He had been a teacher of high school physics, computer science, and mathematics (calculus, algebra, college algebra, geometry, and trigonometry) in Syracuse (Indiana) High School and its successor Wawasee High School for thirty-six years. He felt a call by God and struggled for several years before taking the training to fulfill the requirements in the North Indiana Conference to become a Local Pastor. He had a time of overlap following his appointment to the Brimfield, Indiana church in 1994. During these two years he had also continued teaching. He then devoted himself to the ministry full time. He has served on the Conference Board of Global Ministries and as Chairperson of the Elkhart District and Warsaw District Committees of Global Ministries. Due to some physical problems he felt unable to continue in full-time ministry and received an appointment part-time as associate pastor at St. Andrew's UMC in Syracuse, Indiana in 2004. He has instituted a caring group called Shepherds for the congregation, is especially committed to calling on ill members, preaches on perhaps a Sunday a month, and has been a major help consulting with members about computer needs and problems and other electronic things that can confuse us.

Gary Phillips is a part-time United Methodist Local Pastor at the Calvary United Methodist Church in Dunkirk, Indiana. He has been pastoring small churches in the Muncie District of the North Indiana Conference since 1985 and has been licensed to preach since 1989. He completed the North Central Jurisdictional Course of Study in 1999. He completed the North Indiana Conference Two Year Training Program for Spiritual Formation Leaders in 1989. He has served on the North Indiana Conference Spiritual Life Division while that committee was formulating the Core Values for the North Indiana Conference. He serves on the Conference Committee on Religion and Race and is the Spiritual Director for the Conference Committee on Lay Speaking Ministries. Gary is a board member of the City Wide Church of Muncie and is active in the Jay County Ministerial Association. Gary is married to Kathy Phillips and has four children and six grandchildren. He has worked as a welder, carpenter, machinist, janitor and store clerk. He lives in Albany, Indiana. His hobbies include hunting, fishing, reading, and blacksmithing. He is the president of the Indiana Blacksmithing Association, a member of the Rural-Smiths of Indiana and the National Muzzle Loading Rifle Association.

Saint Andrew's United Methodist Church, Syracuse, Indiana - one of the small group fellowships was very helpful in evaluating the material for group devotional study after the book was finished. Members: Earl Bales, Verna Bales, Richard Brandon, Bonnie Brandon, Rev. Mike Neff (our associate pastor who is a Local Pastor), Charles Morton, Isabel Morton, Gloria Frew, Jack Clark & Carolyn Clark (group facilitator).

David Schramm is a retired Elder (ordained minister) of the North Indiana Conference of the United Methodist Church. As such he *only* works about three days a week doing such things as pulpit supply, teaching Hebrew class at a local church, participating in spiritual growth events, and serving in prayer groups. He has served as a District Superintendent and a member of the Bishop's Cabinet in the North Indiana Conference of the United Methodist Church. He served as Ball State University (Indiana) Chaplain and taught Hebrew and Greek at The World Harvest Bible College (now University of Indiana) in South Bend, Indiana.

Joyce Schramm graduated from DePauw University and holds a master's degree from Northwestern University. She is a former English teacher and presently is doing counseling and leading prayer seminars. She has been active with impassioned praying for the lost, and freely shares with friends the miracle she witnessed in the life of one of her daughters when she was little and the joy that has come into their family from one of their grandchildren who has Mongolism. Joyce's husband is a retired United Methodist pastor. She is a mother of four and a grandmother of fourteen.

George Shaffer at the time this book is written is a ninety-seven year old active participant in life living in Winona Lake, Indiana Grace Retirement Village. He is active in the chapel in the retirement center and a long-time member of Trinity United Methodist Church in Warsaw, Indiana. He started to college to become a chemical engineer, but had to drop out because of the depression of the 1930s. Early employment was as a carpenter working with his father and operating a small printing company with a friend. Most of his life's employment was at Endicott Church Furniture Company in Warsaw. At Endicott at various times he supervised installation of the end-product, was the comptroller, and just before retirement was in charge of the manufacturing in their newly started plastics division. He taught an adult Bible class for years and sang in his church choir at Trinity and led a choir at his and wife Dortha's winter home in Melbourne Beach, Florida. He was a Boy Scoutmaster for many years and received a Silver Beaver Award for his Scouting work.

Larry Sheets worked in business management for thirty-three years. For the last five years, he and his wife Barbra have worked together in their home maintenance business living near Syracuse, Indiana on Dewart Lake. They are members of the Goshen (Indiana) First Brethren Church. Besides being very active in their congregation, they both enjoy all kinds of outdoor activities and see God's boundless creation as testifying to His existence, mercy, love, and power. Larry was born July 13, 1951 to Max and Phyllis (Weaver) Sheets. His mother was very loving and caring. His father was a severe physical disciplinarian. Larry thought this was ok until 1968 when he met Cathrine and Woody Puckett, his future in-laws. Through this relationship, he learned this kind of parenting was not beneficial. He has fond memories of his mother's parents, Mable and Elmer Weaver. Many Saturday evenings would find Larry and his brother staying at the Weavers' home where they would always pray before meals, read the Bible, and pray with the boys before bedtime. They were very kind, Godly people who left a legacy of being humble and caring. Larry shares that he surely misses them and looks forward to seeing them in heaven. Larry was saved by God's grace at the Nazarene church in Goshen, Indiana in 1969. He still shares the awesome feeling of the burden of sin being lifted from his soul, but also shares that he drifted to the way of the world by not holding onto his Savior's loving hands and a lack of daily walk with his Lord and Savior. Larry was first married at age nineteen and had three beautiful sons. He shares that he "played the Christian game" that so many do for many years. The family went to church most of the time when the doors were open, but they failed to open the Word (Bible) daily to allow Christ to take up permanent residence in his heart. At that time Larry felt the way of the world was more important than his daily walk with Him. Larry's mother was tragically killed in an auto accident in 1980. As he looks back at those years that he wasted and didn't grow with his Lord, he regrets that time. Larry's marriage failed after twenty-six years. In three years, he re-married, and most important of all in October 2006, he made a long term relationship with Jesus after reading *The Purpose Driven Life* by Rick Warren and viewing the movie The Passion of the Christ. It helped to realize that he didn't have all the answers. Larry praises God for waiting and the open arms that received him when he returned. Larry has felt very fortunate to have had awesome pastors in his life. The Holy Spirit has always been near when he made wrong choices. From now until Kingdom comes He has determined to make only right choices. "Oh, to be like Jesus." Larry finally read the Bible through, listens to great radio stations and great radio preachers (such as Chuck Swindoll and David Jeremiah, "awesome men of God"). Larry especially praises God for sending his best friend, his loving wife, Barbra, an inspiration along with her God-Loving humble parents. Larry is thankful for the influence of so many people in his life, and he shares his belief that God puts people and things in our lives for one reason. He looks forward to Christ's coming or His calling him to serve Him and gives Him all the praise.

Harlan Steffen is the senior pastor of Wawasee Lakeside Chapel, a Mennonite congregation in Syracuse, Indiana. He is vice president of the Syracuse-Wawasee Ministerial Association. In addition to his pastoral duties Harlan is a realtor in Syracuse, Indiana. Harlan has dedicated much of his ministry to helping people with alcohol and drug addiction and has been instrumental in establishing Rose House, a half-way house, for women with these problems in his community.

Cathy Ann Turner's first recalled independent church experience was a Vacation Bible School in Miami, Florida from which she brought a fish home in a large brandy snifter at the end of the week. The fish didn't live long! Cathy shares some of her life's spiritual journey in her commentary on the question: **How does God feel about people?** Due to her parents' divorce, she attended confirmation classes at a later age than most, but perhaps found them more meaningful because of the wait. She married just after college. She and her husband, Tom, moved frequently due to his engineering jobs. Over the years they joined or attended a wide range of Protestant Churches: three United Methodist, one Lutheran, three Evangelical Covenant, three Presbyterian, two Episcopalian (one that left the Episcopal Church of America and aligned itself with the World Wide Anglican Church) and an Assembly of God church. They currently attend a United Methodist Church in Hope, RI. Of all those Ecumenical experiences, the one where she grew the most was during the six years they were members of the Assembly of God. She had come to a personal understanding and relationship of who Christ was to her when she was 40. She comments that right there, is a telling statement. More information is given in her answer to the above question.

Church responsibilities have included board positions, very active participation in their adult Sunday school, small group ministries, study groups, heading church bazaars, chairing the pie and coffee house after each of ten singing Christmas tree performances that averaged about 150-200 slices of pie each time, chairing the church Christmas decorations for three years, planning and serving two building fund raising dinners, and she was the head of a fund-raising pizza sale that raised over $10,000 for the church. Outside of her church work she has taught in high school and junior high at first as a home economics teacher and then as a substitute teacher. She and her husband have four children; the youngest is now a college sophomore.

Jonathan Ummel is 31 years old. As a young child his family was active in the Faith Assembly, a charismatic congregation near Syracuse, Indiana. When he was some older he was active in St. Andrew's United Methodist Church in Syracuse (serving as a camp counselor), and as an adult he is a member of the Reformed Presbyterian Church of North America in Elkhart, Indiana. He was active in sports as a young person playing Little League baseball (named most valuable player) and later tennis at Wawasee high school (in Syracuse, Indiana – team co-captain in 1994 and most valuable player in 1995). He was Valedictorian of Wawasee's class of 1995 and went on to attend Purdue University (in Indiana) on a full four-year academic scholarship graduating with a Bachelor of Science in interdisciplinary engineering with highest distinction in 1999. His areas of concentration were heat transfer, civil and chemical engineering. Between his junior and senior years, he spent his summer vacation in Valdivia, Chile as a missionary with Campus Crusade for Christ. Following college graduation, he served again with Campus Crusade for Christ two years – first in Ankara, and then in Istanbul, Turkey. All of these involved working with college age students. Three of his siblings also worked in the mission field as did his wife Jennifer. Jennifer, an analytical chemist, was in central China for a year with Campus Crusade for Christ. The Ummels have three children: Ethan, Abigail and Seth. Jon is certified as a professional engineer and has worked as a Civil engineer for Elkhart County (Indiana) and now for the state of Indiana.

Printed in the United States
123144LV00001B/73-166/P